A Landscape of Interactions During the Late Prehispanic Period in the Onavas Valley, Sonora, México

Emiliano Gallaga

Arizona State Museum
THE UNIVERSITY OF ARIZONA.

Arizona State Museum Archaeological Series 205

Arizona State Museum
The University of Arizona
Tucson, Arizona 85721-0026
(c) 2013 by the Arizona Board of Regents
All rights reserved.
Printed in the United States of America

ISBN (paper): 978-1-889747-91-0
Library of Congress Control Number: 2013932270

ARIZONA STATE MUSEUM ARCHAEOLOGICAL SERIES

General Editor: Richard C. Lange
Technical Editors: Laura Burghardt, Alicia M. Vega

The *Archaeological Series* of the Arizona State Museum, The University of Arizona, publishes the results of research in archaeology and related disciplines conducted in the Greater Southwest. Original, monograph-length manuscripts are considered for publication, provided they deal with appropriate subject matter. Information regarding procedures or manuscript submission and review is given under Research Publications on the Arizona State Museum website: *www.statemuseum.arizona.edu/research/pubs*. Information may be also obtained from the General Editor, *Archaeological Series*, Arizona State Museum, P.O. Box 210026, The University of Arizona, Tucson, Arizona, 85721-0026; Email: langer@email.arizona.edu. Electronic publications and previous volumes in the Arizona State Museum Library or available from the University of Arizona Press are listed on the website noted above.

The Arizona State Museum *Archaeological Series* is grateful to the many donors and supporters who continue to make this publication possible.

Cover: This is Figure 7.8 in the text.

Contents

Figures

Tables

Acknowledgments

To my parents Lic. Roberto Gallaga and Lic. Ofelia Murrieta for their love, support, and encouragement that allowed me to be an archaeologist and to achieve my dreams and goals. To my brother Francisco who sent me good vibes from Belgium.

This project was financed by a Dissertation Improvement Grant from the National Science Foundation (BCS-0424743); the Anthropology Department of the University of Arizona, the Arizona Archaeological and Historical Society, and CONACYT. I am grateful for the permission and support of the Consejo de Arqueología, INAH-Mexico. I thank Dr. Paul Fish and Dr. Suzanne Fish for their support, comments, and friendship, as well as Dr. Richard Pailes from the University of Oklahoma and Dr. Charles Spencer and Dr. Christina M. Elson from the American Museum of National History, New York City, for facilitating access to their material collections. Arqueologa Elisa Villalpando and the staff of INAH-Sonora also deserve my gratitude for their academic and technical support. I much appreciate the efforts of Mayela Pastrana† (que en Paz descanse), Cory Harris, Cesar Villalobos, Maricruz Magaña, Coral Montero and "Inge" Armando for providing valuable participation in the field, working and analyzing materials. I would also like to thank Drs. Joel Palka and Elizabeth Paris for their helpful reviews of the manuscript. A very special thank you I extend to the Onavas community and its authorities, who gave the OVAP their support and helped us in many ways, making our stay in their community unforgettable. Last but not least, thanks go to Gillian Newell for her comments, work, and emotional support.

Para Gillian,
Xavi,
Ayla,
y Nopal.

Chapter 1
Introduction

...from north to south, the Magdalena, Sonora, Yaqui, and Mayo. These river valleys undoubtedly served as corridors along which peoples and ideas moved throughout northwest Mexico and perhaps, into the southwest United States (Johnson 1966:28).

Despite the impressive amount of archaeological research conducted in Sonora in the last decades, much of the state remains poorly known. Some initial work has been done in the Onavas Valley, located at the Middle Río Yaqui Valley, but much still remains to be examined. As a crossroad for prehispanic interaction between northern Mesoamerica, the U.S. Southwest, and the Casas Grandes region, the area is critical to understanding regional development and interaction. The present publication is the result of the Onavas Valley Archaeological Project (OVAP) as part of my dissertation research at the University of Arizona. Three field archaeologists and one shell analyst carried out the project. From the beginning, the OVAP utilized a landscape analysis theoretical framework that incorporated ethnohistoric and ethnographic datasets to establish the Prehispanic cultural development of the Onavas Valley.

The OVAP, conducted archaeological investigations between the modern Alvaro Obregón and El Novillo dams (Figure 1.1), was obliged to begin by building a basic archaeological database for the region in order to increase our still fragmentary understanding of the late Prehispanic context of Northwest Mexico. A full-coverage systematic pedestrian survey was undertaken to define the cultural history of the Onavas Valley and to examine extra-regional interactions between the valley and surrounding areas. In addition, the OVAP contributed to the equally important goal of public education (Gándara 1992; Little 2002). The OVAP shared project findings with the people of Onavas about our project to enhance local awareness, recognition, and appreciation of their cultural and historical patrimony. These efforts will promote the protection of archaeological and historic sites in the region and encourage Onavas town members to take pride in their local prehistory.

Although the Rio Yaqui has been generally recognized as an under-studied area in this region, OVAP research faced significant academic challenges as well. The lack of a local or regional chronology, and an almost total absence of site descriptions and locations, required a generalized research design based heavily in regional ethnography and ethnohistory (Dirst 1979). From the beginning it was clear that an interdisciplinary approach was necessary in order to fill the vacuum in archaeological knowledge. All information from nearby projects was gathered, as well as information from relevant Colonial documents and ethnographic research. Landscape analysis and a theoretical framework focused on the role of prehispanic communities were chosen to analyze the archaeological data gathered by the field survey. Both frameworks proved to be flexible enough to overcome the lack of basic data sets and to allow a preliminary interpreta-

Figure 1.1. Location of Onavas Valley in the Middle Rio Yaqui region and points of comparision in the Northwest.

tion of the archaeological context at this initial regional level of analysis.

Landscape archaeology enables a broad analytical focus on an area with a great variety of Prehispanic cultural activity (Anschuetz et al. 2001; Ashmore and Knapp 1999; Canuto and Yaeger 2000; Rapoport 1982; Roberts 1996; Rossignol and Wandsnider 1992). To investigate the cultural landscape of the inhabitants of the Prehispanic Onavas Valley, referred to as the "Nébomes" by the earliest Colonial accounts, the OVAP followed a three-step approach: (I) construction of a local chronology and an inventory of diagnostic material culture; (II) development of an understanding of the landscape structure (settlement pattern and ritual landscape) of the area; and (III) collection and analysis of material remains to investigate the manufacture, use, and exchange of non-local goods.

I: AN INVENTORY OF DIAGNOSTIC MATERIAL CULTURE AND THE CONSTRUCTION OF A LOCAL CHRONOLOGY

Archaeologists in Northwest Mexico generally accept that the Río Sonora archaeological tradition extends from the international border between Mexico and the United States of America to the northern limits of Sinaloa, Mexico, and includes the eastern portion of the Sierra Madre on the Sonora side (Alvarez 1996:212; Dirst 1979; Pailes 1972:6-7, 1994a:81; Villalpando 2000b:249; see Figure 1.2). However, no substantive archaeological evidence suggests that this cultural tradition exists in the Middle Yaqui River Valley region (Pailes 1994a:81).

The suggestion that the Onavas Valley was associated with the Río Sonora archaeological tradition brings certain specific temporal and largely material-based assumptions of cultural affiliation that remain unaddressed. Based on architecture, artifacts, and a few radiocarbon dates from excavated archaeological contexts in the Río Sonora Valley and southern Sonora (Dirst 1979:103-104; Doolittle 1988:36-37; Pailes 1972:328), researchers place the Río Sonora archaeological tradition from around A.D. 100 to 1500, divided into three internal phases (Figure 1.3). To assess the assumptions of material-based cultural affiliation and temporal assignation, as well as further questions

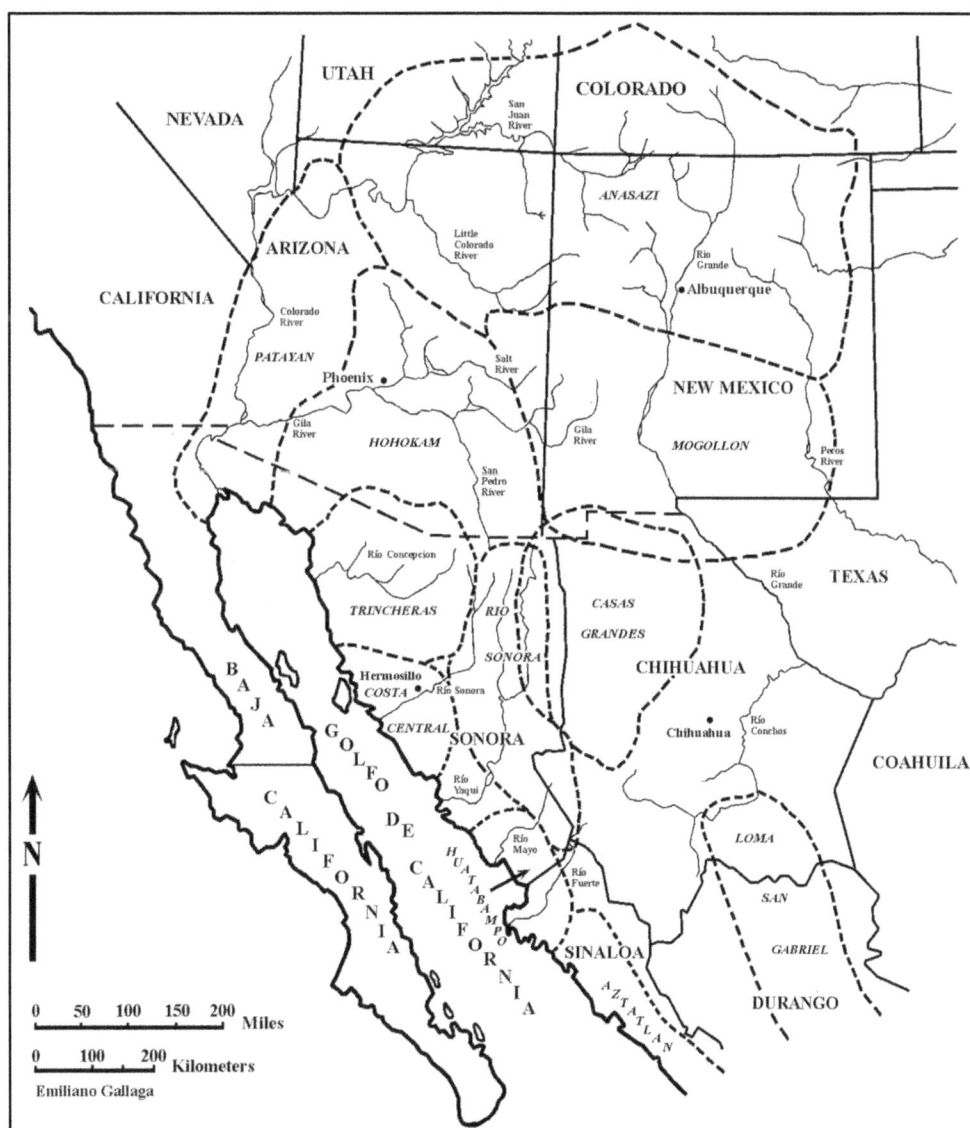

Figure 1.2. Archealogical traditions of Northwest Mexico/U.S. Southwest.

B. C.   A. D.

| | 10000 | 8000 | 6000 | 4000 | 3000 | 2000 | 1000 | 800 | 600 | 400 | 200 | 0 | 100 | 200 | 300 | 400 | 500 | 600 | 700 | 800 | 900 | 1000 | 1100 | 1200 | 1300 | 1400 | 1500 | 1600 | 1700 |

Trincheras Tradition [1]: Paleoindian — Archaic — Atil Phase — Altar Phase — El Realito Santa Teresa Phase — Oquitoa Phase

Central Coast Tradition [2]: Paleoindian — Archaic — Preceramic Phase — Ceramic Phase (Tiburon Liza Tipe) — Historic Seri

Huatabampo Tradition [3]: Paleoindian — Batacosa Phase — Huatabampo — Cuchujaqui Phase

Rio Sonora Tradition [4]: Paleoindian — Early — Middle — Late

Casas Grandes Tradition [5]: Paleoindian — Late Archaic — Preceramic — Plainware Period (Pithouses) — Viejo Period — Medio Period

Loma San Gabriel Tradition [6]: Paleoindian — Pre-Chalchihuites — Chalchihuites I — II — Tepehuan/Historic III

Hohokam Tradition [7]: Paleoindian — Archaic — Late Archaic Transition — Pioneer — Colonial — Sedentary — Classic

Mogollon Tradition [8]: Paleoindian — Archaic — Pithouse Period — Early — Late — Mogollon-Pueblo I II

Anasazi Tradition [9]: Paleoindian — Archaic — Basketmaker I II III — Pueblo I II III IV

Mesoamerica [10]: Paleoindian — Archaic — Early — Formative — Late — Classic Early — Middle — Late — Teotihuacan — PostClassic Early — Late — Toltec Empire — Aztecs

1 McGuire and Villalpando 1993
2 Bowen 1993
3 Alvarez 1990 and Pailes 1993
4 Doolittle 1998, Villalpando 2000
5 Schaafsma and Riley 1999
6 Lazalde 1987
7 Fish 1989
8 Reid and Whittlesy 1997
9 Cordell 1997
10 Fagan 1996

(by Emiliano Gallaga)

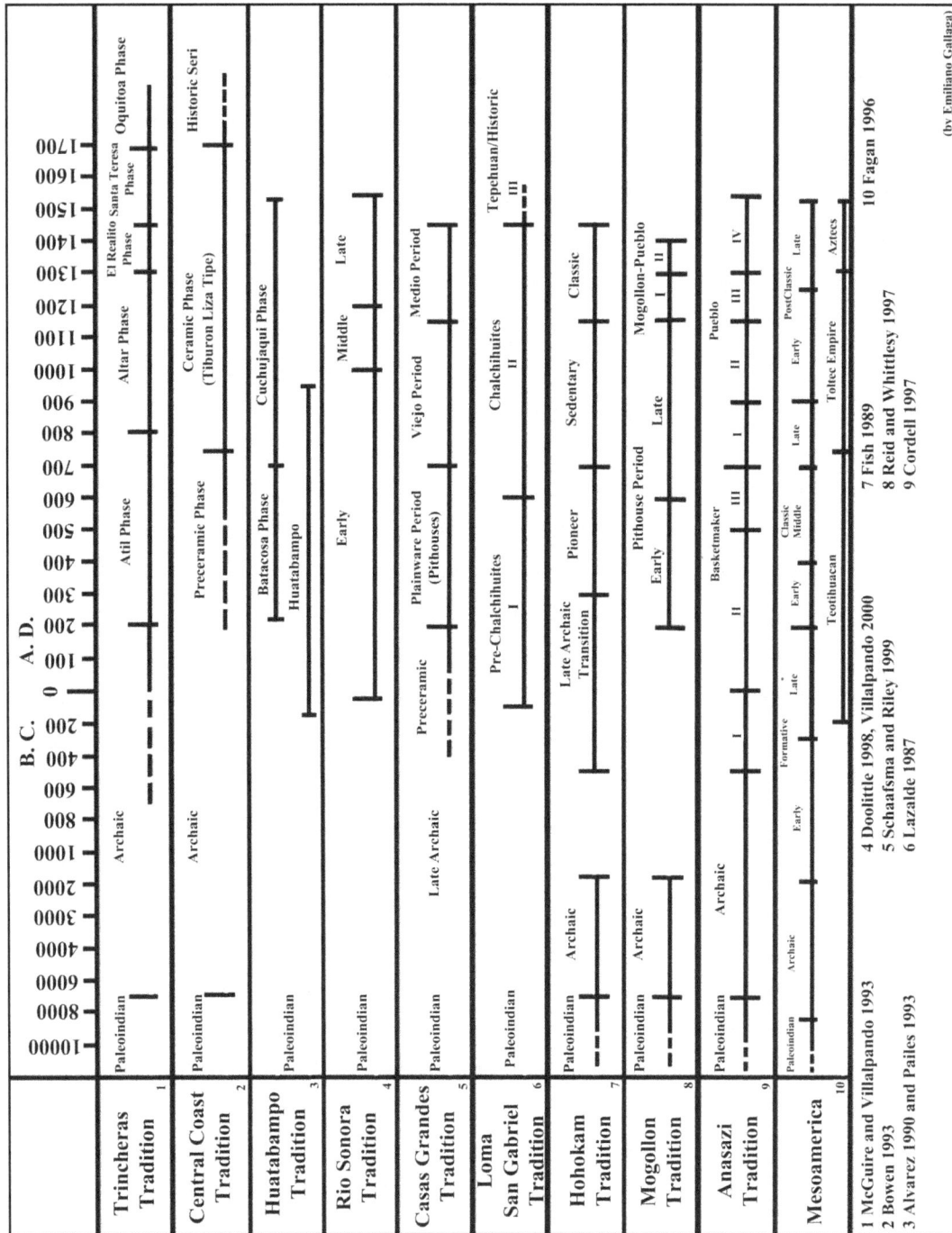

Figure 1.3. Comparative time line of regional archaeological traditions (from Gallaga and Newell 2004).

regarding regional differences and similarities of the Onavas Valley, an inventory of the valley's diagnostic material culture and a local chronology are necessary (Ekholm 1939, 1942; Gallaga 2004b; Pailes 1972).

Moreover, to arrive at an understanding of the valley's extra-regional interactions likewise requires placing sites and material into a temporal and spatial framework. In lieu of excavation and stratigraphically recorded material, the collection and analysis of ceramics and lithic material from the surface provided the preliminary data for a proposed local chronology for the Onavas Valley. Overall, it was expected that the OVAP would clarify the interpretations and speculations already in place.

II: Understanding the Landscape Structure (Settlement Pattern and Ritual Landscape) of the Onavas Valley

Landscape structure analysis methodologically enables the researcher to examine the natural environment and the archaeological remains (sites and materials) in an integrated fashion (Anschuetz et al. 2001; Ashmore and Knapp 1999; Rossignol and Wandsnider 1992). Societies and communities are flexible, diverse, and versatile entities. They are also shaped by local, regional, and extra-regional interactions, as well as social and natural boundaries (Goldstein 2000; Marcus 2000; Minnis and Redman 1990).

For the OVAP, settlement pattern analysis facilitated the examination and determination of patterns of land use, settlement hierarchy, and settlement structure in terms of either dispersed or nucleated, subsistence technology, occupation, and transformation over time in the Onavas Valley. The analysis further allowed a study of population density, temporal changes in ceramics, and the identification of trade and exchange items (Gallaga 2004c). Using human-made and natural markers identified in the valley, the ritual landscape for the Prehispanic communities of this region is provisionally described. Ethnohistoric and ethnographic data proved to be very useful in providing an initial interpretation of the material record and possible perspectives on how the Nébome landscape was perceived. Data used to understand settlement and ritual landscape patterns were gathered by a full-coverage systematic survey in the valley. Similar projects in the Southwest U.S. and Northwest Mexico have already demonstrated the potential of settlement pattern analysis using full-coverage systematic surveys, such as the Trincheras Valley (Fish and Fish 2004), the Casas Grandes region (Whalen and Minnis 2001), or the Marana community (Fish et al. 1992). The cultural landscape of the Onavas Valley was compared with results from those projects to deepen the interpretation of the extent of their development and types of interactions these societies might have created in similar geographical environments. Our understanding of these interactions can be understood through the examination of material culture, including non-local and local goods.

III: Non-Local Goods

Colonial documents describe the transportation of a variety of non-local goods in large quantities around Northwest Mexico and the U.S. Southwest. These goods consisted of turquoise, shell, cotton textiles, copper items, ceramics, feathers, live birds, corn, hides (including those from buffalo), slaves, salt, fish, pearls, dyes, hallucinogenic plants, fruits, and many perishable items (Nuñez Cabeza de Vaca 1993; Pérez de Ribas 1999; Sauer 1932; Villalpando 1997). Unfortunately, the documents neglect to mention the frequency, origin, or destination of such trade endeavors and the items exchanged. Nonetheless, the list of goods illustrates that both common as well as sumptuary goods were transported for trade in local and possibly regional markets.

During the Prehispanic and most of the Colonial periods, the river valleys formed the main avenues of communication in Northwest Mexico (Alvarez 1990; Bandelier 1890-1892; Braniff 1992, 2001; Dirst 1979; Reff 1991; Riley 2005; Sauer 1932; Villalpando 1988; West 1993). Geographical conditions in Sonora, such as rough terrain and the lack of water, restricted effective communication between areas to the north and south, and east to west. Although there is evidence of the use of canoes for sea traveling among the Seris (Bowen 2000:22), there is no data to suggest that indigenous canoes were used for river travel, particularly not over long distances (Pennington 1980:67). With some exceptions along the coast, all Prehispanic interactions had to be undertaken by foot. Because the Yaqui drainage is one of the few perennially flowing rivers in Sonora, it could have been used year-round as a natural communication corridor between the southern coast and the Sierra Madre Occidental, reaching as far north as southern Arizona and central Chihuahua through its tributary rivers, the Bavispe and Moctezuma (Braniff 1992, 2001; Di Peso et al. 1974; Kelley 2000; Riley 1987, 1990, 2005; West 1993; Wilcox 1986a, 1986b).

The excavation at the site of Paquimé, Chihuahua, by Charles Di Peso in the 1960s documented Pacific coast and west Mexican goods at the site. Di Peso (1974:628) proposed that the Río Yaqui may have functioned as one of the main routes used by traders. The geographical location and direction of flow of the Río Yaqui positions this natural causeway as an ideal trade corridor. If the Río Yaqui indeed served as such, to whom, and when were goods traded? Who directed the trade, trade specialists or part time travelers? We know that shell was traded inland, but what was traded in return?

Systematic archaeological research in the Onavas Valley provides the necessary data to hone our understanding of coastal-sierra interactions during Prehispanic times.

REGIONAL CULTURE HISTORY

Sixteenth century Spanish ethnohistorical records describe the Onavas Valley and its surroundings, albeit with the typical and recognizable temporal biases. Ethnohistorically, southern Sonora was described as one of the most highly populated native kingdoms of New Spain (Hopkins 1988; Nentuig 1977; Nuñez Cabeza de Vaca 1993; Pérez de Ribas 1999; Pfefferkorn 1989; Reff 1991). Yet, prior to the OVAP, a mere ten archaeological sites appeared in the site registry of the Instituto Nacional de Antropología e Historia (INAH) for the quadrants SON P:10 and SON P:6 (INAH Sonora Archive 1998). Of those sites, only three were located directly in the OVAP research area (SON P:10:2, SON P:10:3, and SON P:10:4, See Appendix I and II). This scarcity of sites was assumed to be the result of the paucity of research in Northwest Mexico, a trend that recent work has started to reverse (Newell and Gallaga 2004; Pollard 1997; Villalpando 1997; Villalpando and Fish 1997).

Moreover, the ethnohistoric sources indicate that during the Prehispanic period, a considerable variety of indigenous groups characterized this area. Opata people were located to the north, Lower Pimas or Nébomes were found in the center, Guarigio and Tarahumaras lived in the east, and Yaqui people were found to the south (Beals 1943; Moctezuma 1991; Pérez de Ribas 1999; see Figure 1.4). In addition to these sedentary groups, Jesuit Father Pérez de Ribas documented that nomadic Seri Indians from the coast temporarily inhabited this region in the 1620s (Pérez de Ribas 1999:390). Ethnohistorical and ethnographic

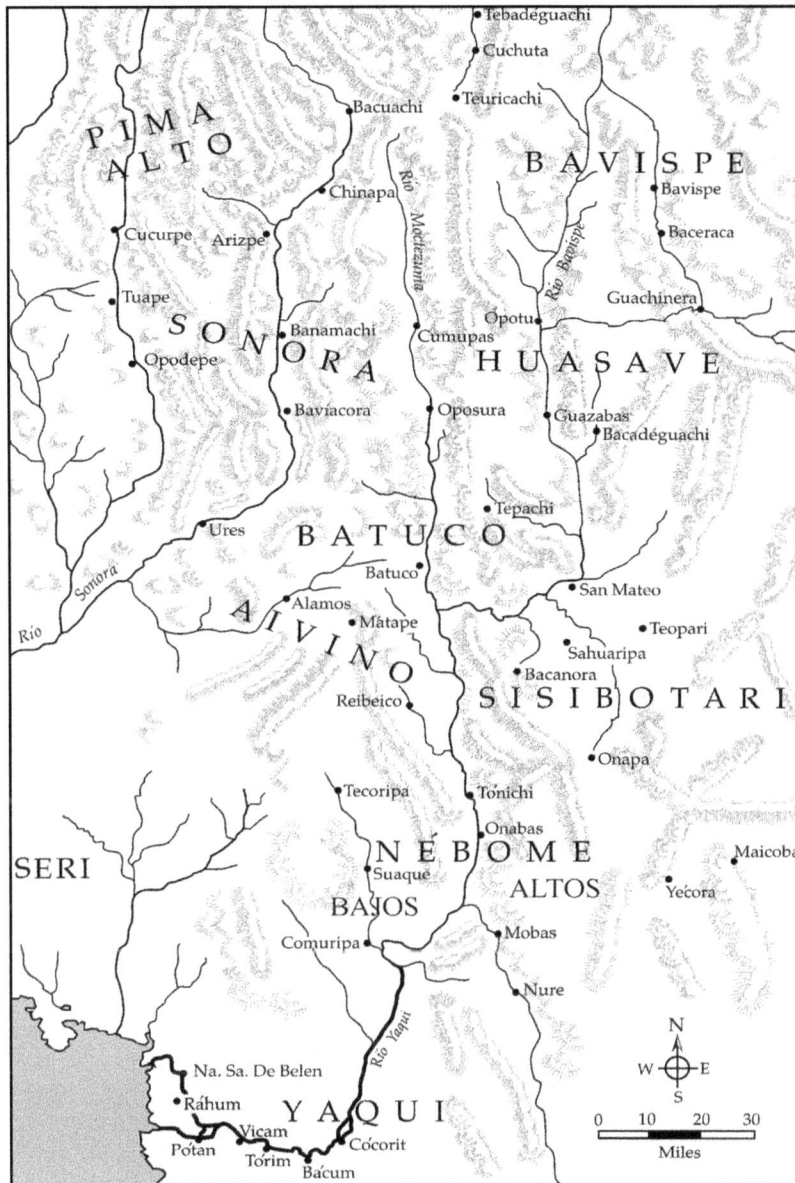

Figure 1.4. Prehispanic Indian groups in the region during the Colonial period (modified from A. de Ribas 1999:325).

data further indicate that the Prehispanic communities that settled in the Middle Río Yaqui Valley area belonged linguistically to the Uto-Aztecan language family (Figure 1.4). These groups are subdivided into several different linguistic groups (Miller 1983; Moctezuma 1991). The Yaquis belong to the Cahita subgroup of the Taracahita people, the Nébomes pertain to

the Tepiman group, and the Opatas belong to the Opatan subgroup of the Taracahita people (Dunnigan 1983; Miller 1983; Moctezuma 1991; Pennington 1980, 1982; Spicer 1994).

The Yaqui Indians settled in the area from the river delta to the present location of the Alvaro Obregón dam. The Lower Pimas or Nébomes, which Pérez de Ribas (1999:401) divided into Upper and Lower Nébomes, occupied the region between the present Alvaro Obregón Dam to the modern town of Soyopa. Pérez de Ribas (1999:401) suggested that the upper Nébomes settled near the east side of the river, whereas the Lower Nébomes resided in the hills on the west side of the river. The northern portion of the Middle Río Yaqui Valley area was inhabited during the Colonial period by different subgroups of Opata Indians. The Opatas from the south, also called Aivinos or Eudeves, lived next to the Lower Nébomes. The Opatas neighboring the Upper Nébomes were named Sisibotaris (Moctezuma 1991; Pérez de Ribas 1999). Thus, ethnohistorical accounts suggested that a high number of habitation sites could be found in this area, as well of remains of water irrigation control, such as canals and terraces.

Chapter 2
Geographical and Environmental History Background

Although Sonora is situated outside the torrid zone, beginning in the twenty-seventh degree of north latitude, it is nevertheless, on the whole, a very warm country (Pfefferkorn 1989:38).

The early European descriptions of the Sonora region recognize the area's environmental challenges but also acknowledge its potential on resources and expansion of the New Spain. The presence of numerous Prehispanic communities offers material evidence that the region consisted of more than a barren desert landscape. This environment did in fact provide people with a functional place for habitation. An understanding of the location and distribution of sites, distribution and exploitation of local resources, and human relationships with the surrounding landscape requires a scrutiny of the geography and environment of the area of research.

The Onavas Valley lies in the south-central part of Sonora, Mexico (28° 28' N, 109° 32' W, 150 m above sea level). The town of Onavas (see Figure 1.1), the center of the OVAP research area, is a small agricultural community of approximately 450 inhabitants. Jesuit Father Diego Vandersipe founded a mission there in 1622 with the name of San Ignacio de Onavas. Today, the village serves as the cabecera (administrative center) of the municipio (equivalent to a U.S. county) with the same name (Almada 1990:468). The village of Onavas is located two hours driving distance (200 km) from the city of Hermosillo, which is the capital of the state of Sonora.

GEOGRAPHY AND GEOLOGY

The study area lies in the middle of the ecological sub-province of Sonora in the Middle Río Yaqui Valley which is characterized by parallel mountain ridges and valleys. Due to its location, this area functions as a transition zone between the Sierra Madre Occidental and the Sonoran Desert (Figure 2.1). The climatic and topographic characteristics of this region are shaped by the proximity of the Sierra Madre Occidental and the Gulf of California. The Sierra Madre Occidental consists of high volcanic tablelands and ranges, and extends from eastern Sonora and western Chihuahua to Jalisco in central Mexico. The Sierra Madre Occidental was created by Cretaceous-Tertiary volcanic activity and consists of igneous rocks—such as rhyolite, basalt, obsidian, and superficial lava, granite, and andesite. With rare exceptions, other lithologies or rock formation originated outside the Sierra Madre Occidental proper or were introduced by recent alluvium, including sedimentary rocks as quartzite and limonite. Silver, gold, and copper ores are present in the area as well and they have attracted miners to this region since Colonial times (Escarcega 1996:51; West 1993:1). In terms of geological time, the coastal plain is a recent event which was the result of the con-

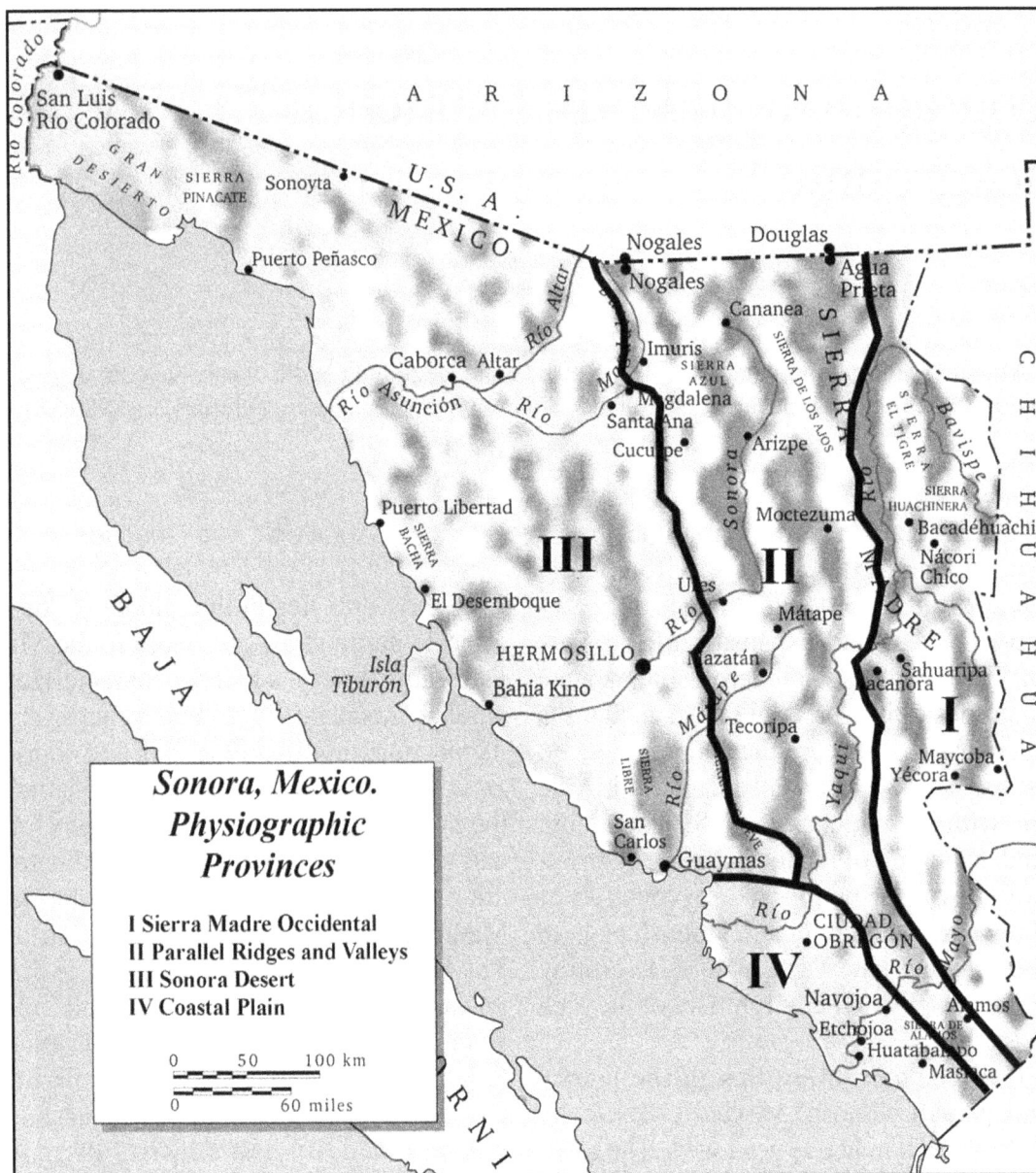

Figure 2.1. Sonora physiographic divisions (modified from Yetman 1996: Figure 1).

tinuing alluvial deposits from the Sierra Madre Occidental. These systems of mountain ranges are rugged and range in elevation from 800 to 2,000 m above the river valleys. Several rivers originate on the highlands and have carved out deep, jagged canyons or barrancas in the Sierra (Almada 1990; Montane 1993; Pérez Bedolla 1996; West 1993).

To the west of the Middle Río Yaqui Val-

ley lies the Sonoran Desert that forms part of the Northwest Mexican Coastal Plain originating in central Nayarit and ending in the Lower Colorado River in Arizona. In contrast to the Sierra, the coastal plain only averages around 100 m above sea level. Geologically, the Sonoran Desert region consists of sediments from Precambrian origin (such as granite, quartzite, limonite, and limestone). Most of the mountains created in the Precambrian have since eroded, leaving only a few scattered remains (Escarcega 1996; Montane 1993; Pérez Bedolla 1996; West 1993:6).

All major rivers in Sonora originate high in the Sierra Madre Occidental. As West (1993:1) mentions, the alluvial floodplains of most of the river valleys created in the Sierra province and in the basin and range sub-province are narrow and rarely exceed more than 2 km in width. Zones with the highest agricultural potential include the large delta plains along the Sonoran coast, particularly those created by the Río Yaqui and Mayo. Filled with alluvium and bordered by Tertiary and Pleistocene gravel terraces, the river valleys prior to reaching the delta plains functioned as rich and highly productive agricultural areas amidst a desert landscape (West 1993:1). In most cases, the gravel terraces have now become sharply cut due to erosion, deforestation, and human activity forming flat-topped or dissected terraces that overlook the rivers.

From an archaeological perspective, those small mesas are important (Figure 2.2). Located above the potential flood zone, the mesas served as habitation sites since Prehispanic times (West 1993:3). As rugged as the Sierra province is, river valleys form logical routes to travel through the Sierra connecting the Sonoran coast with the interior and vice versa. For example, the Onavas Valley is located between 140 to 240 km from the Sonoran coast and around 300 to 350 km west of the Sierra from the Casas Grandes region (see Figure 1.1). Although the distance between these areas does not amount to much, the terrain is difficult and must have taken several days to cross by foot in Prehispanic times and before the construction of modern roads (Carpenter 1996:64). Therefore, the Río Yaqui provides a logical route of commerce and communication.

CLIMATE

Most, if not all, European colonizers describe the Sonoran climate as a hot and dry desert that caused humans and beasts to suffer. The Köppen system normally classifies the Onavas Valley as semi-arid dry-steppe, a transitional climate between the moderate climate of the Sierra Madre Occidental and the arid true desert/dry of the coast (Pérez Bedolla 1996:111-112). Measurements from the La Estrella weather station of the nearby Soyopa municipio show that the average annual temperatures for this

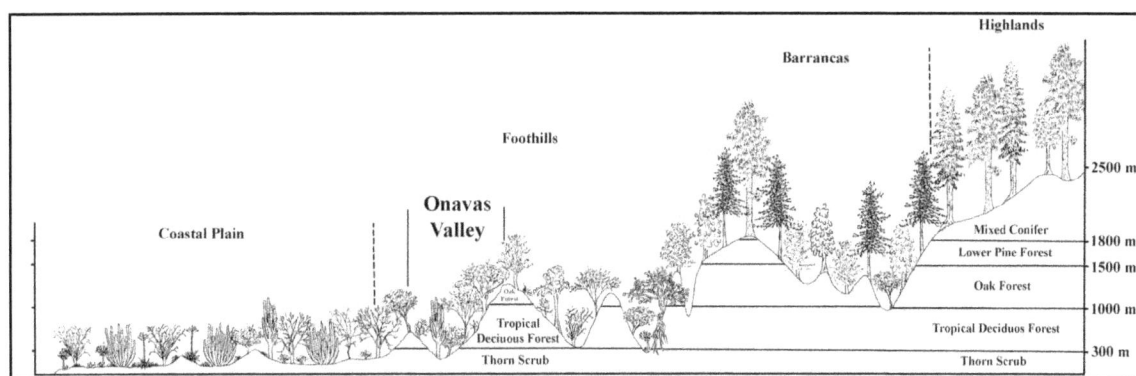

Figure 2.2. A common geomorphic cross-section of a typical river valley from eastern Sonora (modified from West 1993).

region vary between 47° C (120° F) and −10° C (15° F). Annual average precipitation measures 608.5 mm (Escárcega 1996; MacMahon 1985; Pérez Bedolla 1996; West 1993).

Rain in Northwest Mexico falls in two periods or seasons: heavy rains in the summer (July through September), locally named *chubascos,* and a less intense rainy season in the winter (November through February), locally named *equipatas.* Due to the altitude differences between the coast and the Sierra Madre, annual precipitation is greater at the higher elevations, resulting in a shorter rainy season on the coast than in the Sierra by at least two weeks (Gentry 1942:12; Pailes 1972:12-13; West 1993:4). This dual precipitation system allows some regions to have two crops per year, as has been recorded for the Yaqui and Mayo Valleys in the ethnohistoric records (West 1993:6).

VEGETATION

Like climate, vegetation is directly correlated to elevation, humidity, and temperature. The local flora consists of desert scrub brush with riparian shrubs along the drainages, in addition to subtropical trees on the hills and mountains (Figure 2.3). According to Gentry's (1942:27) vegetation classification of southern Sonora, the OVAP research area consists of a short tree forest, also known as a tropical deciduous forest, with a presence of thorn forest and oak forest divisions. The short tree forest mixes with the thorn forest at lower elevations and with oak forest at higher elevations. Short tree forest grows between 300 and 1000 m above sea level, typically reaches between 10 and 15 m in height, and consists of a combination of deciduous trees and tropical species. The most common species for short tree forests are the pochote (*Ceiba acuminata*), torote (*Bursera* sp.), palo blanco (*Ipomoea arborescens*), brazil (*Haematoxylon brasileto*), chino (*Pithecellobium mexicanum*), chirahui (*Acacia cymbispina*), mauto (*Lysiloma divaricata*), tepeguaje (*Lysiloma watsoni*), guásima (*Gsezuma ulmifolia*), and huizache (*Acacia carnesina*).

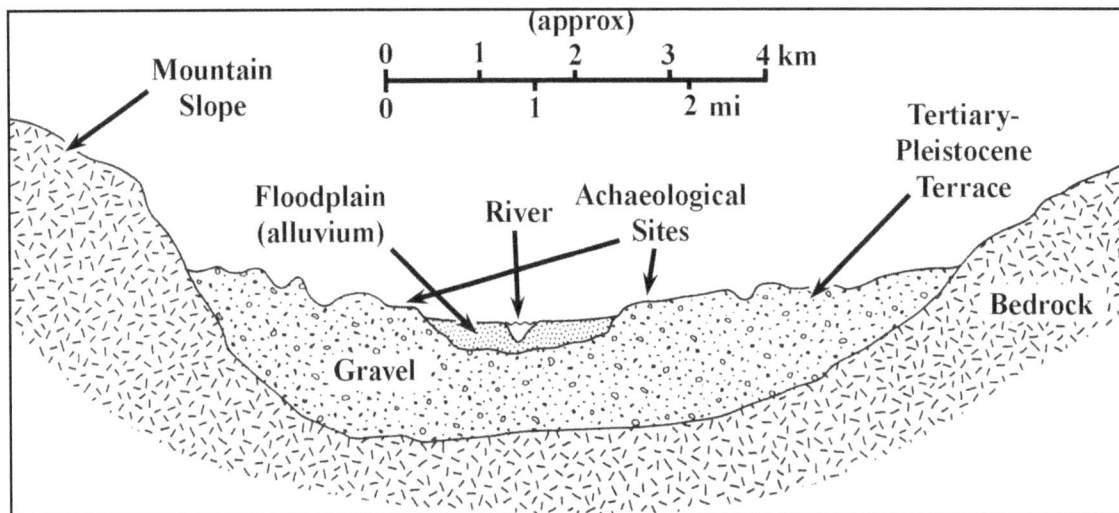

Figure 2.3. Cross-section from the coast to the Sierra showing the location of the Onavas Valley (modified from Gentry 1942).

Thorn forest grows below 600 m above sea level and is characterized by xerophytic deciduous shrubs. The most abundant plants in this vegetation division are pitahaya (*Lemaire-ocereus thurberi*), mesquite (*Prosopis velu-tina*), ocotillo tree (*Fouquieria macdougalii*), paloverde (*Cercidium* sp.), several species of century plants (*Agave* sp.), and prickly pear cactus (*Opuntia* sp.). The last vegetation division, oak forest, grows between 1000 to 3000 m above sea level and contains different species of pine (*Pinus arizonica, Pinus engelmannii, Pinus ponderosa*, and *Pinus chihuahuana*), oak (*Quercus*), and juniper (*Juniperus*) (Pérez Bedolla 1996:125, 129).

The diversity of ecological areas in this region provided the ancient inhabitants of the Onavas Valley with a great variety of natural resources. Several of these plants were used during Prehispanic times as important sources of food. Sonoran people today still use mesquite pods, fruits of various cacti, and the hearts and leaves of agaves in their diet. Other plants were used for construction, such as pine and oak, or for craft production, such as ironwood, leaves, and palms.

FAUNA

Before the European entradas into the area, the Sonoran Desert harbored a great variety of animals that the Prehispanic people utilized. Due to their wide spectrum of adaptation, most of the faunal assemblage of Sonora can be found everywhere, except for some species restricted to a specific ecosystem, such as black bear or bighorn sheep. Later introduction of European stock diminished the number and ecological areas for local fauna. Indigenous fauna species, hunted for food by humans that still can be found in the region include antelope (*Antilocapra americana sonorensis*), mule deer (*Odicoileus hemionus crooki* and *Odicoileus*

virginianus), bighorn sheep (*Ovis canadensis*), peccary (*Dicotyles tajacu*), turkey (*Meleagris gallopavo*), rabbit (*Sylvilagus audubon*), and jack rabbit (*Lepus californicus*). Predator species, such as bobcat (*Lynx rufus*), mountain lion or puma (*Felis concolor*), jaguar (*Felis onca*), ocelot (*Felis paradalis*), black bear (*Ursus americanus*), coyote (*Canis latrans*), and gray wolf (*Canis lupus*), were hunted for their hide or for ceremonial purposes, rather than for food. Other animals common to the area are desert tortoise (*Gopherus agassizi*), several rodents (*Neoto* sp., *Peromyseus* sp., and *Perognathus* sp.), and a variety of birds (MacMahon 1985; Pérez Bedolla 1996; Rea 1998; West 1993).

In addition, the Río Yaqui offers several freshwater food sources, such as catfish and lisa, (the latter a sardine-like fish), freshwater shells, and reeds or water plants. The Sonoran coast supplies a great amount of food and raw materials, such as marine shell, fish, and salt, that was used not only by the coastal Prehispanic communities, but also by people located in the interior.

THE ONAVAS VALLEY

The Onavas Valley is part of the Río Yaqui drainage system (see Figure 1.1). The largest and most economically important river in the state of Sonora, the Río Yaqui has a mean annual discharge of 90,000,000 m³, extends about 740 km, and drains a watershed of some 80,000 km² (Pérez Bedolla 1996:116). The Río Yaqui originates to the west of the Sierra Madre at the junction of the Río Papigochic and Río Bavispe. On its way south to the coast, the major tributaries of the Río Yaqui are the Río Sahuaripa, Bacanora, Moctezuma, Chico, and Tecoripa. Below the Alvaro Obregón dam, the river changes its course westward to drain into the Gulf of California (Pérez Bedolla

1996:116). Currently, the Río Yaqui is the only river in Sonora that flows year-round. Previous to the construction of the Alvaro Obregón (1952) and El Novillo (1963) dams, the Río Yaqui had seasonal floods that irrigated and fertilized an extensive floodplain. This seasonal event, however, no longer occurs, or at least not with the force preceding the construction of the dams. Erosion marks on stone walls on the river banks illustrate that the river previously used to flood its banks at least 15 to 20 m higher than it does today (see Figure 7.1). The distribution of archaeological sites along the Río Yaqui confirms these old flood levels.

Topographically, the Onavas Valley consists of a system of parallel mountain ridges with narrow intermountain valleys and elevation ranging from 100 to 1200 m above sea level. Higher elevations in the area belong to four regional sierras. To the east side of the Río Yaqui lays the Sierra El Encinal with an elevation of 1500 to 1900 m. The Sierra Cabestro, which is 1138 m above sea level, stands at the southern portion of the Onavas Valley. On the west side of the Río Yaqui, the Sierra Varilleras ranges between 900 and 1300 m above sea level and the Sierra de las Huertas is 1300 m above sea level. The Sierra Varilleras encloses the Onavas Valley from the coastal province and it is the reason that the Río Yaqui continue south. Several deeply cut canyons are present in this area. So the Onavas Valley is a narrow strip of arable land that stretches north-south.

The soil regimes for the Onavas valley are mainly borolls (chernozem) and phaeozems on the alluvial floodplains, which are rich in nutrients and organic matter that are very good for farming. Between the hills and the alluvial floodplains it is common to find red soils, or xeresoles luvicos, that are poor in humus and not very good for extensive agriculture activities. Lithosol soils, "stone soils," extend into the mountains and are very thin with a thickness of less than 10 cm. The productivity of these soils depends on rain and vegetation covers (Pérez Bedolla 1996:113, 143).

The geographical diversity of the research area illustrates that the Prehispanic communities had a great variety of resources at their disposal which they most certainly used to their advantage. Natural resources for construction included stone outcrops and wood from the forests. Several natural resources met their craft production requirements, such as clay deposits for ceramic manufacture, in addition to stone outcrops and good quality raw material for stone tools manufacture. Freshwater resources from the Río Yaqui, and wild plants and local animals supplied material for a variety of daily necessities from food to household implements.

The most important of all these natural resources for human populations are perhaps the geographical and physical characteristics of the Onavas Valley area themselves. Over time the combination of rain, wind, and erosion produced a river valley rich in sediments with good soils for subsistence agriculture. These characteristics rendered the area suitable for permanent settlement with fields capable of sustaining large numbers of people. The identification of a large number of habitation sites in the area was expected, as well as the presence of the remains of water irrigation, such as canals and terraces.

Chapter 3
Previous Research in Southern Sonora

Nearly all the information comes from surface reconnaissance, most of this in the northern half of the state. The few excavations conducted have been on a small scale or have not been reported in detail (Johnson 1966:29).

Archaeological exploration, collection, data analysis, and publication of research in Northwest Mexico are comparatively far behind investigations both in Mesoamerica and the U.S. Southwest. As Kelley and Villalpando (1996:71) state:

> Culture history, chronology, definition of areal boundaries, understanding of cultural diversity and adaptation, knowledge of past and present environments, and so on thought a litany of the kind of topics that are of routine interest to Southwestern archaeologists, are for the most part very poorly known south of the international border.

This scenario has started to change over the last few decades with renewed interest from Mexican archaeologists, as well as American and Canadian colleagues (Gallaga and Newell 2004; Kelley and Villalpando 1996; Pollard 1997; Villalpando and Fish 1997). Prior to the OVAP, no researcher had created a model for the settlement pattern of the area and no archaeologists had undertaken a systematic recording and description of the valley's sites. Knowledge of the area's material culture either from artifact types or architecture was still limited. The chronology archaeologists relied upon for the area originated from the distant Huatabampo and Upper Río Mayo regions. Until

the present project, no formal archaeological excavation had been performed in the area or region. In the 1960s, Campbell Pennington (1980), an American geographer, conducted ethnographic research in the region providing a substantial cultural dataset, albeit mostly of contemporary and historic times.

Prior to Pennington's research, the principal source of ethnographic data for the Onavas Valley was Colonial period chronicles, beginning with the early Spanish *entradas* in the sixteenth century. However, the conquistadors' descriptions offer relatively little information about this area other than a few limited passages. Richer accounts about the Nébomes and the Onavas Valley are found in the ecclesiastic reports that the Jesuit fathers penned over 100 years later.

The Jesuits penetrated the Onavas region in 1622 when Father Diego Vandersipe founded the mission of Onavas and the *visita* churches of Tonichi and Rebeico (Ortega 1996:48; Figure 3.1). Over the years many other mission towns and settlements were established throughout the rest of what became the modern state of Sonora (Hu-Dehart 1995; Ortega 1996; Pérez de Ribas 1999; Radding 1997). The establishment of the missionary network together with the constant presence of the Spanish military created a complex administrative structure which produced an impressive amount of bureaucratic record. Reports of various kinds

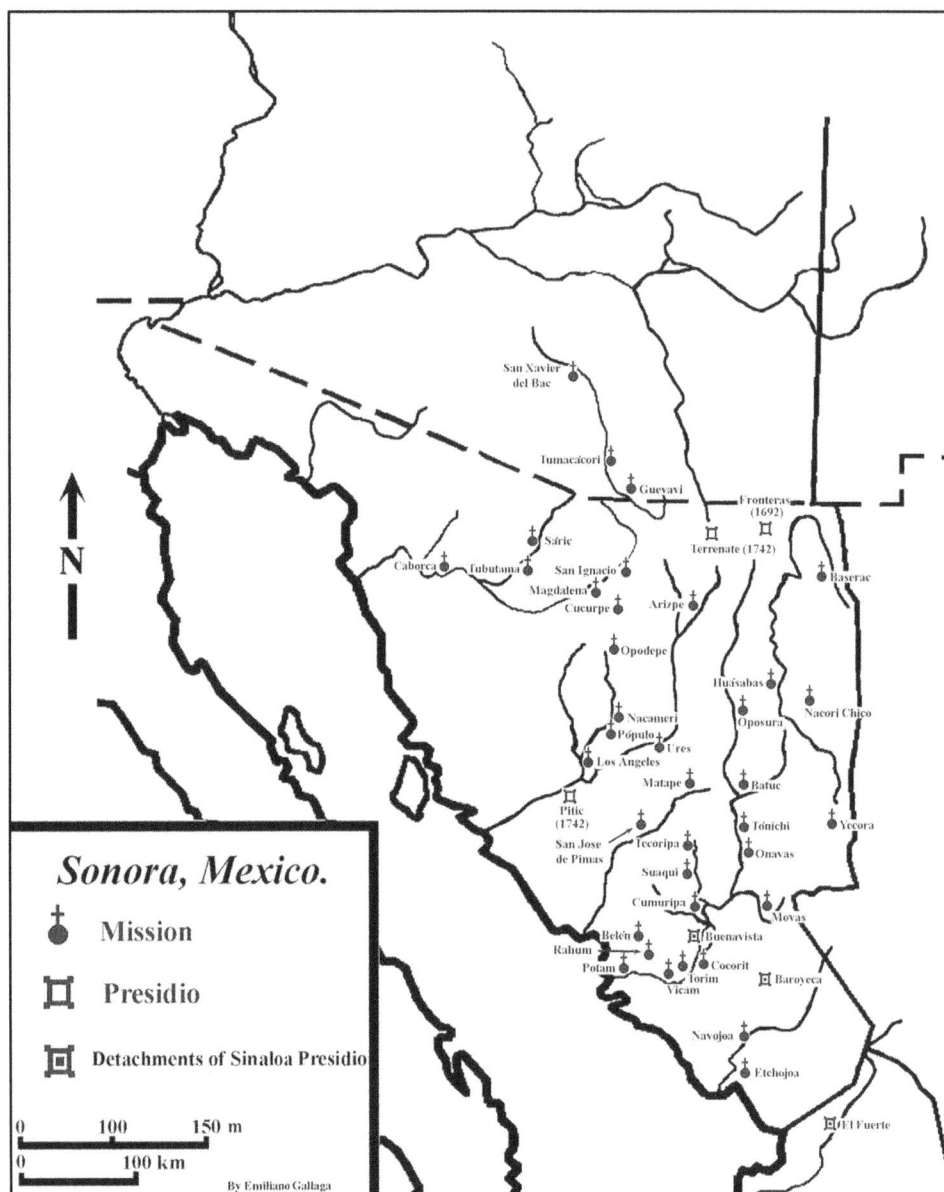

Figure 3.1. Missions and presidios in Sonora in 1742 (modified from Sheridan 1999 and West 1993).

found their way to Mexico City, Spain, and Rome. Yet over time, events such as the expulsion of the Jesuits from the New World in 1767 led to the destruction of documents, and much information has been lost since then.

To summarize the details of these historical documents and earliest missionaries in the Onavas Valley reported that a population of 20,000 Upper Nébomes lived in the area distributed among 90 rancherías and six large towns in the Onavas, Movas, and Nuri Valleys (Guzmán 1615; Pennington 1980:17; Pérez de Ribas 1999:393; Reff 1991:219). To clarify the types of settlements here, the term *ranchería* is used to describe small, scattered, riverine-oriented sites that provided permanent residential areas for the inhabitants. The documents also mention that the rancherías were dispersed along the river valleys. They describe houses made of adobe and irrigated agricultural fields along the river from which the native inhabitants harvested crops twice a year (Hopkins 1988:22; Guzmán 1615; Pérez de Ribas 1999:328). Spicer notes, however, that the description of rancherías for the Nébomes and Yaquis suggests that these regions were more densely settled than other neighboring native communities such as the Tarahumaras (Spicer 1992:12-13).

After Mexican Independence in 1821, several travelers and researchers ventured into Sonora in the late nineteenth and early twentieth centuries. Some produced written descriptions of the region, and others undertook explorations, but none visited the Middle Yaqui River region (Amsden 1928; Brand 1935; Gladwin and Gladwin 1929; Huntington 1912; Lister 1958; Lumholtz 1912; McGee 1895, 1896, 1898, 2000; Sauer and Brand 1931). It was not until the end of the 1930s that the area was first explored archaeologically under the aegis of the Sonora-Sinaloa Archaeological Survey Project.

THE SONORA-SINALOA ARCHAEOLOGICAL SURVEY PROJECT

George Vaillant, a researcher from the American Museum of Natural History in New York, conceived, designed, and directed the Sonora-Sinaloa Archaeological Survey Project. Although Vaillant directed the project, Gordon F. Ekholm, a former graduate student from Harvard University, was appointed project field director. The project's main objective consisted of filling the gap in the archaeological knowledge of the region between the U.S. Southwest and the northern Mesoamerican frontier, covering the area from the international border to the Río Culiacan (Ekholm 1942:33). Unfortunately, while the researchers achieved their objective, the results of the project remain largely unpublished, with the

exception of some general articles (Ekholm 1939), results of the excavation performed at the Guasave site in Sinaloa (Ekholm 1942), and a recent material catalogue compiled by Emiliano Gallaga (Gallaga 2004b).

Over the course of three field seasons of six months each, undertaken between 1937 and 1940, Ekholm surveyed areas within this vast region guided by local knowledge on the location of archaeological sites. Ekholm recorded a total of 175 sites in Sonora and northern Sinaloa (Figure 3.2). Of these, 100 sites lay in Sonora and the remainder in Sinaloa (Gallaga 2004b; see Table 3.1 for Ekholm site list). The sites Ekholm recorded occurred in different geographical areas, where the Prehispanic inhabitants had exploited different resources and followed different trajectories of cultural development. The sites Ekholm discovered in the interior of Sonora typically lay along the river valleys in areas near water sources and good agricultural lands, such as those of the Río Sonora archaeological tradition. The majority of sites Ekholm recorded were identified as Prehispanic (Ekholm 1937-1940).

Ekholm's extensive collections consisted mostly of surface material from 106 sites, but archaeological materials also came from excavations undertaken at the largest sites, including the Guasave site on the coast of Sinaloa. In addition, he purchased existing collections in the region, such as the Bringas collection from the inland town of Soyopa, Sonora (Ekholm 1937-1940; Gallaga 2004b). With the exception of the material from excavations and from private collections, Ekholm encountered mainly ceramic and lithic artifacts on his surveys, although a great variety existed within these artifact categories. Among the ceramic material, plain wares occurred in the greatest numbers. Decorated wares, malacates or spindle whorls, and ceramic figurines also appeared. Greater variety characterized the lithic collection, which included stone axes,

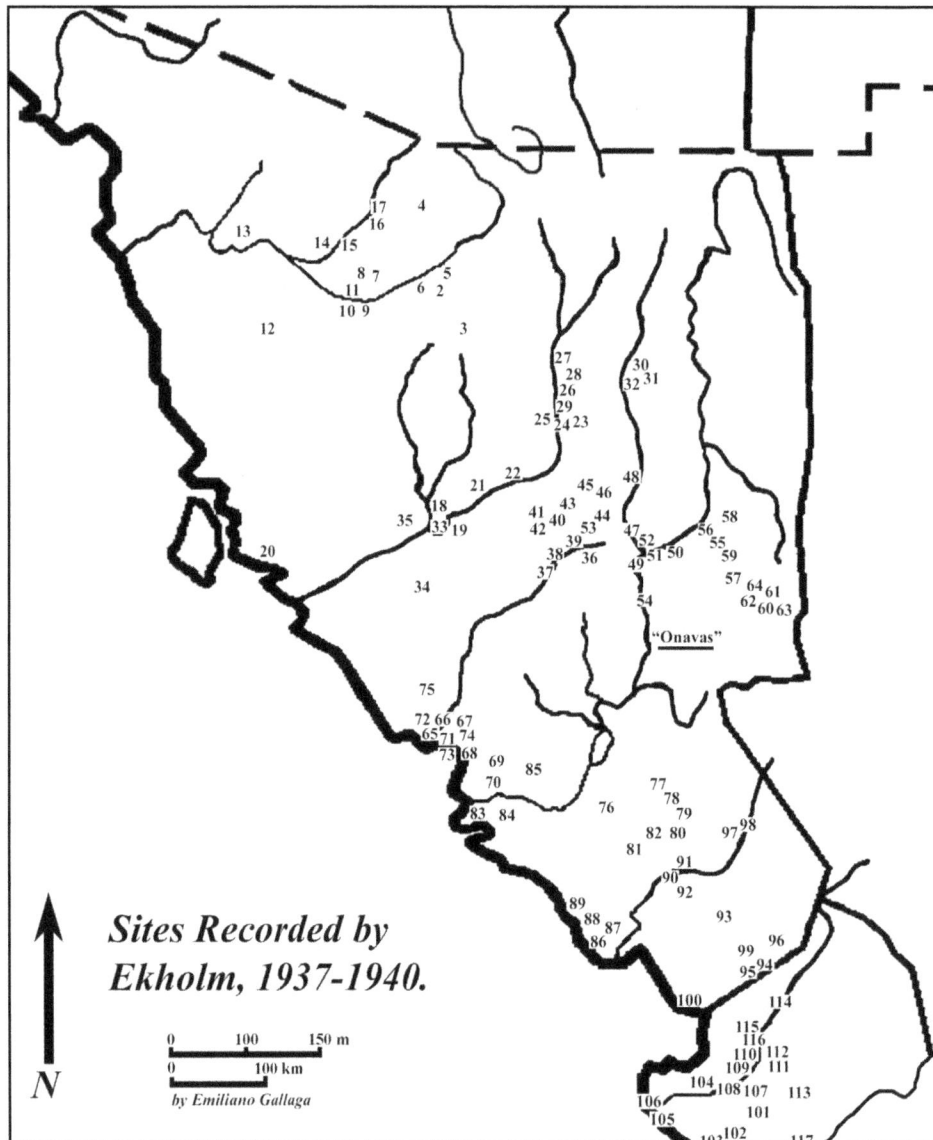

Figure 3.2. Sites recorded by Gordon Ekholm 1937-1940 (modified from Gallaga 2004b).

ornaments, palettes, agave knives, reamers, stone bowls, atlatl handles, and arrow points. Some turquoise beads and mica pendants were recovered as well. Another common material collected by Ekholm was marine shell. Marine shell as artifacts in various stages of productions included raw materials, works in progress, debris, and finished goods, such as beads, pendants, tinklers, or bracelets (Gallaga 2004b).

In general, the great variety of materials

that Ekholm encountered during the project suggests that a considerable movement of goods occurred between the coast and the interior. However, the amount of ancient trade was not to the degree he expected. The kind and degree of exchange found would not support theories of direct, large scale Mesoamerican-U.S. Southwest interaction (Carpenter 1996; Ekholm 1942:136; Gallaga 2004b). Unfortunately, because most of his research results

Table 3.1. Sites register by Ekholm, 1937-40, shown in Figure 3.2

1	Mazatlán, Sin.	46	No name	91	Celina
2	Escondida	47	Batuc	92	E Agua Blanca
3	Cucurpe	48	N San Pedro La Cueva	93	Rancho Gazella
4	El Alamo	49	Batuc II	94	Bacomayo
5	NE Magdalena	50	Rió Yaqui	95	÷Alamos and Rió Mayo
6	W Magdalena	51	Suaqui	96	Cueva del Altar
7	Sin nombre	52	Batuc II	97	San Bernardo
8	La Playa	53	Virgen	98	Bernardo II
9	El Cerrito de las Trincheras	54	Soyopa	99	Rancho los Braziles
10	Cerro de Trincheras	55	Sahuaripa II	100	Agiobampo
11	Misión Alamito	56	Sahuaripa III	101	Los Mochis, Sinaloa
12	SW Bamori	57	Arivechi	102	Topolobampo, Sin.
13	W Caborca	58	Ticorinami	103	Topolobampo II, Sin.
14	N Altar	59	Sahuaripa	104	Suarez, Sin.
15	N Oquitoa	60	Cueva de la momia, Tayopa	105	Delta del Río Fuerte, Sin.
16	Atil	61	Rancho Tayopa	106	San Pablo II, Sin.
17	Santa Teresa	62	Cueva Toyopa	107	Mochicahui, Sin.
18	Punta Cerco	63	Paxson Hayes mommy burial	108	La Haciendita, Sin.
19	Mesa del Seri	64	Toyopa	109	La Palma, Sin.
20	Bahia Kino	65	Guaymas	110	La Palma, Sin.
21	Rancho El Gavilan	66	Empalme	111	San Blas, Sin.
22	San Joaquin	67	Empalme II	112	San Blas II, Sin.
23	San Jose	68	Guasimas	113	Tasajera, Sin.
24	San Pablo	69	Mapoli	114	Paparaki, Sin.
25	La Estancia	70	Pitaya	115	Buenavista, Sin.
26	Huepac	71	Playa Miramar	116	Buenavista II, Sin.
27	Bacachi	72	Guaymas II	117	Guasave, Sin.
28	El Ranchito	73	Playa Miramar II	118	Bacahuarita, Sin.
29	Aconchi	74	Cuevas (playa Miramar)	119	Bacahuarita II, Sin.
30	S Cumpas	75	Aranjuez	120	Bacahuarita III, Sin.
31	La Galera	76	Cajeme	121	Bamoa, Sin.
32	Jecori	77	Tezopaco (Rosario)	122	Bamoa II, Sin.
33	Haciendita	78	Cedros	128	Ocoroni, Sin.
34	La Pintada	79	Tesocoma		
35	W Hermosillo	80	Quiriego		
36	Mazatan	81	Batacosa		
37	Mazatan II	82	Tapahuis		
38	Mazatan III	83	La Luna		
39	Mazatan IV	84	Potam		
40	Rancho de Alamos	85	Torocobampo		
41	El Pueblo Viejo	86	E. Estero Bueca		
42	Rancho de Alamos II	87	Huatabampo		
43	Pueblo de Alamos	88	Tobaris S		
44	Mahacubiri	89	Tobaris N (Echomora)		
45	Rancho Gayago	90	Camoa		

remain unpublished, no general conclusions can be make about the sites, the area, settlement patterns, or even the artifacts. John Carpenter (1996) undertook the first detailed re-evaluation of the Ekholm collection, but focused on the excavated material from the Guasave mortuary mound site and not on the surface material of the entire area Ekholm explored.

In the Middle Río Yaqui Valley, Ekholm found and recorded only five sites. Today, four lay under water as a result of the modern El Novillo dam, also referred to as the Plutarco Elias Calles dam (sites # 47, 49, 51 and 52), while the fifth (# 54) lies close to the modern town of Soyopa (Figure 3.3) and approximately 50 km from Onavas (see Figure 3.2). All are located to the north of the Onavas Valley. Of the five sites recorded, Ekholm excavated only the settlement near the town of Soyopa (# 54), and did so with limited success (Ekholm 1937-1940, 1939). Most of the material Ekholm recovered consisted of plain and redware sherds and a couple of shells (Gallaga 2004b).

THE ARIZONA STATE MUSEUM SONORA-SINALOA PROJECT

In the late 1960s, William W. Wasley directed the Arizona State Museum Sonora-Sinaloa Project and conducted a large survey covering almost all of Sonora. This project, however, excluded the Yaqui region, getting only as close as the town of Bacanora (Bowen 2002; Wasley 1966-1967). Wasley left the Yaqui region unexamined because another archaeologist, Richard Pailes, was working in the southern area of the region at that time. At the end of the Arizona State Museum Sonora-Sinaloa Project, Wasley recorded more than 200 sites, mostly in the Trincheras, Seri, and Serrana regions (Bowen 2002). Unfortunately, Wasley never published

Figure 3.3. Excavation of site # 54 at Soyopa by Ekholm (Ekholm 1937-1940, AMNH archives, NY).

the final report or material analysis. A substantial manuscript generated from this project
exists in the Arizona State Museum archives,
but it lacks relevant information on the Onavas
area (Wasley 1966-1967). Fortunately, Bowen
(2002), one of the student members of the projects, published some of the archaeological data
from Seri and Trincheras regions.

RICHARD PAILES AND THE RÍO SONORA ARCHAEOLOGICAL TRADITION

During the early 1970s, Richard Pailes conducted an extensive archaeological survey and

undertook limited test excavations between
southern Sonora and northern Sinaloa. The
project focus on the river valleys, and aimed
to determine whether the Río Sonora archaeological tradition reached as far as the southern
Sonora-northern Sinaloa region. In addition,
Pailes strove to compose a chronology for
the Huatabampo archaeological tradition and
sought to describe the local Prehispanic cultural
adaptations to this region (Pailes 1972:2).

The final field results of the project
recorded a total of 119 sites and partial excavations at two sites (site YE 27-2 and Cueva
de la Colmena) (Figure 3.4). Pailes also
established the first chronology for southern

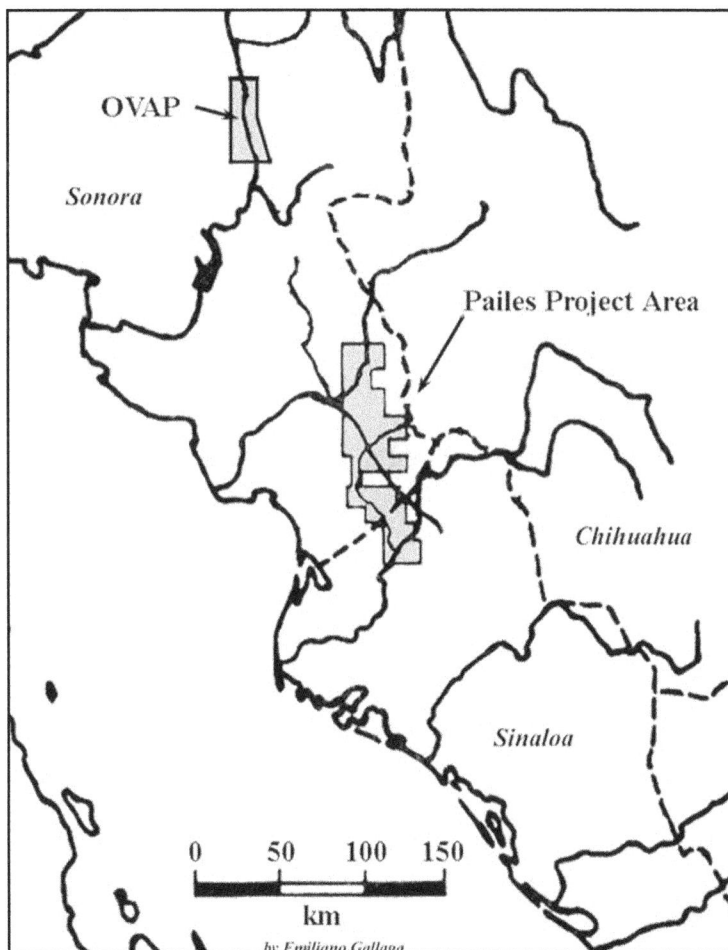

Figure 3.4. Río Sonora Project by Richard Pailes (1972) in relation to OVAP.

Sonora based on eight ^{14}C dates, two obsidian hydration dates, and intrusive Sinaloan ceramics from the excavation of two sites. Thus, Pailes' research resulted in a chronology with an early cultural sequence he called the Batacosa phase (300 B.C.–A.D. 700) and two later cultural sequences, the Cuchujaqui phase (A.D. 700–1500) for the lower foothills, and the Los Camotes (A.D. 700–1200/1300) and San Bernardo (A.D. 1200/1300–1530) phases for the upper foothills (Pailes 1972:329; see Figure 1.3). All these chronological phases have cultural affiliations with the coastal lowlands to the south and west.

Batacosa sites are located in the upper and lower foothills, while the Cuchujaqui sites appear only in the lower foothills. The Los Camotes and San Bernardo phase sites only occur in the upper foothills. Batacosa sites are small, housing probably one immediate or extended family. For this phase, Pailes found no architectural remains and recovered a limited material assemblage consisting of a brown and red plain ware called Batacosa Brown and Batacosa Red, basin metates, manos, and flakes (Pailes 1994a:83). The Cuchujaqui sites are similar to the Batacosa settlements except the former had larger material assemblage. A new ceramic type was identified, which was named the Cuchujaqui Red. A number of northern Sinaloa wares were recorded, such as Guasave Rojo-over-Brown, and were interpreted as an indication of regional contacts. In addition, marine shell objects and stone tools were encountered (Pailes 1994a:83).

In the upper foothills, Pailes found stone structures and some large sites on top of the hills and mesas, dating to the Los Camotes phase (A.D. 700-1250/1300). The material assemblage from this period consisted of Los Camotes Incised ceramics, a brown ware with a geometrical incised decoration, as well as metates, manos (tapered-end type), projectile points, and ¾-grooved stone axes (Pailes

1994a:85). The following San Bernardo phase (A.D. 1250/1300-1530) contained evidence for some cultural change from the preceding period. Site sizes increased from very small to large and the preferred location for sites switched from the hills to the valleys, which were interpreted as evidence for an increase and concentration of population. Residential structures likely consisted of adobe with stone foundations, similar to those found on the Río Sonora. The material assemblage also became larger and more diverse. Three ceramic types were identified: San Bernardo Incised, Corrugated, and Texturized. Several stone tools were identified such as shaft polishers, hoes, stone axes, stone pipes, and even a coarse stone idol was recovered (Pailes 1994a:85-86).

The Río Sonora archaeological tradition was initially defined by Monroe Amsden in 1928; however, his work consists mainly of general descriptions of the archaeological record and materials rather than broader interpretations and synthesis. Pailes' subsequent research in the area defined a Río Sonora tradition based on stone foundations for habitation units composed of two lines of river cobbles, and ceramic material decorated with incising or punctuated geometric designs (Amsden 1928:45; Pailes 1994b:118). The Los Camotes and San Bernardo phases and the sites located at the upper foothills and at the Sierra Madre Occidental are affiliated with the Río Sonora tradition (Pailes 1972:3). The Cuchujaqui phase and sites located on the lower foothills are affiliated with the Huatabampo archaeological tradition (Pailes 1972:334). The expansion of the geographical reach of the Río Sonora tradition toward the border of Sonora and Sinaloa constituted one of the main contributions of the Río Sonora Project.

At the end of the 1970s, Pailes conducted another project, the Valley of Sonora Project, which was located in northern Sonora at the core of the Río Sonora culture. This research merely confirmed Amsden's preliminary arguments and postulations about the Río Sonora tradition. Although both of Pailes' archaeological projects covered an extensive area of the Río Sonora tradition, Pailes did not venture into the Middle Río Yaqui region. He approached the area as close as the northern portion of the Río Mayo to the south and south of the middle portion of the Río Sonora to the north of the Río Yaqui. Instead, he simply and deductively assumed that the Río Sonora tradition of north-central Sonora continued as far as northern Sinaloa. This assessment was based on the similarity of material evidence found at both extremes of this extensive region (Doolittle 1988; Pailes 1972:2-3, 1994a:81; Villalpando 2000b:249). Pailes emphasized, however, that any understanding of cultural homogeneity was speculative due to the lack of research on the central portion of this region (Pailes 1994a:81).

Either way, the study increased the still limited archaeological knowledge of the Río Yaqui area (Dirst 1979; Pailes 1972, 1994a).

THE PIMA BAJO OF CENTRAL SONORA ETHNOGRAPHIC PROJECT

Between 1968 and 1971, Campbell W. Pennington undertook research in the OVAP research area, albeit of a slightly different nature than Pailes' project (Pennington 1980). His research was not archaeological, but ethnohistoric and ethnolographic in nature. He studied the Pimas Bajos (Nébomes) of central Sonora and established his base camp in the community of Onavas (Figure 3.5). In his first volume, Pennington analyzes archives (military and ecclesiastic) from the Colonial through modern periods. Based on the docu-

Figure 3.5. Pedro Estrella Tánori's family at Onavas, Sonora, 1960s (Pennington 1980: frontispiece).

ments, Pennington discussed the contact and interactions between the Pimas Bajos with Spaniards, Mexicans, and other native groups. He also provides a cultural description and historical narrative of the Pima Bajo people. In addition to the ethnohistoric work, Pennington's description of 1960s era Piman life ways offer valuable insights into their culture, including agriculture, animal husbandry, gardening, food preparation, hunting, gathering, fishing, ceremonies, plant use, games, leather goods, fibers, textiles, personal adornments, and dwellings. In a second volume, Pennington presents Pima Bajo (Nébomes) vocabulary, which is an edited version of a seventeenth-century Jesuit manuscript.

Although Pennington collected some archaeological artifacts from the field, such as axes, projectile points, and stone pallets, his project did not include archaeological research. An attempt was made to locate those materials but there was no success. His ethnohistorical data, however, offers a valuable depiction of the Indian communities during the early Colonial period. His insight facilitated the interpretation, understanding, and explanation of the archaeological record recorded during the OVAP by drawing analogies between past and present life ways and material culture, as later chapters illustrate in greater detail.

THE PROCEDE PROJECT

Between the 1960s and the late 1990s, no one conducted archaeological work in the region. Then, as a result of legal changes in the ejido (community land tenure and usufruct) system in Mexico, the Instituto Nacional de Antropología e Historia de México (INAH) carried out a national archaeological survey project on ejido lands called PROCEDE (Proyecto de Certificacion y Delimitacion Ejidal) in 1996. The ejido system was a prod-

uct of the Mexican Revolution and established commonly-held lands for local communities. Until constitutional changes at the end of the 1990s, ejido land passed from father to son, but could not be sold.

The PROCEDE national project in the study region was directed in the State of Sonora by archaeologist Elisa Villalpando of the INAH-Sonora. In the area of the OVAP research, the PROCEDE project recorded five new sites near the Onavas town (INAH 1998). Archaeologists undertook limited surface collection at these sites, designated SON P:6:2, SON P:10:2, SON P:10:3, SON P:10:4, and SON P:10:5 (Appendix I and II). Four of them were located on the east side of the river on the floodplain, and a fifth was situated in the hills on the west side of the river. Of those, three sites fall directly within the OVAP research area (SON P:10:2, SON P:10:3, and SON P:10:4, See Appendix I and II). Archaeologists obtained the locations of those sites fortuitously by tapping into local knowledge from informants. Neither systematic survey nor excavations took place. Moreover, the study refrained from covering the surrounding hills and mountains, and only focused on the floodplain. With the exception of SON P:10:5, nine of the ten sites known in the Middle Río Yaqui region (five recorded by Ekholm and five by PROCEDE) were found in the valley. The material PROCEDE collected consisted mostly of plainware ceramics, red wares, some lithics, and a few marine shell items. Notably, one Babícora Polychrome ceramic sherd belonging to the Casas Grandes archaeological tradition was recovered. Reports also indicate that some shell remains were found at these sites, but no further analysis of this or any other material was conducted during this project. While the final report is on file at the National Council of Archaeology in Mexico City, PROCEDE's final results and material analysis remain unpublished.

ARCHAEOLOGICAL TRADITIONS OF SOUTHERN SONORA

A summary description of the archaeological traditions identified for the southern region of Sonora completes the history of previous archaeological research for the Middle Río Yaqui region. Two traditions require elaboration here: the Río Sonora and the Huatabampo (see Figure 1.2).

Río Sonora Archaeological Tradition

The Río Sonora archaeological tradition is found in the upland portion of Sonora, which has sites located in the valleys and mountains of the eastern Sierra Madre Occidental extending from northern Sinaloa almost to the international border (Alvarez 1996; Dirst 1979; Doolittle 1988; Kelley and Villalpando 1996; Pailes 1980, 1993). Most of the research in this area has focused on the Río Sonora valley and, in particular, on the San José Baviácora site. Research in other areas will inevitably change or elaborate the definition of the Río Sonora tradition. Some researchers view the Río Sonora tradition merely as a manifestation of influence from the Casas Grandes people. Investigators have suggested that it is possible that Casas Grandes attempted to control trade routes to the ocean and/or sent migrants to the region (Braniff 1992:I:18; Pailes 1984:319-325; Riley 1999:199), while others think that the Rio Sonora tradition is a local development (Douglas and Quijada 2005; McGuire and Villalpando 1989; Villalpando 2000b:250). Further research and material evidence is required to verify these interpretations and clarify the general picture of the Río Sonora tradition (Dirst 1979; Kelley and Villalpando 1996; Newell and Gallaga 2004; Villalpando 2000a).

Amsden (1928) undertook the first research project in the area in the 1920s, but research by Pailes in the 1970s (1972, 1980, 1993) and later by Doolittle (1988) provided most of the description for the Río Sonora tradition. In addition, research by John Douglas and César Quijada in the Bavispe drainage has contributed, and continues to add, much information about this tradition (Douglas and Quijada 2004a, 2004b, 2005). John Carpenter's current research in the Upper Río Fuerte drainage will increase Pailes' findings, as will the work of Cristina Moreno who is currently working in the south portion of Sonora registering new sites and performing excavations at sites such as Batacosa that will increase our knowledge of the area. More importantly, their work sheds light on areas beyond the more commonly investigated Río Sonora valley.

In chronological terms, the archaic period of the Río Sonora area remains poorly understood. Between A.D. 250 and 700, the inhabitants lived in ranchería type settlements, evidenced by a significant amount of lithic and ceramic material found without visible domestic structures. Around A.D. 1000-1200, pithouses appeared in the archaeological record of the Río Sonora area (Doolittle 1988:27). The inhabitants seem to have practiced agriculture, while relying on hunting-and-gathering subsistence activities as well. Textured Red-on-Brown ceramic types characterize this phase. Between A.D. 1200-1300, the pithouses were replaced by rectangular structures identified on the surface by stone foundations composed of two lines of river cobbles (Amsden 1928:45; Doolittle 1988:23). The Río Sonora people continued to manufacture textured ceramics although some foreign decorated types were imported mostly from the Casas Grandes region (Alvarez 1996:214). Other imports such as turquoise, pottery types, marine shell, and copper bells also suggest that the area also enjoyed extensive exchange networks, mainly with the Casas Grandes region, the U.S. Southwest, and the Pacific coast (Alvarez 1996;

Amsden 1928; Dirst 1979; Doolittle 1988; Kelley and Villalpando 1996; Pailes 1980, 1993; Villalpando 2000a).

The Río Sonora tradition climaxed between A.D. 1400 and 1500, illustrated by complex farming activities associated with soil-retention and irrigation techniques. The San José Baviácora site became a relatively more complex community with over 180 structures, among them public architecture such as ball courts and elongated platforms. Doolittle (1988:45) determined that by this time, the inhabitants of the region cultivated cotton, tepary beans, and two annual crops of maize.

Unfortunately, the period between A.D. 1500 and the arrival of the Spaniards is currently invisible in the archaeological record. By the time the Spaniards entered the area, Opata groups had settled the region, although Piman groups had lived in that area before the Opata arrived (Sauer 1934:40; Villalpando 2000b:250). Piman groups may have left the region for some still unknown reason, in effect leaving the area open for the Opatas. Alternatively, the Opatas may have pushed the Pimans out during a period of Opata expansion (Sauer 1934:40).

Due to archaeological evidence that illustrated that the Río Sonora Prehispanic societies show a degree of complexity, several researchers argue that the region was organized into "statelets" (Doolittle 1988:59-60; Pailes 1993; Riley 1999:195-196). Riley (1987) coined the term "statelets," but neglected to provide a clear definition. Nonetheless, a general definition is obtainable from other publications. A *statelet* is taken to refer to a level of socio-political organization similar or slightly more complex than that of the Pueblo Indians (Riley 1999:197). Motivated by their research findings, Douglas and Quijada (2004a) mention that the lack of research in the past and the results from new research in this area, lead to questions around the identification of statelets as part of the Río

Sonora tradition.

Huatabampo Archaeological Tradition

First described in the 1930s by Ekholm (1942) and later by Alvarez (1990, 1996) in the 1980s, the Huatabampo tradition is found in the southern portion of Sonora and the northern section of Sinaloa (see Figure 1.2). The inhabitants of this area lived in relatively complex communities: most settlements were located on the coast but were also found on the lower foothills. Surface collections and excavation of the Huatabampo site have provided most of the information known about this tradition today. The pre-ceramic period remains virtually unknown, though it seems plausible that inhabitants of that area lived like their nomadic neighbors, the prehistoric Seris. Around 200 B.C., the inhabitants of this area started to cultivate maize and beans along the major rivers or near water sources, as indicated by relatively substantial sites found in those locations (Villalpando 2000b:246). Early ceramic types include by Huatabampo Brown and Venadito Brown wares, which were later replaced by redwares types. Around A.D. 700 to 750, when farming conditions apparently were favorable, the number of sites in the area increased. Settlements flourished in the Río Fuerte and Río Mayo valleys, on the coastal plain and up into the lower Sierra Madre Occidental (Alvarez 1990, 1996:221; Carpenter 1996).

The Huatabampo site consists of a dispersed village composed of scattered non-contiguous houses made from perishable materials, perhaps lath and mud or adobe. The community also included communal spaces, trash mounds, and cemetery areas. The material recovered from excavations indicates that the Huatabampo people participated in long-distance regional trade networks with people from northern and southern areas. They seem to have obtained turquoise and ceramic figurines from the north and obsidian blades and ceramic vessels from the south, all in exchange for marine shell (Alvarez 1990, 1996; Carpenter 1996; Ekholm 1942; Kelley and Villalpando 1996; Villalpando 2000a).

The Huatabampo community was abandoned abruptly around A.D. 1000, probably due in part to rapid environmental changes. Between A.D. 1000 and 1100 the Huatabampo tradition seems to have continued in northern Sinaloa at the Guasave and Mochicahui sites (Carpenter 1996; Talavera 1995). By the time the Spanish conquistadors entered the area, Cahita speakers (e.g., Yaqui and Mayo Indians) lived in the region (Alvarez 1990, 1996; Carpenter and Sánchez 2001; Ekholm 1942; Kelley and Villalpando 1996; Villalpando 2000a, 2000b). Due to the magnitude of modern agricultural activities in the area, nearly all Prehispanic sites reported on the coast have been destroyed. The areas around the lower sierra and in the Río Fuerte and Río Mayo Valleys have not been researched, but future investigation in these regions could provide valuable information about this tradition and its regional interactions (Alvarez 1990). Currently John Carpenter is running a project on the upper portion of the Río Fuerte drainage: his findings will increase our knowledge of the costal Huatabampo tradition, in addition to the cultures in the foothills, and the Sierra communities.

EVALUATION OF ETHNOHISTORIC DATA FOR THE NÉBOMES

The first mention of Onavas Valley or the Nébomes traces back to early Spanish Colonial documents that consist mostly of descriptions of the Spanish entradas, such as those by Diego de Guzman (Carrera Stampa 1955; Heredia 1969), Francisco de Ibarra (Hopkins 1988), Marcos de Niza (Hallenbeck 1987), Nuñez

Cabeza de Vaca (1993, Covey 1998), and Vasquez de Coronado (Hammond 1940; Hammond and Rey 1940; Nakayama 1974). Contextualizing these and later writings requires a short historical overview.

After the fall of Mexico-Tenochtitlan in 1521, Spaniards embarked on a quest of discovery and conquest of new lands and kingdoms. Exploration of northwestern New Spain was focused on finding a safe and more direct path either by land or sea to Asia, specifically to the Philippines, which had territories and ports that later become part of the Kingdom of Spain (Sauer 1932:3). The process of exploration and conquest was relatively fast in central and north central Mexico and highly destructive for native communities everywhere. By 1523, the villa of Colima was founded by Hernán Cortés and by the early 1530s, Nuño de Guzman founded the villa of San Miguel Culiacán. The latter formed the northernmost Spanish settlement for almost half a century and served as departure point for multiple expeditions bound north and northwest (Sauer 1932:8-9).

In 1533, the Diego de Guzman exploration party reached as far north as the modern location of Cumuripa on the Río Yaqui and returned to Culiacán. Three years later in 1536 and after eight years of traveling, Núñez Cabeza de Vaca and his three companions finished their unexpected journey when they encountered a Spanish slave raiding party between the Río Sinaloa and the Río Mocorito (Núñez Cabeza de Vaca 1993:97; Sauer 1932:20). Their return to Spanish society and their histories motivated further exploration into the northwest of New Spain. In 1536, Fray Marcos de Niza with the black slave Esteban set out in search of the famed cities of Cibola, known today as Zuni (Hallenbeck 1987). After Esteban's death at the hands of the Zuni Indians, a fearful Fray Marcos decided to return to Mexico City before ever setting his eyes upon the cities. In Mexico City, Fray Marcos transformed his ill-fated expedition into a golden tale, in part motivating Vazquez de Coronado's expedition of 1540 (Hammond 1940; Sauer 1932:32). Coronado reached Cíbola at the Zuni pueblos in modern New Mexico and after observing they were no more than pueblos, returned to Mexico City. The fever for northwest exploration languished after the disappointment of Coronado's expedition.

The absence of complex societies and cultural richness such as those present in central Mexico or Peru resulted in a slow Spanish penetration in the northwest region of New Spain and a rather general and limited description of the native population there. The additional realization that this region lacked easy access to wealth or sedentary societies to conquer for labor purposes meant that the area beyond northern Sinaloa drew little interest. Growing rumors of wealth further north, initially under the banner of the Seven Cities of Cíbola, drew the attention of explorers in a different direction (Carpenter 1996:84; Sauer 1932:20). Subsequent exploratory expeditions, until the Jesuit penetration, focused on reaching those cities paying little or no attention to the region in between (e.g., modern Sonora). Travel descriptions focused on geography, such as mountains, distances, or rivers and the availability of resources, especially water. General comments about the area's population center mostly on disposition toward the Spaniards, whether or not the natives showed resistance or formed a particular threat to the conquistador's objectives.

Diego de Guzman provides the first account of the Nébomes. During his expedition in 1533, he reached Cumuripa, the lowermost Nébome village on the Río Yaqui (Carrera Stampa 1955:172; Sauer 1932:12). The account details that the village had been destroyed recently by Yaqui Indians but provides no further description. Several years later, Núñez Cabeza de Vaca was the first to mention the vil-

lage of Onavas. On his way to Sinaloa, his party encountered a Nébome Indian in a settlement, ethnohistorians identify as Onavas, wearing a "sword-belt buckle" with a stitched-on horseshoe nail (Covey 1998:122; Núñez Cabeza de Vaca 1993:94). Again, no further description of the settlement or the Indians is presented. Interestingly, Pennington (1980:55) mentions that nearly 350 Nébomes were among the natives who accompanied Núñez Cabeza de Vaca by the time they reached Sinaloa, and they eventually founded the town of Bamoa in northern Sinaloa (Pérez de Ribas 1999:103, 185-187; Sheridan 1999). Unfortunately, neither Núñez Cabeza de Vaca nor Pérez de Ribas offer more detailed information about this particular group or event.

According to his report, Fray Marcos de Niza and his expedition traveled along the Río Yaqui to the village of Corazones located in the Sonora Valley. Unfortunately, his descriptions only summarize the area as being well-populated and having received great hospitality from the natives (Hallenbeck 1987: lx; Sauer 1932:27). Coronado seems to be the next expedition to pass through the Onavas Valley, but again no mention at all is made of any Prehispanic communities in this area (Hammond 1940: 24; Nakayama 1974:24).

Twenty-five years later, Francisco de Ibarra undertook another expedition to penetrate the northwest in 1565. He founded the Villa of San Jaun Bautista de Carapoa on the banks of the Rio Fuerte River. On his expedition, Francisco de Ibarra passed through the Onavas Valley only to mention that he encountered nearly 500 Nébome warriors with weapons and elaborate clothing decorated with feathers, beads and marine shell (Hopkins 1988:16). After some Nébomes re-supplied Ibarra's expedition he continued on north, but additional descriptions are lacking for the later portion of his journey. On April 30, 1583, Don Pedro de Montoya founded the villa de San

Felipe y Santiago de Sinaloa on the left bank of the Petatlán River.

The reports of almost all of the expeditions of the sixteenth century mention hardly anything about the Middle Yaqui region (Pennington 1980:10)—a region that at this time was considered an integral part of el camino del norte, or the road north (Sauer 1932:1). However, these reports do include descriptions of the Opatas further north. The Opateria area was located at a suitable distance for re-supplying the Spaniards and consisted of a more sedentary and complex community than other indigenous communities they had previously encountered. The Spaniards are likely to have looked favorably upon the Opata nation. The Opata Indians' favorable reception of the Spaniards further contributed to more elaborate descriptions of the Opatas in Colonial documents (Riley 1999:196-197).

In addition to the Spaniard's apparent lack of interest in the region, other than as route of passage, the destruction they brought to the region in the form of disease and violence disrupted and diminished Prehispanic communities in general (Reff 1991:xii; Sauer 1932:7; Spicer 1992:16). Whereas early Colonial documents mention the high population numbers and settlements in the region and emphasize the area's richness, later expeditions describe desolation and abandoned settlements (Covey 1998:123; Nuñez Cabeza de Vaca 1993:95).

While no direct description of the Onavas Valley exists in the early Colonial records, the few references made concerning this region suggest that the area was settled by well-populated communities that were predominantly sedentary. Their inhabitants practiced agriculture and irrigated farming. They engaged in trade as far west as the coast and north as the modern U.S. Southwest. They also undertook warfare with their neighbors, Yaquis, Opatas, and/or Seris (Carrera Stampa 1955; Covey 1998; Hammond 1940; Hammond and Rey

1940; Heredia 1969; Hopkins 1988; Nakayama 1974; Nuñez Cabeza de Vaca 1993; Sauer 1932).

Following initial explorations by the conquistadors, Jesuit Fathers entered the region, and produced a variety of ethnohistorical documents and reports which contain detailed observations on the area. Their rich descriptions of the native communities proved far more informative than the military reports and expedition chronicles. The most significant sources for this period were provided by Father Pérez de Ribas (1999), Father Juan Ortiz Zapata (1678), Father Juan Varela (1626), Father Philipp Segesser (1945), and Captain Diego Martinez de Hurdaide (in Pérez de Ribas 1999, 1610-1617). Most of the cultural interpretation and ideas about the Prehispanic groups that lived in this area originate from these documents; although I hasten to point out that the OVAP did not encounter the requisite archaeological evidence to support all their observations.

After the establishment of the villa of San Felipe and Santiago in 1586 and the realization that military conquest was not the most suitable option to colonize this arid land, Spanish authorities changed their colonization strategy to one of evangelization (Ortega 1996:42). The Company of Jesus, or the Jesuits, took responsibility for this task with ardent zeal and in 1591 the first two Fathers arrived at the villa: Martín Perez and Gonzalo de Tapia. As more Fathers arrived, the villa of San Felipe and Santiago served as the foundation for Jesuit missionization of the native souls further north. Penetration was slow but steady. By 1622, Father Diego Vandersipe founded the mission of Onavas and the visitas of Tonichi and Rebeico (Ortega 1996:48). After the mission was established at least twelve Jesuits Fathers ministered at Onavas before their expulsion from New Spain in 1767 (Pennington 1980:374-384).

Previous to the establishment of the mission in the Onavas Valley, Captain Hurdaide, commander of the presidio El Fuerte and the region's military enterprises, contacted the Nébomes and provided good descriptions of their culture and society. According to Hurdaide, the Nébomes were peaceful, willing to accept Spanish domination, and constantly requesting missionaries to come to their towns. They lived in sedentary settlements of adobe houses, practiced irrigation farming, and were well-dressed (Hurdaide 1614, in Pérez de Ribas 1999:289-290). Reportedly, the Nébomes had learned about Spanish missions and administration well through their relatives from the town of Bamoa in Sinaloa, with whom they maintained constant contact.

After the founding of the missions among the Nébomes, Colonial documents provide some information about them in the early years of missionization, but little is mentioned in subsequent documents. In general, the Jesuit Colonial documents associated with the Onavas Valley describe the status of the mission and, list its accounts, debts, and inventories, or consist of administrative correspondence written by the missionaries stationed at Onavas. Overall, these reports fail to elaborate much on the Indian community. Spicer (1992:88) explains that as the Nébomes were incorporated into the mission system "there is no record of any but routine happenings in these missions for nearly 150 years."

Fortunately, Father Pérez de Ribas, in his magna obra "History of the Triumphs of our Holy Faith amongst the most Barbarous and Fierce People of the New World" published in Spain in 1645, provides some substantial information about the Nébome Indian nation (Pérez de Ribas 1999). Having served as missionary in the region from 1604 to 1619, some of this information draws upon personal experience. Later, through his work as Jesuit provincial and rector at the Colegio Maximo and the Jesuit Casa Profesa, Father Pérez

de Ribas accumulated much experience and knowledge. He also obtained further insights and information on northern New Spain from letters, reports, and annuas from military and missionary personnel who worked at or visited the Onavas mission in the early years of its founding. Apparently, the quick acceptance of Spanish dominion and Colonial system among the Nébome communities and the lack of violence and serious transgressions of this nation toward the Fathers rendered them largely invisible in the Colonial documents. In contrast to their troublesome neighbors, the Yaquis or Seris, who were constantly mentioned by the Spaniards for their opposition, the Nébome required little elaboration.

In that respect, continuous and large-scale conflict between indigenous groups in this region stands out in the ethnohistorical literature. In the case of the Nébome in particular, by the time of Spanish contact, this group had been struggling to maintain its territory from an expansion of the Yaqui and Opata territories, to the south and north respectively. Diego de Guzman noted that when his expedition reached Cumuripa, the lowermost Nébome village on the Río Yaqui, in 1533 the village had been destroyed recently by Yaqui Indians (Carrera Stampa 1955:172; Sauer 1932:12). Apparently, this territorial warfare limited both Nébome contact from outside of their territory and their mobility. The latter is illustrated by the fact that almost 350 Nébomes, who founded the town of Bamoa in northern Sinaloa (Pérez de Rivas 1999:103, 185-187), fled the area with Cabeza de Vaca in 1536. Jesuit reports mention subsequent Nébome groups leaving the area to settle near Spanish communities or that the Nébomes requested constant Spanish military support to keep the Yaquis and Opatas at bay (Pérez de Rivas 1999).

In spite of the rather small amount of descriptive information on the Nébome given the many years of missionization, ethnohistorical and ethnographic research offer a limited amount of data about their culture. The available data indicates that the Onavas Valley was settled by the Nébome nation and that the Lower Nébomes, who lived in the Onavas, Movas, and Nuri Valleys reached a population of more than 20,000 individuals (cf. Carrera Stampa 1955; Covey 1998; Dunnigan 1983; Hammond and Rey 1940; Hallenbeck 1987; Heredia 1969; Hopkins 1988; Hurdaide in Pérez de Ribas 1999, 1610-1617; Nakayama 1974; Nuñez Cabeza de Vaca 1999; Pennington 1980; Pérez de Ribas 1999; Sauer 1932; Segesser 1945; Varela 1626; Zapata 1678). The Nébome were a sedentary culture with permanent communities. Most of their communities consisted of small rancherías dispersed throughout the rich agricultural valley, although larger settlements with local chiefs existed also. Their structures were described as sturdier than those of their neighbors, and made of compact adobe with earthen roofs. Most houses had gardens in which they grew several plants for different uses such as medicine, food, and decoration. They practiced agriculture along the Río Yaqui and other small river drainages. Water control strategies, such as agricultural terraces and irrigation canals, facilitated cultivation especially around the small drainages. Along the Río Yaqui Valley, the native peoples relied on seasonal flooding rather than canals to irrigate crops. In general,

they obtained two crops per year and harvested corn, beans, squash, and cotton. The Nébomes also cultivated agave and gathered natural resources, such as mesquite seeds, cholla buds, prickly pear fruit, and nuts. In addition, the Nébomes were good hunters and fishermen, taking advantage of the abundance of game and fish in their territory. The Nébome were skillful ceramicists, basket makers, and tanners. They also worked with stone, shell, turquoise, and hides. Colonial records mention that they dressed much better than their neighboring nations and wore shell and stone jewelry. Although they engaged in skirmishes from time to time with their neighbors—Yaquis, Opatas, and sometimes the Seris—the Nébomes were not considered a bellicose nation. Due to the fertility of their valley, Seri Indians came to trade hides, fish, and marine shell for food during the harvest season. The Nébome performed communal and secluded ceremonies as well as rituals in their communities, in the nearby hills, and on the Río Yaqui.

This cultural depiction, based on ethnohistorical and ethnographic research, was an important part when formulating the OVAPs research design, and especially useful to have for the landscape analysis. Furthermore, to facilitate artifact and landscape analysis and interpretation, the information gleaned from Colonial documents was contrasted with the archaeological data gathered by the OVAP.

Chapter 4
Theoretical Perspective

Theoretical models and frameworks, developed to interpret the archaeological record of Northwest Mexico have evolved faster than knowledge of the material culture of the region. The international border bisecting this large area has had a substantial effect on research in Northwest Mexico (Kelley and Villalpando 1996:69; McGuire 1997:131). Early and middle twentieth century archaeological research, conducted mostly by non-Mexican archaeologists, focused on finding material evidence for a link between the U.S. Southwest and Mesoamerica. These early models have focused on distant or external agents in local cultural processes rather than depicting the area as having indigenous developments (Whalen and Minnis 2001, 2003).

Increased exploration in Northwest Mexico in the last two decades, however, has shown that local populations, such as the inhabitants of the Trincheras region had little direct influence from Mesoamerican pochtecas or Southwestern traders. More recently, researchers have recognized external influence in the area, but not to the degree suggested by the earlier cultural imperialist or diffusionist models, some of which involve influence or directed change from pochtecas (McGuire and Villalpando 1993, 2011; McGuire et al. 1994, 1999; Minnis and Redman 1990; Whalen and Minnis 2001; Upham 1986). For the OVAP project results and interpretations, I support the latter position, as it serves as a more balanced and dynamic stance where local groups were engaged as actors for their own development and were active participants in local and regional interactions (Blanton et al. 1996;

Kowalewski 1996; Mills 2000; Pauketat 1997, 2000; Peregrine 1992). The data recovered by the OVAP illustrate this perspective.

Due to the previous lack of basic data from the area, the OVAP focused on a regional analysis. Landscape analysis was chosen to build a preliminary description of the valley's archaeological past from the data recovered by a full-coverage systematic pedestrian survey. The identified Prehispanic sites were analyzed through the "community framework," explained in the following pages, which I believe is useful for describing the socio-political structure of the Prehispanic settlement of the valley. Ethnohistory provides additional interpretative frameworks for understanding the material record of this region.

COMMUNITY

In the Southwest U.S. and Northwest Mexico, prehispanic groups exhibited great cultural diversity with different levels of socio-political complexity, settlement patters, economic organization, and interaction. Researchers have employed different terms to describe the socio-political structures of prehispanic societies in Northwest Mexico, namely chiefdoms, *cacicazgos*, middle range societies, pre-state societies, statelets, segmentary states, pristine civilizations, and communities or comunidades (Doolittle 1988; Feinman and Neitzel 1984; Fish 1999a; Lekson 1999; Mills 2000; Whitecotton 1977; Wilcox 1999; Yoffee et al. 1999). The *community* concept was prominently featured in American archaeological jargon for a while, but only in the last decade have researchers used this term to replace the chiefdom concept, which is associated with neo-evolutionary models (Fish and Fish 2000a:164). Originally, the term *community* was borrowed from the Mexican term *comunidad*. The term '*cacicazgo*' was used mostly during the Spanish Colonial period to describe the socio-political structure of indigenous autonomous communities (Fish and Fish 2000a, 2000b; Whitecotton 1977). Researchers interpreted archaeological sites using the community model, especially in the Hohokam region, where material evidence for paramount leaders and/or highly ranked kinship lines failed to emerge unambiguously (Adler 1996; Fish and Fish 1994, Fish et al. 1992; Lekson 1991). Whitecotton (1977:188) defines a community simply as a "large self-governing as well as economically self-supporting [settlement],"—regardless of its socio-political organization. Today's *comunidad* concept is still well-established in the Mexican countryside and can be defined or envisioned as a:

> unit of territory and local administration...typically incorporate[ing] multiple settlements, but hav[ing] an administrative center and a foremost church in a large village...comunidad boundaries guarantee continuing rights to agricultural land and access to resources beyond those available through membership in a single village (Fish and Fish 2000b:381).

From the archaeological perspective, areas can be interpreted accordingly as an area identified by several settlements that shape a community with shared cultural patterns. However, in some cases one of the settlements among that community will have a higher ranked position than the rest, and that could have some influence over the whole community. This community will be autonomous from other equivalent communities found in external areas.

In defining the socio-political structure of a comunidad, researchers further emphasize that it may or may not be kin-based or reliant on a "paramount position of a leader and his highly ranked lineage" (Fish and Fish 2000b:381) as in the case of chiefdoms. Instead, a community is based on a corporal or communal socio-political structure where its people earn membership through their status as elders and participation in communal work, such as construction and maintenance of canals, farming fields, and public architecture (Fish and Fish 2000b:381). As a result, a community is envisioned as a socio-political and territorial unit which can be identified through a set of related settlements representing all its members and surrounding environmental resources. Such a unit not only provides a socio-political framework for its members but also a collective group identity with a strong affiliation with a particular territory.

In the U.S. Southwest and Northwest Mexico Prehispanic region researchers define community as a (Fish and Fish 2000a:160-161):

> set of interrelated sites within a bounded community territory... Such a community contains a center with public architecture of a kind and/or magnitude that is not duplicated in other community sites... Community boundaries presumably demarcated the land and resources wherein primary use-rights were reserved to community members.

Of particular interest is the fact that communities maintain a hierarchy between the settlements that control access to land and resources, and most likely to cultural knowledge and ritual activities as well.

An important element of the community

is the central site(s), which normally functions as the focus of communal activities and decision-making in the community. Researchers believe that public architecture in central sites is the "focus of communal observances on behalf of all members...the inter-linkage of population and settlements are symbolically embodied in the communal structures" (Fish and Fish 2000b:378). Public architecture is envisioned further as a material representation of communal symbols and beliefs shared by members of a community. The labor input represented in the construction of this public architecture "communicate[s] the cohesiveness and prominence of the community" (Fish and Fish 2000b:381). In addition, Doyel and Fish (2000:19) mention that the term "community" has dual meaning or application: one where the community is used to describe "interlinked members of a single settlement" and second where the term is used for "interlinked members of a set of closely related settlements."

In addition to the central site, the hierarchical socio-political structure of a community is made of (Rice and Redman 2000:322):

1) Special activity areas wich are brief to multi-century reuse of the same space, processing/craft areas, or source material procurement location, such as roasting pits, field houses, stone or clay sources, roads, water irrigation control systems, or agricultural fields.

2) Household compound wich consist of two or three rooms for probably one or two related families, who are self-sufficient for their subsistence needs, but are connected to larger communities.

3) Hamlets or rancherías were composed of six to 40 rooms inhabited possibly by more than one family lineage with a full range of subsistence activities

and relatively long-term occupations.

Community size and boundaries depend on population density, natural resources, distance to those resources, intra-community communication, and interactions (both local and regional). In addition, Fish and Fish (2000a:161) mention that the size of a community will depend on the boundaries of neighboring communities, so a community could have territorial affiliation to a single valley or share a given territory with other communities. In the U.S. Southwest, where this model has been applied the most, archaeological community boundaries have been defined by "settlement fall off, where a settlement cluster containing a central site is spatially discrete from other such clusters" and "through a replication of patterned elements at intervals...[or] distribution of central sites with public architecture" (Fish and Fish 2000b:378). Such artificial boundaries probably limited the territory a community controlled.

There is no particular explanation as to how communities arose or were born in the Northwest Mexico and the U.S. Southwest. However, combinations of factors seem to have played a role in this process, such as an increase in population density and competition for natural resources (Fish et al. 1992). These factors would have increased in the labor force available to conduct communal work increasing both resource production and territorial claims. Individuals would have needed to belong to a certain community to have rights to exploit natural resources, and in order to have that affiliation they would have needed to participate on the communal work, community ceremonial activities, and shared community values (Fish and Fish 2000a:164-165).

The community model enjoys enough flexibility to accommodate other models to explain socio-political power and its underlying bases, such as the central site model, landscape analysis, prestige economy, or dual-processual theory (Ashmore and Knapp 1999; Fish 1999a; Fish and Fish 1996, 2000a, 2000b; Fish et al. 1992; Smith 1976). Naturally, the communal socio-political structure indicated by the field data guides the researcher in choosing between these models. Fish and Fish (2000a) push the community concept forward by developing the civic-territorial model. In this framework, individuals were bound together through real and fictive kinship networks while membership in the community was ensured through territorial affiliation and communal work, such as construction and maintenance of irrigation canals. More recently, Varien provided another definition for community (1999:19) who states that, "a community consists of many households that live close to one another, have regular face-to-face interactions, and share use of local social and natural resources…" To this definition, Kintigh (2003) and Gilpin (2003) add several important variables that offer a better range of analysis for a community in the archaeological record. The variables are "a minimum population size for a reproductively viable social unit, a maximum population size given the level of social complexity that we infer for the [U.S.] Southwest, a one-day round trip walking distance and a settlement clustering" (Kintigh 2003:103). On top of these variables, Canuto and Yaeger (2000:11) push the community analysis even further and propose three types of analysis: (1) spatial analyses that examine intra and inter-unit spacing, access patterns, and boundary maintenance; (2) techno-material studies of artifact styles, exotic goods, resource scarcity, and (3) labor investment; and demographic studies of settlement patterning, ecological adaptation, site numbers, and nucleation and dispersion.

The applicability of the community concept is not constrained to the U.S. Southwest and Northwest Mexico region, as the latest archaeological research on community's shows. The community concept has been applied in other regions as well, such as India, Australia, and South America (Canuto and Yaeger 2000), proving its applicability for different archaeological record in different natural environments.

The OVAP will focus on the application of the community model as used in the Southwest, in particular in the Hohokam region (Fish and Fish 2000a), and considers this model the best fit for archaeological findings in the Onavas Valley.

Landscapes and Culture

The origins and use of the landscape concept can be traced as far back as the late nineteenth century in the social sciences, when geographer Friederich Ratzel and sociologist Emil Durkheim debated the role of the natural environment in the social structure of humans and societies (Anschuetz et al. 2001; Hirsch 1994). Formally, Carl Sauer (1925:46) provided the first definition for landscape in archaeology based on his work in geography:

> The cultural landscape is fashioned from a natural landscape by a cultural group. Culture is the agent, the natural area is the medium, and the cultural landscape is the result. Under the influence of a given culture, itself changing through time, the landscape undergoes development, passing through phases, and probably reaching ultimately the end of its cycle of development. With the introduction of a different –that is, alien– culture, a rejuvenation of the culture landscape set in, or a new landscape is superimposed on the remnants of an older one.

Sauer's definition, from his geographical perspective, points to the importance of understanding archaeological sites in relation to their surrounding space and not in isolation. Moreover, his definition emphasizes that landscape is a cultural product of a human group, in conjunction with the natural environment.

Later, the innovation of regional archaeological settlement pattern studies in the 1940s and 1950s indicated that not only does the natural environment shape the cultural landscape, but the latter was also influenced by the dynamics of cultural and human needs (Willey 1953). Gordon Willey (1953:1) defined settlement pattern as "the way in which man disposed himself over the landscape on which he lived. It refers to dwellings, to their arrangement, and to the nature and disposition of their buildings pertaining to community life." Although settlement pattern studies achieved the much needed examination of archaeological sites in relation with other sites, it still lacked the incorporation of other aspects that shape a community, such as ritual landscapes, geographical markers, or ethnic boundaries.

Through the 1960s and 1970s, archaeologists sought to clarify this problem and research "moved beyond descriptive documentation of site distributions and organizational hierarchies within regions to interpretation of the multivariate dynamics underlying archaeologically observed pattern across the dimensions of space and time" (Anschuetz et al. 2001:170).

Since Sauer's work, landscape analysis has been developed into a strong methodology adopted and adapted by the archaeological discipline to understand the cultural perception of a given natural environment in a particular period of time (Anschuetz et al. 2001; Ashmore and Knapp 1999; Potter 2004; Snead 2004). Four interrelated premises provide the foundations for landscape analysis, those are (Anschuetz et al. 2001:160-161):

1: Landscapes are not synonymous with natural environments.

2: Landscapes are worlds of cultural products.

3: Landscapes are the arena for all of a community's activities.

4: Landscapes are dynamic constructions.

By following these premises, researchers of landscapes emphasize human culture and agency and recognize how these elements play into the construction of the world as it is known to the individual. The term "world" is not only used for the material or natural environment, but also entails the metaphysical, mythological, social, and cultural contexts.

Currently, researchers agree that landscape is not a synonym for natural environment or settlement pattern, but something complementary to and beyond those terms (Anschuetz et al. 2001; Ashmore and Knapp 1999; Hirsch 1995; Potter 2004; Rossignol and Wandsnider 1992). In addition, landscape analysis incorporates knowledge gathered by anthropological and ethnographical research, such as ritual activities or the perception of the natural realm. Ashmore and Knapp (1999:1) state that landscape is, "an entity that exists by virtue of its being perceived, experienced, and contextualized by people." So, landscape is a total human formation and has to be analyzed accordingly. A more detailed definition is provided by James Potter (2004:322), who states landscape is:

a conceptual and behavioral process; it is as much about what people perceive and do on the land as it is about what is on the land to begin with. Landscapes are created by human activity, which is influenced not only by the distribution of resources on the land but also by cultural perceptions of human relationships to those resources.

Potter (Potter 2004:322) established three analytical elements for a better understanding of a particular landscape: (1) time, as landscape is being created by human activities and perceptions, it is also bound to its temporal frame; (2) space, as landscape is created by human activities, those actions need space that create a place for them in the environment, shaping human action and enhancing the space significance; and (3) perception or conceptualization of the landscape based on "mythic" and "real" experience of the people or groups on such space and in a particular time period. These elements allow landscapes to be analyzed archaeologically.

The analysis of built structures in a landscape assists archaeologists in identifying and evaluating the interdependent and dynamic relationships between humans and the physical, social, and cultural realms of their environment over time and space (Anschuetz et al. 2001; Ashmore and Knapp 1999; Rossignol and Wandsnider 1992). After all human beings lived and conducted a multitude of activities outside the dwelling areas as well. Consequently, artifacts and features resulting from these activities were deposited in exterior structure areas (Rice and Ravesloot 2001; Wells et al 2004). Likewise, human beings change natural environments into a cultural landscape, sometimes fortuitously leaving material culture behind to record the event. Based on ethnographic research, James Ebert (1992:26-27) estimates that the frequency of tool use outside versus inside the dwelling area is between four to five times greater. In other words, "archaeology research that deals only with residential settlement might ignore 75 percent to 80 percent of the data concerning

the use of the landscape" (Rice and Ravesloot 2001:2).

Recent research in landscape archaeology focuses on identifying relationships and patterns between central settlements, smaller residential units, and varied assemblages of non-habitation/activity features found in a specific locale and for a specific time frame. These components are explicitly studied to understand the interaction between human and nature (Anschuetz et al. 2001; Ashmore and Knapp 1999; Snead 2004). Furthermore, if possible, archaeologists interpret geographical markers or areas to arrive at some understanding of their ritual/ceremonial value to a Prehispanic community, thus increasing understanding of the use of a community's surrounding landscape.

More of this research on landscapes needs to be applied to Northwest Mexico Prehispanic contexts, where archaeological traditions have conventionally been described and defined narrowly by research on a single site or from a survey area. Moreover, much of this research and analysis took place three or four decades ago, if not longer (Newell and Gallaga 2004), with earlier theoretical models and limited methods, both in terms of theoretical perspective, archaeological methodology, and available technology. For example, the development of GIS (Geographical Information System) has done much to enable landscape analysis and to move (practically and theoretically) beyond the preceding one site/area-based interpretation. Augmenting such research, however, requires more full-survey projects that cover large areas to find, describe, and analyze the necessary data to undertake landscape analysis.

Normally, landscape analysis focuses on three contrasting, but complementary elements of analysis yielding an understanding of a cultural landscape. Those elements are: settlement ecology or settlement pattern, ritual landscape, and ethnic landscape (Anschuetz et al. 2001; Ashmore and Knapp 1999; Potter

2004). All three aspects focus on how members of a community define, perceive, use, and shape their surrounding space in a particular period of time and transform general space into a specific place. Yet, each element of analysis provides insight into a particular aspect of landscape use.

Settlement Patterns

In the first element of analysis, past settlement pattern studies focused on the description and analysis of spatial interrelationships among archaeological sites with domestic and/or public architecture to describe what characterized the past. Today, settlement pattern analysis focuses on the explanation of why and how organizational and technological changes occurred in a specific settlement pattern of a region and for a specific period of time (Anschuetz et al. 2001; Willey 1983). As such, settlement pattern functions as the product of a dynamic interaction between the characteristics of the environment and human economic, social, and technical needs. Settlement pattern corresponds to "archaeologically observed patterns of land use, occupation, transformation over time,… raw material needed for physical comfort and health, and items for trade or exchange" (Anschuetz et al. 2001:177). Because settlement patterns are human constructions and conceptions of their surrounding environments, they also are affected by other factors such as time, culture and tradition affiliations. Changes in the settlement pattern over time may signify a change in the human conception of the cultural landscape and could represent changes in the cultural affiliation of the inhabitants.

Ritual Landscapes

The second element of analysis concerned ritual landscape, which Anschuetz et al. (2001:178) defines by seeing ritual landscapes as the results of "stereotyped actions, including specific acts and sequences of acts, that represent the socially prescribed orders by which communities define, legitimize, and sustain their occupation of their traditional homelands." In addition, they emphasize that the

traditional wisdom often is tied to places, thus the landscape is full of history, legend, knowledge, and power that help structure activities and organize relationships. Ethnohistorically known groups have full ritual calendars and a rich cosmology that structure, organize, and inform on much of their landscape, which community members perceive and with which they interact (Anschuetz et al. 2001:178).

As mentioned above, the repetition of acts, such as ceremonies, rituals, or feasts, creates a social memory that enhances community affiliation to a place and enhances integration among communities (Potter 2004; Rappaport 1979). The construction of public architecture (constructed landscapes) or repetition and reuse of a specific area to perform such activities may produce significant or substantial archaeological remains associated to and indicative of a ritual landscape (Anschuetz et al. 2001; Ashmore and Knapp 1999). Such remains can be "public buildings, monuments, squares or plazas, petroglyphs or pictographs, and various vernacular markers" (Anschuetz et al. 2001:178). Natural markers or conceptual landscape markers with insignificant or absent material culture must be included to the previous listing, exemplified by rivers, mountains, forest, water sources, or peaks (Ashmore and Knapp 1999). In Northwest Mexico, the Sierra del Bacatete for the Yaqui Indians (Hu Dehart 1995; Olavarria 1995; Spicer 1983, 1992, 1994) or the Mayo River for the Mayo Indians (Crumrine 1983; Crumrine and Crumrine

1967) can be used as suitable examples.

Ethnic Landscapes

The final element of analysis, ethnic land-scapes, are notoriously hard to identify archae-ologically and are interrelated with land-use and ritual landscapes. Anthropological research establishes that "community members create and manipulate material culture and symbols to signify ethnic or cultural boundaries based on customs and shared modes of thought and expression that might have no other sanction than tradition" (Anschuetz et al. 2001:179). Ethnicity is not directly or automatically tied to physical spaces and may not manifest itself with particular geographic markers. Ceremonies or rituals that identify an ethnic group can be performed outside its original geographical location without losing their community affiliation (e.g. the Yaqui or Jewish diasporic communities that have experienced spatial dislocation over time). Such charac-teristics limit the identification and analysis of ethnic landscapes (Anschuetz et al. 2001; Ashmore and Knapp 1999; Canuto and Yager 2000; Potter 2004; Rapoport 1982; Rossignol and Wandsnider 1992).

Archaeologically speaking, researchers have attempted to establish ethnic 'regions' or 'boundaries' through the recognition of certain cultural material elements considered diagnostic of a particular cultural group. This methodology proves problematic and provides fixed or hard boundaries of past societies which do not necessarily provide an accurate picture. On the other hand, in the absence of a surviving human presence, such identifica-tion of cultural material markers continues as valid in archaeological research to identify archaeological traditions, trade and exchange, migration, or cultural changes. We must remind ourselves, however, that those diagnostic material distributional maps created by the

archaeologist are at best an approximation or partial representation of the Prehispanic spatial interactions that had actually taken place.

Landscape Theory

Given the current state of archaeological knowledge of the Onavas Valley, landscape theory offers an insightful, productive way to begin to understand the social and cultural dynamics of this area in the Late Prehispanic period. The application of landscape theory in the Onavas Valley informs the OVAP's three-pronged research design, as discussed earlier. The final results of the OVAP research and analysis provided a solid database for further archaeological research in the area and allow comparison of this area with neighboring regions. The latter is an important and neces-sary part of research, allowing a better picture of the interactions between different archaeo-logical traditions as expressed through goods, styles and ideas. In addition, landscape archae-ology works in tandem with the community model to provide useful information about the Onavas Prehispanic community.

Comparison of the Onavas Valley with Casas Grandes, Trincheras, and Classic Hohokam regions in the forthcoming chapters will facilitate an understanding of the for-mation of differences in cultural landscapes with similar environmental conditions. Such understanding will form a basis for propos-ing mechanisms of extra-regional interactions between the Onavas Valley and the remaining regions. Comparisons of the different areas will include an examination of public architecture, settlement hierarchy, settlement structure in terms of dispersal and nucleation, subsistence technology, and loci of craft production. The completion of the OVAP finally enabled such systematic comparison among these areas because comparable full-coverage surveys have been undertaken within recent years in all these aspects of the archaeological record (Fish et al. 1994; Fish and Fish 2004; Whalen and Minnis 2001).

ETHNOHISTORY

Another important framework for analysis used by the OVAP is the rich data found in Colonial documents. Archaeologists found that other disciplines, such as history, ethnohistory, and ethnography, can provide data not normally available in the archaeological record which serve to complement archaeological analysis and interpretation of the past (Doolittle 1988; Riley 1990, Sauer 1932; Schuyler 1988; Chang 1967; Webster 1996). This interdisciplinary approach proved useful, especially in proto-historic and Colonial periods of the American continent (Alvarez 1999; Trigger 1985; Reff 1991; Sheridan 1988; Spicer 1992; Villalpando 1989; William 1994).

In the 1950s, ethnohistory appeared as a discipline that served to challenge or confirm historical claims made in court by Native American groups suing the U.S. Government for recovery of damages incurred in the conquest and possession of their lands (Krech III 1991; Spores 1980). In Mexico, due to the complex historical development and the richness of their past and living cultural patrimony, ethnohistory had been an important and robust discipline in Mexican anthropology. Since then, this discipline has developed theoretical frameworks and methods to pursue its object of study and to distinguish itself from history and anthropology (Fenton 1962; Kintigh 1990a; Sheridan 1988; Spores 1980). In the past, the discipline focused on "people without history," referring to groups who lack written documentation of their past (Krech III 1991; Trigger 1983). After long debates among ethnohistorians and colleagues from affiliated disciplines, the trend today seems to be away

from that evolutionary, ethnocentric, and, in some cases, eurocentric definition and focus has shifted to any group of people. Currently, ethnohistory may be defined as a discipline that focuses on changes in culture over time and space, using methods from history, political economy, archaeology, ethnography, and cultural anthropology, written and oral source analyses, combined into a multidisciplinary approach (Fenton 1962; Schuyler 1988; Sheridan 1988).

Several authors (Adams 1981; Alvarez 1999; Chang 1967; Schuyler 1988; Spores 1980; Trigger 1983; Villalpando 1989; Wilson 1993; William 1994) state that interdisciplinary research between archaeology and ethnohistory can complement each other precisely due to their similarities and their differences. Ethnohistory offers a perspective on relatively shorter periods of time than does archaeology, a common practice in Mexican research (López 1973, 1995; López and López 2001). Further, ethnohistory supplies information regarding human behavior, cultural changes, and information on social contexts that fail to appear, or are not accessible, in the archaeological record. Archaeology provides knowledge about relatively longer periods of time, material analyses, and material evidence that can support or counter information obtained from written and oral documents. Yoffee (2005:31) cautions to avoid direct projection into the archaeological record, especially when the ethnohistorical and ethnographical data "have been snatched out of time, place, and development sequence."

Although the veracity of information in Colonial documents is always a concern, these documents provide detailed insights into a cultural context that no longer exists and facilitate the understanding of both post-contact and Prehispanic communities (Gasco et al. 1997; Lightfoot 1995; Majewski and Ayres 1997). When compared to archaeological data, the rich ethnohistorical record of the Río Yaqui serves as a mixed blessing.

The varied ethnohistorical sources provide a set of expectations regarding what might be encountered archaeologically, yet the archaeological record may contradict these expectations. In addition to ethnohistorical data and research, recorded oral history from local Mexican Indians such as the Yaquis and the Mayos was also analyzed. Thus, the OVAP incorporated the analysis of ethnohistorical and ethnographical data to create a provisional understanding of Prehispanic and proto-Historic period conditions to be tested with data collected in the field. Ethnohistorical information was used to inform and aid in the interpretation of the data recorded in the archaeology of the region. Hence, they offer possible scenarios for understanding the configuration of polities, social and political organization, regional and local interactions, and population at the time of Spanish contact and probably for the Late Prehispanic period. Likewise, archaeological material analysis assisted in the determination of the temporal and spatial, or possibly the cultural group affiliation associated with the archaeological sites.

Chapter 5
Fieldwork

Besides the oddity of living in the jail, the villagers thought we were rather curious and perhaps a bit nutty, "walking in the middle of the day in the bushes, up the hills, over the fences, looking for something in the ground." (Gallaga 2004c:14).

Following the river's course, the OVAP focused on the middle section of the Río Yaqui in southern Sonora, Mexico, between the modern Alvaro Obregon and El Novillo dams (see Figure 1.1). This is an area of roughly 1600 km² of dry, warm, and rugged terrain. As mentioned before, very little archaeological research has been conducted in the Middle Río Yaqui area (Gallaga 2004c; Newell and Gallaga 2004). Consequently, to start building an archaeological baseline of knowledge about this area, including site types, site distribution, material assemblage, and building a tentative chronological sequence, the OVAP fieldwork design consisted mostly of a pedestrian survey. To determine the cultural landscape structure of the valley, the pedestrian survey located Prehispanic communities, natural resources, possible trail networks, and the network of activity areas in the landscape.

Onavas Valley Archaeological Project Survey

Logistics

The Onavas Valley Archaeological Project field work lasted 10 weeks, from early June to mid August of 2004, with the Onavas town serving as the middle point of the research area. Previous visits to the town allowed us to become acquainted with community members, as well as with the local authorities such as the Presidente Municipal, Nardo Buelna Valenzuela; the comisario ejidal, José Navarro Esparza; and the chief of police. In addition, the Centro INAH Sonora provided us with letters of introduction to the local authorities. In lieu of a decent suitable house for rent in the community the municipal president offered the use of the new jail as our field work house, which was just two months old and located behind the presidencia municipal. This place turned out to be perfect since it was a secure space to leave the equipment, the material, and it had plenty of space for the accommodation of project members and lab analysis. The project crew consisted of three individuals in addition to the project director, Emiliano Gallaga. These were two Mexican undergraduate archaeologists, Maricruz Magaña and Cesar Villalobos, and Gillian Newell—a graduate student from the University of Arizona. Coral Montero and "Inge" Armando, two Mexican colleagues, participated in the project for a few days. All crew members recorded sites, took notes, filled out forms, and helped with lab activities such as washing, cataloguing, and sorting. Three members of the community were hired, two to help with the logistics in the field and one to cook for the crew.

Before and after the field work, the project director, Emiliano Gallaga, staged a series of public presentations for the members of the community of Onavas to present the project goals and procedures, as well as the results. Copies of the project results, such as Gallaga's dissertation and publications, were given to the presidencia municipal, the public school, and to the community members who helped with the project.

Methods

The OVAP fieldwork survey consisted of two phases: intensive background research; and a full-coverage systematic pedestrian survey in the summer of 2004 in the center of the valley. The first phase consisted of gathering all the existing archaeological data for the area to know as much as possible about the archaeological remains in or around the research area. As I mentioned before, field notes, maps, site descriptions, and archaeological collections were consulted from the PROCEDE project at the INAH, Sonora archives, the Pailes collection at the University of Oklahoma, and the Ekholm collection at the American Museum of Natural History (AMNH) in New York. As a result of this phase, a field catalogue of archaeological materials was produced (Gallaga 2004b). In addition, two exploratory trips were made to the research area to get acquainted with the terrain, the community, and the logistics to start the field project.

The second phase was a full-coverage systematic pedestrian survey area with transects spaced at 10 to 25 m intervals depending on the terrain, from approximately 9 km to the north to 5 km to the south of Onavas. To the east and west the limits were set from the Río Yaqui to the 200 m above sea level mark, which created transects ranging between 2 and 5 km long transects (Figure 5.1). Such arbitrary limits were set with the intention to cover the entire Onavas Valley, investigating the terrain between the Río Yaqui and the nearby foothills of the Sierra Madre Occidental, but avoiding the very rugged terrain beyond 200 m above sea

level. At the end of the field season, the archaeologists had covered more than 67 km².

A survey team of at least three archaeologists systematically walked the 67 km² intensive study area at an approximate spacing of 20 to 25 m between surveyors in open fields and 10 to 15 m in dense vegetation. In steep areas, such as the bajadas or foothills, survey members covered all ridgelines, piedmont spurs, and hilltops, while steep slopes that were unlikely to have had settlement were checked less intensively.

With the help of a compass, GPS, topographic maps, and natural and cultural landmarks, transects were set in the field and marked with toilet paper. To maintain control of the survey area, transects were kept perpendicular to the Río Yaqui as much as possible.

Due to a special set of conditions triggered at the Onavas town at the time of the field work, a small excavation unit of 2 x 4 m was made at the site of SON P:10:08 (Appendix I and II). Description of the process of the excavation and of the material analysis found is considered in Chapter 6.

Data Recording

All the features potentially used by people in Prehispanic times were recorded on maps or annotated in the field data log for the subsequent analysis. Not all features were recorded as archaeological sites, especially if no archaeological material was found in association with features. Hence, what was considered a site? At OVAP, an archaeological site was defined as:

> …any place where archaeological material exists, especially in a cluster and with defined limits, the distribution of which resulted from human activity. These clusters could range from a simple activity area to a settlement unit, with a depositional range

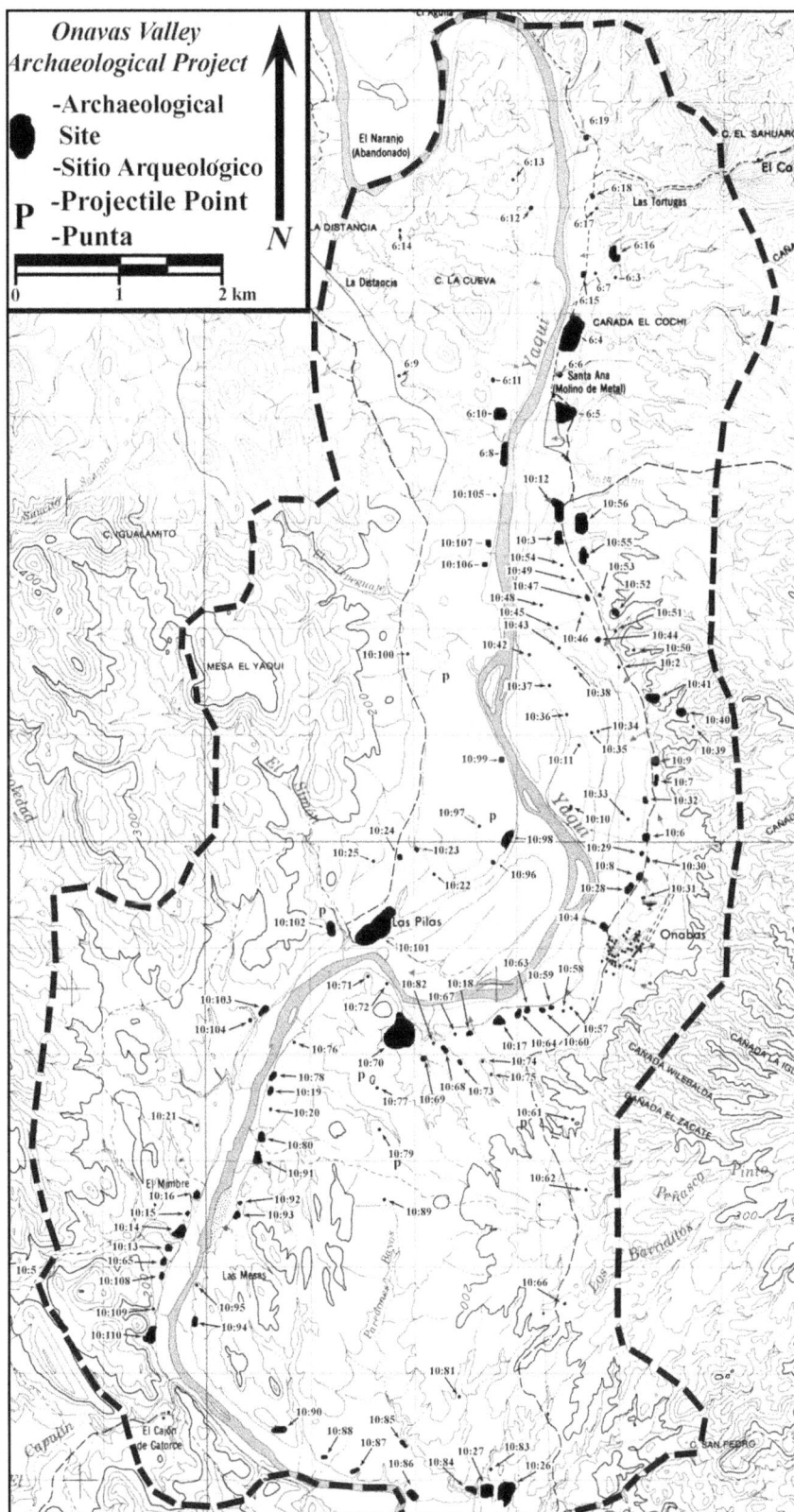

Figure 5.1. OVAP research area and total sites recorded.

that varies from a single occupation to all the archaeological deposits found in a sequence in that space and within defined depositional limits (López 1984:109; author's translation).

How many sherds or flakes make a site? Fish and Gresham (1990:162) mention that in the Georgia piedmont, a site is defined as greater than 10 artifacts in close proximity, while less signifies it is an "occurrence." To circumvent distinctions and to overcome the differences in concepts, OVAP employed the field work standards for site registration from the anthropology department of the Universidad Nacional Autonoma de Mexico (UNAM) where a minimum of six sherds or any combination of six archaeological materials constitutes a site. Fewer than six elements or archaeological items, when encountered, were recorded, marked on maps, and collected as isolated items but not recorded as a site. Only eight isolated items were recorded by OVAP.

After the location and recording of a site in the field, a further distinction or classification of the archaeological sites was undertaken in the lab and during analysis. Based on the evidence recorded, sites were classified either as residential settlement or non-residential temporary camps (Rice and Ravesloot 2001). Residential settlements were identified by the presence of:

> 1) "midden deposits, 2) a diversity of artifacts and features representing a range of processing and production activities, 3) the remains of architecture indicative of a shelter or habitation areas" (Rice and Ravesloot 2001:5).

Although the presence of midden deposits or a variety of processing or production related artifacts or features may also indicate non-residential temporary camps, the absence of the remains of a shelter served to indicate that these sites were not as permanent as the residential settlements.

Once a site was defined as a residential settlement, a further division served to distinguish between: (1) household or rancherías, (2) hamlets or aldeas, (3) villages, and (4) regional centers (Doolittle 1988:36; Rice and Ravesloot 2001:5; Rice and Redman 2000:324). This settlement classification was based mostly on Doolittle's (1988:36) research on the Río Sonora Valley, an area geographically and archaeologically similar to the Onavas Valley. The classification adapted to OVAP is as follows:

> 1) Household or Rancherías: Small, scattered and riverine-oriented permanent habitation sites with sites composed of one or two nucleated families (Doolittle 1988:36).

> 2) Hamlets or Aldea: Sites occupied by between 10 to 100 people, but lacking in public architecture with the presence of residential units (Blanton 1972:20; Doolittle 1988:36; Parsons 1990:22).

> 3) Villages: Sites with a minimum of 100 and a maximum of 1000 people, composed mostly of residential units with minimal public architecture (Blanton 1972:20; Doolittle 1988:36; Parsons 1990:22).

> 4) Regional Centers: Large, nucleated, and architecturally complex sites with large public architecture and a population between 1,000 and 2,000 (Blanton 1972:20; Doolittle 1988:36; Parsons 1990:22).

The non-residential temporary camps proved more difficult to discern archaeologically. Ethnographic research, fortunately, provides some insight to better understand the complexity and use of the natural environment of a Prehispanic community. These studies suggest that four to five times more activities are located outside residential settlements and more tools are been used as well (Ebert 1992; Rice and Ravesloot 2001; Wells et al. 2004). As a result, a significant number of such sites can be expected around residential settlements, such as those that result from the procurement activities of prickly pear fruit, cholla buds, mesquite, and leguminous seeds. Other examples include: agave agriculture and processing areas, agriculture field camps, flaked stone knapping stations, ground stone quarries, and clay and wood procurement areas. Hunting areas, paths, pot-break sites, shrines and altars serve as examples of some of the activities or loci associated with non-residential temporary camps identified in geographical areas similar to the OVAP also (Doyel et al. 2000; Fish and Kowalewsky 1990; Pennington 1980; Rice and Ravesloot 2001). As Christian Wells et al. (2004:631) mention, "in general, these activities were conducted in locations away from residential settlements, resulting in the deposition of artifact in small, low-density clusters and as isolated artifacts, or locations." In other words, to understand how a Prehispanic community operated, it is important to find these temporary work sites as well.

For the OVAP, the non-residential temporary camp sites were divided into five different types or categories, taking into account the most probable activities performed at each site by its Prehispanic residents based on the material recorded and the location in the field. Those activity types were:

> Type 1: Food gathering (prickly pear fruit, cholla bud, mesquite/leguminous seed, and agave) activities, as well as travel/trails and pot-burst events.

> Type 2: Agricultural field camps, and travel/trails and pot-burst events.

> Type 3: Stone, clay, temper, wood gathering, work areas and travel/trails and pot-burst.

> Type 4: Hunting, travel/trails, pot-burst areas.

> Type 5: Shrines, altars, ceremonial/ritual areas, and travel/trails and pot-burst.

Type 1 camp sites were identified by their association with rock-piles for growing agave and roasting pits for cooking of agave or other foods, as well as concentrations of ceramic sherds or pot-bursts, but no residential structures. Type 2 sites, were small concentrations of mostly ceramic materials (pot-burst events), with no permanent residential structures, which were located on the floodplain where farming agriculture likely took place. Type 3 sites were small concentrations of material associated with outcrops of stone or clay resources, or were near the foothills for wood gathering. Type 4 sites were mostly isolated projectile points and small concentrations of similar sherds identified as a pot-burst or breaking event. The latter were also associated with travel or human movement in the area. The last camp sites, Type 5 were features associated with ceremonial/ritual activities such as stone shrines, geoglyphs, pictographs, or stone alignments. On the whole, classification and final identification of all sites took place at the laboratory, in conjunction with material and data analyses. The classification pattern used by the OVAP to identify and interpret the data recovered is only a model to fit the data and to attempt to produce a good approximation of the Prehistoric daily life in this region.

For the entire research area, all transects, site boundaries, and isolated finds were plotted on topographic maps after pinpointing their locations by Global Positioning System (GPS) readings. Sites were recorded on forms matching the standards and criteria for the Centro INAH Sonora as approved by the Dirección de Registro Publico de Monumentos y Zonas Arqueológicas (DRPMyZA) (Department of the Public Registry of Archaeological Monuments and Zones) in Mexico City. At the same time, the site registration forms from the Arizona State Museum site registration office were also filled out. Employing 1:50,000 INEGI topographic maps and aerial photographs, surveyors identified the limits of the sites and marked representative features. Sites were fully recorded, including gathering information about the geographical position and a physiographical and archaeological surface description, as well as a map of the site, a photographic record of it, and a description of observed surface material.

In addition, crew members collected surface material for further analysis at every site recorded. Originally, the archaeological material collection method consisted of the oft-employed strategy of circle-shaped collection units of 1-m radius (so-called dog-leash sampling). However, due to a high level of site destruction and scattering of archaeological material at the surface by mechanized farm machinery, it was quickly decided to gather artifact samples in an unsystematic fashion. Although collection was unsystematic, collection nonetheless a minimum of 100 objects were gathered from each site, mostly ceramics and lithics, to have an acceptable representation of the whole site. In many cases, all the archaeological materials visible on the surface were collected from the site, due to the low density of surface material. To summarize, two artifact collection types were employed by the OVAP:

Total Collection: Applied to sites with fewer than 100 surface arti-

facts. All the archaeological material was collected except heavy metates and ground stone fragments. General Collection: Collection of 'local and common' artifacts, such as ceramics and lithics, as well as diagnostic, intrusive, or non-local material, such as shell.

At sites where material density was higher, more than 100 objects were collected. During previous fieldwork in the study area (summer 2003) and later during the summer 2004 season, it was determined that average artifact density of about 30 artifacts per m² was common at the larger sites while fewer than 10 artifacts per m² were found at the smaller sites. Artifacts were bagged by type (ceramics, lithic, shell, ground stone, bone, and diagnostic) in the field. In addition to unsystematic collection, sites were scouted to recover diagnostic and special artifacts, such as marine shell, projectile points, or decorated ceramics. These were collected and bagged separately. Ground stone material was collected and bagged as well, as were specially diagnostic or distinctive objects, such as stone pallets, points, small metate fragments, or three-quarter grooved axes. Only big and heavy pieces were left in situ. For example, when a metate was encountered, crew members took its measurements, plotted its location and association, if any, recorded its geological raw material type, metate type, and other important characteristics, and made a photographic record, but left it in the field. Diagnostic or distinctive objects were point-plotted on site maps.

By the end of the fieldwork a total of 10,740 sherds—(more than 113.550 kg of ceramic material)—and 2,363 lithic items (more than 64 kg) had been collected from the surface. Also, my expectation that Onavas was suitable research area to measure extra-regional interactions was fulfilled as a grand total of 1,191 marine shell pieces (1.113 kg) were found (Gallaga 2004c; Magaña 2004). In the field laboratory, all material bags were catalogued and the material was washed. All visual analysis of the material was performed at the field laboratory in Onavas. Emiliano Gallaga analyzed the ceramic material, debitage, and miscellaneous material, Cesar Villalobos and Gillian Newell undertook the preliminary analyses of ground stone, obsidian, and chipped stone tools, and Maricruz Magaña performed the shell and turquoise analysis. Data such as measurements and observations of the collected artifacts were digitally recorded on a laptop computer in the field, as well as photographs and drawings of the artifacts. In the following chapter, I present the final results of the artifacts analyses, discussed by category. At the end of the season, all archaeological materials were boxed and turned over to the INAH-Sonora facilities in Hermosillo for curation and storage.

The research and description of the different material analyses will serve for two research goals set by the OVAP: a preliminary local chronology base on the ceramic and lithic analyses and a diagnostic inventory of the material culture of the Prehispanic communities of the Onavas Valley. The descriptions of the collected and analyzed artifacts will provide afforded insights into the manufacture, use, and exchange of trade goods among the Onavas Valley Prehispanic communities, particularly that of marine shell. The information generated by the OVAP will provide a base line to start understanding the cultural development of the area, as well as help us identify the archaeological traditions of the Nébome that will allow researchers to compare it with that of other regions.

Limitations of the Data Set and Possible Bias Factors

As the archaeological record illustrates, the Onavas valley has been occupied from the Paleoindian period until the present. Such long term occupation is reflected in the archaeological record despite disturbances on the surface caused by intense agriculture, ranching, and mining activities, construction of communication lines (highways, roads, and electric lines), and amateur pot hunting or gold mining activities. Accessibility to water and good quality farming land make the floodplain desirable for settlement. It is in this area where most of the archaeological remains were recorded. Unfortunately, for the same reasons, the area where Prehispanic activities were focused coincides with the most intensive modern farming and cattle herding activities areas. Due to mechanized agricultural activities and land leveling, many architectural features have been destroyed, especially those located near or in the modern agricultural fields. Such destruction of sites, also expose a lot of material to the surface increasing the density and diversity of material collected from those sites. This situation created a non-realistic difference between sites that has been considered in the analysis of material distribution at each site. In addition, escalating amateur pot hunting activities have caused significant site destruction on the floodplain and in the foothill areas. Regardless, sites were still visible and recorded based on the scattered materials left on the surface.

In addition to these human actions, natural events have to be considered as well. Before modern dams were installed, the Río Yaqui was notorious for its floods, carrying an impressive amount of water that easily could have washed away archaeological features. These natural events may also have deposited a large quantity of soil and sand, potentially covering any cultural remains. Modern erosion and cuts on tributary drainages in the research area revealed that at least 3 to 4 m of deposits covered old floodplain surfaces. Most likely, ancient archaeological sites located on

Figure 5.2. Rio Yaqui tributary drainage cut on the floodplain (Photograph by Emiliano Gallaga).

the floodplain are covered by these layers. All cuts and drainages were carefully examined for cultural remains, but none were found (Figure 5.2). The landscape analysis will show a possible explanation for these results.

The survey was conducted from June through August and inevitably the summer rainy season caught us in the middle of the survey. To minimize the growing vegetation as a potential biasing factor on the site identification and artifact collection procedures, it was decided to survey flat areas first and more sloped landscapes later. In addition, the distances were shortened between crew members in areas of denser vegetation ensured full survey coverage. Although the vegetation changes between the dry and rainy season were striking,

bushes, grass, and weeds did not start to grow until the end of the field season. Therefore, ground visibility was not compromised.

Finally, the major limitation imposed upon this archaeological analysis is the fact that most of the dataset comes from surface contexts only. While conscious of this potential limitation, I am confident that such surface data has provided valuable information and insights into the Prehispanic past and will serve to structure research in the near future. Although the OVAP performed a full systematic survey in the most accurate way possible, it is likely that a few sites or features were missed and others misidentified. Nonetheless, a reliable data set was recovered providing a good approximation of the Prehispanic reality.

Chapter 6
Onavas Valley Material Culture

The archaeological material analyses completed by the OVAP were geared toward defining and describing material types and varieties to summarize the material assemblage of the Onavas Valley Prehispanic communities. The material analyses focused on obtaining both stylistic and functional information. Analytical and descriptive analyses of the archaeological materials were performed during the field season and at the INAH-Sonora facilities in Hermosillo, Sonora, due to Mexican legislation requiring that all archaeological materials stay in Mexico, unless the analysis performed is faster and/or less expensive to do than in México. Artifact collections and records of sites are stored at the INAH-Sonora facilities. The following chapter will provide a full description and analysis of the archaeological materials recovered by the OVAP.

CERAMICS

The Nébomes equivalent of olla was **aha**, which is analogous to the present-day term, **haha**. An olla used to carrying water was called **vaicarha**, and the act of making it was **vaicarh'ta**. An olla used for storing water was called aha **sudagui toacarha** (Pennington 1980:313; bold for emphasis).

In the last couple of decades, new research in Northwest Mexico, particularly in Sonora, is filling the existing gap in archaeological understandings of the region left by previous investigations. This research has provided new data and archaeological materials for several portions of the state of Sonora that had previously been investigated. The OVAP ceramic analysis required the creation and definition of new ceramic types as well as the reuse of established ceramic types. In the absence of a local ceramic typology, I developed a preliminary classification system based on the type-variety method and defined new ceramic types for the region. The presence of known non-local ceramic types allowed the use of existing typologies employed by Alvarez (1990), Braniff (1992), Bowen (1976a, 1976b, n.d.), Di Peso (1974, 1956), Gallaga (1997), Hinton (1955), and Jácome (1936).

The ceramic analysis consisted of obtaining both stylistic and functional information through the gathering of data on the following variables: ceramic type, vessel form, sherd count, weight, part of vessel (base, body, shoulder, neck, or rim, handle, and leg), rim form, and method of interior finishing (plain, brush, or shell) (Banning 2000; Gallaga 1997; McGuire and Villalpando 1993). As mentioned above, new ceramic types were identified and named, and existing typologies were also used to classify material. Generally, the sherds we recovered were medium to small in size, with an average radius of about 5 to 6 cm and weighing an average of 10.6 g. However, the sherd sizes were adequate for analysis. Whenever possible we identified vessel forms, based on rim forms, bases, and interior and exterior polishing.

Sherds were classified into eight ceramic forms. *Bowls* were open ceramic vessels with outcurved, and in some cases incurved, walls. The rim diameter is greater or equal to the maximum diameter of the vessel body and the interior is usually polished. *Jars* had closed rims with or without a neck, with a rim diameter that was equal or less than the maximum diameter of the vessel body. *Seed Jars* or *Tecomates* were spherical neckless ceramic vessels with a rim diameter that was substantially less than the maximum diameter of the vessel body. *Plates* were shallow, open ceramic vessels with wide outcurving walls and a rim diameter equal or more than five times the height of the vessel, and often had polished interiors. *Comales* were similar to plates but were shallower and normally exhibited remains of a burned base. *Scoops* were open ceramic tools with elongated forms, and were commonly used for pouring or heating liquids. *Partial vessels* were identificated through several refitting sherds from the same vessel. The majority of ceramic materials were classified as unknown or undetermined when the vessel form could not be determined.

Four additional types of ceramic artifacts were also identified. *Figurines*, which is a modeled ceramic object (animal, human, thing) made of fired or unfired clay. *Worked Sherds* were fragments of ceramic vessels with evidence of being worked into tools by humans, such as pottery scrapers or pendants. *Sherd Discs* were sherds shaped into a circular form, normally with rounded edges. These were probably used for games or were pre-forms of spindle whorls. *Spindle Whorls* were similar to sherd discs but with a hole drilled through the center and most likely used for weaving activities. In addition to the vessel types described above, two vessel parts were also recorded as they are unusual in the ceramic assemblage of Northwest Mexico. *Handles* were portions of ceramic vessels used to lifting them. And *vessel feet* were appendages attached along the circumference of the base that raises the body.

The interior finishing of the vessels received special attention. As McGuire and Villalpando (1993:25) state, "coarse parallel striation of uneven depth and width, usually on the inside of vessels, are a common feature of several ceramic types in northwestern Sonora." The ceramic material recovered during the OVAP proved no exception. Three types of interior finishing were identified: plain, brushing, and use of a shell scraper. The identification of these three types indicates the use of coil-and-scraped ceramic vessel manufacture (Gallaga 1997; Johnson 1960; McGuire and Villalpando 1993; Rice 1987). In addition, the identification of sherds with an interior scraped by a marine shell tool proved significant because researchers have identified similar ceramic manufacture technique for southern Sonora Prehispanic communities, such as Huatabampo (Alvarez 1990; Ekholm 1942; Pailes 1972).

Complete drawings of all rims from each form identified among the several ceramic types found in the analysis were made. The drawings have a ratio of one-to-one and indicate the interior and exterior of the vessel. The main attributes used for the description and identification of the new ceramic types were technological attributes, including, paste (color, presence of charcoal, texture, resistance, hardness, and temper), characteristics of the exterior and interior surfaces, presence of slip, thickness, rim types, and vessel forms (Banning 2003; Gallaga 1997; McGuire and Villalpando 1993; Rice 1987). Description and identification of the ceramic types found by the OVAP follow, but detail only the newly identified ceramic types. Type descriptions of ceramics previously identified and classified elsewhere are not fully reproduced here, and are only provided in summary form.

By the end of the field season, a total of 10,740 sherds—more than 113.550 kg of ceramic material—was recovered from the surface. Of these, 23 sherds and 0.072 kg (0.22 percent and 0.06 percent) were Majolica (two sherds), modern (14 sherds), and unidentified post-Prehispanic ceramic types (seven sherds), which were subtracted from the total. Those 23 non-Prehispanic sherds will not be described here.

Table 6.1 illustrates that the 96.50 percent of the sample is represented by plainwares while the decorated sherds only amount to 3.50 percent. Within the plainware ceramic cluster, four ceramic types were identified: Onavas Plain, a plainware likely made locally; Smooth Orange Slipped Ware; Coarse Red Slipped Ware; and Smooth Red Slipped Ware (Table 6.2). The decorated ceramic cluster consists of nine ceramic types (Table 6.3) divided into three main groups: local, non-local, and undetermined.

Vessel Form and Artifacts

Only 16.58 percent (1,777 sherds) of the total assemblage could be assigned a vessel form or artifact category. The remaining 83.42 percent (8,940 sherds) had to be designated as indeterminate forms. A total of 11 vessel forms/artifacts were identified: bowls, jars, seed jars or tecomates, plates, comales, scoops, figurines, spindle whorls, ceramic discs, and worked sherds. Some handles and vessel feet were also found (Table 6.4). A total of three partial vessels were found, in total 305 sherds and 7.5 kg, all plain jars. Those were incorporated into the total count of jar sherds.

Table 6.4 illustrates that jars, bowls, and tecomates were the most represented vessel forms. Of these 10,717 sherds where vessel form could be identified, 685 sherds were recorded as rims. The analysis of these sherds provides further information on the vessel assemblage of the Prehispanic communities of the Onavas Valley. This analysis indicates that these communities manufactured a wide variety of vessel types of different sizes, including jars, bowls, and tecomates, but plates, comales, and scoops as well. Although all rims were analyzed, the results of the rim sherd analysis mainly parallels the results of the rim analysis of the Onavas Plain and Onavas Purple-on-Red ceramic types, as these types comprised 90 percent of the rim sherd sample (Table 6.5 and Figure 6.1). The high ubiquity of these types provides support for the hypotheses of their local manufacture.

According to the rim analysis and identi-fication of Onavas Plainware bowls (see Table 6.5) Onavas potters appear to have manufactured hemispherical, outcurved, and incurved bowls. Some sherds exhibit exposure to fire, especially the larger vessels. Jars included straight collared jars, jars with outcurved or flaring rims, incurved jars (somewhere between bowls and neckless jars), and tecomates or seed jars. Some of the jars show exposure to fire while others that lack such evidence probably were used for storage and water containers. Jars were made in all sizes from miniature jars to large containers. The OVAP discovered specimens 121 mm thick with a plain interior, likely from large water jars such as those described in the ethnohistoric records by Pérez de Ribas, who mentions the use of these types of vessels among the Nébomes (1999:289). Additionally, two possible jar lip sherds were found which had never before been recorded in Sonora, and were most likely created to facilitate pouring. Plates included forms without a rim, with a straight rim, or with an outcurved, flaring rim. Comales were made without a rim, and had a plain interior surface, and a coarse/burned exterior surface. Scoops appeared in different sizes. Due to the fact that at least three different forms for vessel feet were found, we concluded that the vessel forms included tripod vessels, which occur in all areas surrounding Sonora, but have not previously been reported in Sonora itself.

Onavas Purple-on-Red rims (see Table 6.5) suggested that vessels of this type included hemispherical, outcurved, and incurved bowls; straight collar, outcurved or flaring rim jars, and tecomates or seed jars; and straight rim plates.

Ethnographic research and ceramic data collection undertaken at the end of the 1960s by Pennington (1980) suggests that some of the vessel forms depicted for the Prehispanic period were still in use, mainly jars. The knowledge and custom of making other vessel forms, appears to have become lost or replaced dur-

Table 6.1. Total OVAP ceramics

	Number of Sherds	%	Weight (kg)	%
Plainware	10,338	96.5	109.056	96.1
Decorated	379	3.5	4.446	3.9
Total	10,717	100	113.502	100

Table 6.2. Plainware ceramic type distributions in the sample

	Number of Sherds	%	Weight (kg)	%
Onavas Plain	10,102	94.3	107.833	95.1
Smooth Orange Slipped	61	0.6	0.463	0.4
Coarse Red Slipped	101	0..9	0.304	0.3
Smooth Red Slipped	74	0.7	0.456	0.4
Decorated	379	3.5	4.446	3.9
Total	10,717	100	113.502	100

Table 6.3. Decorated ceramic type distributions in the sample

	Number of Sherds	%	Weight (kg)	%
Onavas Purple on Red	360	3.35	4.323	3.8
Ramos Polychrome	6	0.05	0.048	0.1
Babícora Polychrome	6	0.05	0.021	0.1
Huérigos Polychrome	2	0.02	0.002	0.001
Carretas Polychrome	1	0.01	0.002	0.001
Nogales Polychrome	1	0.01	0.024	0.029
Incised	1	0.01	0.016	0.010
Corrugated	1	0.01	0.005	0.004
Unknown	1	0.01	0.005	0.004
Plainware	10,338	96.46	109.056	96.1
Total	10,717	100	113.502	100

Table 6.4. Ceramic vessel form distributions in the sample

	Number of Sherds	%	Weight (kg)	%
Indeterminate	8,940	83.42	80.01	70.49
Jars	1,064	9.93	22.65	19.95
Bowls	484	4.50	7.08	6.23
Tecomates	105	0.98	1.81	1.59
Plates	48	0.47	0.67	0.59
Discs	37	0.34	0.58	0.50
Worked Sherds	12	0.11	0.25	0.21
Comales	6	0.05	0.1	0.08
Scoops	5	0.04	0.13	0.11
Spindle Whorl	5	0.06	0.06	0.05
Figurine	4	0.04	0.08	0.07
Handles	4	0.04	0.06	0.56
Vessel Leg	3	0.03	0.03	0.02
Total	10,717	10	113.502	100

Table 6.5. Rim sherd sample analysis

Onavas Plain

Vessel Form	Rim Type	Diameters (cm)	Mean (cm)
Bowls	Straight	16 – 50	30.5
	Outcurved	10 – 46	30.0
	Incurved	14 – 50	29.5
Jars	Straight	14 – 46	30.0
	Outcurved	14 – 44	28.5
	Incurved	26 – 48	32.5
	Miniature	4	4.0
Tecomate	Neckless	2 – 48	23.0
Plate	Straight	42 – 46	44.5
	Outcurved	18	18.0
	Neckless	20 – 48	33.5
Comal	Neckless	24 – 50	34.0
Scoop	Straight	N/A	N/A

Onavas P/R

Vessel Form	Rim Type	Diameters (cm)	Mean (cm)
Bowls	Straight	32 – 42	38.5
	Outcurved	14 – 46	30.5
	Incurved	16 – 44	26.5
Jars	Straight	16 – 36	26.5
	Outcurved	18 – 28	24.0
Tecomate	Neckless	14 – 40	21.5
Plate	Straight	40	40

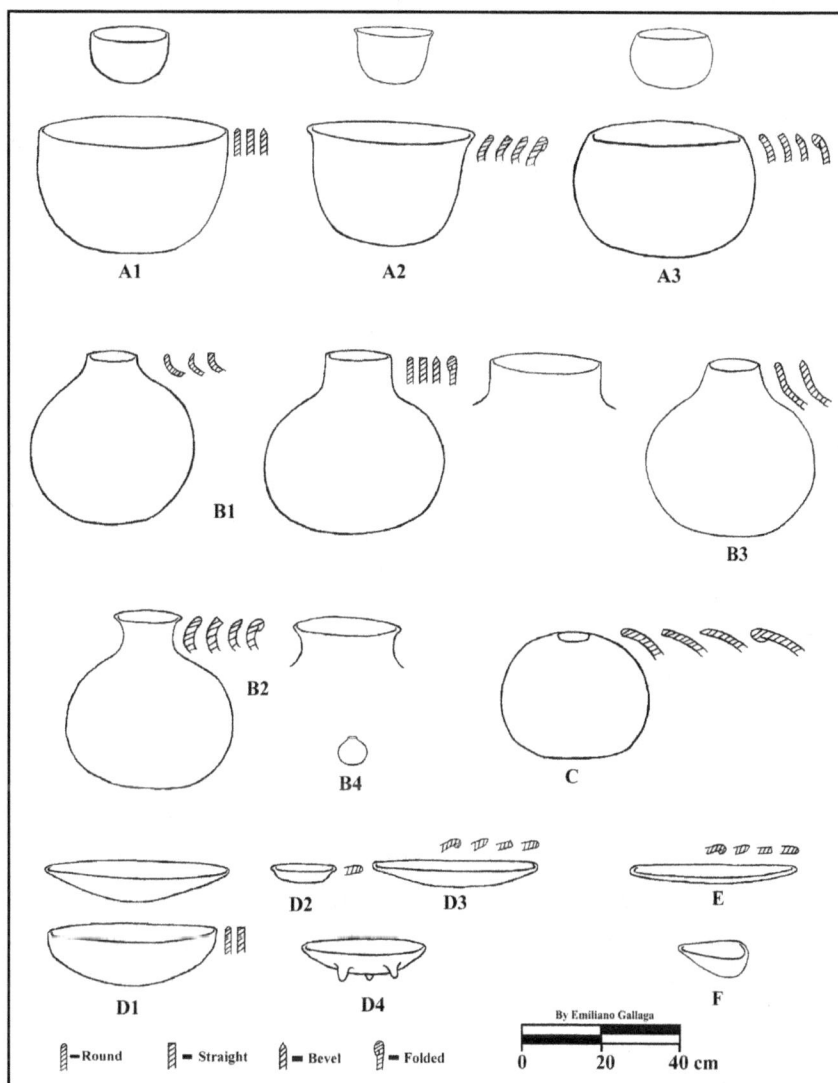

Figure 6.1. Vessel Forms: A) Bowls (straight-A1, outcurved-A2, incurved-A3); B) Jars (straight-B1, outcurved-B2, incurved-B3, miniature-B4); C) Tecomates; D) Plates (straight-D1, outcurved-D2, neckless-D3, plate with legs-D4); E) Comal; and F) Scoops.

ing or after the Colonial period. Additionally, none of the bottle forms (*botellones*) from the Huatabampo tradition (Alvarez 1990:48) or northern Sinaloa (Ehkolm 1942:75) were found in this assemblage.

Plainware Ceramics

The field crew collected more than 10,338 sherds weighing 109.056 kg representing four ceramic types. Redware variants were classified within the plainware category. Plainware made up 94.26 percent of the total sample by count and the 95.02 percent of the sample by weight. Redware was less common, represented only by 2.2 percent by count and 1.06 by weight.

Onavas Plain Ware

Sherds (n): 10,102
Weight: 107.833 kg.
Synonyms: None. No previous report or analysis of this type.

Manufacture: Coil-and-scrape. Ethnographic account established that Pima bajo ceramic manufacture is made by coil-and-scrape technique (Pennington 1980:312), as well of other Indian groups in southern Sonora (Alvarez 1990; Crumrine 1983; Spicer 1983). Most of the time the interior is plain, without marks. A few samples exhibit some scraping marks, however (60 sherds and 0.667 kg; representing 0.55 percent and 0.58 percent respectively of the total sample). These marks or striations appear to have likely been made by a "brush" tool. Other sherds show evidence of scraping with a shell tool (40 sherds-0.37 percent and 0.470 kg-0.41 percent respectively of the total sample).

Paste: Coarse, with 30 to 40 percent non-plastic material. Color: Variable from grayish brown (7.5YR 6/2), orange (5YR 6/8), to red (10R 5/6 and 7.5R 4/6) on the interior and exterior edges with a clear, slightly dark brown core. This diversity of color may have resulted from uneven burning in open fires.Carbon Streaking: None, or rarely. Texture: Mostly coarse, but some fine examples were identified. Fracture: Crumbling. Hardness: Soft, 2 to 3 in the Mohs scale. Temper: Abundant quartz and rock fragments; with sand, heavy minerals, and feldspars. Size ranged between medium (0.25-0.5 mm) to large (+ 0.5 mm).

Exterior: Seldom polished, but in most cases very eroded. Non-plastic inclusions visible on the surface, giving a sandpaper-like appearance. In a few samples a burnished surface is identified. It is possible that a thin layer of fine clay slip was applied to the surface before pol-

ishing. Color: A great diversity of color surface: grayish brown (7.5YR 6/2), to orange (5YR 6/8), and red (10R 5/6 and 7.5R 4/6).

Interior: Mostly plain or polished depending on the vessel form. A few sherds exhibited evidence of scraping by a brush or by a shell tool. On some occasions non-plastic material was identified on the surface. No anvil marks or finger impressions were present.

Slip: In some cases, a fine clay slip was applied for finishing surface techniques, but in most cases, no slip was present.

Thickness: Ranging from 4.5 and 6 mm to 15 and 20 mm with an average of 6 mm. Rims: Straight (129 sherds), incurved (90 sherds), outcurved (199 sherds), and neckless (143 sherds).

Forms: The total sample of this ceramic type consisted of the following forms: Jars (# 878), bowls (# 303) tecomates (# 93), plates (# 42), disk (# 34), worked sherds (# 11), comales (# 6), scoops (# 5), spindle whorl (# 5), figurines (# 4), and undetermined (# 8718). Handles and vessel feet were identified for this ware, probably used in bowl and plates.

Decoration: None. Comments: Due to the quantity reported in the field, I concluded that this type was locally manufactured. Ceramic vessels experimentally made with local clay in cooperation with local potters from the Onavas community produced similar ceramic material to those found in Prehispanic contexts. In addition, the manufacturing technique exhibited on the Onavas Plain Ware, the coil-and-scrape technique, differs from other ceramic traditions, such as those employed in the Trincheras area paddle-and anvil, but appears similar to those from the Río Sonora and Southern Sonora. Furthermore, the use of a marine shell for scraping some of the vessel interiors is consistent with the ceramic type descriptions from the southern Sonoran coast, illustrating a similarity with those ceramic types from coast Prehispanic communities.

Time Period: Unknown, Prehispanic period.

Onavas Valley Distribution: This common ware was found in 106 sites, from camps to villages. The sites with more representation were SON P:10:08 (n = 2,648), SON P:10:56 (n = 414), SON P:10:27 (n = 336), SON P:6:05 (n = 329), SON P:6:04 (n = 243), SON P:10:41 (n = 221), and SON P:10:98 (n = 213) (See Appendix I and II). The rest of the sites had an average of 60 sherds. Site SON P:10:08 (Appendix I and II) had a high number due to its soil perturbance. Due to the fact that the ceramic analysis is based on surface material, this particular plain and utilitarian ware could be associated with early, intermediate, and/or late phase Prehispanic occupation in the valley.

Smooth Orange Slipped Ware

Sherds (n): 61
Weight: 0.463 kg.
Synonyms: None. No previous report or analysis of this type. Possible Huatabampo Red, Cuchujaqui Red, Techobampo Red, or Batacosa Red.

Manufacture: Coil-and-scrape. The interior is generally plain without marks, although a few examples show some scraping marks. These marks or striations were usually made by a brush tool (2 sherds-0.018 percent or 0.014 kg-0.012 percent respectively of the total sample). Some sherds show evidence of scraping with a shell tool (3 sherds-0.027 percent and 0.015 kg-0.013 percent respectively of the total sample).

Paste: Fine, hard, and very little temper with around 10 to 15 percent non-plastic material.

Color: Orange (5YR 6/8). Carbon Streak: None. Texture: Fine. Fracture: Straight. Hardness: Hard, 3-5 on the Mohs scale. Temper: Fine size (0.1-0.25 mm), consisting of sand mixed with quartz, feldspars, and some rock fragments and mica.

Exterior: Well-finished polishing eroded in some instances. Temper is visible on the surface at times. Surface probably burnished with a stone tool. Color: Orange (5YR 6/8).

Interior: Surface mostly found plain or eroded yielding a sandpaper surface. Only a few examples were found with scraping marks, made with a brush or a marine shell tool (Figure 6.2). Pailes (1972:225) mentions similar treatment of Techobampo Red wares. Depending on the vessel form, the interior was burnished or at least polished. Color: Orange (5YR 6/8).

Slip: Most likely. Probably a fine clay slip.

Thickness: Ranges between 5 and 6.5 mm with an average of 6 mm. Rims: Incurved (2 sherds), outcurved (6 sherds), and neckless (1 sherds).

Forms: From the total sample for this ceramic type: Jars (# 7), bowls (# 10), tecomates (# 1), and undetermined (# 43).

Decoration: Usually none, but at least one rim sherd has a serrated decoration (Figure 6.3). Pailes (1972:223) mention similar decoration on Cuchujaqui Red wares. This type of decoration appears to be crafted with the point of a finger pressing perpendicular into the rim, hence leaving a nail and finger print.

Comments: No previous record of this ceramic type or variant has been reported in the Sonoran archaeological record. Its low frequency strongly suggests a non-local origin. It is possible that this type is similar to some fine orange or redwares, such as Huatabampo Red, Cuchu-

Figure 6.2. Interior shell tool scraping and dented rim decoration (Photograph by Emiliano Gallaga).

jaqui Red, Techobampo Red, and Batacosa Red (Alvarez 1990; Ekholm 1942; Gallaga 2004b; Pailes 1972). Redware types in Northwest Mexico are not well-defined and studied, such as those in the American Southwest. However, as mentioned above these sherds probably come from a ceramic tradition from northern Sinaloa and/or the coast (Huatabampo?) due to its characteristics, indicative of interaction between these areas and the Onavas Valley.

Time Period: Unknown, probably ca. A.D. 800-1200.

Onavas Valley Distribution: This ware was found only on 18 sites. The majority of these sherds were found at SON P:10:18 (n = 14), SON P:10:08 (n = 10), and SON P:10:16 (n = 6) (See Appendix I and II), all of them small sites. The rest of the sites had an average of 1.6 sherds of this type. Its presence may dates to early phases of occupation in the valley, just like similar material found in other areas in Sonora.

Coarse Red Slipped Ware

Sherds (n): 101
Weight: 0.304 kg.
Synonyms: Possibly Huatabampo Red, Cuchujaqui Red, Techobampo Red, or Batacosa Red.

Manufacture: Coil-and-scrape. No scraping marks were found on the interior of sherds; all samples for this type exhibited plain interiors. No fingerprints were found in the interior, either.

Paste: Coarse, with around 20 to 25 percent non-plastic material. Color: Paste color is dull reddish orange (10R 6/4), some sherds had a gray to black core, and a red slip on the surface (7.5R 3/6, 4/6, 4/8). Carbon Streak: Occasionally. Texture: Generally, coarse. Fracture: Crumbling. Hardness: Soft, 2 to 3 Mohs scale. Temper: Lots of quartz and rock fragments, but also sand, heavy minerals, and feldspars. The

Figure 6.3. Onavas Purple-on-Red decoration sample (Photograph by Emiliano Gallaga).

size of temper ranges between medium (.25 - 0.5 mm) to large (+ 0.5 mm).

Exterior: Usually polished, but some examples of well-burnished exteriors were reported, with shiny surfaces. Other sherds exhibit opaque surfaces. A thin layer of red slip was applied to the surface and later polished. Color: Dark red to red (7.5R 3/6, 4/6, 4/8).

Interior: Depending on the vessel form, the interior could be plain or polished. Red slip is present only for bowls and on most examples, slips are in relatively good condition.

Slip: Present, a thin layer of red slip is applied to the surface. The surface layer is mostly polished or burnished, but in a few instances the surface is not polished at all, giving an opaque surface finish.

Thickness: Ranging between 5 and 6.5 mm with an average of 6 mm. Rims: One outcurved sherd and 12 unidentified rims (too small).

Forms: From the total sample for this ceramic type consisted of the following forms: Jars (# 16), bowls (# 5), disk (# 1), and undetermined (# 79).

Comments: It is possible that this ceramic type was one of the redware types reported for southern Sonora, such as Huatabampo Red, Cuchujaqui Red, Techobampo Red, or Batacosa Red (Alvarez 1990; Ekholm 1942; Gallaga 2004b; Pailes 1972). Unfortunately, as mentioned above, redware material remains poorly reported, studied, or described. From the analysis of manufacturing techniques, the southern Sonoran redware found in the Onavas Valley appears to differ from similar redware types from the north of Sonora (coil-and-scrape versus paddle-and-anvil)—an idea that needs further testing. It is low frequency suggest a non-local origin, probably the coast.

Time Period: Probably ca. A.D. 200-1000 (Early Ceramic phase).

Onavas Valley Distribution: Only in 19 sites containing this ware were identified. The most representative site was SON P:10:89 (n = 52), identified as a camp (pot-burst event). The rest of the sites had an average of 2.7 sherds. These sites could represent an early/middle occupation of the valley in Prehispanic times.

Smooth Red Slipped Ware

Sherds (n): 74
Weight: 0.456 kg.
Synonyms: Possibly Huatabampo Red, Cuchujaqui Red, Techobampo Red, or Batacosa Red.

Manufacture: Coil-and-scrape. Most of the sample has a plain interior surface with occasional marks caused by slight dislocation of the non-plastic material during the polishing process. Six sherds exhibited scraping marks made with a marine shell tool. No finger prints were spotted on the interior of the sherds.

Paste: Fine, with 10 to 15 percent non-plastic material. Color: Dull reddish orange (10R 6/4), no gray or black core, and the surface shows some tones of red (10R 5/6, 4/6). Carbon Streak: None. Texture: Fine. Fracture: Straight. Hardness: Hard, 3 to 5 on the Mohs scale. Temper: Fine size (0.1-0.25 mm), consisting of sand mixed with quartz, feldspars, and some rock fragments.

Exterior: Mostly plain with an opaque surface, some sherds seem to have been polished but unlike the Coarse Red Slipped Ware.

Interior: Depending on the vessel form, some plain interiors revealed a red slip.

Slip: A thin layer of red slip was applied to the surface. In most cases the surface layer is just plain giving an opaque surface finish.

Thickness: Ranging between 4 and 5.5 mm with an average of 5 mm. Rims: Straight (2 sherds), incurved (2 sherds), outcurved (3 sherds), neckless (2 sherds), and undetermined (3).

Forms: The total sample for this ceramic type consisted of the following forms: Jars (# 18), bowls (# 24), tecomates (# 6), plates (# 1), and undetermined (# 25).

Comments: Same as the Coarse Red Slipped Ware.

Time Period: Probably ca. A.D. 200-1000 (Early Ceramic phase).

Onavas Valley Distribution: This ware was recovered at a total of 27 sites, particularly at SON P:10:08 (n = 8), SON P:10:12 (n = 7), SON P:6:04 (n = 7), SON P:10:18 (n = 6), SON P:6:15 (n = 6), SON P:10:64 (n = 5), and SON P:10:69 (n = 5) (See Appendix I and II). The rest of the sites had an average of 1.5 sherds. These sites could represent an early/middle occupation of the valley in Prehispanic times.

Decorated Ceramics

Decorated ceramics were recovered in lower numbers than plainware ceramic types. The collection of several decorated sherds of non-local origin and the identification of a previously unreported local decorated ceramic type provide considerable information about the region's possible cultural interactions and development. More than 379 decorated sherds weighing 4.446 kg were identified. The decorated ceramic material made up 3.54 percent of the total sample by count and the 3.92 percent of the sample by weight. Nine ceramic types were present, divided into three subdivisions or groups: (1) local, (2) non-local, and (3) undetermined (see Table 6.3).

Local Onavas Purple-on-Red

Sherd (n): 360
Weight: 4.323 kg.
Synonyms: None, previously unreported. This type is similar to the Trincheras Purple-on-Red ceramic in terms of purple color decoration.

Manufacture: Coil-and-scrape. Most of the sample shows a plain interior surface, occasionally some marks were created by the dislocation of the non-plastic material during polishing. Depending on the vessel form, decoration was either on the interior or the exterior. The surface was well-polished. No finger prints existed on the interior of the sherds.

Paste: Coarse, with 30 to 40 percent non-plastic material, although some exceptions exhibited a finer paste. Color: Paste color runs from red (10R 5/6), orange (2.5 YR 6/6), dull orange (5YR 6/3), to grayish brown (5YR 6/2). Some sherds have a gray or black core, and the surface shows some tones of red (10R 5/6, 4/6), orange (2.5 YR 6/6, 6/8, 7/8), and grayish brown (5YR 4/2, 5/2, 6/2). Carbon Streak: Only occasionally present. Texture: Coarse to fine. Fracture: Crumbled for the coarse sherds and straight for the finer paste ceramics. Hardness: In general, hard, 3-5 on the Mohs scale. Temper: Abundance of quartz, feldspars, and rock fragments, with sand and mica or pyrite. The size ranges between medium (0.25-0.5 mm) to large (+ 0.5 mm) for the coarse sherds, and fine (0.1-0.25 mm) for the fine sherds.

Exterior: Well-polished or plain. In general, the temper is not visible on the surface. It is possible that a fine clay slip was applied to the surface in preparation for painting. All jars of this type always had decorated exterior surfaces, while bowls were most often had decorated interiors.

Interior: Similar to the exterior. In the jars the interior is unpolished and smooth.

Slip: It is possible in some cases that a fine clay slip was added to the surface.

Decoration: The color used for decoration ranges from a dark purple or red (7.5R 3/4) to a light red (10R 4/8). The change in color intensity could have resulted from the way the vessel was fired. This purple color lacks the specular mica used in the Trincheras decorated wares. The color used may have a mineral base, but it is less resistant than the Trincheras wares. The color used on the Onavas Purple-on-Red wears off easily, especially when wet. From the sample collected for this project, the designs were mostly lines and geometric figures. In some cases, solid figures or bands were depicted (Figure 6.3). The design types are different from those used for the Trincheras wares. Generally, bowls carried designs on the interior and jars on the exterior, although jars occasionally had designs inside around the neck-rim area.

Thickness: This type shows a great range in thickness, from 3.4 mm to 16.3 mm. Rims: Straight (15 sherds), incurved (22 sherds), outcurved (23 sherds), and neckless (5 sherds).

Forms: From the total sample for this ceramic type consisted of the following forms: Jars (# 149), bowls (# 141), tecomates (# 5), plates (# 1), disk (# 1), and undetermined (# 63).

Comments: This local decorated ceramic type, found during this survey, has not been previously recorded. The variety of vessel forms, number of sherds, and similarity to the physical characteristics and manufacture of the Onavas Plain suggest that this ceramic type was also manufactured in the Onavas Valley region. More research in the area, excavation, and testing of clay sources is required to confirm this hypothesis.

This local type appears similar to those from the Trincheras region (Purple-on-red and Purple-on-Brown), with purple or reddish decoration on a background which is most often red, but also occasionally grey or brown. In spite of their appearance, however, the Onavas types lack some key characteristics of the Trincheras wares, such as brushed interiors, specular hematite pigment, and particular decoration designs. It is possible that the Onavas decorated ceramic types were a local imitation of Trincheras types, but any speculation in this regard remains inconclusive until researchers undertake further ceramic research in surrounding areas as well as in the Onavas Valley.

Onavas Purple-on-Red was found on the surface in association with Casas Grandes ceramic types. Originally, it was thought to be close or contemporaneous to the Medio Period (A.D. 1200-1450). However, ceramic analysis and regional comparison suggest that the Onavas Purple-on-Red could be an early type (A.D. 1000-1200). Similar decorated ceramic types in Sonora point to this conclusion. In the Trincheras region, the local Trincheras Purple-on-Red and Purple-on-Brown decorated types had a time span of A.D. 700-1150 (Gallaga 1997; Heckman 2000; McGuire and Villalpando 1993). At the Bavispe Valley, located near to the core of the Rio Sonora region, new research has placed local Red-on-Brown ceramics around similar dates (Douglas and Quijada 2005). Northern Sinaloa Red-on-Brown ceramics (John Carpenter personal communication 2005) and probably Convento Red type (Di Peso et al. 1974) are also thought to date to this period. In terms of vessel forms, jars and bowls formed the majority of the

assemblage, but some tecomates/neckless seed jars were also manufactured. The presence of tecomates supports the notion of an early ceramic type.

I should mention that initially, two new types were named in the field: Onavas Purple-on-Red and Onavas Purple-on-Grey. However, after the completion of the ceramic analysis it was decided to unite the two types into one: Onavas Purple-on-Red. The gray color may be the result of a non-homogeneous burning rather than indicative of a different type.

Time Period: Probably A.D. 800-1200 (Onavas II Phase).

Onavas Valley Distribution: A total of 27 sites were reported to have this local decorated ware. The most representative sites were SON P:10:08 (n = 223), SON P:10:98 (n = 34), SON P:10:44 (n = 15), SON P:6:05 (n = 13) SON P:10:29 (n = 11), and SON P:10:70 (n = 10) (See Appendix I and II). The rest of the sites had an average of 2.5 sherds. These sites could represent an early/middle occupation of the valley in Prehispanic times.

Non-Local

In total, five types were reported belonging to one of two archaeological traditions (Figure 6.4). The first of the two archaeological traditions identified was the Casas Grandes tradition, of which four ceramic types were identified in the OVAP sample, all belonging to the Medio Period (A.D. 1200-1450): Ramos Polychrome, Babícora Polychrome, Huerigos Polychrome, and Carretas Polychrome. These Chihuahuan types, associated with the Casas Grandes region, had been identified before on the west side of the Sierra Madre Occidental at sites in northern and central Sonora (Braniff 1992; Bowen n.d.; Dirst 1979; Gallaga 1997; Sauer and Brand 1931). However, this is the first report of Chihuahua types in the mid-southern portion of Sonora, and hence is relevant to understanding the Onavas valley Prehispanic extra-regional interactions. In an ongoing project, Carpenter has reported finding Chihuahua ceramic types in the Río Fuerte Valley in northern Sinaloa (Carpenter, personal communication 2005). The second archaeological tradition identified in the decorated ceramics was the Trincheras region, which were represented by a single Nogales Polychrome sherd recovered from the surface.

Undetermined

Three ceramic types composed this last group: incised, corrugated, and a possible northern Sinaloa type. The first two types are roughly identified or related to the Río Sonora archeological tradition (Amsden 1928; Pailes 1972), whose ceramics are often textured. The last type may have originated from northern Sinaloa.

Incised

Through minimal research conducted in the Sonoran portion of the Sierra Madre Occidental it has been established that certain types of incised decorated wares belong to the extended Río Sonora archaeological tradition (Amsden 1928, Doolittle 1988, Douglas and Quijada 2004a, 2004b; Pailes 1972). This tradition appeared to stretch from the current international border to the border of Sinaloa state (Pailes 1972). For unknown reasons, incised material seems to have enjoyed popularity among Prehispanic communities in the northern and southern Sierra Madre Occidental portions of Sonora. However, in the Onavas Valley only one sherd (0.01 percent), weighing 0.016 kg (0.01 percent), was recorded. This small sherd shows some incised decoration but not enough to establish the presence of an incised type as recorded for the north or south

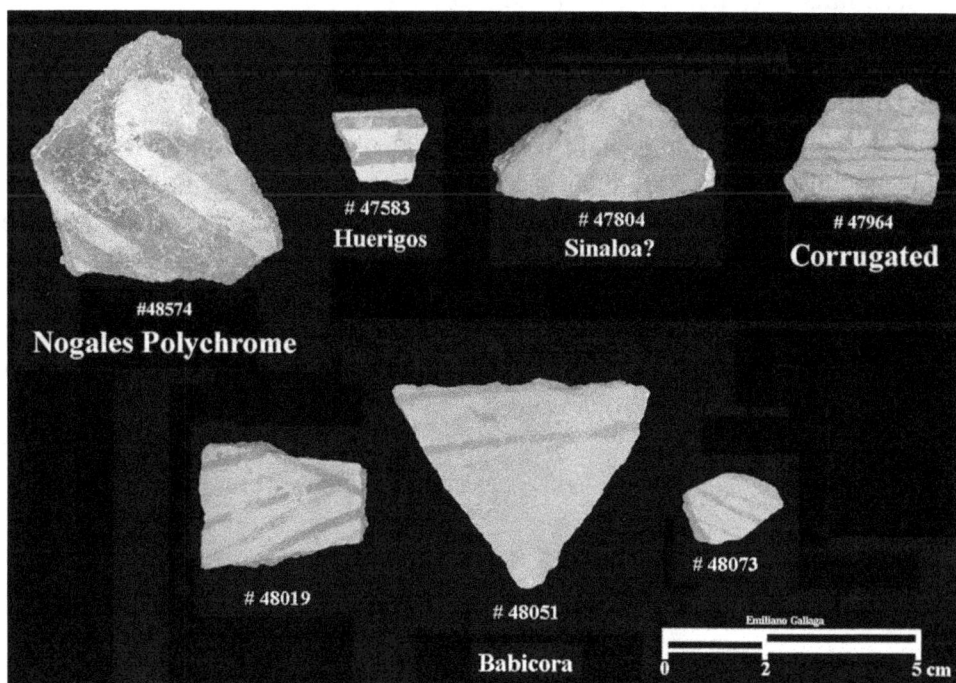

Figure 6.4. Non-local decorated ceramic types (Photograph by Emiliano Gallaga).

of the state (Pailes 1972). The sherd belongs to a bowl and the decoration is on the interior. This sherd was found at SON P:10:08 (Appendix I and II).

Corrugated

This ceramic type is not abundant in Sonora. Some examples are reported from southern Sonora (Pailes 1972) and from the Río Sonora tradition (Douglas and Quijada 2004b; Pacheco 2003), but it remains a relatively rare ceramic type. Only one sherd (0.01 percent), weighing 0.005 kg (0.004 percent), was reported. This sherd was a straight jar rim. Manufactured by the coil-and-scrape technique, only the interior of the jar was plain, while the coil marks were left exposed on the exterior (Figure 6.4). This sherd was found at SON P:10:08 (Appendix I and II).

Unknown

Only one sherd falls into this category (0.01 percent), weighing 0.005 kg (0.004 percent). This sherd exhibited a fine paste, plain interior, and polished exterior surface. The exterior had at least two distinguishable colors: light gray (10YR 8/1) and dusky red (7.5R 4/4). The first color formed a small band and the second decorated two thirds of the sherd. Its characteristics do not resemble any known ceramic type in Sonora. Thus, it may possible that this sherd came from northern Sinaloa (Figure 6.4). This sherd was found at SON P:10:26 (See Appendix I and II).

Ceramic Artifacts

Figurines

Four small figurine fragments were collected during the survey (Figure 6.5a). As their paste was similar to those used for the manufacture of the Onavas Plain ceramic type, the figurines may have been manufactured locally. None had decorations. Three of the fragments consisted of the trunk of a body without any parts of the legs, arms, or head attached. Two of the four fragments appear to represent female figures (# 47585 and # 48324). The fourth fragment is a portion of a possible head (# 48176) that shows only a nose. It is unclear if it represents a human or an animal figure. The lack of faces or other distinctive decorative features does not allow us to compare these figurines with those of neighboring regions, such as the Huatabampo tradition (Alvarez 1990), the Southwest U.S. (Haury 1976), or those reported by Ekholm (Gallaga 2004b). In Gilberto Carlos' personal collection at Onavas, a ceramic ear was recorded (Figure 6.5b). The piece illustrated a delicate and skilled example of ceramic manufacture, is not possible to establish if it is a local or non-local piece. The lobe had at least 6 holes, possibly depicting the use of earrings or another sort of ear decoration.

Spindle Whorl

In Sonora, spindle whorls are generally made from flat sherds that have been worked into disks perforated through the center, and were used for fiber/cord manufacture (Figure 6.5c). However, some Mesoamerican-style spindle whorls are reported for Sonora. To date only four examples have been found in three areas: southern Sonora described by Pailes (1972:261-263), Huatabampo (Ekholm 1942:88), and the Trincheras region (Sauer and Brand 1931:11). On the other hand, 27 Mesoamerican-style spindle whorls were reported from the Guasave site, but no perforated sherd disk-style spindle whorls were recovered (Carpenter 1996:258). Unfortunately, no Mesoamerican-style spindle whorls were found by the OVAP; only five Sonoran-style spindle whorls were identified.

Only four of the perforated sherd spindle whorls were considered to be complete (# 47710, 47871, 48242, and 48514). The remaining one (# 47625) had the hole in the center, but lacked a round shape. This spindle whorl may have broken, leaving only the center portion. Alternatively, it may represent an unfinished spindle whorl, and may have been left unfinished because it was broken while being perforated. Three of the spindle whorls measured 4 cm in diameter, while the fourth spindle whorl measured 2 cm in diameter, and the last one could not be measured with regard to diameter due to its unfinished state.

Ceramic Disks

A total of 37 ceramic disks were identified during the ceramic analysis (Figure 6.5d). All disks consist of ceramic sherds worked into a disk shape. None were actually manufactured and fired as a disk. Of the whole sample, one disk belongs to the Coarse Red Slipped Ware ceramic type (# 47594), one to Onavas Purple-on-Red (# 47987), and one to the Smooth Orange Slipped Ware type (# 48071). The rest, a total of 34, were identified as Onavas Plain Ware sherds. In addition, they ranged in size from 1 to 16 cm in diameter. One measured 1 cm in diameter, three were 2 cm, five were 3 cm, thirteen were 4 cm, three were 5 cm, four were 6 cm, one was 7 cm, five were 8 cm, one was 14 cm, and the last one was 16 cm in diameter. This diversity in sizes may indicate that their use may have differed depending on their size. Perhaps the smaller ones were game pieces, while the middle ones corresponded to spindle whorls in progress, and the larger ones could represents vessel covers.

Worked Sherds

Twelve examples were found during ceramic analysis. These items exhibit evidence of grinding or flaking in all or some portion of the sherd, but lack the roundness of a disk. Six take on a clearly rectangular shape and may be unfinished ceramic pendants. The latter arti-

facts measure on average 4 x 3 cm. All sherds were identified as Onavas Plain Ware, with the exception of one Babícora polychrome sherd (# 48073). None were drilled or perforated.

Ceramic Summary

The quantity of ceramic material recovered from the surface illustrates that the Prehispanic communities were sufficiently sedentary to produce high densities of ceramic refuse. The ceramic analysis indicates that most of the wares appear to be of local manufacture using local clay sources. The OVAP also identified at least two new ceramic types: Onavas Plain Ware and Onavas Purple-on-Red.

The Smooth Orange Slipped, Coarse Red Slipped and Smooth Red Slipped wares present interesting avenues for future research. First, it must be determined whether these types are of local manufacture or are non-local ceramic types imported from elsewhere. As several researchers state, the lack of analysis of orange and red wares in Northwest Mexico have resulted in a diversity of similar ceramic types divided only by region or area of research, but not by a systematic typology (Braniff 1992; McGuire and Villalpando 1993; Gallaga 1997). Some of the identified red slipped monochrome sherds could be part of the ceramic assemblages from the south of Sonora such as Huatabampo Red, Cuchujaqui Red, Techobampo Red, or Batacosa Red (Álvarez 1990; Ekholm 1939, 1942; Pailes 1972). The ceramic analysis further indicates that the manufacture of the Onavas wares was coil-and-scraped and could belong to the coil-and-scraped tradition of brown wares from the Guaymas area and the Huatabampo tradition (Río Mayo and Río Fuerte) (Alvarez 1990, 1996; Bowen 1976a). The latter is interesting considering that Upper Pima and Hohokam ceramic wares were made with the paddle–and–anvil technique. However, more comparative analysis is needed. In addition, compositional analyses from sherd

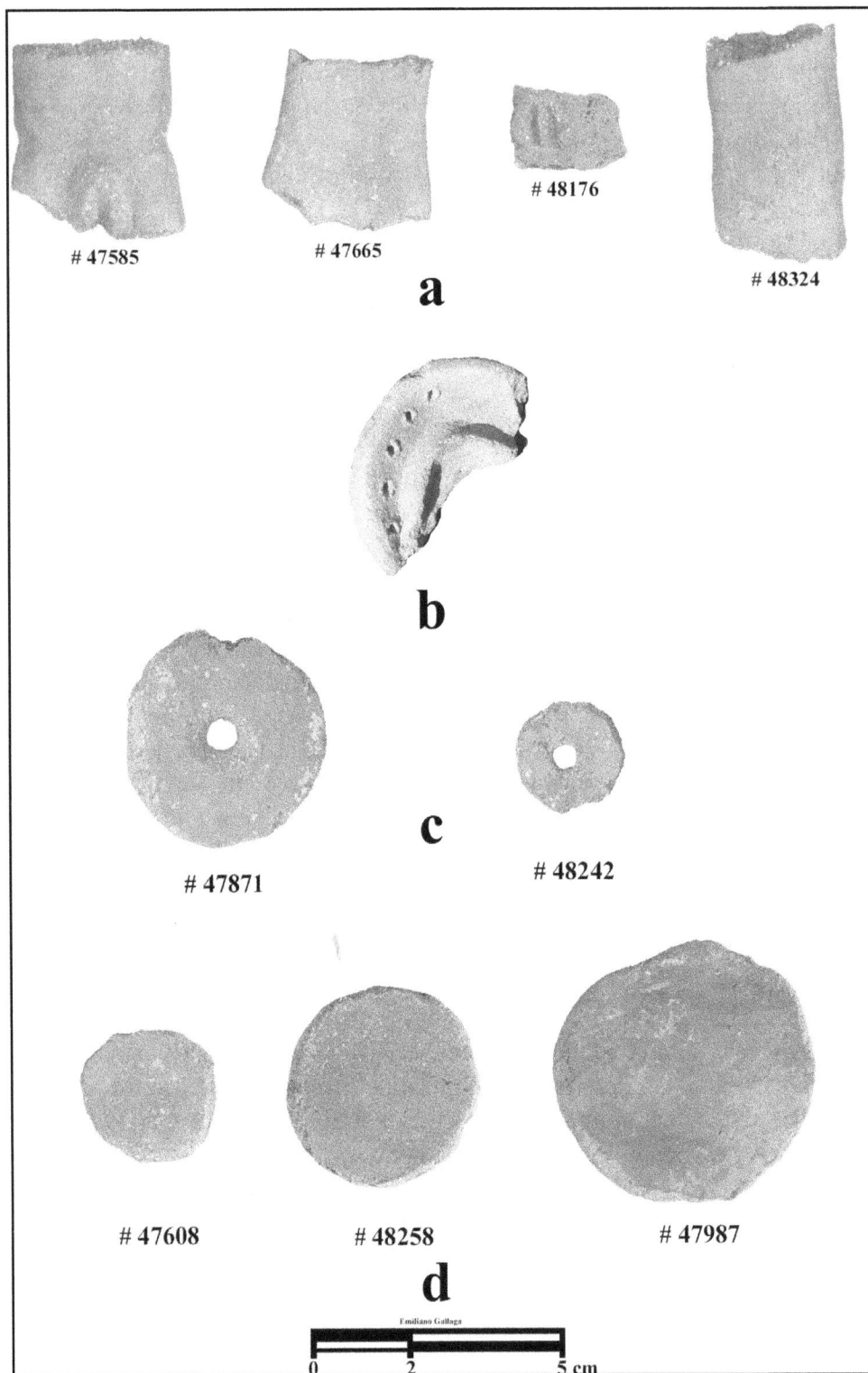

Figure 6.5. Ceramic Artifacts:a) figurines; b) ceramic ear (Gilberto Carlos collection); c) spindle whorls; and d) ceramic disks (Photograph by Emiliano Gallaga).

samples and local clay sources could determine the origin of those ceramic types.

In the field, a couple of sherds were identified as possibly belonging to the Seri "eggshell" ceramic type. During later ceramic analysis such identification was discarded, and the sherds were instead identified as very thin Onavas Plain sherds. It is important to remember that the Jesuits documented the presence of Seri bands in the Onavas Valley during the harvest season, who visited the area to trade coastal items for food and sierra items (Perez de Ribas 1999:390). The very thin sherds, therefore, might have been local "eggshell" vessels made by Seri Indians with local Onavas clay.

The decorated wares were fewer in number than local wares, but provide important evidence for extra-regional interactions and the possible role played by the Onavas Valley Prehispanic inhabitants. The identification of 17 non-local sherds (Ramos Polychrome, Babícora Polychrome, Huérigos Polychrome, Carretas Polychrome, Nogales Polychrome, and a possible northern Sinaloan type) is relevant for several reasons. The identification of these non-local sherds in the Onavas Valley expands the known spatial distribution of these ceramic types. Their presence in Onavas serves as physical evidence of some sort of interaction between different archaeological traditions. Additionally, these types provide the first material evidence for the use of the Río Yaqui as a possible trade route between the southern Sonoran coast and the Sierra Madre Occidental.

The recovery of more than 15 sherds from the Casas Grandes region is important considering the distance between the two areas, more than 300 km of rough terrain, and is particularly notable in light of similar surveys such as the Cerro de Trincheras Settlement and Land Use Survey Project (1998) in the Trincheras area. During this project only one Casas Grandes sherd was found (Paul and Suzanne Fish personal communication 2004). Yet, the Cerro de Trincheras Archaeological Project (1994 and 1996) uncovered 824 sherds originating from the Chihuahuan region in excavated contexts, which represent only 0.078 percent of the total sample (Gallaga 1997; see also McGuire and Villalpando 2011). The prevalence of Chihuahuan sherds found during survey and excavation, as well as the identification of 15 Chihuahuan sherds during the OVAP suggests that the Onavas Valley may reveal more Chihuahuan sherds during future excavation of Onavas valley sites. The presence of Chihuahuan sherds in the Trincheras area is also interesting as the area has long been considered one of the major marine shell suppliers for the community of Paquimé (Braniff 1992; Di Peso et al. 1974; Nelson 1991). Yet, the low numbers of Chihuahuan ceramics suggest that the interaction between those two areas was not as intensive as previously thought (Gallaga 2004a). Furthermore the shell manufacturing technology from Cerro de Trincheras is quite different from that of Paquimé (McGuire and Villalpando 2011; Vargas 1999, 2004), and no Trincheras ceramic types have been found in Paquimé. Other areas likely functioned as the shell suppliers of the Paquimé community. The Río Yaqui may have served as such a conduit.

An important result of the ceramic analysis is the near absence of Río Sonora ceramic types, such as the incised and punctated wares identified by Amsden (1928) and Pailes (1972). Of the 10,740 sherds collected and analyzed, only one sherd was identified as incised, representing only 0.009 percent of the total ceramic sample, and not a single punctated sherd was recovered in the entire research area. The almost complete absence of Río Sonora ceramic types in the Onavas Valley shows a spatial discontinuity in the Río Sonora archaeological traditions as had been proposed by Pailes (1972, 1994a, 1994b). Pailes, who conducted research projects in the south of Sonora as well in the Río Sonora area, found similar material remains in both areas, such as stone foundation habitation areas and ceramic types (the incised and punctuated wares). These findings led him to state that the Río Sonora archaeological tradition runs from the northeast area of Sonora to the southern border of Sonora with Sinaloa (Pailes 1972, 1994a, 1994b). However, the lack of material evidence of the Río Sonora tradition in the Onavas Valley, such as the incised and punctated ceramic types in the middle of this region, raises some crucial questions regarding the spatial extent of this archaeological tradition as it has been characterized to date in the archaeological literature.

In summary, the ceramic analysis identified a late Prehispanic ceramic assemblage with a diverse and skillfully manufactured array of vessels and tools. Potters in the area were not only producing ceramic vessels to fulfill household needs, but also spending the time, effort, and resources to manufacture stylistically better ceramics. However, further excavations of sites in the area are needed to provide sufficient data to establish clear temporal affiliations of ceramic forms and types.

Lithics

By far the most important stone item used by the present-day Pima Bajo is the metate. There are two types —a very smooth legless slab called **mátur** and a rough legless slab called **istusk**…(Pennington 1980:313; bold for emphasis).

By the end of the field season, 2,363 lithic items had been collected (64.051 kg). The lithic sample consists of 1,871 debitage flakes and cores (15.948 kg), 231 pieces of obsidian (0.252 kg), 15 pieces of turquoise (0.019 kg), 125 pieces of stone tools (46.515 kg), 21 bifacial tools (0.815 kg), and 107 projectile points (0.502 kg). This discussion of the lithic sample was divided into three categories: (1) raw material types, (2) debitage, and (3) stone tools. Of the stone tool types, three sub-categories were distinguished: ground stone, chipped stones, and projectile points. Due to the absence of previous research in the area, this lithic analysis aims principally to provide a description of the lithic assemblage for the Nébome inhabitants.

Raw Material

Researchers mention that good quality material for lithic tool manufacture exists in limited and discrete distributions in Northwest Mexico and the Southwest U.S. (Pacheco 2003). For chipped stone tools, good quality material consists of obsidian and cryptocrystalline rocks, such as quartz, chert, chalcedony, and jasper. However, cryptocrystalline raw materials were not always available in optimum quantities or sizes. Therefore, igneous rocks (rhyolites, andesites, lava rock, or basalts) or sedimentary material (sandstone or slate) were mostly used in the Onavas Valley.

Lithic analysis of the material recovered during the OVAP shows that a great variety of raw material was used by the Prehispanic craft producers of the Onavas Valley, such as rhyolite, basalt, chert, vesicular basalt, quartz, slate, sandstone, lava rock, obsidian (green, gray, and black), and turquoise. Apparently, the Prehispanic flint knappers used local, non-local, and cryptocrystalline and non-cryptocrystalline raw materials. However, the intended use of an object determined what kind of rock was best. Local material appears to have consisted mostly of volcanic origin rocks, such as andesite, rhyolite, lava rock, basalt, and vesicular basalts. Sedimentary rocks, such as sandstone or slate, and some cryptocrystalline rocks were used as well. These rock types are available in local gravels and secondary deposits along the valley.

High-quality material was also available in the area, such as obsidian, chert, and chalcedony. In the case of the obsidian, specific local sources remain unidentified, but may have been utilized prehispanically. Local miners have mentioned that obsidian may be found in the area in drainages or high up in the Sierra Madre as small nodules (approximately 5 cm) commonly referred to as "Apache tears"(Pacheco 2003). The color of this local obsidian is black or gray. The OVAP recovered evidence of the manufacture of small projectile points from such nodules. In addition, larger obsidian tools such as bifaces were also found, but it is highly possible that they are not local and arrived in the area as finished tools via trade. Some of those bifaces are translucent gray and green and based on their physical characteristics and visual identification, they may have come from northern Mesoamerica, most likely from Nayarit or Jalisco (Alvares 1990; Spence et al. 1993). Further analysis would be required to determine this for certain.

Turquoise presents a different and more complicated picture. The turquoise items found by the OVAP was fine and colors ran from light green to an intense green or blue. Three small pieces of raw material were identified, and this evidence may indicate either exploitation of a local sources or trade of raw material from areas outside the valley. A lack of research on turquoise in the Onavas Valley leads to the assumption that these turquoise items or raw materials possibly originated somewhere in the U. S. Southwest, probably from sources in New Mexico, such as Cerrillos or the Azure site, or in Arizona, such as Courtland or Gleason (Ekholm 1942; Pailes 1980; Weigand and Hardbottle 1993).

However, local sources for this material exist in the Sierra Madre Occidental, but the paucity of archaeological research or analysis prohibits any determination as to the use or degree of use of these Sonoran sources during the Prehispanic period (Alvares 1990; Pogue 1912; Weigand and Hardbottle 1993, 1995). Weigand mentions seven mines or sources of turquoise in northeast Sonora that were probably used in Prehispanic times. The sources are Cananeita, Campo Frío, Arroyo Cuitaca, Los Campito, Nacozari de García, El Verde, and San Felipe, but no further information is provided (Weigand and Hardbottle 1993:162-163). Of those sources, the El Verde and Nacosari sources are the closest to the Onavas Valley, located about 200 km away to the north. Hence, it is possible that the turquoise found and used in the Onavas Valley originated from these Sonoran sources and not from the U.S. Southwest.

Debitage

The analysis of the debitage assemblage followed the "production stage approach" (McGuire and Villalpando 1993; Rice 1985; Slaughter 1993). The methods of lithic analysis classification followed those of the Marana Archaeological Project directed by Paul and Suzanne Fish and followed the "Chipped Stone Coding Form-2001/02" for the Marana Mound Site. The 1,871 pieces of flake material were divided into eight categories: (Table 6.6).

Raw material

The raw material was divided into five different material types depending on material quality. The categories were: (1) fine-grained volcanic: lithics of volcanic origin with a fine or glassy matrix, such as andesites and rhyolites ,with few small crystalline inclusions, and often with reflective surfaces; (2) medium-grained volcanic: lithics of volcanic origin with a fine-medium matrix such as basalts and rhyolites, with crystalline inclusions and dull surfaces; (3) coarse-grained volcanic: lithics of volcanic origin with a coarse-grained matrix such as vesicular basalts and rhyolites, with large crystalline inclusions, high porosity, and dull surfaces; (4) cryptocrystalline: lithics of sedimentary origin characterized by a fine-grained matrix such as cherts, chalcedony, and jasper, with surfaces which may reflect light, and in some cases had a banded matrix; and (5) other: lithics that fail to exhibit any of the above characteristics, such as quartz, quartzite, granites, schist, slate, or sandstone. Obsidian was analyzed separately.

Primary flakes

They represent the initial flakes removed from a nodule or core that exhibit 50 perceny or more cortex on the exterior surface (n = 263).

Secondary flakes

These pieces had less than 50 percent cortex on the exterior surface, and represent the core reduction and core preparation process (n = 314).

Tertiary flakes with cortical platform

They are also known as thinning flakes from which tools or bifaces can be made, they are also product of tool-making (Sliva 1997; Pacheco 2003; McGuire and Villalpando 1993) Cortex is present only on the striking platform. (n = 266).

Tertiary flakes without cortex present

They are also called thinning flakes because they do not show cortex on the striking platform or on any flake surface. (n = 884).

Angular debris or indeterminate

No diagnostic feature of a flake or core is present to analyze (n = 125).

Core

This material is a piece of rock that displays one or many striking platforms and clear flake removal scars (n = 18).

Core tool

Cores that have been modified by retouching or wear and use as stone tools (n = 1).

Finally, after assigning the material to the above categories, the weight of all flake debitage bags collected at the sites was obtained. Combining the flake debitage previously divided by material category, the total weight of the flake debitage collected during the OVAP amounted to 12.935 kg, while the cores and cores tools amounted 3.013 kg.

The debitage flake analysis indicates that the medium-grained volcanic material was the most frequently used material by the lithic crafters of the Onavas Valley, followed closely by fine-grained volcanic material. Good quality raw material was well represented in the sample by weight and artifact count: (see Table 6.6). Although cryptocrystalline rocks were the most frequently utilized material for flakes, it only represents 16.27 percent of the weight. The least represented material was the "other" stone. These figures suggest that the Onavas crafters used both high and lower quality material available either from local or non-local sources for stone tool production. The diversity in raw material quality is most likely the result of the type of tools Nébome crafters wanted to produce. Analysis of tools revealed that points and bifaces were made mostly of good quality material such as cryptocrystalline and fine-grained volcanic stone, while other tools required stronger material such as coarse-grained volcanic stone.

The analysis seems to indicate that lithic production in the valley included the early stages of production, rather than exclusively late-stage production from preforms. Such is the case of the identification of tertiary flakes, the most numerous in the sample (n = 1,150/62.10 percent), and most likely resulting from tool shaping and core trimming indicated

Table 6.6. Debitage flakes analysis

Material	Primary Flake	Secondary Flake	Tertiary-cortical platform	Tertiary-not cortex present	Angular debris/Indeterminate	Total	%	Weight (kg)	%
Fine Volcanic	78	88	64	144	5	379	20.47	2.725	21.07
Medium Volcanic	81	99	77	171	16	444	23.98	5.592	43.24
Coarse Volcanic	32	23	26	41	59	181	9.77	2.141	16.55
Cryptocrystalline	69	97	96	515	37	814	43.95	2.161	16.70
Other	3	7	3	13	8	34	1.83	0.316	2.44

that much flaking occurred in the production of tools, bifaces, and preforms. This type of flakes has an average length of 1.5 cm. The presence of angular debris (n = 125/6.74 percent), while limited in number, indicates core preparation and/or reduction of raw material at the sites (McGuire and Villalpando 1993; Pacheco 2003; Sliva 1997). In addition, the number of tertiary flakes collected from surface seems to illustrate that the Nébome crafters spent a lot of time on projectile point manufacture.

With the exception of SON P:10:8, which yielded 447 pieces of debitage material, the average number of debitage flakes per site was around 23 pieces. The sites with above average quantities of debitage were SON P:10:56 (n = 97), SON P:6:5 (n = 89), SON P:10:6:4 (n = 72), SON P:10:28 (n = 72), and SON P:10:26 (n = 69) (See Appendix I and II).

More than 231 obsidian flakes were collected (0.252 kg). Of those, more than the 95 percent of the flake material is black, translucent, or dark gray in color. The remaining 5 percent of the sample were green translucent which may point to a non-local source. Apparently obsidian from local sources is black. Flake size, in general, was small (<1 cm) suggesting they originated from small nodules (average of 5cm), probably from the area or possibly eroded away from the Sierra Madre (Pacheco 2003). After the analysis of 231 obsidian pieces, 15 fragmented nodules were identified with evidence of being worked. A total of 216 flakes were recorded, of those, 81 had remains of the cortex. Furthermore, 14 flakes show evidence of retouching or being artifacts in process, such as points. In the sample no obsidian blades, characteristic of Mesoamerican lithic technology, were identified. Obsidian was found in 34 sites, and SON P:10:98 (n = 60), SON P:10:8 (n = 47), SON P:10:101 (n = 32), SON P:10:103 (n = 14) (See Appendix I and II) had an above-average number of obsidian artifacts, while all other sites had fewer than 10 items each.

Stone Artifacts: Non-Chipped Stone

A total of 125 lithic artifacts was identified.

Ground Stone

Commonly, ground stone artifacts are related to food processing, but can also be connected with several other activities, such as clay and pigment preparation, medicine, craft production, or rituals (Adams 1997; Pacheco 2003; Woodbury 1954). Either way, the identification of function of these items is important in order to determine the activities performed at site(s) or in areas. During the analysis (Figures 6.6 and Figure 6.7), 21 stone tools types were identified.

Abraders

"Handstones that have a rough surface for shaping the surface of other items" (Adams 1997:11). Three abraders were identified (Figure 6.6a). These items, commonly referred to as "shaft polishers," had U-shaped grooves and most likely were used for the shaping or polishing of cylindrical objects, such as arrow shafts, prayer sticks, wooden spindles, awls, strings, or beads (Adams 1997; Jernigan 1978). Although abraders are numerous in the southwest U.S., few have been reported in the literature for Sonora. Known examples include, two from the Rio Mayo region (Pailes 1972:315), three from the La Playa site (Johnson 1960:123), and two from the Guasave site, Sinaloa (Ekholm 1942:107).

Axes

Made or designed for chopping, cutting, digging, or hoeing, these stone tools had to be hafted to a wooden handle in order to truly function, although hand axes existed as well (Adams 1997). The type of groove used to haft the axes facilitates identification of the different axe types. In total, nine axes were identified (Figure 6.6b). Two examples belonged to the "full groove" type, four to the ¾-groove type, and three were blank or had no groove. The full-groove axes are usually identified or related to the northern Anasazi dating to A.D. 700, and made their way south (in the direction of Paquimé, Chihuahua) ca. A.D.1200 (Adams 1997:15). The ¾-groove axe is commonly identified as of Mesoamerican origin and made its way into the north ca. A.D. 900 (Adams 1997:15; Woodbury 1954). This type had been found throughout Sonora (McGuire and Villapando 1993; O'Donovan 2002; Pailes 1972). Two specimens of the blank type were similar to those found by Ekholm in southern Sonora and northern Sinaloa (Gallaga 2004b). A big flake from a large cobble was retouched on the edges and notched on the side for hafting. The remaining blank axe, made of reddish rhyolite, had no groove but a very pointy edge and a good grab base. It was probably used as a hand axe (# 48412).

Bowls/Vessels

These are ground stone items made and designed to use as a container. On some occasions they had been used as portable mortars for mixing or crushing and have to be identified as mortars (Adams 1997). In some instances, the use and shape of these items warrants further identification as a vessel instead of a bowl. In the OVAP, one stone bowl and one stone vessel were identified (Figure 6.6c). The former was a basalt stone bowl with a flat bottom that exhibited grinding. The vessel likewise was made of basalt, but was shaped in a cubic form with a flat bottom. Its use remains unknown. The interior of the vessel shows small remains of some white plaster that appears to be stucco or a similar material. One stone bowl was reported for the Rio Mayo region (Pailes 1972:305) and nearly 30 stone vessels had been reported for the Trincheras region (Johnson 1960:117;

McGuire and Villalpando 1993; O'Donovan 2002:93). The one identified at Onavas is similar to those reported in the Trincheras region. Neither the bowl nor the vessel had feet.

Chopper

Irregularly shaped rocks with primarily bifacial edges, usually big and heavy, which can be hafted or not (Adams 1997; Pacheco 2003). These tools were normally used with a forceful stroke against another surface, material or object. A total of eight choppers were recorded, four made of basalt and four of rhyolite.

Disks

There are stone items designed and crafted into tabular circles or round shapes (Adams 1997). The most common interpretation for their use is as gaming pieces (Brooks and Brooks 1985). Some stone disks have a perforation or a hole in the center, and these were probably used as spindle whorls. Only two flat, non-perforated disks were recorded by the OVAP, and their use or function is unknown. More than 75 of these items have been reported in the Trincheras region, mostly at the site of La Playa (Johnson 1960:138) and some at the Cerro de Trincheras (Gallaga 1998).

Doughnut

Another category for the perforated disks is that of the "stone ring" or "doughnut" (Haury 1976; Di Peso et al. 1974). Their use remains elusive, although some researchers think they could be used as weights or as a weapon (mallet or macana) (Haury 1976; Di Peso et al. 1974). Ethnohistorically, the Jesuit priest Pérez de Ribas mentions the use of macanas among the Indians in this region (1999:90). In the OVAP, one fragment of a doughnut type was identified. While no apparent use exists for the donut, it may be a weapon. This item seems to be found throughout southern Arizona and northwestern Sonora. A total of eight were reported for the La Playa site (Johnson 1960:138) and one in the Altar Valley (McGuire and Villalpando 1993:51).

Drills

These are bifacial tools with elongated distal portions forming a bit with diamond to square-shaped cross sections (Sliva 1997; Pacheco 2003). Some hafting elements can be present. They are normally used for drilling wood, bone, antler, shell, leather, and ceramics. Only one drill was identified.

Hammerstones

Irregularly shaped rocks that have been selected for their useful size, shape, durability, and weight to smash or chip away unwanted material from another item (Adams 1997; Pacheco 2003, Woodbury 1954). A total of 21 specimens were identified in the field, but not collected. Their presence was recorded only on the site registration form. Two specimens were taken from the field as samples.

Handstones

Adams (1997:21) defines this category as those stone items that "are hand-held tools without specific attributes that allow them to be categorized as manos, polishing stones or pestles." Three handstones were identified, although with undetermined use or specific tool type. Two were semi-rectangular and the was round in shape.

Hoes

Thin rectangular stone tools, similar in shape to axes that had to be hafted in order to function properly (Adams 1997; Haury 1976; Di Peso et al. 1974). They were commonly used in agricultural activities and may or may not show evidence of hafting. At least three hoes were identified for the Onavas Valley. These tools were very thin with one sharp and polished edge (Figure 6.6d). One shows evidence of having been hafted. Hoes had been reported for Snaketown (Haury 1976:285) and at Casas Grandes (Di Peso et al. 1974:360), but apparently none have been reported in Sonora. Sometimes they are identified as axes.

Lapstones

Stone tools that "served as bases upon which other artifacts were shaped or intermediate substance processed with a small handstone" (Adams 1997:21). They are different from stone palettes due to their lack of decoration and designs. The OVAP collected two lapstones. One was made of andesite with a flat-pecked surface. The second, made of basalt, had a semi-flat, concave surface (probably due to use) and several V-groove markings. The V-groove is characteristic of polishing or working pointed objects, such as points or awls. These items were probably used for lapidary work or, more likely for shell jewelry manufacture. Lapstones have been reported in Sonora, mostly in the Trincheras region. Twenty-three were reported for the Altar Valley (McGuire and Villalpando 1993:47), and at least four were reported at Cerro de Trincheras (O'Donovan 2002:92).

Metates and Manos

As Adams (1997:23) states, these are "two components of food-processing equipment... the metate is the netherstone, and the mano is the smaller, hand-held component" (Figure 6.6e and f). Both stone tools are used in grinding activities. Manos and metates are classified or identified by their use pattern. Three metate types were identified: (1) basin, (2) flat-concave or slab, and (3) trough. These types fit with

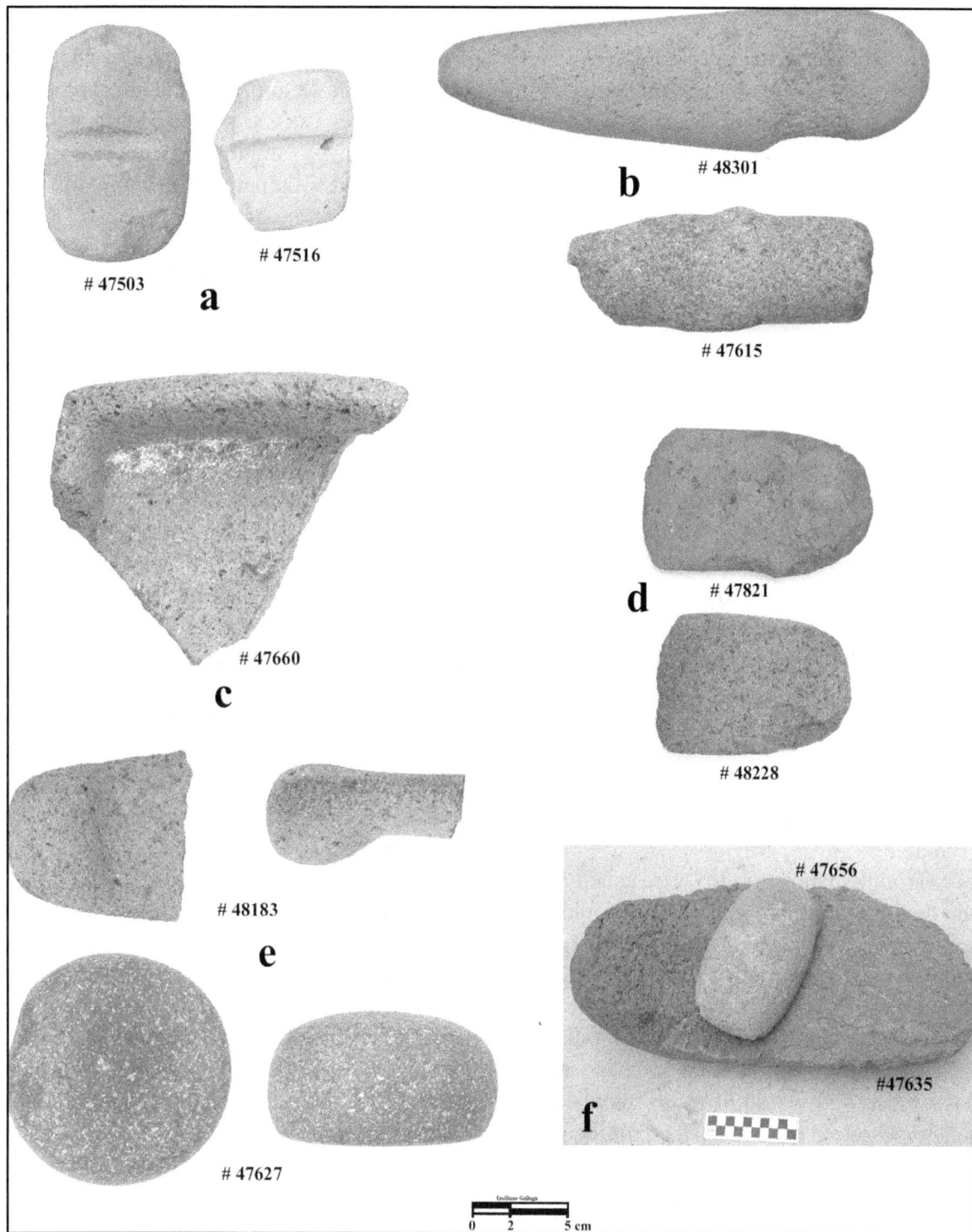

Figure 6.6. Lithic Tools I: a) abraders; b) axes; c) stone vessel; d) hoes; e) manos; f) metate (Photograph by Emiliano Gallaga).

traditional southwestern metate type classification (Haury 1976; McGuire and Villalpando 1993). A total of 57 metates were identified, of which only eight were collected, the rest were recorded on site forms but not collected. With the exception of a single flat-concave metate (# 47635), the rest of the collected metates consisted of fragments.

The basin metates (n = 15) are large, unmodified, cobbles presenting an oblong depression in the center from using a mano in rotary motion. The flat-concave/slab metates (n = 32) are large, unmodified, flat stones only one surface worn down from using a mano in circular motion. The trough (n = 10) metates are the most elaborate of all. In general they are large, shaped cobbles with a deep channel from using a mano with a back-and-forth motion. None of the metates had feet. More than half of the metates were made on basalt (52.8 percent), while the rest were made on andesite (27.8 percent) and rhyolite (19.4 percent).

Three different types of manos were distinguished: (1) trough, (2) flat/circular, and (3) "overhanging." Six manos were collected from surface, and 21 others were identified and reported in the field, but not collected. Usually, each mano type was used on a different type of metate.

Trough manos (n = 20) were usually large and oval-rectangular in shape, and would have required the use of both hands. This type is usually used on trough metates. Basalt (80 percent) was the preferred material, while rhyolite was also used (20 percent). Flat-circular (n = 5) manos were circular in shape with a flat surface and would fit in a person's hand. This types were used mostly on flat-concave/slab metates. Most of them were made with basalt (90 percent) while the rest were made with rhyolite (10 percent). The "overhanging" (*extremos colgantes*) manos, which is a common mano in northern Mesoamerica (Ekholm 1942; Haury 1950; Pailes 1972; Tolstoy 1971), is a mano larger than the width of flat/slab

metates, that with constant use wear down the contact area between the two items but not the edges of the mano. Only one incomplete mano of this type was identified, made from rhyolite. Some examples of the latest type had been found at Classic period Hohokam sites (Haury 1976:348) and in the Trincheras region (McGuire and Villalpando 1993:48), and they are numerous in the Rio Mayo region (Pailes 1972:287), Huatabampo (Alvarez 1990:57), and in northern Sinaloa (Ekholm 1942:107). No manos for basin metates were found or identified.

Mortars

Mortars are stone items that are made and designed as containers, but in their interior "substances were reduced through the crushing and grinding actions of a pestle" (Adams 1997:26). Mortars that are formed directly into bedrock or rock outcrops are called bedrock mortars. None of this type was recorded in the OVAP research area. Two mortars were recorded, one small portable bowl and one made of a big basalt stone. The latter was not collected. Pennington (1980:319) described the use of stone bowls and mortars at Onavas in the 1960s.

Ornaments

Stone items that are made or modified only to wear or use as an ornament. Several items made this category, such as beads, pendants, mosaic tesserae, nose plugs, bracelets, rings, figurines, crescents, and geometrics (Adams 1997; Di Peso et al. 1974; Jernigan 1978). A total of 19 items were identified as ornamental: nine stone pendants, four stone beads, and six geometrical or Sonoran palettes (Figure 6.7a).

Pendants (n = 9) typically are flat plates of rock that have been smoothed, and perforated with a suspension hole located nearer one end. All the seven turquoise pendants found had these characteristics. Other pendants include a small elongated piece of andesite with small notches on the upper portion for hanging on a cord, as well as a piece of quartz crystal that had a small groove for hanging on one side. The point of the quartz exhibits some abrasion. In total, six of the turquoise pendants were rectangular in shape and measure on average 10.9 x 6.5 mm and 2 mm thick, while one was almost circular in shape (# 48225). Three pendants had a conic perforation, two had a bi-conic perforation, and the rest remained unknown as they were fragments without perforation.

Beads (n = 4) are items "perforated with a suspension hole that extends approximately through the middle from side to side so that the edge or perimeter of the ornament is most visible when strung" (Adams 1997:28). All the stone beads identified were made of turquoise. On average they measured 5.55 mm in diameter, were of circular shape, and two had a conic perforation and two had a bi-conical perforation. Most of the turquoise beads, as well as the turquoise pendants, were associated with human burials identified on eroded surfaces.

Several geometrical items were identified in the field as palettes, but they do not resemble those of Hohokam manufacture. Five are flat and square, while one is flat and rectangular in shape, manufactured of black andesite, and stands out because it was side-notched and had an incomplete perforation which probably would have been used to suspend the palette on a cord (# 47855). Four are well-polished and the other two appear to be still in the process of manufacture. None of them had an incised border on the edges. These items are similar in shape and finishing to those reported by Ekholm in the southern Sonora and northern Sinaloa area (Gallaga 2004c). Johnson (1960:122) reported three stone pallets for the La Playa site. Although he mentions that they do not resemble those of Classic period Hohokam, they are similar to those from the Pioneer period. Because of their unique characteristics, I named them Sonoran palettes in order to differentiate them from those found in the Hohokam area. However, Pennington (1980) drew a stone palette found at the Onavas area very similar to those of Hohokam origin with an incised border. Unfortunately he does not provide a photograph of it for further comparison. It it possible that Sonoran Palettes were used more for everyday tasks (lapidary work or shell jewelry making) rather than ritual, such as the Hohokam palettes (McGuire and Villalpando 1993:51).

Polishing Stones

Stone items defined as "handstones of a smooth surface texture involved in the final stage of the manufacturing or production of other items" (Adams 1997:32). Seven items were identified as polishing stones (Figure 6.7b). These were most likely used for ceramic production, especially those manufactured of a hard, durable, iron-like material. Similar items had been reported all around Sonora.

Reamers

Stone tools that "had projections that were used in a rotary motion to shape holes in other artifacts" (Adams 1997:34). These tools are commonly used for shell working, in particular to shape bracelets and rings (Haury 1976; McGuire and Villalpando 1993; Vargas 1998, 1999). Twelve reamers were identified and collected in the field (Figure 6.7b). Further analysis confirmed their probable use in shell production in the area, particularly shell bracelets. Reamers have been reported for the Hohokam area (Haury 1976) and the Trincheras region (Johnson 1960) which were identified as shell jewelry manufacturing communities. No reamers were reported for the Huatabampo area (Alvarez 1990), however.

Tabular knifes or Agave knives

Thin stone items designed and shaped into a general rectangular form, with one sharp side and the other extreme possibly notched to take a haft. These items were thought to have been used for severing leaves from the agave hearts or to cut and shred other fibrous desert plants (Fish et al. 1992; McGuire and Villalpando 1993). A total of seven Agave knives were identified (Figure 6.7c): three of them were recorded in 2003 in the field but not collected at that time. Some agave knifes had been reported in Sonora, mostly in the Trincheras region, including three in the Altar Valley (McGuire and Villalpando 1993:49) and two at the Cerro de Trincheras (O'Donovan 2002:92).

Weight/Net Sinkers

These are flat stone items with a hole near the edge, grooved, or with sides notched for hanging from a cord and used as a weight. A total of seven of these items were identified: five with grooved sides and two with a hole (Figure 6.7d). They vary in size and may have been used as net sinkers for fishing. The Río Yaqui has numerous freshwater fish—a resource that was exploited by the Prehispanic communities judging by the numerous fish bones found on the surface of several sites. Only one possible net sinker at the site of Guasave, Sinaloa has been reported (Carpenter 1996:272).

Undetermined

Stone items that exhibited evidence of human modification but without identifiable use or purpose. A total of 11 items were classified in this category. Two could be stone ornaments in progress, while others may be tools in progress.

Chipped Stone Artifacts

Here, all the stone items with flaked or chipped modifications are described, with the exception of the projectile points, which are discussed later. A total of 36 stone items comprise this sub-category in the following manner.

Cores

Raw material from which stone tools can be manufactured (Adams 1997; Sliva 1997). Normally, these items were not collected, but only recorded in the site records. A total of 23 cores were recorded in the field, and one rhyolite and one andesite core were collected under the initial assumption that they were lithic tools. Closer analysis concluded they were not tools. These items show evidence of flaking, but much of the cortex still remained. The 23 cores recorded amounted to a total of 2.966 kg and were identified as 13 volcanic and 10 cryptocrystalline raw materials.

Bifaces

Stone artifacts made from flakes and worked on both faces, either by percussion or pressure, generally of oval shape. These items may have served as a preforms for the manufacture of other items, used as knifes, or spear points (Pacheco 2003, Sliva 1997). A total of 21 bifaces were identified: nine of rhyolite, seven of basalt, three of andesite, and two of obsidian (one dark grey and one green). The obsidian bifaces were reduced by percussion in early stages and by pressure in later stages. Due to the length of them, these probably served as preforms for spear points. The rest of the bifaces seem to have been made by percussion alone, because they do not show any retouching or fine flaking. Seventeen of these artifacts were identified as general bifaces, three were preforms for projectile points, and one was a biface in process.

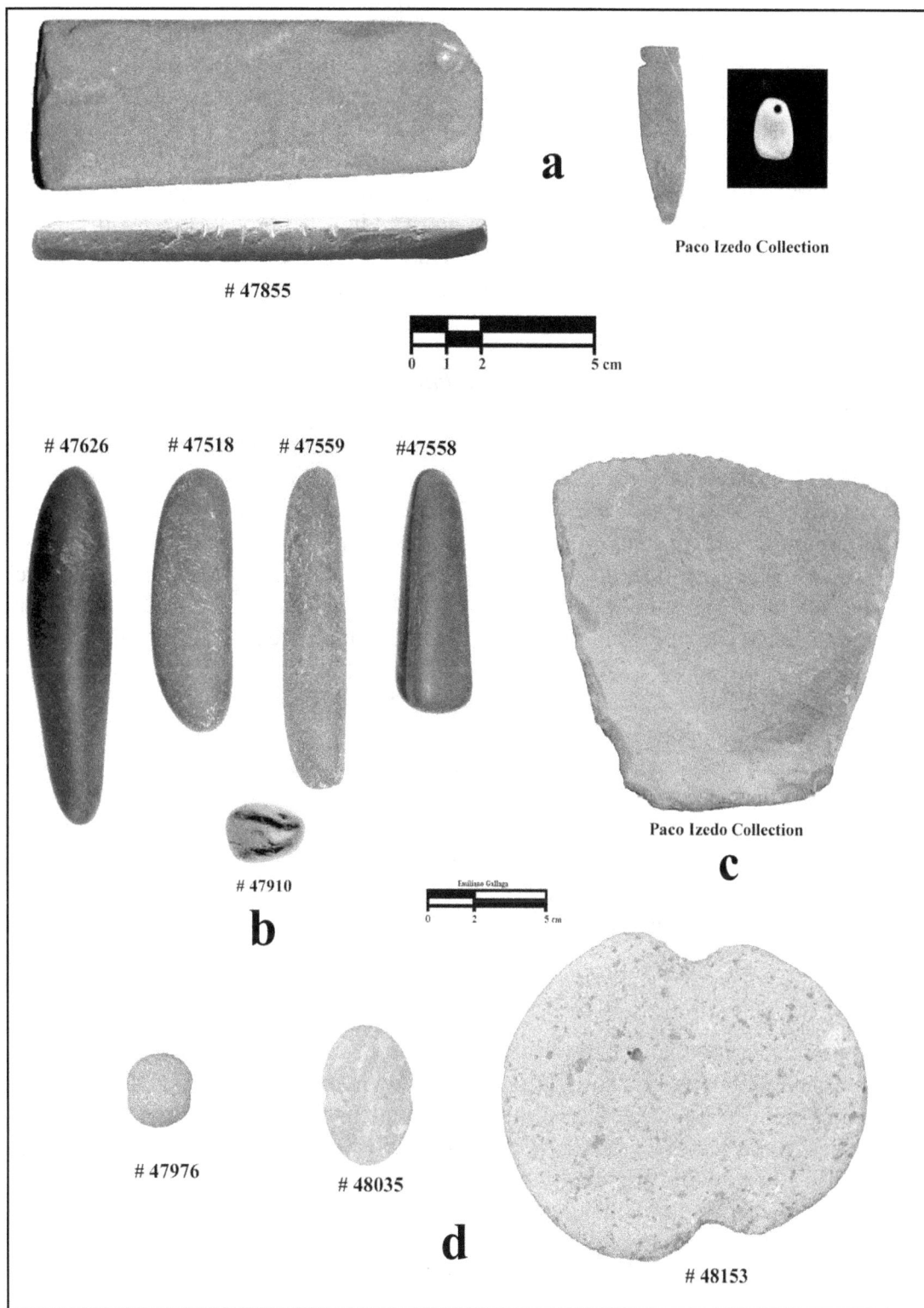

#47855

Paco Izedo Collection

0 1 2   5 cm

#47626   #47518   #47559   #47558

a

b

#47910

Paco Izedo Collection

c

#47976

#48035

d

#48153

Emiliano Gallaga

0   2   5 cm

Figure 6.7. Lithic tools II: a) ornaments (palletes, stone and turquoise pendants); b) reamers and polishing stone; c) agave knife; d) possible net-sinkers (Photograph by Emiliano Gallaga).

Scrapers

A stone tool made of a flake from a larger piece of stone designed for cutting or scraping off unwanted material. Depending on the scraper type, the edge may have been worked by percussion and/or retouched by pressure (Adams 1997; Barnett 1991; Pacheco 2003; Sliva 197). A total of 13 scrapers were identified. Based on Sliva's (1997:38-39) flaked stone analyses, four were endscrapers, seven were sidescrapers, and two were composite scrapers.

Projectile Points

In total, 107 projectile points were collected, 99 were recovered at sites and eight were recorded as isolated findings. The diversity in different point styles has been used to identify cultural affiliations, interactions, or trade with other regions and to assign chronological periods to archaeological sites (Ansley 1993; Di Peso et al 1974; Pacheco 2003; Pailes 1972; Sliva 1997; Figure 6.8). With the completion of the OVAP's projectile point analysis, 14 types or clusters of points were identified. Due to the lack of previous research in the area, some of the projectile points—46 specimens in total—were identified by their physical characteristics rather than as already known types (Table 6.7).

Paleoindian

Only one possible Paleoindian point was identified: a proximal fragment of a straight dark grey obsidian point with a concave base (Figure 6.8a). This piece was initially worked by percussion and finished by fine pressure flaking. The shape of the item suggests the complete piece may have measured around 8 and 10 cm. The base is concave and had a noticeable central notch. The item could be older than 8000-7000 B.C. and similar points can be found from Alaska to Tierra del Fuego.

Pinto (n = 6)

The specimens of this type have a concave-sided expanding stem, a concave straight base, a blade that is often serrated and narrower than the stem (Sliva 1997:50; Pacheco 2003; Figure 6.8b). Pinto points date roughly into the Middle-Late Archaic (ca. 5000-1500 B.C.). This type had a large distribution, all across the western U.S., including northern Mexico (Justice 2002:146).

Pandale (n = 3)

This is a "stemmed type with a twisted profile due to extreme beveling...[this] occurs on stem as well as blade so that the edge often forms a curve" (Justice 2002:171; Figure 6.8c). This type dates from Middle to Late Archaic (4000-2500 B.C.) and its distribution ranges from northern Mexico to central Texas (Justice 2002:171). Very few specimens of this type had been found in Sonora.

Cortaro (n = 1)

This type is characterized by a triangular point without a stem or notching, with a concave base that varies in the depth of concavity (Figure 6.8d). Researchers mention that this type enjoys great morphological variability and some specimens could be hafted bifaces rather than projectile points (Sliva 1997:50). This type has been dated to the Late Archaic to early intermediate periods (3000 B.C.-A.D. 150) and is found in southern Arizona, southwestern New Mexico, and northern Mexico (Justice 2002; Sliva 1997).

Cienega (n = 9)

This type is characterized by a well-marked corner notch, together with an expanding stem, narrow neck, concave base, long triangular blade, and sometimes serrated edges (Sliva 1997:51). There are several morphological variations of this type (Figure 6.8e). Cienega points date between the Late Archaic and the Early Agricultural Period (500 B.C.-A.D. 550) and their distribution ranges from central/southern Arizona, to central/southern New Mexico, to northern Sonora and Chihuahua (Justice 2002; Sliva 1997, Pacheco 2003).

Parallel and Tapering Stemmed Points (n = 20)

This type is characterized by a triangular outline with a wide and short/large stem that is parallel-sided or slightly tapering (Figure 6.8f). The base typically runs from concave to convex (Sliva 2003, Pacheco 2003). This category was the most numerous found on the OVAP. It is possible that some points were misidentified and were actually another known type, such as San Pedro or Datil. These points date to the Late Archaic, probably near the transition to the Early Agricultural Period (500 B.C.-A.D. 550). Their distribution could be similar to Cienega points (Justice 2002; Sliva 1997).

Leaf-Shaped Points (n = 10)

Projectile points with a triangular blade with pronounced unnotched convex bases that in general resemble a leaf shape (Figure 6.8g). This cluster has been dated to the Archaic period (circa 7000-800 B.C.) and its distribution is not well defined, but is found in southern Arizona (Marshall and Bostwick 2003).

Serrated (n = 12)

Very similar to the Classic thin triangular and Classic side-notched point types, this type has serration along the entire length of the blade, stem edges, and concave bases (Sliva 1997:55; Figure 6.8h). It is also similar to the Classic

serrated. This type has been dated to A.D. 1150-1350 and is distributed throughout central Arizona (Sliva 1997). Similar points have also been identified along the Sierra Madre on the Sonoran side (Pacheco 2003).

Unnotched, Concave Base Points (n = 4)

The points in this category are similar to the leaf-shape points, except for the base which is concave rather than convex (Figure 6.8m). None were serrated. There is no temporal affiliation for this cluster.

Triangular (n = 5)

Two points had a thin triangular body, were un-notched, had a straight base, and were short, similar to the Classic triangular points (Sliva 1997:55; Figure 6.8i). Three others are similar in form to the latter type but had a significant concave base or notched base and stem edges, similar to the Sobaipuri type (Slaughter et al. 1992; Figure 6.8j). The Classic triangular point dates to A.D. 1000-1450 and can be found in central/southern Arizona, the Colorado Plateau, and northern Mexico (Sliva 1997; Pacheco 2003). Sobaipuri points on the other hand, date to the Historic period (A.D. 1500-1800) and are distributed in the southern U.S. and northern Mexico (Justice 2002).

Desert Side Notched (n = 5)

In general, this type of point is distinguished by its small triangular form with notches on the sides and one notch at the center base (Figure 6.8k). These are similar to the Harrell and/or Toyah point types (Slaughter et al. 1992; Pacheco 2003). Its temporal affiliation and distribution is similar to the Sobaipuri points (A.D. 1540-1665).

Side Notched Point (n = 1)

Tipology	Site	Bag #	Material	Condition	Cronology	Length (cm)	Thickness (cm)	Weight (gr)
Paleoindian	SON P:10:101	48305	6	F	Paleoindian	4.3	1.3	11
Pinto	SON P:10:3	47673	2	C	5000-1500 B.C	2	0.5	1
Pinto	SON P:6:5	47792	4	F	5000-1500 B.C	1.8	0.5	3
Pinto	Isolated	47944	4	C	5000-1500 B.C	1.8	0.4	1
Pinto	Isolated	48277	1	F	5000-1500 B.C	1.2	0.4	1
Pinto	Isolated	48380	2	C	5000-1500 B.C	1.9	0.5	1
Pinto	SON P:10:13	48436	4	C	5000-1500 B.C	1.6	0.3	1
Pandale	SON P:6:5	47782	5	F	4000-2500 B.C	1.7	0.5	2
Pandale	SON P:10:86	48154	4	C	4000-2500 B.C	3.9	0.6	6
Pandale	SON P:10:101	48295	1	F	4000-2500 B.C	2	0.8	3
Cortaro	SON P:10:87	48157	4	C	500 B.C.- A.D.550	4.9	0.6	8
Cienega	SON P:10:101	48310	2	C	500 B.C.- A.D.550	5.3	0.6	10
Cienega	SON P:10:101	48307	2	F	500 B.C.- A.D.550	2.2	0.6	5
Cienega	SON P:10:101	48291	2	F	500 B.C.- A.D.550	1.1	0.3	1
Cienega	SON P:10:104	48353	2	F	500 B.C.- A.D.550	1.5	0.7	4
Cienega # 1	SON P:10:17	47849	4	C	before 400 B.C.	3.5	0.5	2
Cienega # 3	SON P:10:101	48294	4	C	500 B.C.- A.D.550	3.2	0.4	2
Cienega # 3	SON P:10:96	48204	4	C	500 B.C.- A.D.550	3	0.5	4
Cienega # 3	SON P:6:5	47788	3	C	500 B.C.- A.D.550	2.9	0.4	3
Cienega # 3	SON P:6:8	48392	4	C	500 B.C.- A.D.550	4	0.5	3
Parallel & Tapering Stemmed	SON P:10:56	47702	5	F	Archaic	2.1	1.4	4
Parallel & Tapering Stemmed	SON P:10:26	47794	1	C	Archaic	4.2	0.7	7
Parallel & Tapering Stemmed	SON P:10:26	47795	4	C	Archaic	2.5	0.5	3
Parallel & Tapering Stemmed	SON P:10:26	47810	2	F	Archaic	2.4	0.5	3
Parallel & Tapering Stemmed	SON P:10:84	47957	1	C	Archaic	4.3	0.6	6
Parallel & Tapering Stemmed	SON P:10:86	48152	2	F	Archaic	2.9	1	7
Parallel & Tapering Stemmed	SON P:10:101	48299	4	C	Archaic	2.6	0.4	3
Parallel & Tapering Stemmed	SON P:10:101	48302	1	C	Archaic	5.5	0.7	12
Parallel & Tapering Stemmed	SON P:10:101	48303	4	C	Archaic	3.7	0.6	6
Parallel & Tapering Stemmed	SON P:10:101	48304	4	F	Archaic	1.5	0.5	2
Parallel & Tapering Stemmed	SON P:10:101	48315	1	C	Archaic	5	0.7	9
Parallel & Tapering Stemmed	SON P:10:102	48331	4	C	Archaic	3	0.5	3
Parallel & Tapering Stemmed	SON P:6:10	48359	4	F	Archaic	1	0.4	3
Parallel & Tapering Stemmed	SON P:6:10	48360	1	F	Archaic	2.6	0.5	2
Parallel & Tapering Stemmed	SON P:6:10	48362	2	C	Archaic	2.8	0.4	6
Parallel & Tapering Stemmed	SON P:6:10	48365	2	F	Archaic	2.6	0.7	5
Parallel & Tapering Stemmed	SON P:6:10	48396	4	C	Archaic	2.5	0.3	1
Parallel & Tapering Stemmed	SON P:10:16	48408	2	F	Archaic	1.6	0.7	2
Parallel & Tapering Stemmed	SON P:10:108	48446	1	C	Archaic	3.6	0.5	7
Parallel & Tapering Stemmed	SON P:10:98	48484	1	F	Archaic	2.9	0.5	6
Leaf-Shaped	SON P:10:26	47801	1	C	Archaic	3.9	1.3	7
Leaf-Shaped	SON P:10:70	47917	4	C	Archaic	3.4	0.9	8
Leaf-Shaped	Isolated	47926	4	C	Archaic	3.1	1.3	1
Leaf-Shaped	SON P:10:99	48282	2	C	Archaic	2.8	0.7	3
Leaf-Shaped	SON P:10:101	48316	1	C	Archaic	3	2	5
Leaf-Shaped	SON P:10:102	48329	2	C	Archaic	3.7	1.8	6
Leaf-Shaped	SON P:10:104	48349	4	C	Archaic	2.4	0.5	2
Leaf-Shaped	SON P:10:104	48350	2	C	Archaic	2.4	0.5	1
Leaf-Shaped	SON P:10:104	48354	1	C	Archaic	5	2	10
Leaf-Shaped	SON P:6:11	48401	4	C	Archaic	2.6	0.4	2
Serrated	SON P:10:13	48433	6	F	A.D. 1150-1350	1.6	0.4	1
Serrated	SON P:10:56	47709	4	F	A.D. 1150-1350	1.3	0.2	1
Serrated	SON P:10:8	47974	6	F	A.D. 1150-1350	1.1	0.1	1

Table 6.7. Description of the projectile points recorded by the OVAP

Tipology	Site	Bag #	Material	Condition	Cronology	Length (cm)	Thickness (cm)	Weight (gr)
Serrated	SON P:10:8	47988	6	C	A.D. 1150-1350	1.5	0.2	1
Serrated	SON P:10:94	48197	6	C	A.D. 1150-1350	2.4	0.2	1
Serrated	SON P:10:98	48251	6	C	A.D. 1150-1350	1.8	0.3	1
Serrated	SON P:10:99	48281	4	C	A.D. 1150-1350	3.1	0.6	3
Serrated	SON P:10:101	48297	1	F	A.D. 1150-1350	1.3	0.4	1
Serrated	SON P:10:103	48342	6	F	A.D. 1150-1350	1.1	0.3	1
Serrated	SON P:10:103	48343	6	C	A.D. 1150-1350	2.3	0.3	1
Serrated	SON P:6:8	48374	4	C	A.D. 1150-1350	2.5	0.3	1
Serrated	SON P:10:98	48480	2	C	A.D. 1150-1350	2.8	0.5	2
Triangular	SON P:6:8	48378	5	C	A.D. 1000-1450	2.5	0.8	3
Triangular	SON P:10:103	48337	6	C	A.D. 1000-1450	2.7	0.4	1
Triangular (Sobaipuri?)	SON P:10:103	48338	2	C	A.D. 1540-1665	2.1	0.5	5
Triangular (Sobaipuri?)	Isolated	48285	5	C	A.D. 1540-1665	3.8	0.8	7
Triangular (Sobaipuri?)	SON P:6:10	48397	5	C	A.D. 1000-1450	2.3	0.6	3
Desert Side Notched	SON P:10:8	47478	6	F	A.D. 1540-1665	0.7	0.1	1
Desert Side Notched	SON P: 10:8	48054	4	C	A.D. 1540-1665	1.6	0.2	1
Desert Side Notched	SON P:10:8	48122	2	C	A.D. 1540-1665	1.3	0.1	1
Desert Side Notched	SON P:10:8	*	4	F	A.D. 1540-1665	1.8	0.2	1
Desert Side Notched	SON P:10:8	*	4	C	A.D. 1540-1665	1.8	0.2	1
Side Notched (Ensor)	SON P:10:26	47803	2	F	1500 B.C.-A.D.1000	2.0	0.4	3
Blades	SON P:10:14	48419	1	F	A.D. 700-1100	3.7	0.9	11
Blades	SON P:6:5	47783	2	C	A.D. 700-1100	5.0	5.0	25
Blades	Isolated	48166	1	F	A.D. 700-1100	3.8	1.0	14
Blades	SON P:10:98	48266	3	C	A.D. 700-1100	7.7	0.8	21
Blades	SON P:10:104	48355	3	F	A.D. 700-1100	6.0	5.0	58
Unotched & Concave Base	SON P:10:70	47904	1	C		3.2	0.3	1
Unotched & Concave Base	SON P:10:101	48293	3	C		3.6	0.7	6
Unotched & Concave Base	SON P:10:101	48309	1	C		4.7	0.7	7
Unotched & Concave Base	Isolated	48317	2	F		4.1	0.6	5
Unknown	SON P:6:5	47781	2	F		2.2	0.6	2
Unknown	SON P:10:26	47793	2	F		2.7	0.7	3
Unknown	SON P:10:26	47796	4	F		2.3	0.6	3
Unknown	SON P:10:26	47797	4	F		2.7	0.7	3
Unknown	SON P:10:26	47798	1	F		3.0	0.7	4
Unknown	SON P:10:26	47799	2	F		3.4	0.6	5
Unknown	SON P:10:26	47800	2	C		4.0	1.0	5
Unknown	SON P:10:26	47802	2	F		2.5	0.6	3
Unknown	Isolated	47928	2	F		3.2	0.5	5
Unknown	SON P:10:8	48031	1	F		1.0	0.4	1
Unknown	SON P:10:8	48039	1	F		0.8	0.2	1
Unknown	SON P:10:91	48179	1	F		3.2	0.7	5
Unknown	SON P:10:91	48184	4	F		3.2	1.0	8
Unknown	SON P:10:101	48292	1	F		3.7	0.6	4
Unknown	SON P:10:101	48298	1	F		1.2	0.6	1
Unknown	SON P:10:102	48326	1	F		3.2	0.5	4
Unknown	SON P:10:92	48332	1	F		3.7	0.9	1
Unknown	SON P:10:104	48352	2	F		3.8	0.8	9
Unknown	SON P:6:10	48361	4	F		4.5	0.7	5
Unknown	SON P:10:106	48391	4	C		3.3	0.6	4
Unknown	SON P:6:10	48394	2	F		2.8	0.4	1
Unknown	SON P:10:16	48411	6	C		2.0	1.0	1
Unknown	SON P:10:14	48422	2	C		4.5	0.9	10
Unknown	SON P:10:14	48423	3	F		1.3	0.4	1

Table 6.7. Description of the projectile points recorded by the OVAP cont'd

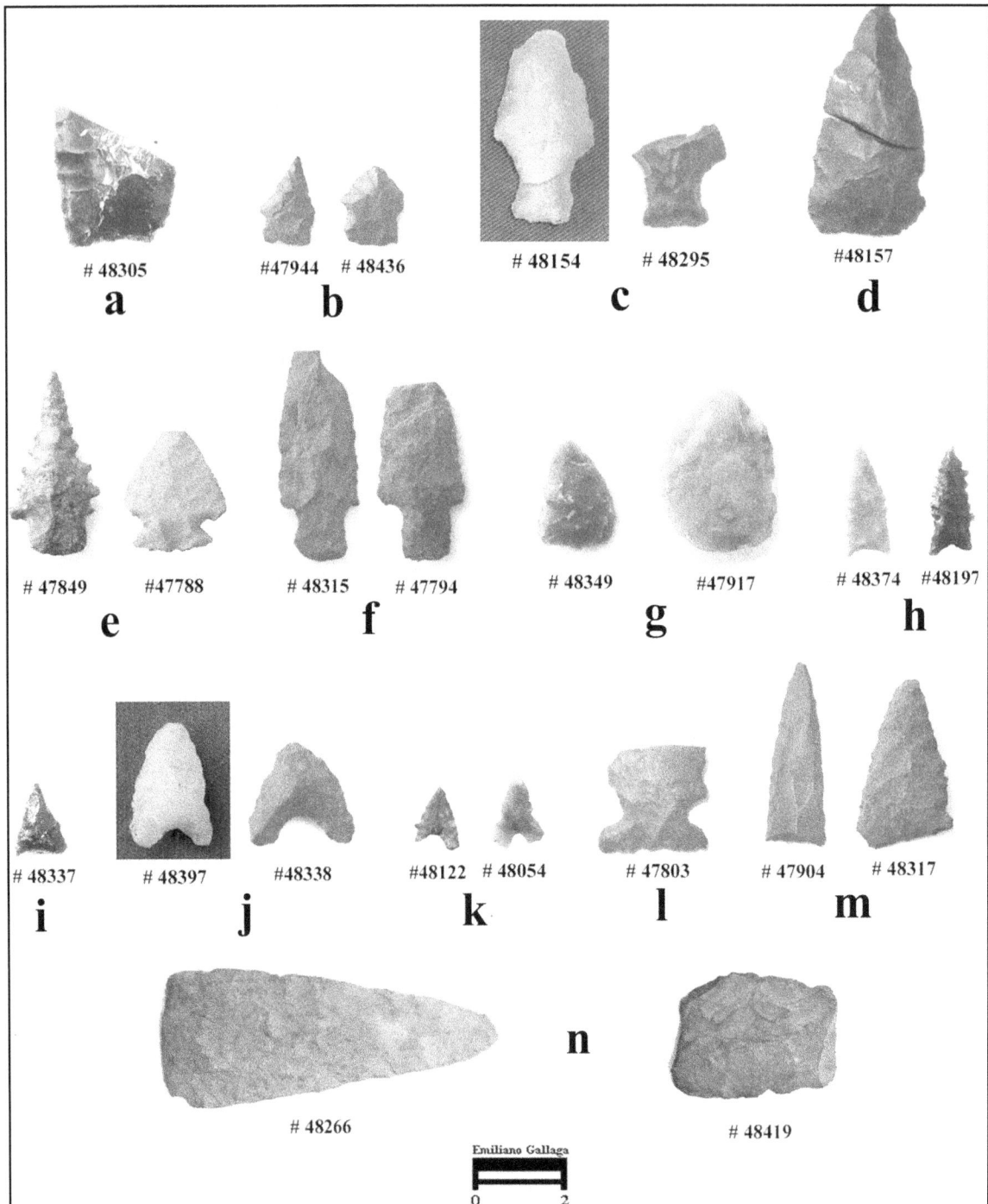

Figure 6.8. Projectile points: a) Paleoindian; b) Pinto; c) Pandale, d) Cortaro; e) Cienega # 1and # 3; f) Parallel and Tapering Stemmed; g) Leaf-Shaped; h) Serrated; i) Triangular; j) Triangular-Sobaipuri?; k) Desert Side Notched; l) Ensor; m) Unnotched and Concave Base; and n) Blades (Photograph by Emiliano Gallaga).

This point is triangular in form with side notches close to the base and with a straight wide base. The point is similar to the Ensor point type (Lazalde 1992:60-61; Figure 6.8l). This type had a long period of use from 1500 B.C. to A.D. 1000, and its distribution extends from southern U.S to northern Mexico as far as Durango (Lazalde 1992).

Blades (n = 5)

In general, blades were long, triangular, and thin with straight bases, and no notches or stems. Two of them were made on fine basalt and one on andesite (Figure 6.8n). They could be knives, if hafted to a handle, or spear points if hafted to a long shaft (Gladwin et al. 1938; Pacheco 2003). For the Hohokam area, this type has been dated to the Sedentary Period (A.D. 950-1150). There is no information for temporal and spatial distribution of this type in Sonora.

Undetermined (n = 25)

In large part, the inability to assign these specimens to specific types was because the only portion available was the distal end of the point. Without the proximal portion or the base, it is almost impossible to identify point type (Lazalde 1992; Slaughter et al. 1992; Sliva 1997, Pacheco 2003).

Lithic Summary

The lithic assemblage from the Onavas Valley revealed several interesting results. First, the raw material used by the local crafters is generally good quality, composed of either fine volcanic or cryptocrystalline material that provides a good flaking material for the manufacture of projectile points and other bifacial tools. Low-quality raw materials locally available in the Onavas Valley, such as rhyolite, basalt, or andesite, were also used, to manufacture stronger lithic artifacts or tools. The type of raw material used depended on the tool and its intended use by the crafters. Although not many cores or hammerstones were collected, some were observed in the field and noted on site forms. These implements suggest that lithic production was performed at the sites. Flaking debris analysis indicates that crafters likely worked cores and preforms into stone tools at numerous sites throughout the region.

Analysis of obsidian materials indicated that flint knappers drew mostly on small dark obsidian nodules that were probably from local sources. Non-local obsidian also appears at these sites, although in smaller proportions, either in the form of raw material or finished goods. The source of this non-local obsidian is unknown, but there is a small possibility of some artifacts originating from as far away as Nayarit (Alvares 1990; Spence et al. 1993). The turquoise poses interesting research questions: was this material exploited locally in Sonora or did it arrive through trade from the U.S. Southwest? To what degree and in what form did Prehispanic Sonoran communities participate in the mining and manufacture of turquoise, or did they trade for finished products? Material evidence from sites in the region illustrate that turquoise is very common in Sonora. In Huatabampo, more than 200 turquoise pieces were reported (Alvares 1990:58-62). At the Guasave site, 99 pieces were found (Ekholm 1942:105) and sites along the Río Alamos in Sinaloa have yielded some turquoise pieces as well (Carpenter, personal communication 2005). Descriptions of nearby cultural groups also offer possible indications of the use of certain materials. Pérez de Ribas emphasizes the use of cotton, turquoise, and the color blue as corporal decoration among the Yaqui:

> They adorned their ears by piercing the edge of the ear and hanging some little charms from ribbons of blue cotton thread. Even the men

did this, in addition to hanging some small, valuable emerald-like stones [turquoise?] from the cartilage of their nose (Pérez de Rivas 1999:329).

Pérez de Ribas mentions that almost all the Indian nations from the region decorated themselves in this manner. Several turquoise pieces were recorded by the OVAP suggesting prolific use of this material in the area. That Pérez de Ribas mentions the use of turquoise among the Yaquis may further point to inter-regional interactions and suggests that this precious material could be obtained via the Río Yaqui, which passes though the Onavas Valley. However, to answer these questions it is necessary to start searching for local sources (Alvarez 1990; Weigand and Hardbottle 1993, 1995).

The analysis of the projectile point assemblage shows a long and continuous human presence in the area. Interestingly, the projectile point sample shows a different history than the ceramic analysis does. While most of the ceramics were identified as Middle-Late Prehispanic, most of the projectile points appear to be Archaic point types—a total of 52—leaving 26 specimens to Late Prehispanic and five to proto-Historic periods. The rest, 18 points, were of styles with unknown temporal provenience. This suggests that the recorded sites had a long occupation, probably from Archaic to Late Prehispanic and/or proto-Historic periods and that mechanized agricultural activities and heavy erosion in the area has mixed artifacts of different temporal provenience at the surface. Sites where Archaic and the Paleoindian points were collected also had ceramic and local decorated material from the Late Prehispanic period. Only the excavation of key sites will clarify this issue. Another possible explanation for this scenario could be the incipient but rising pot-hunting activities in the area, which has caused formal projectile points to be disproportionately collected. In addition,

smaller points are more easily washed away with the heavy summer rains and thus may be underrepresented in the sample.

The apparently lack of defensive sites or compound walls suggests that the projectile point manufacture was oriented toward hunting activities rather than warfare or protection against raids, at least at the Onavas Valley. Ethnohistorical documents indicate skirmishes and warfare between Nébomes and neighboring groups such as the Yaquis, Seris, and Opatas at the boundaries of their territories. But these documents also suggest that in most cases, the Nébomes were on the defensive and not attacking (Pérez de Ribas 1999). If the projectile points were used for hunting, it is likely that they were used for large game (Nelson 1996:141-142), such as deer or wild pig (*javalina*) which is abundant in the valley. Small game could also be hunted with small projectile points. However, ethnographic data suggest that small game was most likely trapped or killed with other weapons (Anell 1969; Pennington 1969, 1980). Colonial documents mention that the Nébomes area was well known for its abundance of deer and the skillfulness of their craftsmen in tanning and working deer skin (Hopkins 1988:22; Pérez de Ribas 1999:391-392). The size of the projectile points allows inferences to be made about their use; small point were used as arrow points while larger points as atlatl darts or lance heads (Nelson 1996:172). The identification of an atlatl handle at the Site # 54 near Soyopa by Ekholm illustrates the used of atlatls in the region (Gallaga 2004b).

The lithic tool analysis indicates that the Onavas Valley Prehispanic communities manufactured a diverse range of stone tools. The lithic assemblage and the ethnohistoric/ethnographic data suggest that the ground stone implements were used for processing both cultigens and wild plants, such as corn, beans, mesquite pods, and agave. The lack of bedrock mortars in the area, the number of manos and metates, the presence of hoes and axes, and the feasibility of performing farming agriculture in the area support the idea that cultigens formed the basis of the local subsistence system as opposed to the gathering of wild plants. In addition, the stone tool kit shows that fishing was an additional food resource for these communities.

It is also possible that the grinding tools were not only used for food processing, but for other processing activities, such as pigment manufacture or clay processing. At SON P:6:4 (Appendix I and II) a whole basin metate was found with remains of red pigment on it, demonstrating that some groundstone tools were used for grinding mineral pigments. The groundstone tool assemblage also suggests that the Onavas Prehispanic communities were utilized for not only food production activities, but also ceramic production (clay processing, polishing stones, pigment manufacture), weaving (spindle whorls), and shell manufacture (lapstones and reamers).

Upon completion of the analysis, with the exception of the debitage refuse, 65 sites were recorded that yielded at least one stone item. Sites with multiple stone items were: SON P:10:8 (n = 78), SON P:10:98 (n = 41), SON P:10:101 (n = 37); and SON P:10:103 (n = 20) (See Appendix I and II). These sites may represent activity areas for farming, stone tool manufacture, or other types of craft production, that were not necessarily associated with habitation areas. However, the sample is too small to delve into this type of analysis.

Shell

...Among them came an Indian more conspicuous than the others, wearing a black cloak like a scapulary decorated with ornately worked pearl shells in addition to many small figures of dogs, birds, and deer among other

things... (Hedrick and Riley 1976:47)

The bet is for a string of small sea snail shells that they prize and wear as ornaments (Perez de Ribas 1999:94).

Marine shell remains received special attention by the OVAP for two major reasons: (1) their relevance as trade goods (Braniff 1989; Di Peso et al. 1974; Nelson 1991), and (2) their excellent degree of preservation in the arid field conditions (Bradley 1993; Vargas 1998). Analysis of the species and the type of remains (raw material, worked debitage, and finished goods recorded) allows contrasting models of marine shell trade from coastal to northern inland areas to be evaluated. Hence, future research will investigate whether there was a preference for particular species and types of goods, and will compare marine shell worshops in Northwest Mexico with those of the U.S. Southwest.

The marine shell analysis from the OVAP establishes that the Prehispanic communities had access to this type of material, not only in the form of finished goods but also as raw material. Of the 117 sites identified as Prehispanic, shell artifacts were collected from the surface of 46 sites. Of the 1,191 total shell artifacts collected (1.113 kg), 446 artifacts were identified as finished goods or works in progress, 732 as worked debitage, 11 as pieces of raw material, and 2 as utilitarian items (Magaña 2004). The final results of the shell analysis are presented below.

Species

Of the 1,191 marine shell artifacts collected, only 928 items (78 percent) could be identified to species. The OVAP collected specimens of nine families, 10 genera, and 14 species of the Pelecypod class. For the Gastropod class, the OVAP recovered specimens of 10 families, 10 genera, and 15 species (Abbot 1996; Keen

1971; Magaña 2004; Suárez 2002). Most of those pieces originated from the Gulf of California (84 percent, n = 995), while the remaining 16 percent (n = 196) came from freshwater sources, most likely from the Río Yaqui, the closest and only major freshwater source in the area. Only one unidentified freshwater species was found in the sample.

Laevicardium elatum was the most commonly occurring species (n = 357), followed by *Glycymeris* (n = 235), the unidentified freshwater species (n = 196), *Olivella dama* (n = 77), and *Petaloconchus complicatus* with 52 examples. The remaining species had a presence of one to less than 40 pieces each (Table 6.8).

Finished Goods

Upon completion of the shell analysis, 448 finished goods, whole or fragmentary, were identified. They represented 37.62 percent of the total shell sample. Of that amount, 446 were classified as ornamental (99.5 precent) and only two pieces as utilitarian (0.5 percent).

The ornamental category consisted of two rings, 163 beads, 181 pendants, and 100 bracelets. Two possible shell awls were classified as utilitarian.

Beads (n = 163)

A total of 163 beads were collected and six different types of beads were identified (Figure 6.9a).

Cylinder (n = 3)

The shell pieces were cut into a cylindrical shape and perforated length-wise. All specimens belong to the Petaloconchus complicatus species.

Disk (n = 86)

Most of these consisted of thin, small beads, of which 48 had a plain face and 11 a convex face. Most were perforated using the biconical technique, while 24 were cylindrical and 14 had a conical perforation. These were the most numerous in the sample, of which 27 were *Laevicardium elatum*, 14 *Spondylus*, four *Glycymeris gigantea*, one *Pinctada mazatlanica*, and 40 unidentified.

Spherical (n = 1)

Only one fragmented item was identified with a plain surface. No species could be identified for this fragment.

"Wheel" type (n = 24)

This type shares similar characteristics with the disk type, but it is thicker. From the total, 11 were *Spondylus*, one was *Petaloconchus complicatus*, and the remaining 12 could not be identified to species. Ten specimens exhibited plain faces. Eleven items had cylindrical perforations, nine had biconical perforations, and three had conical perforations.

Square section (n = 1)

All sides were worked to give the specimen a squarish shape. This bead was manufactured from a freshwater species.

Tubular (n = 48)

This type represents the second most numerous bead type found on the OVAP. Forty one specimens belonged to the *Petaloconchus complicatus* species, six to *Strombus galeatus*, and one species remained unidentifiable. Thirty

Table 6.8. Shell species and their frequencies

Shell Species	Quantities
Anadara grandis	5
Anadara grandiarca	1
Anadara tuberculosa	4
Argopecten cicularis	9
Conus fergusoni	36
Conus californicus	3
Conus ximenes	13
Conus purpurascens	2
Conus perplexus	1
Conus princeps	4
Cerithidea mazatlanica	6
Chione fluctifraga	2
Chione cortezi	1
Diplodonta inezensis	1
Glycymeris gigantea	235
Jenneria pustulata	1
Laevicardium elatum	357
Nassarius livescens	1
Nerita picea	16
Olivella dama	77
Pecten vogdesi	16
Petaloconchus complicatus	52
Pinctada mazatlanica	25
Polinices reclusianus	1
Pteria sterna	25
Spondylus	24
Spondylus princeps	1
Strombus galeatus?	6
Strombus gracilior	1
Transennella llahumilis?	1
Turritella leucostoma	1
Fresh Water	196
Unidentified	67

nine specimens had cylinder perforations.

Sites with greater number of bead were SON P:10:8 (n = 76) and SON P:10:98 (n = 72). In much lower quantities beads appeared at SON P:6:4 with four, SON P:10:55 and SON P:10:70 with three, SON P:10:14 and SON P:10:56 with two, and SON P:10:12, SON P:10:41, and SON P:10:91 with one bead each. (See Appendix I and II)

Bracelets

In total, 100 bracelet fragments were identified, none were complete (Figure 6.9b). One fragment was ¾ complete with the umbo forming part of the decoration, 16 bracelets were identified as works in progress, while the rest were finished items. Only seven show signs of having been burnt, probably in association with cremation. All the bracelets, with the exception of one, were identified as *Glycymeris gigantea*. The exception was one bracelet of *Anadara grandis*. On average, the bracelets measured 6.5 cm in diameter, with 8 cm representing the largest and 4 cm the smallest example. On average, they reached 0.77 cm in width (0.15 cm minimum and 3 cm maximum) and 0.42 cm in thickness (0.14 cm minimum and 0.74 cm maximum).

The technology for bracelets manufacture seems to be different from other regions, such as the Hohokam, and also does not have the extra decorative work found on Hohokam pieces. All the bracelets from the Onavas Valley are plain without any decoration. Only three bracelets still had the umbo of the original shell, possibly as decoration, but none were incised or otherwise decorated. In terms of the manufacturing process, it is notable that none of the upper valves (*tapas*) were found. In analysis, several pieces of shell debitage belonging to the *Glycymeris* species were identified, but not for the upper portion or "tapas." This suggests that the initial steps of the bracelet production may have been conducted outside the valley,

perhaps at the coast, and then finished in the Onavas Valley. Alternatively, manufacture from raw material by direct or indirect percussion on the upper valve seems unlikely due to the low frequencies of debitage present on the surface; current evidence suggests that the valley got most of its raw material pre-worked.

Bracelets were concentrated on two sites: SON P:10:8 (n = 43) and SON P:10:98 (n = 19). In addition five bracelets were found at SON P:6:4; four at SON P:10:110; three at SON P:10:12, SON P:10:70, SON P:10:91, and SON P:6:8; two at SON P:10:28, SON P:10:56, and SON P:6:5; and one at SON P:10:14, SON P:10:27, SON P:10:40, SON P:10:41, SON P:10:65, SON P:10:80, SON P:10:96, SON P:10:101, SON P:10:102, SON P:10:105, and SON P:6:16. The only bracelet fragment of *Anadara grandis* was found at SON P:10:105. (See Appendix I and II)

Pendants

Numerically, this category was the largest of all types of finished shell goods (Figure 6.9c), represented by 181 pieces. The general categories set for these items were *automorphs* and *xenomorphs*. *Automorphs* included all items where modification was minimal, preserving most of the integrity of the shell, while *xenomorphs* exhibited extensive modification of the shell's natural characteristics.

The subdivisions in the automorphos category were made by species rather than by shape. The most represented species were: *Olivella dama* (n = 80), *Conus fergusoni* (n = 15), *Nerita picta* (n = 13), *Cerithidea mazatlanica* (n = 5), *Conus ximens* (n = 5), *Petaloconchus complicatus* (n = 2), and *Anadara grandis*, *Conus perplexus*, *Conus purpurascens*, *Nassarius limacinus*, *Polinices reclusianus*, *Transennella humilis*, and *Turritella leucostoma* (n = 1 each). All these items have a polished surface where a hole was manufac-

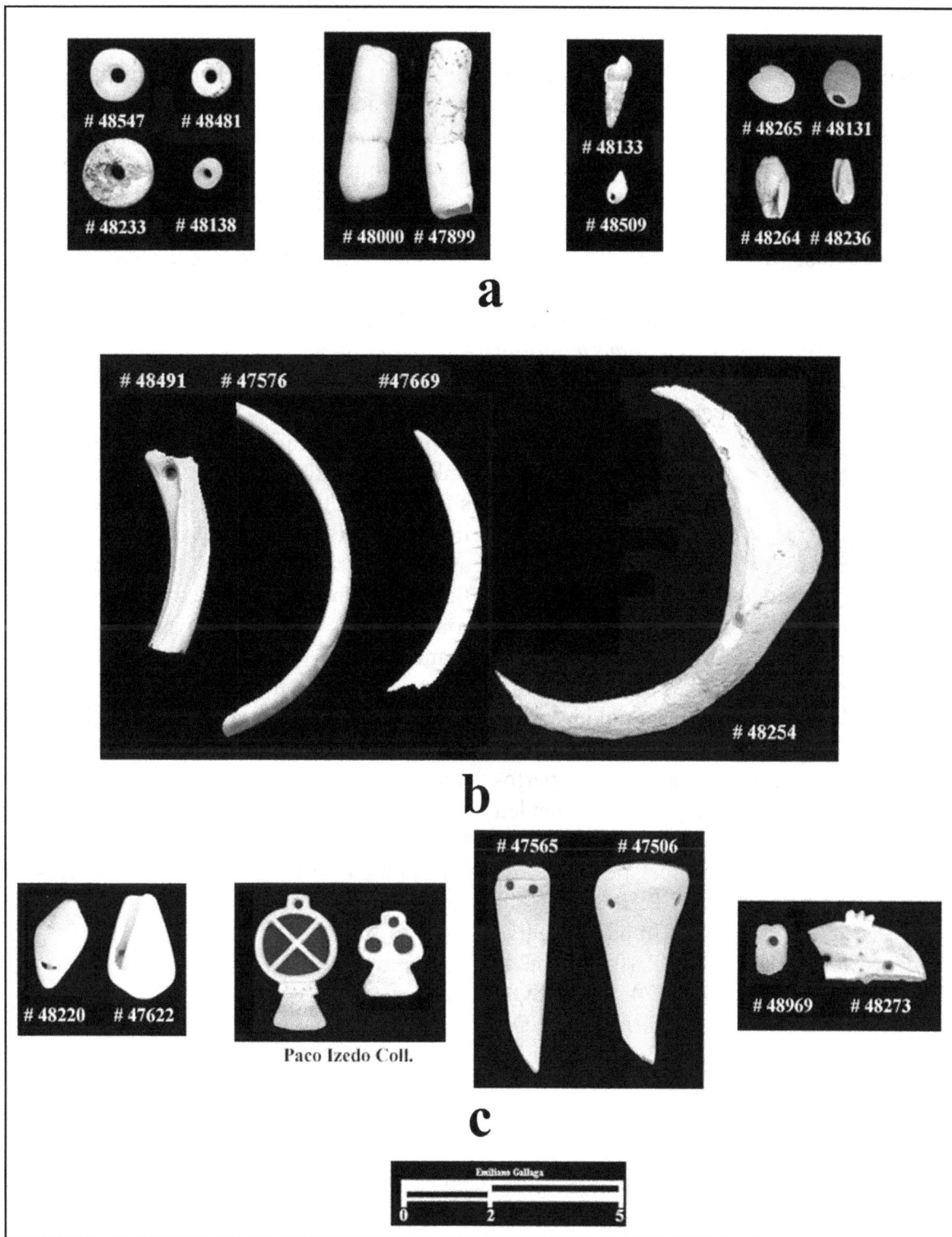

Figure 6.9. Shell goods: a) beads; b) bracelets; c) pendants (Photograph by Emiliano Gallaga).

tured to hang the item. No further modifications were made.

In the second category, the xenomorphs, the shell was fragmented by percussion or in some cases by abrasion and polished into a desirable shape. At times, holes or lateral notches were preformed for the piece to be suspended. As a result, the items were classified by shape: circular (n = 7), square (n = 10), rectangular (n = 15), triangular (n = 9), oval (n = 2), gastropod (n = 2), and irregular (n = 9). The species identified in this category were *Anadara grandis* (n = 1), *Conus fergusoni* (n = 6), *Conus princeps* (n = 1), *Glycymeris gigantea* (n = 10), *Laevicardium elatum* (n = 8), *Pecten vogdesi* (n = 1), *Pinctada mazatlanica* (n = 10), *Pteria sterna* (n = 9), *Spondylus* (n = 3), *Strombus gracilior* (n = 1), and unidentified (n = 4).

For this variety of pendants, some specimens were slightly modified, such as the perforation of a gastropod shell for suspension, while others were skillfully and extensively modified, as in the case of the circular pendants. Some pendants may have been tinklers, such as those made from the *Conus* species. Most of the triangular pendants had a cut or perforation suggesting that they were suspended vertically.

The sites with the most pendants, of either category, were SON P:10:8 (n = 80) and SON P:10:98 (n = 72). In addition, five pendants were found at SON P:10:56; three at SON P:10:18 and SON P:10:70; two at SON P:10:17, SON P:10:27, SON P:10:55, and SON P:6:5; and one at SON P:10:12, SON P:10:14, SON P:10:28, SON P:10:44, SON P:10:84, SON P:10:90, SON P:10:96, SON P:6:4, and SON P:6:16. (See Appendix I and II).

Rings

Only two ring fragments were identified. They were made of *Lithoconus fergusoni*, have a small diameter of 1.7 cm, a circular shape, and polished edges. They are 0.94 and 2 cm in width, and 1 and 1.5 cm in thickness, respectively. They lack any decoration, not like those found in Cerro de Trincheras which had very complex and geometrical designs similar to the ceramic decoration in the Ramos Polychrome type. The first ring was found at SON P:10:70 and the second one was found at SON P:10:8 (See Appendix I and II). However, to date, very few such items have been recovered from sites in Northwest Mexico (Braniff 1989; Suárez 1974; Velázquez 1999).

Awls

As mentioned earlier, the OVAP recovered only two utilitarian shell specimens, both shell awls. Unfortunately, species identification was not possible for either artifact. The awls were crafted from the central column of the shell. One was polished into a perfectly rounded stick, whereas the second had been manufactured with less sophistication but with use had worn to a similar roundedness. The first measures 6 cm in height and 0.6 in diameter and the second 3 cm in height with a 0.5 diameter. Such items are usually rarely found in the archaeological record due to their fragile nature (Braniff 1989; Suárez 1974; Velázquez 1999). One awl was found at SON P:10:70 and the second at SON P:10:18. (See Appendix I and II)

Debitage

As mentioned above, no upper valves (tapas) were found by the OVAP, but more than 732 pieces were identified as debitage representing 61.46 percent of the total shell sample. Almost all of the material shows evidence of breakage by percussion. Less than 5 percent of the pieces appear to have been abraded before breakage. Only three pieces, manufactured from *Glycymeris gigantea*, provide some evidence of the initial manufacturing having taken place in the Onavas Valley. Apparently, this was not the norm for the manufacture of bracelets. Most of the pieces are very small rendering identification of their intended final from impossible. Nonetheless, form the larger pieces it appears that bracelets, beads, and pendants were the products desired for manufacture. The amount of Laevicardium elatum identified in the sample revealed that this species was the preferred raw material of local shell crafters, and was favored for the manufacture of beads and pendants.

The species with the greatest representation in the debitage material were as follows: *Laevicardium elatum* (n = 322), *Glycymeris gigantea* (n = 125), *Pecten vogdesi* (n = 17), *Pteria sterna* (n = 15), *Conus fergusoni* (n = 15), and *Pinctada mazatlanica* (n = 14). The rest of the material was distributed between 14 other species, as well as unidentified species (n = 186). Debitage was concentrated at five sites: SON P:10:8 (n = 239), SON P:10:98 (n = 87), SON P:6:4 (n = 71), SON P:10:12 (n = 54), and SON P:10:70 (n = 54). (See Appendix I and II).

Raw Material

A total of 11 pieces were identified as raw material representing only 0.92 percent of the shell sample. These items were found without any work or modification, although they had been broken. The species identified were: *Conus ximens* (n = 5), *Nerita picta* (n = 2), and *Cerithidea mazatlanica, Conus purpurascens, Glycymeris gigantea*, and *Pteria sterna* (n = 1 each). Most of it was found on site SON P:10:65 (n = 5) and SON P:10:8 (n = 3), while the rest was found on sites SON P:10:70, SON P:10:103, and SON P:6:4 all with one piece each. (See Appendix I and II).

Shell Summary

The number of shell items found by the OVAP

and the shell analysis (Magaña 2004) illustrate that shell jewelry manufacture played an important role in the craft production of the Onavas Valley Prehispanic communities. As Colonial documents mention, shell was common among the Nébome: "they would hang some type of votive or offering, such as the white beads made from little sea snails with which they adorn themselves" (Pérez de Ribas 1999:404). Such shell items, among others, were found by the OVAP (see Figure 6.9). The quality of the finished goods recovered reveals that the valley's crafters were skillful in their manufacture, but not to the level of sophistication of Hohokam crafters in the Southwest U.S. Some of the manufacturing techniques identified in the shell items were from the typical basic production methods, such as percussion, pressure, friction, and sawing. More than 95 percent of the finished goods are plain and have no decoration at all, suggesting that Onavas crafters either lacked the skills and techniques to decorate their jewelry, or preferred not to do so. The few items found with decoration were made by hatching and boring techniques, mostly to obtain geometric designs.

The presence of raw material in the shell sample indicates that the Nébomes from the Onavas Valley were not only exchanging finished shell items, but also that they were part of the manufacturing process and worked raw shell themselves. At this point it is too early to establish or even differentiate whether the foregoing confirms local production or non-local production, but the available archaeological evidence from the surface demonstrates that the amount of Onavas Valley shell jewelry manufacture was high. This is supported by the fact that more than 61 percent of the shell sample consists of work refuse. Furthermore, the identification of stone tools used for shell goods manufacture, such as more than ten reamers and two lapstones, illustrates that local shell workshops existed in the Onavas Valley Prehispanic communities.

The shell assemblage of the Onavas Valley further reveals several interesting interaction patterns. The valley received or acquired shell material from coastal communities, as 83 percent of the sample came from the Gulf of California. At this point, three scenarios to account for this pattern have been suggested. First, coastal communities, such as Prehispanic Yaquis may have served as the connection and supplier of marine shell to the valley. Seri bands also participated in this shell trade, as described in Colonial documents (Pérez de Rivas 1999:390). Second, shell may have been directly acquired from the coast by the Nébomes. Colonial documents mention that the town of Comuripa was the lowest Nébome community on the Río Yaqui (Carrera Stampa 1955:172; Sauer 1932:12), just 60 km away from Guaymas on the Sonoran coast. And third, the Nébomes may have used a combination of these strategies to acquire shell.

Some shell items arrived in the valley without modification and were worked there, such as *Conus* and *Nerita*. Other species arrived with the initial manufacture steps already completed, such as *Glycymeris gigantea*, and were finished in the valley. The shell analysis further indicates that a portion of the shell jewelry manufacture was for local consumption, although a good percentage of that production appears to have been for regional and possible extra-regional trade. It is still too early, however, to establish to whom these shell goods were traded; Paquimé could have certainly been one receiving community.

The analysis presented here focuses on the description and analysis of the marine shell artifacts recovered on the surface of sites in the Onavas Valley: how many, what type, which species, and where they were found. But what about the use of shell items in the social realm: who used them? Why? What do they represent? Did all members of a community use marine shell artifacts? Is there a social distinction based on artifact type and /or species? This is a

research avenue that the OVAP did not pursue for the current project, but is a very interesting topic for future research in the region.

The shell analysis also illustrates that this material was concentrated at four sites: SON P:10:8 (n = 442), SON P:10:98 (n = 250), SON P:6:4 (n = 80), and SON P:10:70 (n = 66), together representing 70.4 percent of the total sample. Current data suggests that these sites were both shell manufacturing locales as well as consumer sites. SON P:10:8, however, was identified as a mortuary mound with extensive modern disturbance, possibly biasing shell quantity and representation in the surface collection. SON P:10:70 was identified as a village, while the remaining two, SON P:6:4 and SON P:10:98 were identified as rancherías. (See Appendix I and II).

BONE

Few bone items were recorded by the OVAP, especially because it was decided not to collect exposed bones fragments from human inhumations. With the exception of the two human inhumations recorded at the excavation unit at the cemetery mound SON P:10:8, these type of features were recorded on the site record form and on the site map only. In some instances, a sample of human teeth was collected when they appeared loose on the surface. Upon completion of the OVAP, the bone sample consisted mostly of animal bones, human teeth, and two bone awls.

Animal Bones

More than 90 percent of the sample consisted of fish bones (n = 75); most were identified as vertebra (Olsen 1968). No fish species was identified, but most are likely from catfish (*Arius*), which is a common local species of the Río Yaqui. The finding of fish bones at the surface in significant amounts affirms that the

Prehispanic communities exploited this fresh-water food resource (Figure 6.10). In addition, the finding of several stone weights identified as net sinkers, described earlier, supports the idea that fishing was a supplementary activity that served to compliment a menu based mostly on legumes (beans and mesquite seeds), corn, and agave.

The remaining 10 percent of the animal bone sample consisted of Canis sp. teeth and a fragment of tortoise carapace (Figure 6.11). It was not possible to distinguish to what species of canine the teeth belonged, but they may have been from domesticated dogs, although it is also possible they were from a wolf. The archaeological record indicates that Sonoran Prehispanic communities such as Huatabampo and La Playa raised dogs (Alvares 1990:70; Villalpando 2001a:215). However, current evidence suggests that the dogs were raised as pets, guards, or vermin hunters, and not for food.

The only tortoise carapace fragment reported did not exhibit any human modification (# 47980). This artifact may have been food refuse, or possibly a tool, or perhaps both. In any case, tortoises are well known to be part of the indigenous menu and the carapace was often used as a tool in Prehispanic communities (Olsen 1968; Pennington 1980). Recent archaeological excavations at the site SON P:10:08, the cemetery mound, uncovered several individuals. One of them had a tortoise carapace on top of his chest (INAH 2012). So it is possible that what we found was part of an offering.

Human Teeth

A total of 38 human teeth were collected from the surface. No analyses were performed on these materials. A visual examination, however, determined that most came from adults, although a few originated from infants. The adult teeth show a great degree of wear and use,

probably caused by a subsistence system based mostly on seeds, corn, and beans. While not conclusive, the physical appearance of the teeth appears to indicate a healthy population.

Bone Awls

Only two bone awl fragments were recovered. Both corresponded to the distal portion of the tool, measuring 5 x 1.5 cm and 6.5 x 1.5 cm each. They are made from split cannon bone of a large mammal, most likely deer, and the points were polished from use. These tools probably were used for making holes while sewing skins, in weaving, basketry, or for similar uses.

PRELIMINARY CHRONOLOGY FOR THE ONAVAS VALLEY

Because of high frequencies of local decorated pottery, considerable variability in the plain ware, the frequent occurrence of imported types that have been dated elsewhere, and considerable variability in projectile points, an initial and reasonably refined chronology emerges as a productive goal of the OVAP (Douglas and Quijada 2004b). Of course in this case, a local chronology is a work in progress, especially because of the limitations imposed by working only with surface material, and some of the periods such as the Early Ceramic is largely conjectural and largely inferred on that basis of analogy to other areas (Figure 6.12). Nonetheless, the presence and identification of several dated ceramic types from the Chihuahuan and Trincheras region provide a reasonable basis from which to start. Well-known Chihuahuan ceramic types, dated to around A.D. 1200-1450 in the Casas Grandes area (Ravesloot et al. 1995; Whalen and Minnis 2003), were found alongside the local Onavas Purple-on-Red ceramic type. One sherd of Nogales Polychrome was also found, dating to around

Figure 6.10. Young boy holding fish he just caught along the Río Yaqui (Photograph courtesy of the University of Arizona, Arizona State Museum, Photographic Collections, Edward H. and Rosamond B. Spicer Collection, Album VIII:7).

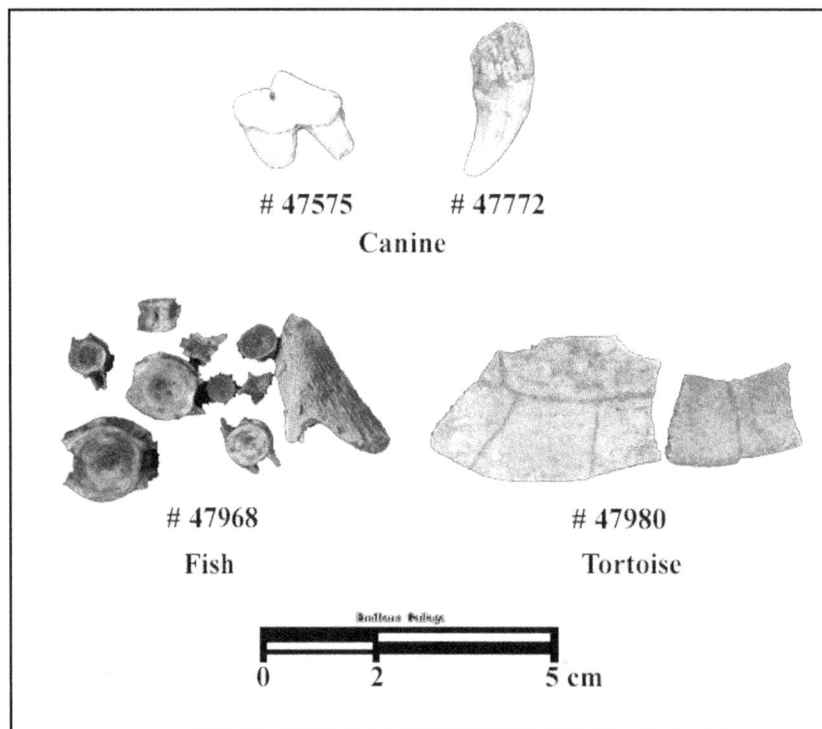

Figure 6.11. Animal bone remains (Photograph by Emiliano Gallaga).

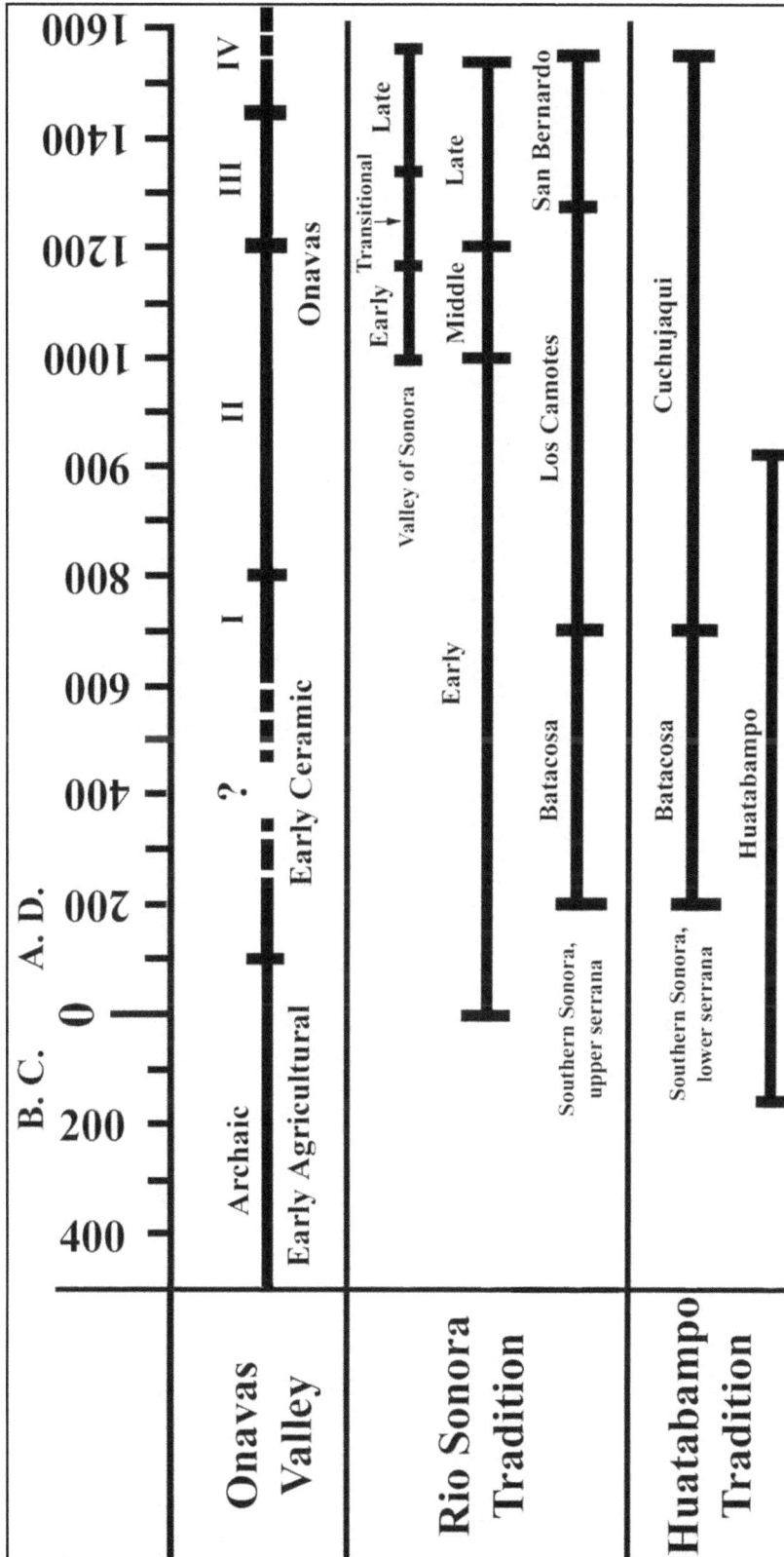

Figure 6.12. Preliminary and comparative regional chronology. Sources: Rio Sonora (Doolittle 1988; Pailes 1972), Huatabampo (Alvarez 1990; Pailes 1972).

A. D. 700-1150 (Gallaga 1997). Provisionally, four periods may be proposed:

Paleoindian-Archaic Period (10,000 B.C. to A.D. 150)

This period is based mostly on the projectile point analysis. Early sporadic non-continuous occupation of the valley is suggested, based on the identification of a possible Paleoindian projectile point (# 48305), as well several Early and Middle Archaic points. In addition, identification of megafauna remains such as horse (SON P:10:82, Appendix A and B), and information from locals of mammoth bones in the region, illustrate that the area could have provide plentiful resources for hunter and gatherer groups. Archaic sites are not numerous, only four were recorded, but a great number of Archaic projectile points were found throughout the research area also. Figure 6.13 illustrates the distribution of identified Archaic sites and sites with Early and Middle Archaic projectile points that suggest Archaic occupations. The few Archaic sites recorded are located mostly on the foothills, rather than on the valley bottom. On the contrary, multicomponent sites with Archaic points are located close to the river on the valley bottom, but interestingly enough not in the farming areas identified later in time. In general, Archaic sites are dispersed on the valley, close to water sources but also to the foothills where they could exploit the resources that area offers, such as game and plants. Occupation of the valley increased during the next period.

Late Archaic-Early Agriculture Period (800 B.C. to A.D. 150)

This period is defined by the projectile points, such as Cortaro, Cienega, Parallel &Tapering Stemmed, and Leaf-Shaped types. It's possible that this is a period of transition between hunting-gathering and early agriculture groups

in the area. Figure 6.14 illustrates those sites that had Late Archaic points. People move from the foothills to the valley bottom. Those sites were close to water but also to the foothills where abundant game could be found. In this period, sites increase in number, but remain dispersed within the valley, closer to the river and further from the foothills. Fish bones remains indicate that fishing was an important activity at this point. They also became permanent and inhabitants probably started to practice farming on the rich valley bottom. Figure 6.14 also depicts three possible Late Archaic communities or aggregations: one at the northern portion of the valley, one at the center, and another at the bottom of the valley. Some of these Archaic sites later became major Prehispanic sites, such as SON P:6:5 and SON P:10:70 (See Appendix I and II). As mentioned earlier, it is possible to have mixed material at surface through modern farming activities performed on top of sites that had a long occupational history in the valley.

Early Ceramic Period (A.D.150 to 500/600)

This period is not well defined, and probably dates between A.D.150 to 500/600. Population may increase in the valley, reflected in an increase in the number of sites. These could be permanent and were located mostly on the valley bottom near arable land and water. Temporary camps were located near or on agricultural fields, or in the foothills for hunting, gathering or occasional use during travels. At this point of the analysis no sites or material evidence can be confidently associated with this period, but it is possible that crude plain wares may date to this era.

Onavas Period (A.D. 500/600-1550)

This period is provisionally divided into four phases, based mostly on ceramic material, projectile point analysis, and chronologies from neighboring regions (see Figure 6.12).

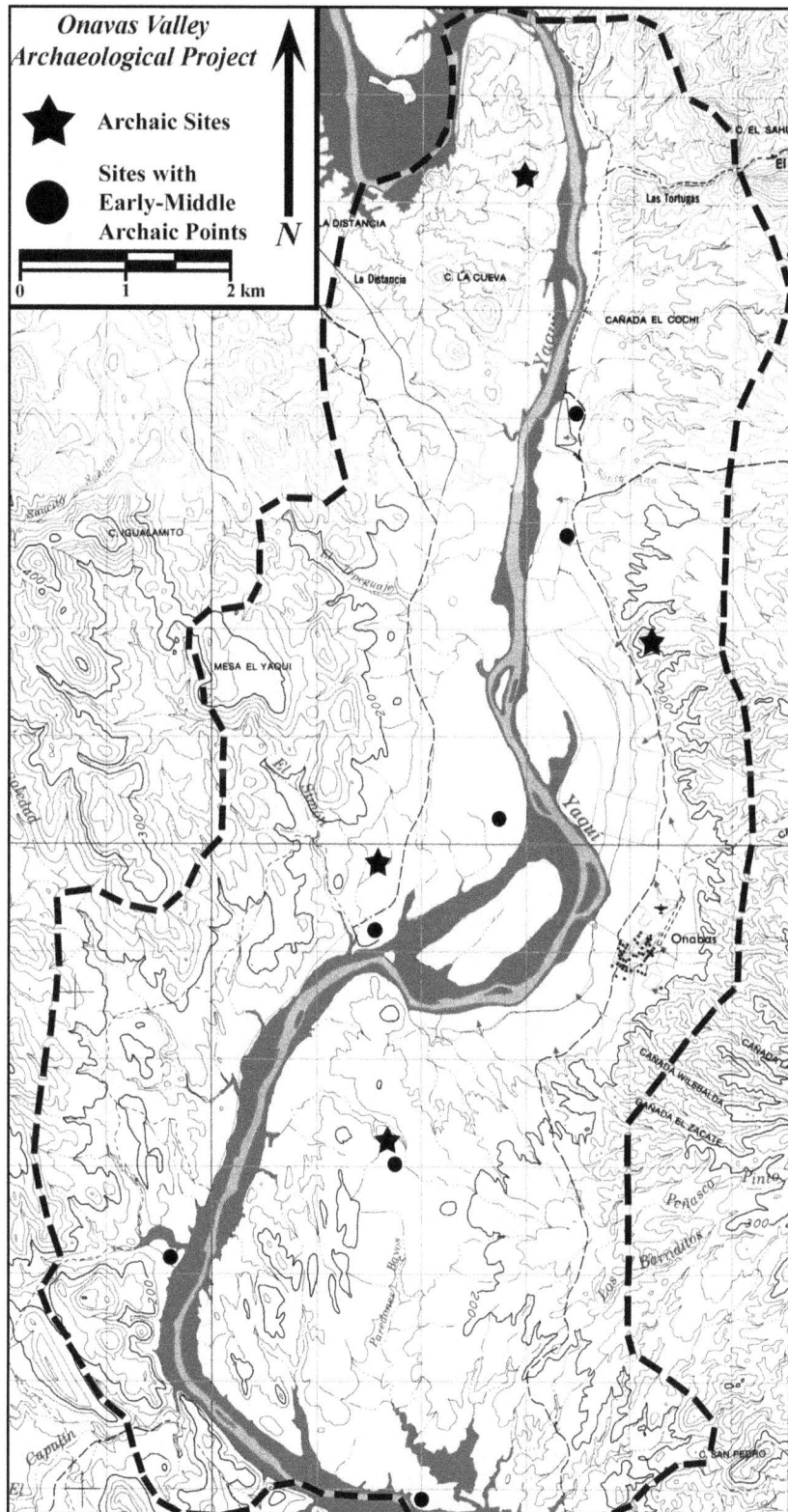

Figure 6.13. Distribution of Archaic sites and sites with Early and Middle Archaic points.

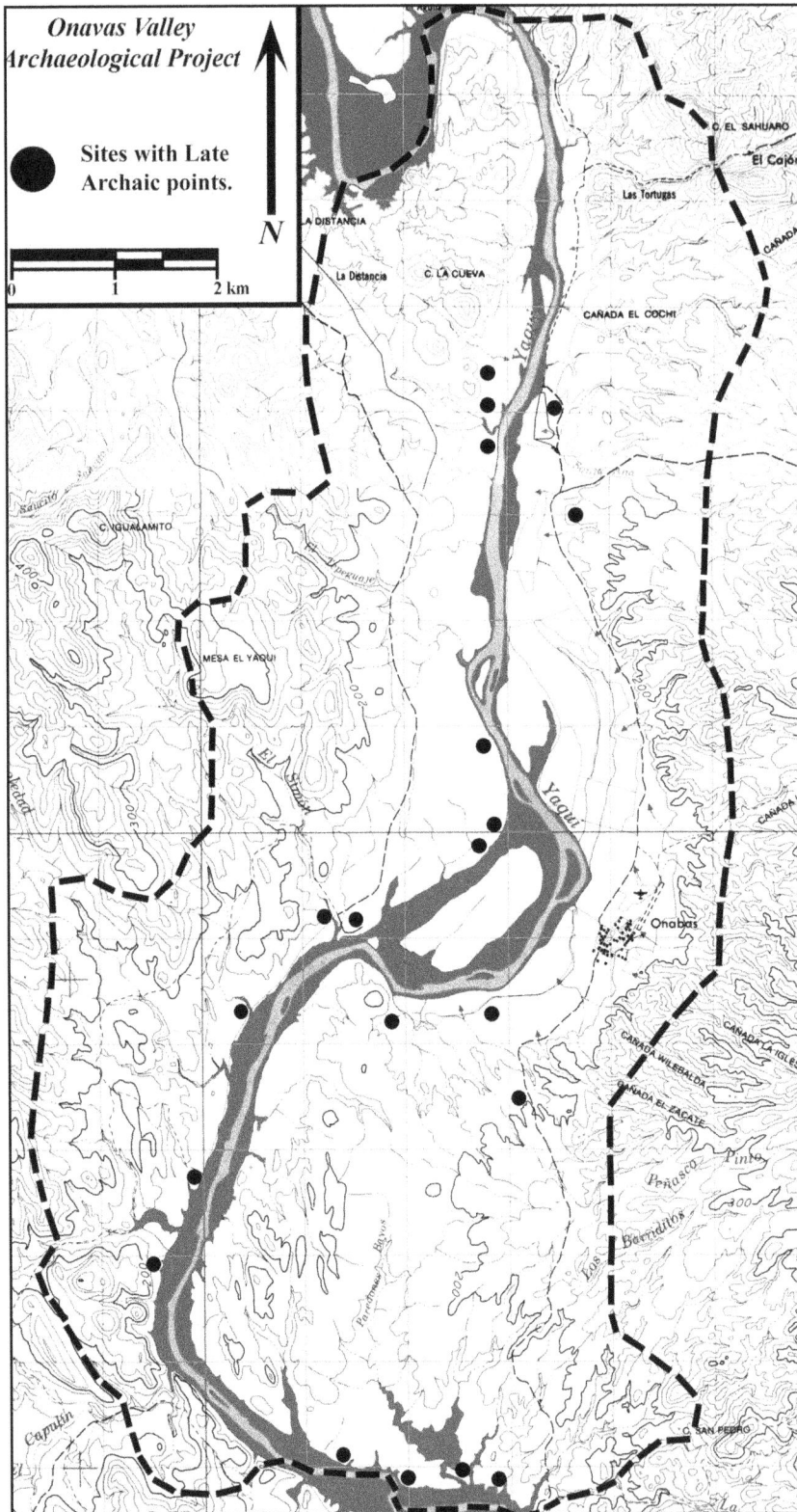

Figure 6.14. Distribution of sites with Late Archaic points.

Onavas I Phase (A.D. 500/600-800)

This phase is not well defined, and is most likely a continuation of the Early Agricultural Period. Ceramic assemblages were dominated by better quality plainwares, possibly Onavas plain and red wares. It is possible that the red wares identified at the Onavas Valley are Hua-tabampo Red, Guasave Red, or Cuchujaqui Red ware types (Alvarez 1990; Ekholm 1942; Pailes 1972). The identification of significant numbers of red wares also suggested that the valley had some sort of interactions with the coast that can be traced with marine shell at Onavas sites. Figure 6.15 illustrates sites where red wares were identified. This figure indicates that sites increase in numbers and most likely the population of the valley increased as well. The settlement pattern for this phase illustrates that the Nébome communities concentrated on the valley bottom, but during this phase settlements also start to be located at the center of the valley where the most productive arable land is concentrated. In addition, Figure 6.15 shows a small concentration of sites near the Onavas town, probably depicting the future location of the regional center. There is not a clear nucleation pattern, but increasing quantities of sites were located in particular areas of the valley, including the south bottom, the southwestern portion, the center, and the northern portion of the valley. It is possible that the areas outside the center of the valley, where the best farming land lays, focused on different strategies for food production such as agave cultivation. In particular those sites at the southern portion of the valley where several hearths were identified, suggesting this type of activities.

Onavas II Phase (A.D. 800–1200)

This phase continue to be dominated by plainware ceramics, such as Onavas Plain and red wares. However, a local decorated ware, Ona-vas Purple-on-Red, was also found at sites in the region during this phase. This ceramic type presents an interesting situation. Although the local decorated ceramic type was found alongside Chihuahuan polychrome types dating to A.D. 1200-1450 on the surface, it is highly possible that this local type dates earlier. Similar ceramic decorated expressions in Northwest Mexico, such as in the Trincheras region (Gallaga 1997; McGuire and Villalpando 1993), Casas Grandes area (Di Peso 1974; Dean and Ravesloot 1993), the Bavispe River (Douglas and Quijada 2005), and northern Sinaloa (Carpenter personal communication 2005), range between A.D. 800-1200. The identification of a Nogales Polychrome (Gallaga 1997) sherd along side with Onavas Purple-on-Red on the surface also points to this conclusion. Figure 6.16 shows a total of 27 sites where Onavas Purple-on-Red sherds were identified. From those settlements, two were identified as villages, three as aldeas, 14 as rancherías, and the rest as camps. Again, it is interesting to note that several of these sites were concentrated near the Onavas town, probably representing the regional center of the community, a northern portion of this center, the production/distribution area of this ceramic type, or all of the above.

During this phase, the sites noticeably increased in the valley and probably had above-ground structures. In terms of regional interactions, the valley continues to maintain its relations with the coast but also with other areas which participated in the Trincheras tradition. It is not clear how those relations were with the later, however. Only one Nogales Polychrome sherd was found from that tradition. Marine shell continues to be consumed by the Nébomes as both finished and unfinished goods and not only for local consumption but for long-distance trade as well. Metates and manos are abundant, showing an increase in food production activities.

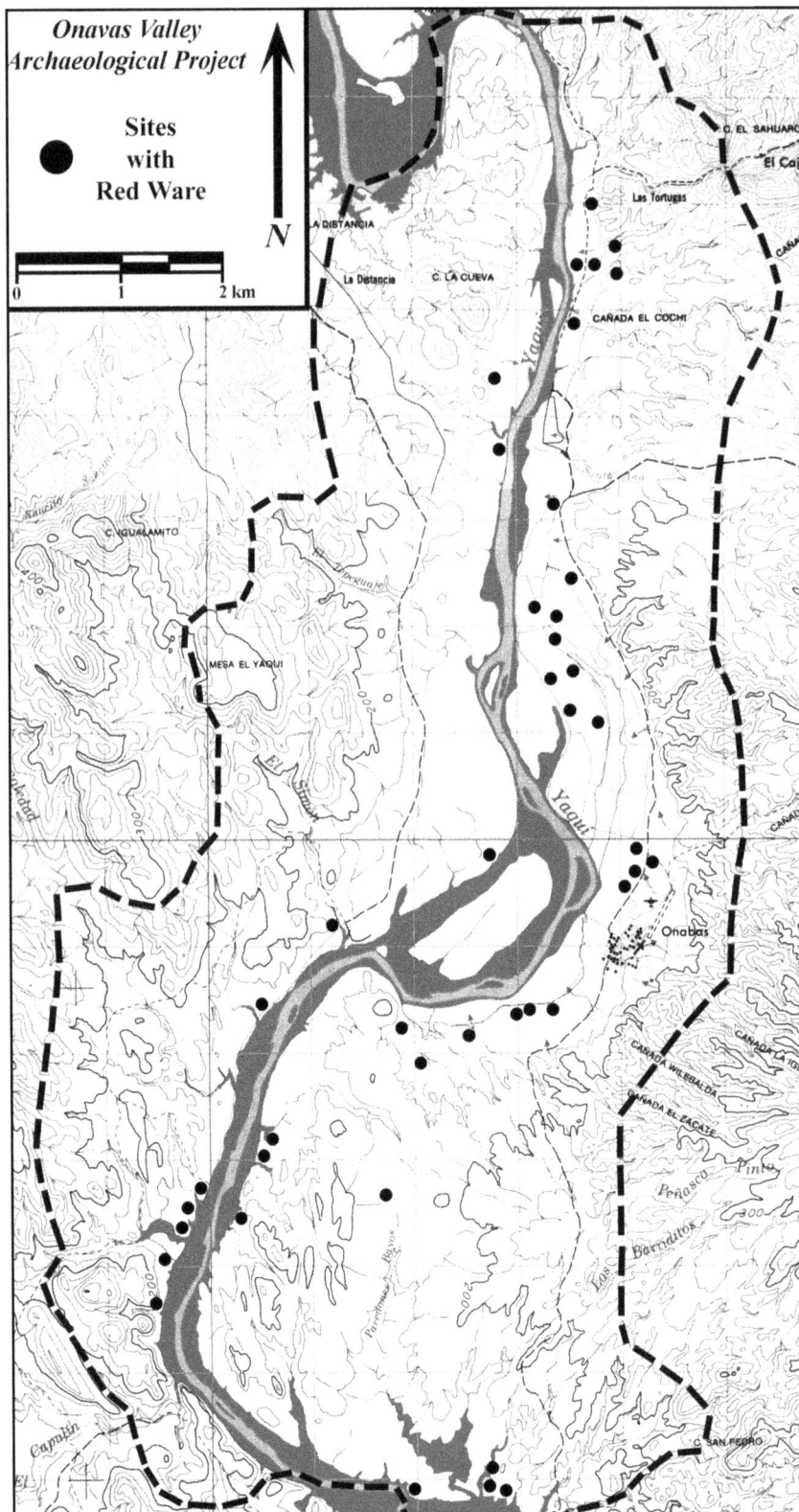

Figure 6.15. Distribution of sites with Red ware.

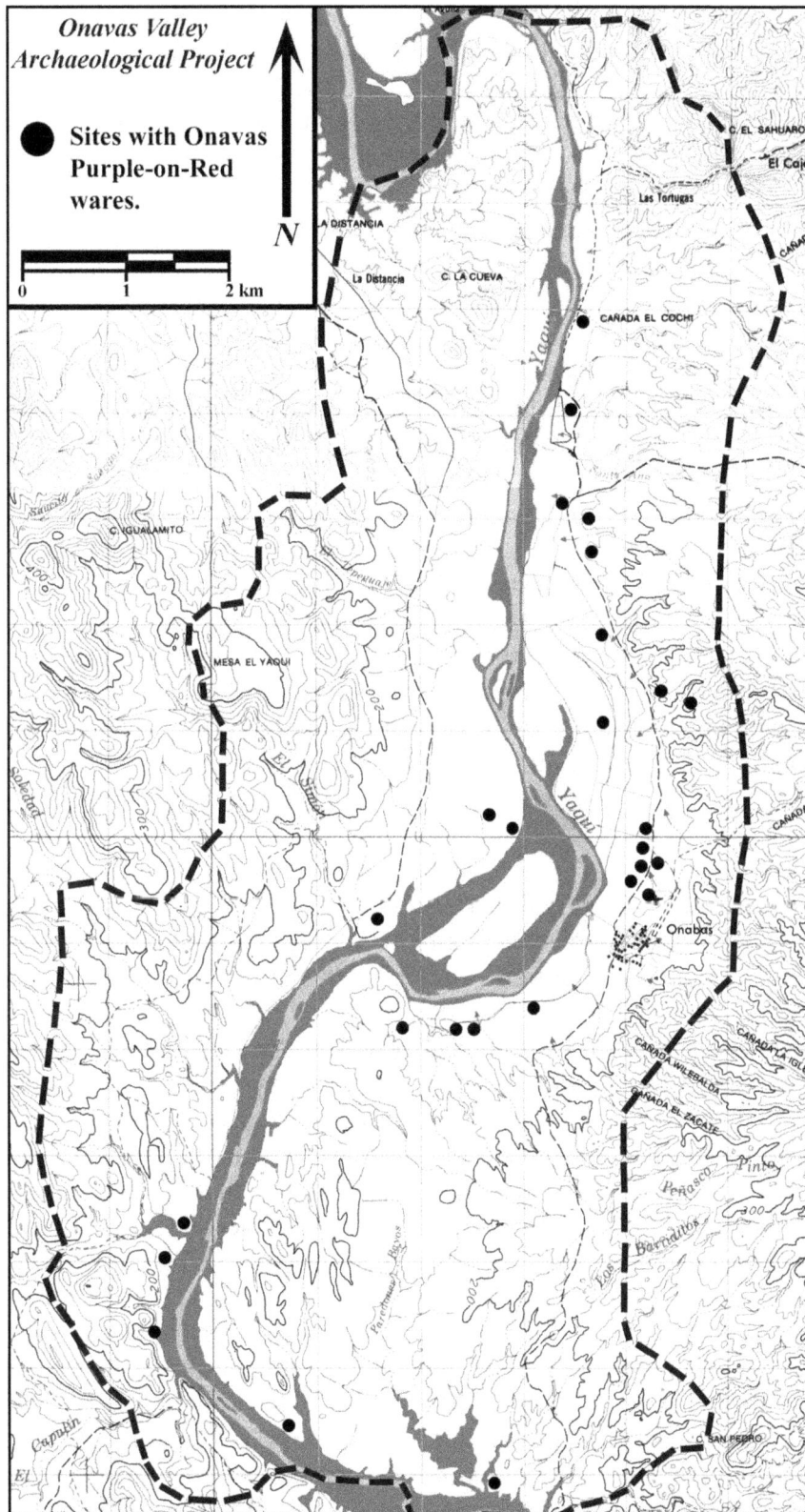

Figure 6.16. Distribution of sites with Onavas Purple-on-Red ware.

Onavas III (A.D. 1200 – 1450)

The valley continues to be occupied and its communities seem to increase in size and number. The higher-ranked sites seem to be distinguished from the rest by the construction of non-habitation structures such as stone altars and platforms. It is not possible to know if Onavas Purple-on-Red was still made in this phase or when it was replaced by non-local decorated types, but those ceramic types arrived in the valley during this time. Chihuahuan polychrome ceramic types were found only at two sites (SON P:10:08 and SON P:10:59, Appendix I and II). However, these are a sign of the diversification and how the extra-regional interactions of the valley with outside areas took off. Marine shell continues to be an important element in the valley goods production through its contact with the coast and eventually with trade farther inland probably for turquoise and decorated ceramics.

Onavas IV (A.D. 1450-1550)

This phase is poorly defined and is based on the identification of particular projectile point forms, such as Triangular, Sobaipuri, and Desert Side Notched types and on ethnohistorical records. The valley seems to be occupied continuously until and after the arrival of the Spanish. Sites continued to be located at the valley bottom near water, sources of fish, and farming land. Sites in the foothills were also utilized during this phase, but only as camps, not permanent residential sites. At the time of contact, Colonial documents reveal a highly populated area exhibiting extra-regional interactions with neighboring communities, such as the Opatas, Yaquis, and Seris, but also with a socio-political structure capable of controlling and defending its territory from the expansion of its neighbors as well.

The chronology suggested for this area, albeit preliminary, is a first attempt to place the Prehispanic communities identified in the Onavas Valley in time. Moreover, it enables a chronological comparison of the area with neighboring regions, and the ability to trace cultural connections and interactions over time. The analysis suggests that the Onavas Valley was constantly occupied, transforming its occupation from temporary and dispersed camps to permanent and nucleated settlements; and from the foothills to the valley bottom. Future excavation of key sites in the Onavas Valley may provide further insights and elaborate this tentative chronology.

EXCAVATION UNIT # 1 AT SON P:10:08 (EL CEMENTERIO)

The local members of the Onavas town had long known about this site, and a member of the community, Rafael Mungia, showed us the site in the summer of 2003 during one of the preliminary trips to the area. The site is located in the valley on the east side of the Río Yaqui, just 800 m away from the town on the side of the old dirt road to the highway. Several activities are currently endangering the site and have already partially destroyed the site. An old dirt road leading to the modern village of Onavas (10-12 m wide) has erased about a quarter of the eastern portion of it. At some point in the past, an irrigation canal was dug through the west side of the site. In 1999, another concrete-lined irrigation canal was excavated on the east side of the river and running parallel to the dirt road to Onavas. Together, these canals have destroyed a substantial portion of the site. In 2003, an electric line was erected with electrical posts that disturbed portions of the ground surface. And agricultural activities performed at the land had been erasing the site as well (Figure 6.17). According to the local informant and the owner of the property at the time, the site had inhumations and cremations. Several of those features were spotted, pot-hunted,

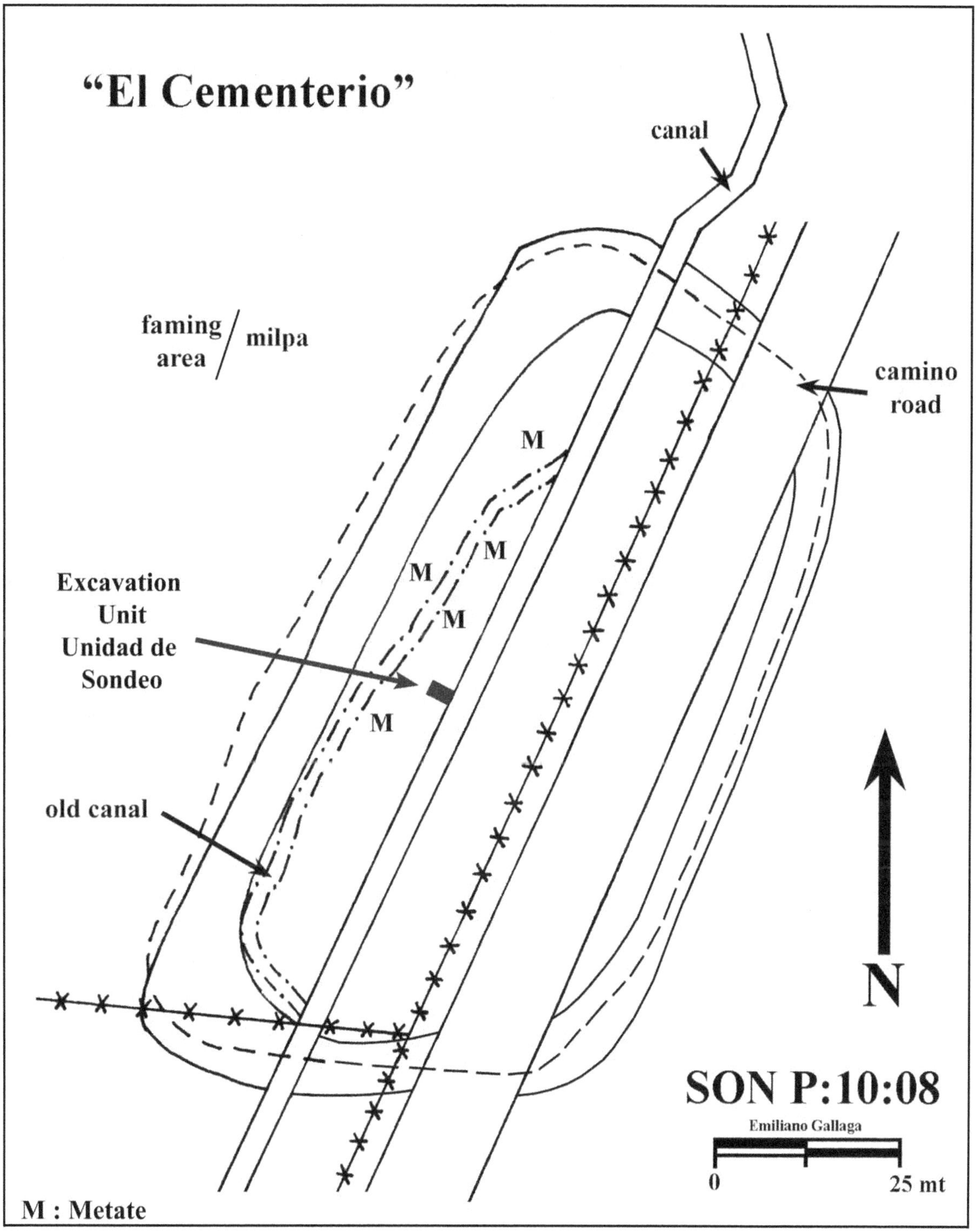

"El Cementerio"

canal

faming area / milpa

camino road

M

Excavation Unit Unidad de Sondeo

M

M

M

M

old canal

N

SON P:10:08

Emiliano Gallaga

0   25 mt

M : Metate

Figure 6.17. Location of the excavation unit on site.

and destroyed during the 1999 canal building. As a result of this construction, to this date a variety of archaeological material is visible on either side of the canal. Although no house remains were observed, some pieces of adobe with roof impressions were found, suggesting that at some point some earth structure was located on the top of this cemetery mound or nearby, as well as domestic material such as manos and metates.

In the preliminary visit in 2003, we just recorded the site with no material surface collection. We talked to the owner, Francisco Isedo, about the importance of the site and its preservation, a situation that he was aware of. He mentioned that he keeps away pot-hunters and private collectors from it, as much he can.

In the summer of 2004, when the OVAP field work was conducted, we received the sad news that the owner, Francisco Isedo, had passed away, and that the family members were fighting among themselves in court for the property rights. The situation had not changed as of 2008. The interest in following the legal situation, of course, is out of concern for preservation of the site.

Site Description

This site measures 100 x 50 m. It is an artificial earth mound approximately 2 meters high. Due to its proximity, it is highly possible that this feature has direct association with the Prehispanic site, presumably situated at the same location as the Onavas town identified as the regional center of the Onavas Prehispanic community.

The site shows a great variety and quantity of surface archaeological material. Agave knives, hammerstones, polishing stones, bifaces, metate fragments, manos, flakes, stone pendants, and lap stones were recorded. In addition, several pieces of gray obsidian, turquoise beads and pendants, chert, quartz, and rock crystal were found. Ceramic material recorded consisted of a large quantity of red and brown Onavas plain ware sherds, several local decorated Onavas Purple/Red sherds, and some non-local decorated sherds, such as Ramos polychrome, Babícora polychrome, Huerigos, possible Carretas, and one sherd of Trincheras polychrome. Worked sherds and ceramic figurine fragments were also collected at the site. In addition, human bone fragments were recorded at the surface, probably from the cremation and inhumation contexts, noted above. Animal bones were also recorded, such as fish and canine. A great quantity and variety of shell material was found at the site as well.

Due to the richness of the context and the relevance of the site to be a potential cemetery mound, a small excavation unit was undertaken. The location of the unit was at the highest place of the mound, on an area that looked undisturbed, and near to the concrete irrigation canal where the informants mentioned that they saw the inhumations (see Figure 6.17). The main objective of the unit was to test the information about the presence of mortuary remains at the site, as well as to establish the cultural deposition and the stratigraphy of the mound, and to recover cultural information about the interior of the mound.

Initially, a small excavation unit (2 x 4 m) was placed west of and perpendicular to the concrete irrigation canal. This unit was established to clear the disturbed deposits from the excavation of the canal and explore intact deposits underneath. The debris from the canal contained a lot of cultural material and was recorded and excavated as Level 1. When the original site surface was reached, and not knowing what the stratigraphy of the site was, it was decided to excavate by artificial 30 cm levels. When the excavations were completed, four levels had been assigned (a depth of 120 cm). In order to avoid compromising the integrity of the canal, the dimensions of the unit were decreased in the lowest level.

The lowest level was only 1 x 2 m (see Figure 6.18). All of the fill was screened through ¼-in mesh screen.

Description of the Stratigraphy

After the excavation, five cultural levels were identified at the analysis of the mound stratigraphy from the unit walls.

Level # 1 (0-50 cm)

This level was a disturbed layer of earth that was originally fill from the mound but dumped to the sides during the irrigation canal excavation in 1999. This layer was 50 cm thick at its highest portion, with a great amount of cultural material from the interior of the mount but displaced from its original deposition context. The material was collected and registered as surface material with no context and analyzed with the rest of the surface material collected on the site.

Level # 2 (50-80 cm)

The excavation unit was 2 x 2 m, in order to not damage the integrity of the irrigation canal, as requested by the community. This layer

was a dark brown clayish/organic earth (6/1 YR brownish gray), semi-compact, with high density of ashes and material culture. No features were identified in it. The material found in this level was ceramics, lithics, shell (work refuse, beads, bracelets, and rings), projectile points, abraders, and bone (human, animal, and fish).

Level # 3 (80-110 cm)

The size of the unit remained the same, 2 x 2 m. The layer continues to have the same physical conditions as level # 1: dark brown clayish/organic earth (6/1 YR brownish gray), semi-compact, with a high density of ashes and material culture. No features where identified on this level. At the end of the level a noticeable change of layer was perceived.

Level # 4 (110-140 cm)

The excavation unit was reduced to a 2 x 1 m. At this level a change was identified from semi-compact to hard compact with a lot of small (less than 0.2 cm²) pieces of charcoal and some small layers ash. The color of the layer change from dark brown clayish/organic earth to light brown (7/2 YR dull orange) sandy earth. Also,

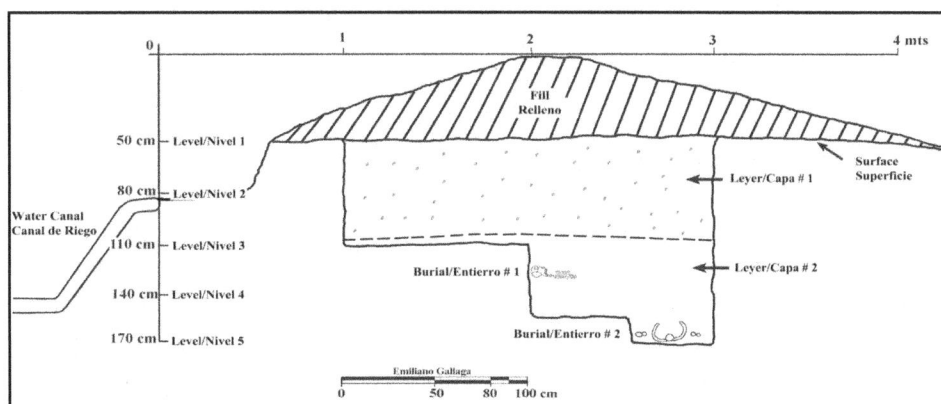

Figure 6.18. Stratigraphic cut from unit # 1 at the cemetery mound SON P:10:08.

the density of cultural material decreased considerably, but there was an increase of human bone fragments. One feature was found in this level in the SE corner of the unit.

Feature 1

Identified as Burial # 1, infant human remains were found, approximately 4 to 6 years old, face up, but incomplete. The remains were oriented E-W, and were not associated with any additional cultural material. However, a few small sherds and lithics were found in the screened earth from around the burial. No tomb or edges of a hole were identified, nor was an intrusion visible that cut the rest of the body in half to explain the missing parts. The skeletal remains were recorded and collected for lab analysis. Currently, Burial # 1 is at the INAH Sonora facilities.

Level # 5 (140-170 cm)

One more level was excavated with the same dimensions as Level 4, but the entire level was not excavated. The layer had the same physical conditions as Level # 4, but with much less cultural material and more charcoal and ash in it. At the bottom of this level, another feature was identified. We did not continue the excavation to bedrock so as not disturb feature # 2.

Feature 2

A second interment of human remains was found, identified as Burial # 2. This was another inhumation, face-up, extended, adult, and probably male. The body was well-preserved oriented N-S, but only half of it could be excavated, and the rest of the body continued into the interior of the north wall of the unit. No material culture was found in association with it, and neither were the remains of a tomb or hole identified either.

Unit # 1 Analysis

The excavation of Unit # 1 reveals evidence of at least two occupational phases at the mound (see Figure 6.18).

First occupation (layer 2)

At some point in the occupation of the valley, the site was used as cemetery mound area probably during the proposed Onavas II phase (A.D. 800–1200), based on the associated cultural materials. The two inhumations found at the site and the high amounts of fragmentary human remains, seems to confirm the use of this site as a cemetery mound. Although no cremation interments were found at the unit, the high quantities of charcoal, ash, and burned bones identified on the earth used as fill of the mound, could be the material evidence of crematory activities. No cultural or material offerings were found in direct association with the two inhumations found, just a couple of ceramic sherds and lithics that were recovered from the burial fill. Also it is possible that the size of the units did not allow us to locate them. Local informants mentioned the presence of complete ceramic pots, shell necklaces and bracelets in clear association with the human remains found at the site.

Second Occupation (layer 1)

Probably due to a change in the socio-ideological belief structures of the Prehispanic community of the valley, the cemetery mound ceased to function as such near the end of the Onavas II phase. Based on the type and quantity of the artifacts recovered from the youngest occupational layer that covered the mound, it seems that the site was re-used as a garbage pile during the Onavas III phase, which would explain the high density of domestic materials recovered from the top of the mound. Similar contexts are found in other areas, such as the

Hohokam or in Sinaloa, where cemeteries and middens are often combined in a single feature (Gallaga 1999).

Material Analysis

Only the material from levels # 2 through 5 is presented here, as they are from undisturbed contexts from inside the cemetery mound.

Ceramics

A total of 1,009 ceramic sherds (9.570 kg) was recovered from the unit. Over 95 percent of the sample is plain sherds, while less than 5 percent are decorated. From the plain type sherds, 99 percent of the sample was identified as Onavas plain. From the 59 decorated sherds recorded, over 95 percent of this sample was identified as Onavas Purple-on-Red, but 5 sherds from the Chihuahuan Prehispanic traditions were also found. The latter confirms some type of relation with that cultural area. In addition, these ceramic types are well-dated to the Medio Period (A. D. 1300-1500), which suggests a similar date of occupation of the Unit 1 mound.

A little less than 20 percent of the sample could be identified to vessel form. From those, 11 percent were jars and 5 percent bowls, followed by ceramic discs. No complete pots were identified. It is important to mention that only four tecomate sherds were identified, which suggests that the mound was occupied late in time and not early. In addition, the vessel shape analysis seems to indicate a domestic refuse context.

Lithics

Very few lithic materials were recovered at Unit # 1, only 108 artifacts. From those, 103 were identified as flakes and there was also one projectile point (Desert Side Notched, A.D. 1540-1665), a shell reamer, an abrader, a stone disc, and one turquoise pendant. With the exception of the flakes, all the lithic objects were found complete with considerable wear use. No broken tools or partially worked tools were found. Although most of the lithic material was identified as flakes, their numbers were not high in comparison with other areas of collection from sites in the valley. Material analysis shows that more than 70 percent of lithic artifacts are made from volcanic material. In general, the lithic analysis indicates a refuse area context.

Shell

In total, 27 shell pieces were found. From those, five were identified as freshwater from an unknown species and the rest were marine species: four *Glycymeris*, three *Conus*, three *Olivella*, and one from *Pinctada*, *Laevicardium*, and *Diplodonta*. Seventeen of the pieces were identified as debitage, and the other 10 as finished items: eight beads, one pendant, and one bracelet fragment. Of the finished items, the species included: *Glycymeris* (1 bracelet, 1 bead), *Spondylus* (3 beads), *Petaloconchus* (3 beads, 1 pendent) and one bead from a freshwater species.

Bone

Several bone fragments were recovered in unit # 1. Most of them were fish vertebrae and other elements (n = 34) identified as *Arius* species (cat fish) (Olsen 1968), which is very common on the Yaqui River today. Other animal bones were recovered in very bad condition (fragmented and burned), and their small size prevented further identification. The most interesting animal material recovered was two *Canis* sp. teeth without any evidence of being worked or used. A small tortoise carapace fragment was also recovered.

In addition, several very small human bones were recovered, but could not be identified, and were not counted towards the number of individuals present in the sample. Most of the sample shows evidence of burning, probably from crematory activities.

Burial Descriptions

Burial # 1

This individual, a child, was found on the southeast corner of Unit # 1 about 73 cm depth from the original mound surface in Level 4. Bones were found articulated and in anatomical position, indicating a primary burial context. Most of the bones, from the cranium to the hips were found, but from below the pelvis all the bones were missing. The pelvic bones were in a very bad shape, so it is possible that the rest of the body disintegrated. However, there is no clear evidence on why this would occur. Within the excavated units there was no evidence of intrusive features or holes that could give the reason for the missing body parts. It is possible that the skeleton was deposited as a secondary burial in its present condition.

The body was placed face up, most likely in extended position, with the skull oriented east. The right humerus bone was parallel to the rest of the body with the radius and ulna bones oriented slightly towards the center-line of the body. The left arm was missing. The skull was lifted up a little, possibly resting on an earth bench, and the lower mandible was missing. Taking in consideration that the vertebrae were not fused, and that the remaining teeth from the upper mandible were permanent and deciduous, the individual was likely a child between 4 and 6 years of age (Coral Montero personal communication 2004).

No burial hole or trench was identified and no cultural materials or offerings were identified, although a few sherds and small flakes were recovered from the fill. The body was recorded, recovered, and is counted at the Centro INAH in Sonora.

Burial # 2

This individual is an adult, possibly a male, located in the northwest corner of the unit at 105 cm from the original surface (see Figure 6.19). The body was placed face up in an extended position with the skull oriented to the south. The body was exposed to the hips only because the rest of the body was inside of the mound on the north wall of the unit. Like Burial #1, the bones were found articulated, suggesting a primary burial context. Both arms were positioned parallel to the body. A preliminary analysis of the skull suggested that it could be brachycephalic. Based on the bone structure, the wear and conditions of the teeth, the body was estimated to be about 20 to 25 years old. The individual lacked its incisor teeth, but they seemed to be a postmortem loss.

Some of the measurements taken from the body are; 1: the maximum distance between molars is 13 cm apart. 2: the distance between the base of the pelvis far extreme and the "bregma" of the skull is 81 cm. 3: the maximum opening of the nose is 3 cm. 4: the maximum width of the skull is 17 cm (Coral Montero personal communication 2004).

Similar to Burial #1, no burial hole or trench was identified during excavations. Additionally, no offerings were associated with the burial. Due to the fact that only the half of the body could be excavated, it was decided to leave the body in situ. A modern item was deposited at the level of the chest, to leave evidence of the excavation done in 2004 (before the unit was covered).

Discussion of Unit # 1

Although it was not possible to reach the sterile layer of the mound, it is fair to estimate that the mound could have reached an elevation of 120 to 150 cm from the original valley living surface to the top of the mound. Based on the material found, mostly on the few Chihuahuan

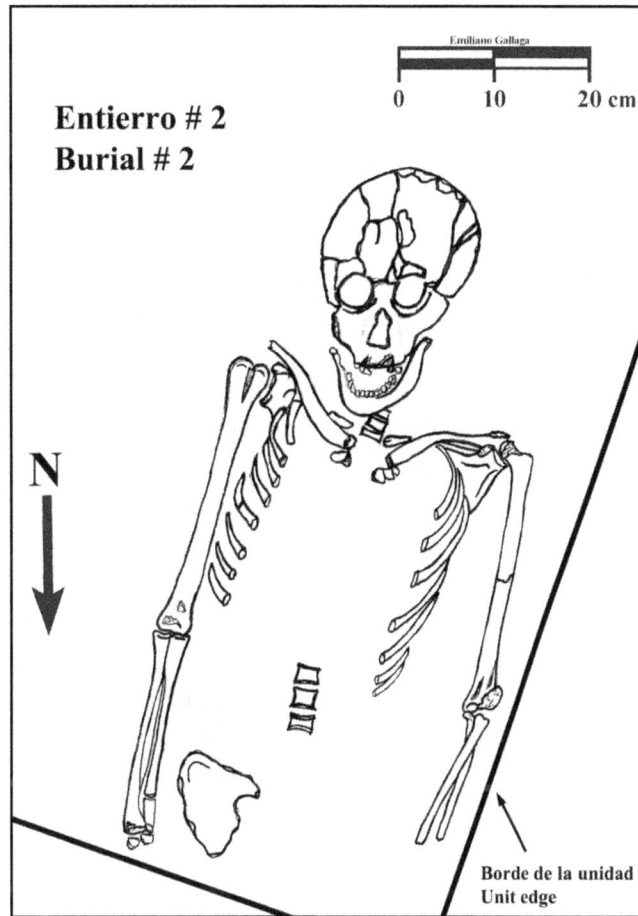

Figure 6.19. Detailed drawing of Burial # 2.

sherds identified, the mound seems to be in use between A.D. 1300-1500. However, recent research on this site provides some dates for the human remains found at the same level of the one previously found in 2006 between A.D. 900-1200 (INAH 2012). Following the proposed chronology for the valley in this work, the cemetery mound seems to be used around the middle of the Onavas II through early/middle of the Onavas III Phase, most likely at the highest point of the Prehispanic Nébome occupation of the valley.

The identification of two human burials, in a very limited excavation area of the mound, confirms that the SON P:10:08 site was indeed a Prehispanic cemetery mound. In 2012, INAH did additional work at El Cementerio. Other cemetery *areas* have been recorded at

the Sonora archaeological sites, such as the one located at the site of Cerro de Trincheras (McGuire and Villalpando 1995, 2011), but this is the first example of a cemetery *mound* recorded in the State of Sonora, and the third for Northwest Mexico (Ekholm 1942; Gallaga 2004b; Talavera 1995). This is important to start understanding funerary traits among the Nébomes. More details of the recent INAH work may be found on-line by searching "El Cementerio" or viewing the website at *http:// www.inah.gob.mx/index.php/boletines/17- arqueologia/6285-descubren-cementerio- prehispanico-en-sonora*. Additionally, the excavation and analysis of the material recovered and the stratigraphy of the site identified two clear episodes of use of the mound:

1: In an early phase, this area started to be

used as cemetery area for the nearby communities. We have material confirmation of inhumation practices, but ethnohistorical documents suggest that cremation was practiced as well. Based on the dimension of the mound (100 x 50 m) and from quantities of the material found, it seems that this mound was either used for a long period of time or very intensively for a short period of time.

2: Probably at the beginning of the Onavas III, the function of the mound changed drastically from cemetery area to a midden disposal area, creating a deposit of about 50 and 60 cm thick.

It is important to mention, that these preliminary thoughts about the cemetery mound are based on a very limited excavations, and more research and excavation at the site are necessary in order to contrast this and to further understand the cultural development of the site and the valley. The most relevant aspect of the excavation is the identification of a cemetery mound for the Nébome Prehispanic community. This feature indicates that the Nébome had a more complex ceremonial/religious structure that we thought on the beginning. The site indicates the establishment of an specific area for the deposition of the dead, which could also have functioned as a community marker, a place for community affiliation, and a material element for space appropriation or land claim. This feature may have played a very important role in the landscape analysis and how the Nébomes envisioned their surroundings.

MATERIAL CULTURE DISCUSSION

This analysis provides a first framework to understand how these Prehispanic communities may have used and exploited their natural resources in the Onavas Valley. Some of the activities conducted in the valley in Prehispanic times are related to farming, such as cleaning and clearing fields, opening and maintaining canals, building terraces, and cultivating and harvesting agave plants. Other activities most likely consisted of gathering food such as mesquite pods, pitaya, prickly pear fruit, or hunting and fishing activities; as well as the crafting of different items, such as weaving, ceramic, basketry, and shell and stone jewelry. Most of these activities were recorded in the Colonial documents and described as late as the 1960s by Pennington (1980). Since then, modernity and plastic have led to the disappearance of these craft activities. At the time the OVAP was conducted none of those craft activities were performed by the local inhabitants of Onavas.

In terms of raw material, the Prehispanic local crafters generally appear to have spent time getting both local and non-local material to produce their tools. The Onavas area is rich in local resources, such as clay deposits of good quality, stones for tools, and construction materials, forest for wood, flowing water year-round, and animal and plant resources from different eco-zones within a one day radius that the Nébomes exploited to their advantage, taking the Onavas community as the starting point.

The analysis also illustrated that the Prehispanic Onavas Valley communities appear to have productive regional and extra-regional interactions. The valley may have served as a link in the material connection between the Sonoran coast and the Sierra Madre Occidental or interior beyond. Clearly, additional research is necessary to test this hypothesis, not only in the Onavas Valley but also at the coast and the Sierra Madre Occidental. In the cultural interactions research field it is furthermore important to ask who is undertaking the trade. Which communities were involved and to what degree? Did the Prehispanic Nébomes travel to the coast to get the marine shell, did coastal groups travel to Onavas to make the trade, or did they meet mid-way? The same questions can be asked about the acquisition of obsidian and turquoise suggesting fertile research grounds yet to be pursued in the area and certain neighboring regions.

The material site distribution suggests some additional initial patterns of interest. Apparently, Onavas crafters and members of the communities had access to non-local raw material as well as to finished goods such as obsidian, turquoise, polychrome ceramics, and marine shell. The amount and type of archaeo-logical material present at each site varied, but in general two sites stand out: SON P:10:8 and SON P:10:98. The material represented at these sites may be biased by the fact that they were heavily disturbed by human and/or natural formation processes that exposed more of the archaeological material for collection. Regardless, both sites revealed a richness of archaeological materials and data potential beyond that of the other sites recorded. They certainly warrant further excavation. The remaining sites also exhibited abundant and diverse assemblages, especially considering that the OVAP consisted of surface survey collection only.

The preliminary material site distribu-tion analysis demonstrates that Prehispanic communities in the Onavas Valley had access to raw materials and finished goods, although some differentiation existed between camps and habitation sites, as well as among the habi-tation sites based on size and artifact density. Future analysis of material distribution will establish whether a system of restricted access to particular goods and materials existed among the different communities or if certain sites were primarily craft production locales, such as SON P:10:8, SON P:10:98, SON P:6:4, and SON P:10:70 (See Appendix I and II), which may prove to have functioned as possible shell jewelry workshops or sites that control prestige goods.

As the material analysis illustrated, the valley seems to have a strong connection and similar development to those communities in the Huatabampo region (Alvarez 1990, 2003), albeit with characteristics of the lower Sierra (Pailes 1972), and not much similarity with the Rio Sonora archaeological tradition.

In summary, the material assemblage of the Prehispanic communities of the Onavas Valley provides a baseline for further local and regional comparative analyses. The analysis of different material types facilitated the distinc-tion of possible activities performed at certain sites and the identification of site type. In addi-tion, site classification aids in understanding how the Prehispanic Nébomes might have envisioned their landscape and might have used that natural environment.

Chapter 7
The Onavas Valley Cultural Landscape

...in order to maintain their territorial boundaries and lands,
which each recognizes as its own... (Pérez de Ribas 1999:87).

Almost all the people were farmers and recognized each other's lands
(Pérez de Ribas 1999:391).

Establishing the cultural landscape of the Prehispanic community of the Onavas Valley during the late Prehispanic period helped to achieve two research goals: 1) define the local archaeological tradition, in this case the Prehispanic Nébome, and 2) compare this cultural landscape with other defined archaeological cultural landscapes in neighboring regions. As discussed in Chapter 4, landscape analysis focuses on three different but complementary analytical concepts: (1) settlement ecology or settlement pattern for archaeology, (2) ritual landscape, and (3) ethnic landscape (Anschuetz et al. 2001; Ashmore and Knapp 1999). The Onavas Valley landscape analysis will focus on the first two, as they can be better addressed using the material evidence collected, but some preliminary thoughts about the ethnic landscape will be presented. The interpretation presented here was based on the complete analysis of the archaeological material recovered by the OVAP, and available ethnohistoric and ethnographic data for the area.

At the outset, it is important to review the natural environment of the research area to understand its cultural development. For the time frame to be examined the Onavas Period (A.D. 800-1450), the natural environment appears to have been similar to what it is today, a complete review of this topic is presented in Chapter 2 (Pérez Bedolla 1996; West 1993). The only significant change in the natural environment in the past centuries, which is highly relevant for the landscape analysis of this period, concerns the water level of the Río Yaqui (see Figure 7.1). Prior to the construction of the modern Alvaro Obregón and El Novillo dams, the Río Yaqui ran freely and had seasonal floods that irrigated and fertilized a large amount of the floodplain farming land. These seasonal events do not occur any longer or at least not with the same force as before (Pennington 1980; Pérez de Ribas 1999). Colonial accounts mention that the Rio Yaqui was one of the largest rivers in the north and that it made the valleys around it so productive for agriculture. Erosion marks on the river banks indicate that the river level used to flood up at least 15 to 20 m higher than it does today. Figure 7.2 posits what the river level may have looked like during the late Prehispanic period. Interestingly, the distribution of sites near the river illustrated that no Prehispanic occupations seems to occur under the water level identified on the river banks. There may have been evidence of Prehispanic activities and occupation under thick sediment deposits from these annual floods; alternatively, these floods may have washed out nearby sites.

Figure 7.1. Old eroded river bank (the black arrows show old river level) (Photograpgh by Emiliano Gallaga).

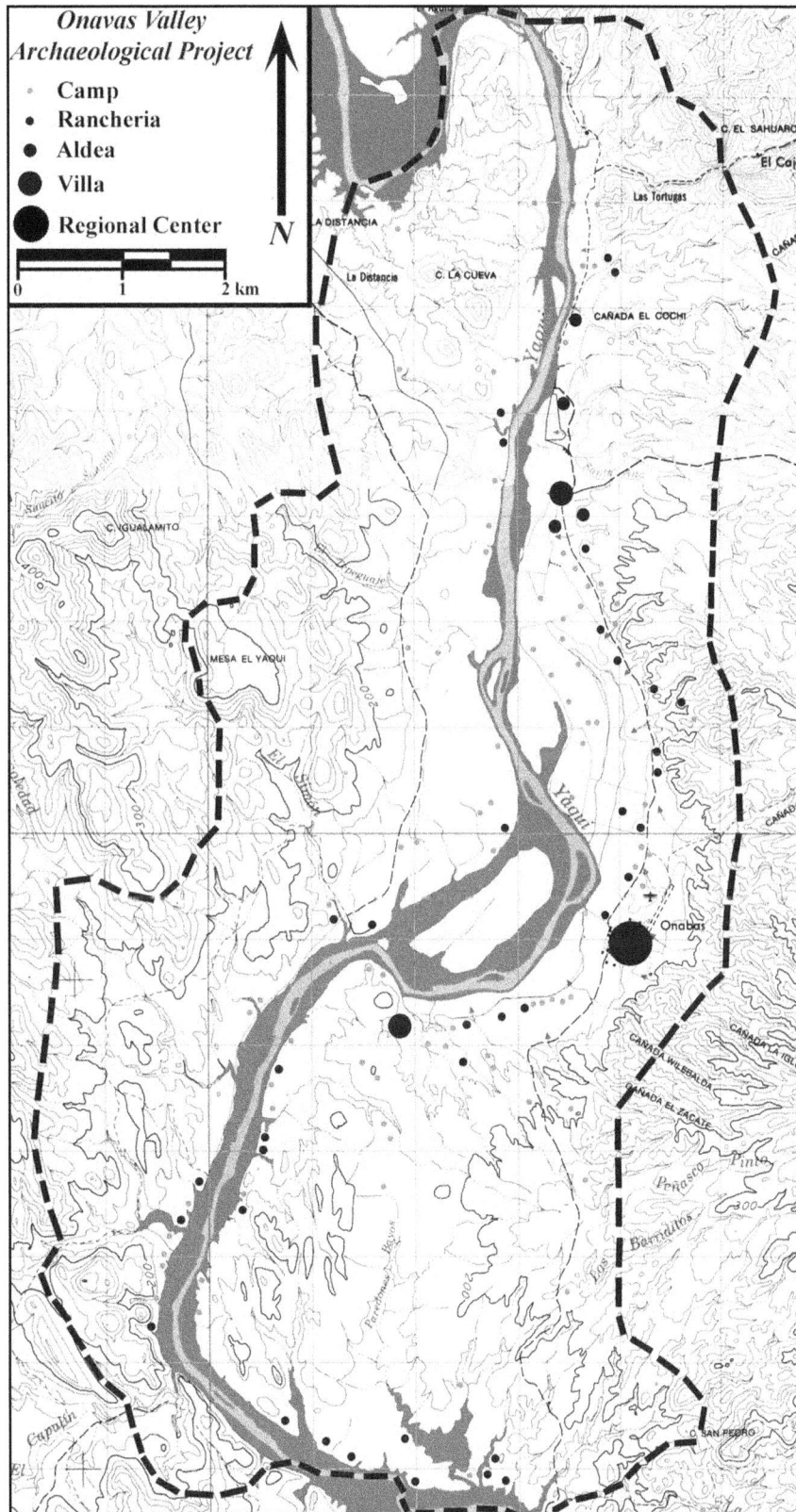

Figure 7.2. Distribution of prehispanic sites and the water level of the Yaqui River at that time.

SETTLEMENT ECOLOGY/SETTLEMENT PATTERN

Of the three analytical components of landscape analysis, settlement ecology/settlement pattern is perhaps the most accessible due to its close relation to settlement patterns and systems approaches (Anschuetz et al. 2001; Ashmore and Knapp 1999; Potter 2004). Settlement ecology envisions landscape as the product of a dynamic interaction between the physical characteristics of the natural environment and the technical, social, and economic necessities of human beings, with an emphasis on, "archaeologically observed patterns of land use, occupation, transformation over time, ... essential subsistence resources, [and] other raw material needed for physical comfort and health, and items for trade or exchange" (Anschuetz et al. 2001:177).

In spite of intense modern agriculture, ranching, mining activities, construction of communication networks (highways, roads, and electric lines), and amateur pot-hunting or gold mining activities in the region, a total of 122 new sites and eight isolated projectile points were recorded in the SON P quadrant during the field work of the OVAP. Adding those to the four sites recorded by the PRO-CEDE project in 1998, a total of 126 sites have been recorded for the Onavas Valley. Of the 126 sites, 117 sites were identified as Prehispanic, including four Archaic sites and one paleontological sites (Figure 7.2). The last consists of the remains of a horse (*Equus* sp.) without the presence of any apparent human association. In addition, six historic sites were recorded, two of which also had Prehispanic occupations as well.

Settlements

Some have thought that these were mountain people because their land is surrounded by gentle hills and mountains, but this is not the case. Their pueblos and cultivated fields are situated in level valleys and all the inhabitants are very peaceable (Father Pedro Méndez letter (1628) in Pérez de Ribas 1999:413).

Site distribution in the Onavas Valley proved relatively homogenous. More than 119 sites were encountered on elevated areas in the valley or on the alluvial plain near the Río Yaqui, as expected from the ethnohistorical data. The remaining seven sites were recorded just above the 200 m above sea level mark. Of these, an Archaic camp was found on top of a hill. Of all 126 sites, only one site was recorded in the mountains more than 3 km away from the river (rock art site SON P:10:5, which is not shown on the research area map as it is located outside of it). This site had been recorded by the PROCEDE project, years prior to the OVAP. Though showing the potential for future research, this site falls outside the OVAP research region and no attempts were made to locate it or others like it in its vicinity or elsewhere in the high mountains.

The physiographic setting of the Onavas Valley is rather narrow, bounded by the Sierra Madre Occidental to the east and by very narrow mountain passes to the north and south. As a result the short tree forest floodplain is the optimal zone for settlement of Prehispanic communities due to the abundant location of primary resources such as water (the Río Yaqui), food (agriculture land), and fuel. One hundred twenty-two sites were located in this area. Above the short tree forest, the thorn forest ecological zone is less suitable for settlement due to its broken terrain and lack of water sources, with the exception of arroyos. Only three sites were found in this area—all of them were small camp sites. The next suitable area is the oak forest high up in the Sierra Madre Occidental. Local informants mentioned the presence of archaeological sites, but the

OVAP has not confirmed these. Father Pedro Méndez also made similar observations of the settlement pattern in these regions on his trip to the Sisibotari (Opata) Indian communities early in the seventeenth century (Pérez de Ribas 1999:413).

At first glance, it appears the Prehispanic communities settled along the river on terraces just above the floodplain, but still close to the river and arable lands in the Onavas Valley. This Prehispanic settlement pattern is consistent with those identified in other river drainages in Sonora, such as the Río Sonora and Rio Bavispe in northern Sonora or the Río Cuchujaqui and Río Mayo in southern Sonora (Doolittle 1988; Douglas and Quijada 2004a, 2004b; Pailes 1972).

Of the 126 archaeological sites recorded in the Onavas Valley, 32 sites were located on the west bank of the river and the rest (94) were located on the east bank. This suggests that both banks of the river were used during Prehispanic times, although the east bank appears to have had a greater number of settlements, with almost three times as many. In addition, the east bank of the river is better suited for flood farming than the elevated west bank. It is possible that this uneven distribution of Prehispanic communities may have been what missionaries later described as Nébomes Altos and Nébomes Bajos in Colonial records describing the communities settled in Onavas during the late seventeenth century (Pérez de Ribas 1999:401). The Jesuits mentioned, however, that the Prehispanic communities on the west side were located high up in the mountains, not along the river bank.

In the absence of a firm local chronology or regional ceramic seriated typology prior to the current project, it was a challenge to establish whether the Prehispanic sites in the Onavas Valley were contemporaneous or not. Initial analyses of ceramic and other materials seem to illustrate that at least six sites are likely to be historic, at least 117 sites likely belong to the Prehispanic period dating to around A.D. 800-1500, four sites date to the Archaic (6000-200 B.C.), and one to the late Pleistocene (12,000-10,000 B.P.).

Many of the sites had temporarily mixed material assemblages due to destruction by mechanized agriculture activities. For example, SON P:10:101 (Figure 7.3) had seed jar (tecomate) sherds that are considered to be an early ceramic vessel form in association with a possible Paleoindian point, late local and non-local decorated ceramic material, and historic material as well. It is possible that Prehispanic communities re-used optimal habitation areas again and again due to the lack of flat areas in the valley suitable for habitation above the floodplain and for farm lands. Only excavating key sites could hope to clarify this hypothetical scenario and examine if early material underlies the late Prehispanic record.

One of the reasons for choosing to do a full-coverage systematic pedestrian survey of the core of the Onavas Valley was to be able to maximize the diversity of the sites found to allow a comprehensive landscape analysis of the region. For the purpose of this analysis, the historic (n = 4), the Archaic (n = 4), and the paleontological (n = 1) sites will be excluded, leaving 117 Prehispanic sites. Of those, 75 sites were identified as camp sites while the remaining 42 sites were identified as residential settlements (see Figure 7.4).

Camp Sites

For the sake of analysis, I added the eight isolated projectile points recorded in the area to the total number of camp sites, yielding a total of 83 camps (Figure 7.5). From those, eight sites were identified as camp type 1 (9.5 percent); 53 as type 2 (65.5 percent); two as type 3 (2.5 percent); 16 as type 4 (19 percent); and three as type 5 (3.5 percent) (see pp. 47 for

Figure 7.3 SON P:10:101 (Photograph by Emiliano Gallaga).

camp site type description). The geographical distribution of camp sites illustrate that all the sites identified with farming activities were located in the floodplain. Food gathering activities were located on the foothills, just above the floodplain. Although more than two clay or stone resource areas were identified, only two had archaeological material associated with them. Those sites were located less than a day walking distance from their most proximal settlements. Isolated projectile points and pot-bursts events were recorded throughout the research area indicating possible hunting areas and trails. In all, the camp sites indicated that numerous activities were performed outside the residential settlements, mostly between the floodplain and the nearby hills.

Rancherías/Households

Only 36 sites were identified as rancherías/ households (Figure 7.5). These sites were identified by a combination of features, such as the presence of residential structures, site area, and/or material assemblage. As seen in Appendix I, some of the ranchería sites did not have residential structures but the artifacts were widely distributed over a large area of the ground surface, and the high density and diversity of archaeological materials suggested subsurface residential contexts. Figure 7.2 illustrates that ranchería sites were located along the valley on the floodplain on both sides of the Río Yaqui, most likely associated with farming activities.

Aldeas/Hamlets

Only four sites were identified as aldeas/hamlets, SON P:6:4, SON P:6:5, SON P:10:03 and SON P:10:56 (See Appendix I and II), all of them recorded on the northern portion of the valley. Those sites were identified as aldeas mostly by site area, presence and number of residential structures, and a high density of archaeological material. Figure 7.2 illustrates that all the aldeas were located only on the east side of the river, as expected.

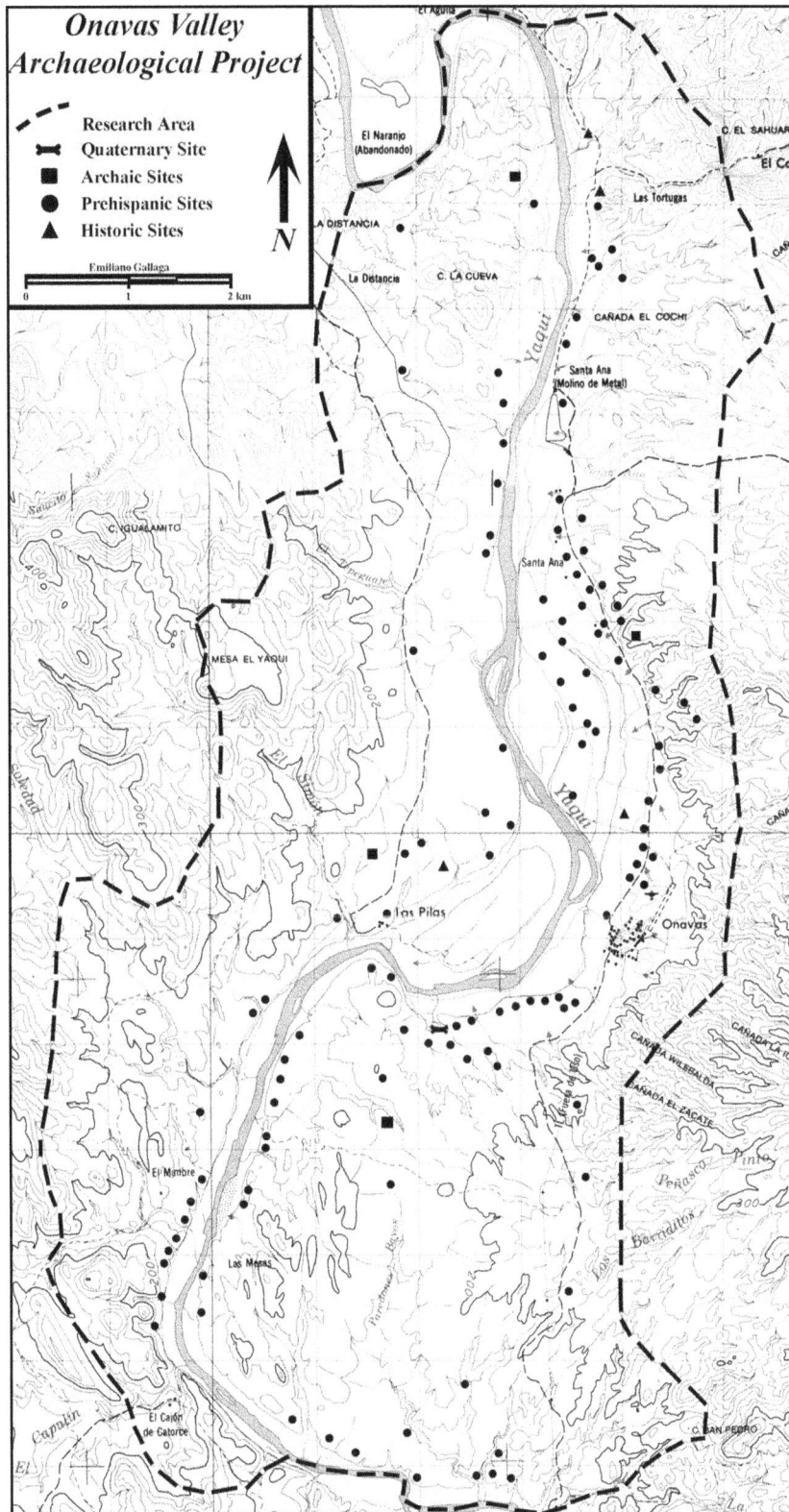

Figure 7.4. Geographical distribution of sites by period.

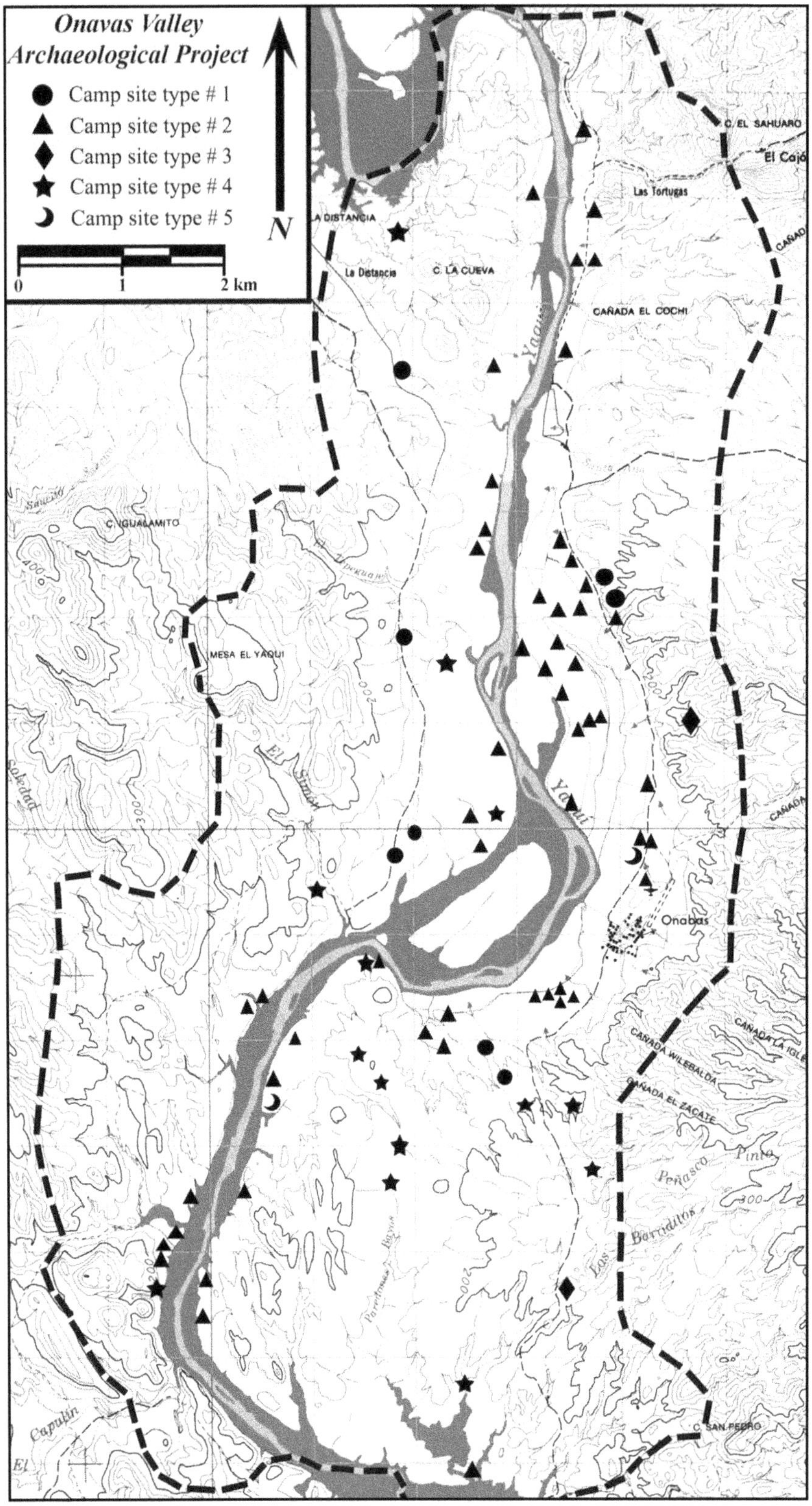

Figure 7.5. Camp site geographical distribution.

Villages

Of all the sites recorded, only two had the characteristics needed to be considered villages: SON P:10:12 and SON P:10:70. (see Figure 7.6) The main characteristic that distinguished these sites from the rest was the presence of public architecture: on SON P:10:12 (a possible earth mound) and on SON P:10:70 (a possible stone altar and a plaza). The locations of villages was distinct from that of the aldeas in the valley. SON P:10:12 was located in the northern area surrounded by aldeas, while SON P:10:70 was located in the southern area of the valley.

Regional Center

No regional center was recorded in the survey. Some evidence does point to the possibility that the location of the Onavas town corresponds to the Prehispanic regional center of the Nébome communities, however. Ethnographic research suggests that part of the name, Onavas, was a Nébome word (Pérez de Ribas 1999:389) meaning "place for collecting salt" (Pennington 1980:7). This description is suggestive of a pre-existing Indian community of importance (Pennington 1980:352). Materially speaking, in and around the Onavas town, considerable archaeological material has emerged, not only on the surface of patios but as part of the mixing adobe walls from the old houses and even at the mission structure. In addition, the stone used for the base of the mission church and some old houses in town are similar to those slab stones used for construction in some of the Prehispanic sites, such as SON P:10:70 and SON P:10:102 (see Figure 7.7). It is conceivable that a Prehispanic stone structure was robbed for the mission foundation or for its construction, which was a common practice in Colonial times. Normally, mission churches or "cabeceras" were located the largest or most important Indian community of a region to take advantage of local human labor, infrastructure,

Figure 7.6. SON P:10:70 (Photograph by Emiliano Gallaga).

Figure 7.7. SON P:10:102 (Photograph by Emiliano Gallaga).

and natural resources already exploited by the locals (Olavarria 1995; Ortega 1996; Radding 1997). Furthermore, there are several small sites located just outside of Onavas town to the north, which could be the remains of a northern compound of the regional center. In addition, the cemetery mound is also located in this cluster. The quantity and diversity of material remains collected and identified from this mound, such as high quantities of marine shell, local and non-local decorated wares, and turquoise, could also be related to the higher ranking position of this particular area or a site (e.g. the Onavas regional center). In addition on the Ibarra expedition Obregón mentioned the town of Oera, which Reff (1991:218) equated

with Onavas, as a large town with more than 1000 excellently grouped flat-roofed houses (Hammond and Rey 1928:108).

Oral history provides additional support for the presence of a regional center here. In the early 1940s, Giddings recorded several Yaqui oral histories of myths and legends. One in particular, "War between the Yaquis and the Pimas," states:

> The Pimas wanted permission
> to borrow the image of San Juan
> from the Yaquis in order that they
> might carry it to their pueblo, that
> is, to Onabachi (Giddings 1993:91).

This narrative illustrates that the town of Onabachi, which was most likely Onavas, was indeed a Pima or a Nébome town of enough importance to bear the religious image and still retains a relevant place in the memory of their neighbors, the Yaquis. In addition, Pérez de Ribas provides another clue on the subject, when he mentions that:

> The Nébome advised the Nure that this could be achieved more easily if they reduced themselves to a principal place (which they did), abandoning their rancherías (Pérez de Ribas 1999:399).

The comment suggested that the Nébome were concentrated in an already existing principal community, such as Onavas, to obtain the services of missionaries. Furthermore, the Onavas town is located on an elevated area at the center of the valley where the best arable land is found. Most likely, every year seasonal flooding of the river irrigated and fertilized the surrounding lands. In addition, its elevated position offers a good view of both river banks lending further credence to the idea that the Nébome regional center was located at the same location of today's *cabecera*, the modern Onavas town.

Residential Structures

> The Nébome lived along the banks of good flowing streams. Their houses were better and more permanent than those of other nations because they had walls made of large mud adobes and were covered with flat earthen roofs (Pérez de Ribas 1999:391).

A total of eight types of habitation structures were identified in the research area. Six of them were Prehispanic features, of these, five were surface structures and one was a "pit house." The Prehispanic habitation structure types were:

1) Alignment of river cobbles, one cobble in width with spaces in between cobbles (n = 52).

2) Alignment of stone slabs, one slab in width with spaces in between slabs (n = 4).

3) Double alignment of river cobbles without spacing between them (n = 4).

4) Stone platform (n = 3).

5) Stone circle (n = 1 recorded structure).

And the "pit house" type is a:
6) Rectangular depression composed of thick river cobble walls (n = 2).

In addition to these Prehispanic types, a seventh type includes historic structures (n = 5). The eighth type (n = 12) was added later during analysis to describe features identified in the field as possible Prehispanic habitation structures but that failed the test of unambiguous identification in later analysis. Adding all the habitation structures together, a grand total of 83 habitation structures were recorded by the OVAP, divided over the eight types of structures (Table 7.1).

It is important to mention that the actual number of houses in the valley could be much higher, taking into account the destruction of sites and the possibility that not all the Prehispanic habitation units were made of adobe and stone foundations. If houses were of the ramada or *bajareque* type it is almost impossible to find remains on the surface and difficult to find remains via excavation. Ramadas and bajareques are structures made of perishable material, had a use life of 10 to 20 years according to local knowledge, depending on maintenance,

| | | | | | | | | | Table 7.1. Habitation structure type distribution |

Site	# 1	# 2	# 3	# 4	# 5	# 6	# 7	# 8	Total
SON P:6:3			1						1
SON P:6:4	4								4
SON P:6:5	13						1	3	17
SON P:6:8	1								1
SON P:6:16	1								1
SON P:6:18							1		1
SON P:6:19							1		1
SON P:10:2								3	3
SON P:10:3								1	1
SON P:10:7								1	1
SON P:10:14			1						1
SON P:10:17								1	1
SON P:10:27			2						2
SON P:10:40								2	2
SON P:10:55	3								3
SON P:10:56	10								10
SON P:10:70		2		1					3
SON P:10:73	6								6
SON P:10:78	4					1			5
SON P:10:80								1	1
SON P:10:83						1			1
SON P:10:88	3								3
SON P:10:90	1								1
SON P:10:93				1	1				2
SON P:10:98	2								2
SON P:10:101	4						2		6
SON P:10:102		2		1					3
Total	52	4	4	3	1	2	5	12	83

and were thus very ephemeral.

Amsden (1928:45) and later Pailes (1994b:118) characterize the habitation structures of the Río Sonora tradition as a double alignment stone foundation, similar to the third type described for the Onavas Valley Prehispanic communities (see Figure 7.8). However, Doolittle (1988:25) mentions that habitation structures at the Río Sonora region also appear with one alignment stone foundation. This particular construction technique is also very common throughout eastern and northwest Sonora, along the Sierra Madre Occidental, western Chihuahua, and northern Durango, making it difficult to tie this structure into a particular archaeological tradition without further material association or research (Douglas and Quijada 2004a, 2004b; Newell and Gallaga 2004).

Currently that type of habitation structure, identified as Type # 1 for the Onavas Valley, is the most abundant (n = 52). Pit houses, clas-

sified as Type # 6, were also recorded in the Río Sonora region by Doolittle (1988:27-28) and according to his research are believed to be an early style of dwelling. Types # 2 and # 4 (one slab stone alignment and stone platform respectively) have not been reported before in the Sonora archaeological record and may exemplify a local variant with northern Sinaloa similarities. Stone slab structures, which resemble those found at the Onavas Valley, were recently found and are currently under excavation in the Río Fuerte Valley, northern Sinaloa (John Carpenter personal communication 2005).

In sum, the habitation structures analysis for the Onavas Valley illustrates that structures in the area are consistent with the rest of the Sierra region (Type # 1), but also show similarities with specific archaeological traditions, such as the Río Sonora in Type # 3 and northern Sinaloa in structure Types # 2 and # 4.

With the exception of Type # 8, "unde-

Figure 7.8. Stone house foundation, SON P:10:27 (Photograph by Emiliano Gallaga).

termined," and Type # 6, "pit house," house foundations were normally rectangular in shape with an average area of 20 m². Foundations of the surface structures measured approximately 4 x 5 m, but we also recorded larger houses, measuring 4 x 8 m. House walls were probably made of puddled adobe, stakes-and-brush, or wattle-and-daub, and roofs most likely consisted of earth-covered thatch. Evidence to support such construction methods was encountered at one of the sites where a piece of earth adobe with remains of the wattle was recorded. Furthermore, in spite of the high level of destruction by mechanized agriculture in the research area, some sites appeared to reveal remains of possible melted adobe that may have been from standing adobe structures.

Normally, recorded structures had a single room. Several multiple-room variations were also recorded, such as three rooms in a row at SON P:10:88, an "L" shape room block at SON

P:10:78 (Figure 7.9 and 7.10), and "U" shape room block at SON P:6:5. No material evidence was found for walled enclosures or compounds at these sites, but their absence is also not confirmed. It is important to note that in spite of Colonial accounts describing multiple-storied structures (Hammond and Rey 1940; Nuñez Cabeza de Vaca 1993; Pérez de Ribas 1999), no material evidence was found in the research area to support such descriptions.

Archaeologists use the presence and absence, number, and density of different artifact categories to infer community organization. Small residential sites composed mainly of houses are interpreted as family households associated with agricultural activities, while sites with public/ceremonial architecture are identified as political, economic, and religious centers of some sort (Doolittle 1988).

The same interpretation appears to hold true for the Onavas Prehispanic communities. A

Figure 7.9. SON P:10:88 (Photograph by Emiliano Gallaga).

Figure 7.10. SON P:10:78 (Photograph by Emiliano Gallaga).

settlement pattern characterized by a few, scattered, small sites has been interpreted as a dispersed settlement pattern exhibiting a limited intraregional interaction. On the other hand, if the settlement pattern shows "one large, a few intermediate-sized, and several small settlements, all uniformly spaced" (Doolittle 1988:35) researchers identify this as a formal and structured clustered settlement pattern with a high intra-site interaction (Doolittle 1988; Grove et al. 1976; Johnson 1972).

From the site classification and analysis of the OVAP area, the clustered settlement pattern appears to best fit the Onavas Valley Prehispanic communities. The distribution of Prehispanic sites in the valley suggests that the possible regional center located at the center of it served to connect the rest of the communities in the valley with the help of two secondary sites (villages) through some sort of influence or social assignment. In the northern part of the

valley, three of the four aldeas identified were located around the northern village. This close spatial relationship raises the possibility that this village (SON P:10:12) and two of the closest aldeas (SON P:10:3 and SON P:10:56) were actually one large community, if they were occupied contemporaneously. If that proves to be the case, one large village may have had more influence on this portion of the valley than previously thought. Rancherías were located along the river valley interspersed between the villages and the regional center. The material evidence and geographical characteristics of the area illustrate that the southern rancherías were possibly not engaged in general agricultural activities but in other subsistence strategies, such as agave cultivation, vineyards, and hunting. No aldeas/hamlets were found in the southern portion of the valley, probably due to a lack of large tracts of good arable land there. With the regional hub at the geographical center, surrounding sites could have been reached and controlled in less than a day by walking in any direction from there. The lack of large flat areas for habitation and the competition for farming areas in the valley probably encouraged the nucleation of communities that the OVAP identified.

Following the regional center in the community hierarchy, the OVAP identified two villages (SON P:10:12 and SON P:10:70), both situated on the east side of the river. SON P:10:102 was situated approximately 4 km to the north of the regional center and SON P:10:70 around 2.5 km to the southwest. These two villages, or secondary site types, stand out due to the presence of public/ceremonial structures or features that required communal work for their construction. It is interesting to observe that the village sites are located at both ends of the best arable land in the valley.

Aldeas or hamlets, the next residential site type in the community hierarchy, show an interesting pattern. These sites consisted of habitation units representing more than a nucleated family, but less than roughly 100 community members. Only four were identified (SON P:6:4, SON P:6:5, SON P:10:3, and SON P:10:56, See Appendix I and II), all located in the northern portion of the valley on the east bank of the river. SON P:10:3 and SON P:10:56 were very close to the northern village of SON P:10:12. Due to the destruction of the area it is not possible to say if these three sites were actually a single site or satellite hamlets. Interestingly, no aldeas/hamlets were found at the southern portion of the valley, probably due to a lack of large tracts of good arable land there.

As expected, the smallest residential sites, rancherías/households, were distributed all along the river valley filling the space between the regional center, the villages, and the aldeas/hamlets sites. A total of 36 rancherías/household sites were identified. Two areas in particu-

lar emerged as exhibiting the most rancherías/households in the valley: 1) an area between the two village sites with 18 sites (3 on the west bank and 15 on the east bank) and 2) the south portion of the valley with 8 sites, all on the east bank of the river. As mentioned above, the central portion of the valley contained the best agricultural lands, and in this section of the valley comparatively more sites were located. The material evidence and geographical characteristics of the area illustrate that the southern rancherías/households were possibly not engaged in general agricultural activities but in other subsistence strategies, such as agave cultivation, vineyards, and hunting.

Similar to the distribution of rancherías/households, camp sites were located throughout the river valley on both sides of the river. Including the eight isolated projectile points found by the OVAP, 83 camp sites were identified. Of these, eight (9.5 percent) sites were identified as camp type 1; 53 (65.5 percent) as type 2; two (2.5 percent) as type 3; 16 (19 percent) as type 4; and three (3.5 percent) as type 5. First, as Figure 7.5 illustrates, most camp sites are located close to the river valley. Secondly, 59 sites were recorded on the east bank of the river, while the rest were located on the west bank of the river. The latter suggests that the east side experienced more activity than the west side. Most of the camp sites related to agricultural activities areas are at the center of the valley, between the regional center (Onavas) and the northern village. Camp site type 4 is the most numerous and this type of site is dispersed all over the research area, illustrating that the activities undertaken at this type of site were performed at a certain distance from the communities, especially hunting. In addition, the identification of "pot-burst" areas, or locations of single broken pots, was essential for the identification of possible paths around the research area. More than three ceremonial/ritual activity areas were identified by the

OVAP, but only three were classified as camp sites. Those camps were not in direct contact or association with habitation sites and probably represented more secluded areas, excluding the cemetery mound. One of those sites (SON P:10:5) is not on the map (see Figure 5.1), due to its location far in the hills.

The distribution of Prehispanic sites in the Onavas Valley suggests that the possible regional center located at the center of the valley served to connect the rest of the communities in the valley with the help of two secondary sites (villages) through some sort of influence or social assignment. With the regional hub at the geographical center, surrounding sites could have been reached in less than a day by walking in any direction from it. Rancherías were located along the river valley interspersed between the villages and the regional center. To the north of the valley, three of the four aldeas identified were located around the northern village. This close spatial relationship raises the possibility that this village (SON P:10:12) and two of the closest aldeas (SON P:10:3 and SON P:10:56) were actually one large community, if they were occupied contemporaneously. If that proves to be the case, one large village may have had more influence on this portion of the valley than previously thought. The lack of large flat areas for habitation and the competition for farming areas in the valley probably encouraged the nucleation of communities that the OVAP identified.

Population Density Analysis

Using Colonial data, Pennington postulated that a total of 3,000 Nébomes inhabited the middle Río Yaqui by 1645 (Pennington 1980:34). Later on, Daniel Reff (1991) estimated a population limit for the Upper Nébomes of 20,000 distributed over 90 rancherías in the Onavas, Movas, and Nuri Valleys, just prior to the arrival of Europeans around A.D. 1500. Reff bases his

numbers on Colonial documents, such as the annuas and the Jesuit reports (Guzmán 1615; Pérez de Ribas 1999:393), and also extrapolates his figures based on the decimation of the Indian population after European contact (diseases, warfare, and labor demands). Dividing Reff's number equally among the three areas, the Onavas Valley may have had roughly 6,600 inhabitants.

Although the archaeological remains recorded do not provide clear population figures, particularly in light of the destruction (human and natural) of the archaeological record, the archaeological record still serves as contrast against information gleaned from the Colonial documents. Because Colonial documents often report numbers that are largely exaggerated by their authors to impress their readers, especially colonial authorities in Spain from whom they were seeking support, additional analysis is required to get a better idea of the population density. Consequently, several examples of analysis from neighboring areas will be applied to the Onavas Valley and compared to Reff's calculations. Those analyses estimate potential population from agricultural assessments and settlement data based mainly on house remains (Doolittle 1988; Fish and Fish 1994; Craig 2000).

Some population density studies base population figures on the number of hectares necessary to sustain a family in certain geographical conditions (Doolittle 1988; Fish and Fish 1994). Drawing upon such logical estimations, Fish and Fish (1994) have gained insight into the subsistence requirements for a Piman family. If a family is composed of five members and that live in a similar desert environment like the Onavas Valley such as southern Arizona (where many or most Pima live today), a family requires a minimum of 0.86 ha and can use a maximum of 2.15 ha. Taking into account that today the Onavas Valley has around 1500 ha of canal irrigated and floodwater land (INEGI 1993), the valley itself could have supported a Prehispanic community of 3,488 to 8,720 people. This equation does not include the resources that the Río Yaqui and the surrounding mountains provide. Considering these additional resources, the valley could have reached the population Reff suggests for the Late Prehispanic period.

Other researchers base population density estimates on the residential space or site area of a particular region and use an estimate of 10 persons per hectare to get a figure (Craig 2000:159). The estimated residential space for the Prehispanic sites of the Onavas Valley amounts to a total of more than 415,696 m², a little more than 41.6 ha. That amount represents 6,204 m² of site area per km². Using Craig's calculation, the Onavas Valley was occupied by a total of 416 people.

Taking a different perspective and analytical approach, the material evidence recorded by OVAP shows that 83 houses were recorded in the research area. From that total, 73 were identified as Prehispanic. Assuming for the sake of calculation that all 73 houses were contemporaneous and each served as a family residence for three to six individuals, the valley could have had a population from 228 to 456 persons—a slightly lower, but similar figure to the one acquired with Craig's population estimate. It is important to take into account 1) that the number of houses present at the valley may have been much higher due to the destruction of sites, 2) the possibility that not all Prehispanic habitation units were made with adobe and stone foundations, and 3) the possibility that a single family may occupy more than one residence.

Drawing on different data and using divergent reasoning, two main population density figures result. The first estimate calculated a range of 3,488 to 8,720 people, while the second estimated a range of 228 to 456 persons. The material evidence and the settlement space analysis produced the lower population number diverging considerably from the estimation based on Colonial description and ethno-archaeological reasoning. It is important to keep in mind that the Onavas Valley and the sites throughout this area have suffered a significant degree of destruction from mechanized agriculture.

Thus, the number of habitation structures was likely much higher, resulting in higher population figures. Taking a middle stance between these minimum and maximum figures, an estimation of around 3,000 Nébomes living at the Onavas Valley for the Prehispanic period emerges as a plausible number. The latter is a very rough estimation, however, and must be considered as such. After the Spanish contact, Nébome population reduced drastically. Based on Colonial documents and on nineteenth and twentieth century reports, the Onavas population was reduced to no more than 500 inhabitants after the eighteenth century and that population level has been maintained until today (INEGI 1993; Pennington 1980; Reff 1991).

In terms of number of inhabitants per km², using the estimate of 3,000 people, a figure of 46 Nébomes per km² resulted. On the contrary, if the estimate of 500 inhabitants is used, the figure reaches to 7.5 Nébomes per km². The latter suggests a low population density for the valley, while the former estimate indicates a medium density, which seems more acceptable when taking the number of sites recorded into account, the estimated food resources, and the flat valley surface for habitation and agricultural capacity.

Classification and Distribution of Land Types in the Onavas Valley

A systematic survey uncovers not only the location of a great diversity of archaeological sites, but also possible economic use in the region and the human utilization of the land. Furthermore, a proposed land use distribution by the prehispanic communities of the valley is important. These analyses are based on the archaeological record, the natural environment, and cultural factors.

Arable Land

The ecological conditions of the valley render the floodplain and the floor of large arroyos the most suitable for agricultural activities today. It is likely that the same arable land was used in Prehispanic times. Based on the INEGI database (1994), the ejido of Onavas currently uses a little more than 1500 ha of the valley bottom for agricultural activities, while the rest of the area is used mostly for cattle grazing. Most of the 1500 ha suited for agricultural activities is located at the valley center, 5 km to the north of the Onavas town and 2 km southwest of the valley along the river banks. Small pockets of usable land are located on the west bank to the southwest and at the south end of the valley.

An interesting correlation between the current distribution of arable land and the Prehispanic locations on such land in the Onavas Valley is also evident. More than 90 percent of the Prehispanic sites were located in areas where agricultural activities are currently practiced and it is reasonable to believe that Prehispanic Nébomes used the same areas for agricultural activities. Based on Colonial documents, agriculture was irrigated with overflow in the valley bottom, as well as by canal irrigation from arroyos for areas far from the river (Pennington 1980:154; Pérez de Ribas 1999:289, 328, 413).

This pattern further facilitates a classification of possible arable land during the Prehispanic period. The arable land was divided into primary and secondary arable land (Figure 7.11) based on INEGI data, soil and terrain conditions, access to water, and archaeological

information. Primary arable land corresponds to the area covering the northern to the southwest-central portion of the valley bottom on both sides of the Río Yaqui. Secondary arable lands are located at the northern tip of the valley on either side of the river, the southern end of the valley, and the southwestern portion close to the west and east banks of the river.

Colonial documents emphasize that Prehispanic communities along the Río Yaqui produced at least two crops of maize per year: one main crop after the overflow of the river in summer, and one of less importance in the rainy season. Pérez de Ribas stated:

> When the river rises and overflows, which ordinarily happens almost every year, the fields are irrigated so that summer planting is possible. Rainfall is therefore not needed for their crops to ripen and for them to enjoy abundant harvests. The Indians have already harvested one crop [by the time] the river overflows, which is usually at the beginning of July. This crop is their main harvest, but nevertheless, during the rainy season some of them plant again, although this harvest is of less importance...(Pérez de Ribas 1999:328; words in brackets sic in original).

A similar strategy was practiced in the nearby valley of Sonora (Doolittle 1988) and in Colonial times in the Onavas Valley (Pennington 1980). Hence, it appears likely this strategy worked and was used in the Onavas Valley during Prehispanic times. The Colonial records mention that the main crops in the region were maize, beans, squash, agave, and cotton (Dunnigan 1983; Pennington 1980; Pérez de Ribas 1999:328, 413). Excavation and analysis of botanical remains is necessary to test this information for the Onavas Valley.

Additionally, Colonial documents indi-

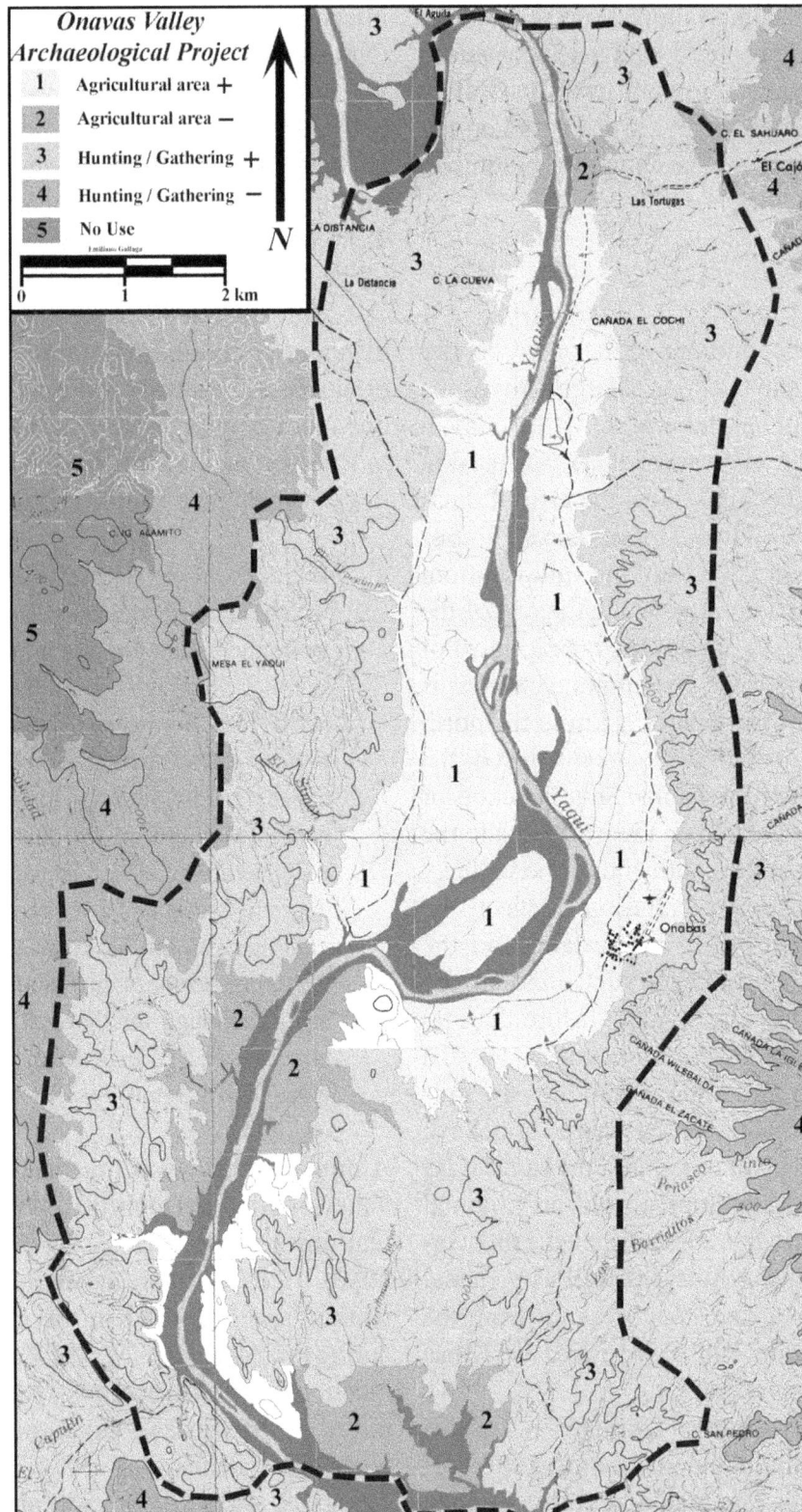

Figure 7.11. Classification and distribution of land types in the Onavas Valley.

cate canals and terraces were used in order to increase arable land (Nuñez Cabeza de Vaca 1993; Pérez de Ribas 1999; Hopkins 1988), as in this report made by Captain Hurdaide on a rescue mission at the Nébome region in 1614:

> They are great farmers and cultivated using irrigation. They manage {their} reservoirs and canals as skillfully as Spanish farmers (Captain Hurdaide letter (1614) in Pérez de Ribas 1999:289).

Father Pedro Méndez also mentions the use of irrigation a few years after the mission of Onavas was established:

> ...these are located in two very fertile valleys that produce maize and various legumes. They skillfully irrigate their fields with fresh and healthful waters drawn from streams... (Father Pedro Méndez letter (1628) in Pérez de Ribas 1999:413).

Only a small section of a likely agricultural terrace was found at site SON P:10:12, indicating the use and presence of such water control techniques in the area. In the 1960s, Pennington mentioned that "a number of drainage ditches are visible in shallow arroyos leading to the Río Yaqui...just north of Onavas" (1980:154). However, none were recorded by the OVAP in 2004.

Within these proposed arable lands, not only farming or crop raising activities, but also agave cultivation and the gathering of wild food, such as prickly pear fruit, cholla bud, mesquite and other leguminous seeds either in the wild or in gardens took place. Pérez de Ribas describes these activities for the Nébomes as:

> In some places with a good lay of land

they had irrigated fields, using ditches to bring the water from their arroyo. In addition to this, they planted next to their houses a vineyard of sorts with a plant that the Spaniards call lechuguilla [*Agave bovicornuta*], because it is similar to leaf lettuce in shape but its leaves are much firmer. It takes one or two years for it to grow and mature. Once it is ripe they cut it and roast the root with a few of the leaves, which serves them as food (Pérez de Ribas 1990:391).

Such activities and gardens have been described in the Colonial documents and by ethnographic accounts as a means to diversify and complement agricultural food resources (Dunnigan 1983; Hopkins 1988; Nabhan 2004; Pennington 1980; Pérez de Ribas 1990). Pennington describes that "the Onavas Pima make much use of fruits and some nuts, which give variety to the rather uninteresting staple foods that, characterize the middle Yaqui country" (1980:221). The identification in the research area of at least one agricultural terrace, several possible hearths, and agave knives, may indeed confirm the description provided by Pérez de Ribas. Such activities appear to have taken place at the valley bottom. Several sites (SON P:10:27, SON P:10:28, and SON P:10:84, See Appendix I and II) seems to exhibit more agave cultivation and processing other farming activities, given the amount of hearths and possible agave pits recorded. Their location on poor arable land locations may further serve to confirm these horticultural uses. In the 1960s, Pennington described the Onavas gardens and their cultigens as (Pennington 1980:165):

> Plants that are source of edible fruits and tubers, condiments used in the preparation of meat and vegetables dishes, leaves and stems used in the preparation of medicines or refreshing drinks, dye-

stuffs, quelites, and ornamental plants appear in what may be described as a jumble of vegetation in virtually all of the gardens maintained by Onavas Pima.

His detailed report of the plant diversity in those gardens illustrates that not only edible plants were cultivated, but also medicinal and ornamental species. In neighboring Lower Pima Indian communities, similar ethnographic reports were made (Dunnigan 1983; Spicer 1983). The Nébomes may indeed have had similar gardens.

Hunting and Gathering

Aside from farming activities, hunting and gathering produced a good percentage of the food resources of the Prehispanic Onavas communities. Pérez de Ribas (1999:391) mentions that the Nébome, "hunted the game that abounds in their montes, especially deer. They are very skillful in shooting these, as well as birds of the air, which are plentiful." Also, around and beyond the arable lands, the gathering of other types of resources, such as clay, wood, or stone, were identified archaeologically. Similar to the arable land, these areas were divided into primary and secondary hunting and gathering areas based on distance to river or water sources, altitude, different ecosystems, and archaeological evidence, such as isolated projectile points associated with hunting activities (Figure 7.11).

In these areas today, it is still possible to hunt deer, javelina, rabbits, hares, rats, and turkeys. At higher altitudes, antelope and bighorn sheep can still be found, and puma, jaguar, wild cat, and black bear were probably hunted also for their hides (Dunnigan 1983; Pennington 1980; Pérez de Ribas 1999). Such hides were reported in the Colonial documents to have used as insignias for war chiefs or elite community members (Pérez de Ribas 1999:329).

In fact, Colonial documents emphasize that the Nébome nation was well known for its use of deer hides, as deer were abundant in their montes (Hopkins 1988:22; Pérez de Ribas 1999:391-392). Pérez de Ribas describe local dress as:

In their dress [the Nébomes] are the best attired of all the nations in Sinaloa. This was due to the fact that they had a large number of deer hides, which they knew how to tan to make very good, durable buckskin. These serve the woman as covering, in the manner of skirts. They are very long that they drag on the ground…The young women also decorated these buckskins with red ocher. They covered their upper torsos with mantas woven from cotton or fibers from another plant such as agave (Pérez de Ribas 1999:391-392).

Also, Cabeza de Vaca (1993) chronicles that about 400 deer hearts were offered to his expedition on their journey down to Sinaloa by the Indians in a community from this general region. Pennington (1980) also describes hunting these animals, the hunting techniques, and the uses for these animals by the Onavas Pima around the twentieth century.

In addition to the farming lands and community gardens, local residents obtained other resources, such as wood from the nearby forest, clay from hills and streams, and stone. Clay deposits were observed in several places throughout the area, especially at eroded streams and nearby hills. Pennington describes that clay used by the Onavas Pima was gathered "from veins located east of Onavas" (1980:312). One of those veins was used by the OVAP members for a ceramic workshop with Raymundo Navarro, a local contemporary Onavas amateur potter, in 2004. In terms of the acquisition of stone, one quarry from where the masonry stone for the construction of the mission church may have been taken was identified. The stone quarry is located about 1 km southwest of the Onavas town. This quarry might also have been used in Prehispanic times. Although no Prehispanic material was found nearby, several sites were identified in its immediate vicinity (SON P:10:57, SON P:10:58, SON P:10:59, SON P:10:60, SON P:10:63, and SON P:10:64, See Appendix I and II).

In addition, the Río Yaqui itself must be included in this category of hunting and gathering, due to all the freshwater resources available for collection and use in addition to the water, such as fish, freshwater shell, river cobbles, and reeds or water plants. Colonial documents mention that Indians in general practiced a great deal of fishing, not only at the open ocean, but also alone the rivers as a complementary food resource (see Figure 6.10). Pérez de Ribas (1999:85), states that the Indians, "fish with nets…some fish with bow and arrow." Although the comment is not related directly to the Nébome nation, possible fishing net sinkers collected and the presence of fish bones at the sites reveals the practice of this activity in the Río Yaqui by the Nébomes (see Figure 6.7 and 6.11). Similar information was gathered by Pennington (1980) at the end of the 1960s.

Although no material data was collected in this regard, Colonial documents mention the domestication of animals such as turkeys and/or chickens by the Nébome communities (Captain Hurdaide letter (1614) in Pérez de Ribas 1999:289). Dogs also are a possibility due to some canine teeth collected at the sites. Dog remains were found in archaeological record in Huatabampo communities (Alvarez 1990:70).

Unused Land

Another category to consider in terms of land use concerns those pockets of land that apparently lack a particular use, reveal no significant material record, or where the activities performed fail to leave an indicative material record. For the valley, "unused land" corresponds mostly to areas located above the 300 m mark (Figure 7.11). This distinction was based on local knowledge confirming a lack of archaeological material at these areas (not verified by the OVAP), a lack of water sources, problems of accessibility, and rugged terrain. It is important to note that the "unused land" category does not imply that the Nébomes never frequented those areas. Rather, it means that use was not as frequent as that in other areas of the valley or failed to preserve an obvious archaeological record in the material record. Of course, the same can be said for the other land categories as well. Hunting and gathering may have been pursued in the agricultural areas and vice versa. The land classification merely serves to indicate that a particular activity was the most persistent or main activity performed on that land.

Trails/Paths

> It must be pointed out that even though they were two hundred leagues from their own lands and were traveling through territory with deep gorges and mountains that were often uninhabited, they never got lost or perished (Pérez de Ribas 1999:175).

The Onavas Valley is rather narrow, enveloped by the Sierra Madre Occidental to the east and by very narrow mountain passes to the north and south. From such geographic characteristics, there are not many ways to get around and out of the valley. Thanks to the systematic survey of the research area, several possible Prehispanic paths are been proposed. Some of them were identified by the presence of archaeological material, such as "pot-burst" events along clear narrow paths. Others may have been destroyed by modern dirt roads and the train tracks, and few other possibilities are speculation at most. Figure 7.12 outlines a series of paths around as well as leading in and out of the valley.

First, in the central portion, the flat valley bottom permitted access between the different sites and activity areas without noticeable obstacles, but most trails have been between the northern communities and the regional centers on both sides of the river bank.

Secondly, two trails were identified beyond the central valley bottom, at the southern portion on the east bank of the river. One path ran between the river and the foothills connecting the southern bottom communities with those on the south-central portion of the valley. The second path started near the regional center, cut closer to the hills, and later joined the Río Yaqui at the bottom, exiting the valley in the direction of the southern portion of today's state of Sonora. By following this path along the Río Nuri a traveler eventually could reaches the Río Mayo and the coast.

Thirdly, on the west bank, on the southern portion of the valley, two more paths were identified. One path ran up to the mountains passing along the perennial water source now known as El Obispo. On this perennial stream, site SON P:10:5 is located, which is the only rock art recorded in the area to date. According to local informants, by following the El Obispo stream into the mountains one arrives at cliff dwellings. This information remains to be verified, but might indicate that this trail was used to cross the west mountains and thus arrive at the coast. Although the Colonial documents refrain from mentioning where the Seris that arrived in the valley for trade departed from, this trail may very well have served these groups as the access route to the valley. The second trail could have followed the river course downstream and eventually

reached the Yaqui communities and the coast. Probably the same trail used by the early Spanish expeditions.

In the northern portion of the valley, on the east side of the river another set of paths are located. One trail extends from the river up into the east to the Sierra using the Las Tortugas stream as a natural pass between the valley and the mountains. Following that direction, the Sisibotari area may be reached as well as the upper Sierra Madre Occidental region. The second trail follows the river course north and connects the Onavas Valley with the Tonichi Valley, which is part of the Upper Nébome region, and further north with the Opatas.

Finally, a single path was distinguished on the west side of the river in the northern portion of the valley. This trail cuts between the river and the foothills following the river's course north out of the valley. Not far away from this location, to the northwest, a natural pass in the mountains exists that connects this inner valley with the coastal plains. This could have served as another possible Seri route into the Onavas Valley.

The identification of some probable paths suggest that at the interior of the valley all Prehispanic communities were connected, while other paths could be trails that served to connect the valley with neighboring regions outside of it, such as the Seri region, the Huatabampo area, the west and northern Sierra, and the Opata region. As the archaeological materials indicated, the area received considerable amounts of non-local material, such as marine shell, Chihuahua polychrome, and turquoise. Considering these observations, the Onavas Valley was not isolated and had some regional and extra-regional interaction.

Ritual Landscape

Anschuetz et al. (2001:178) define ritual land-

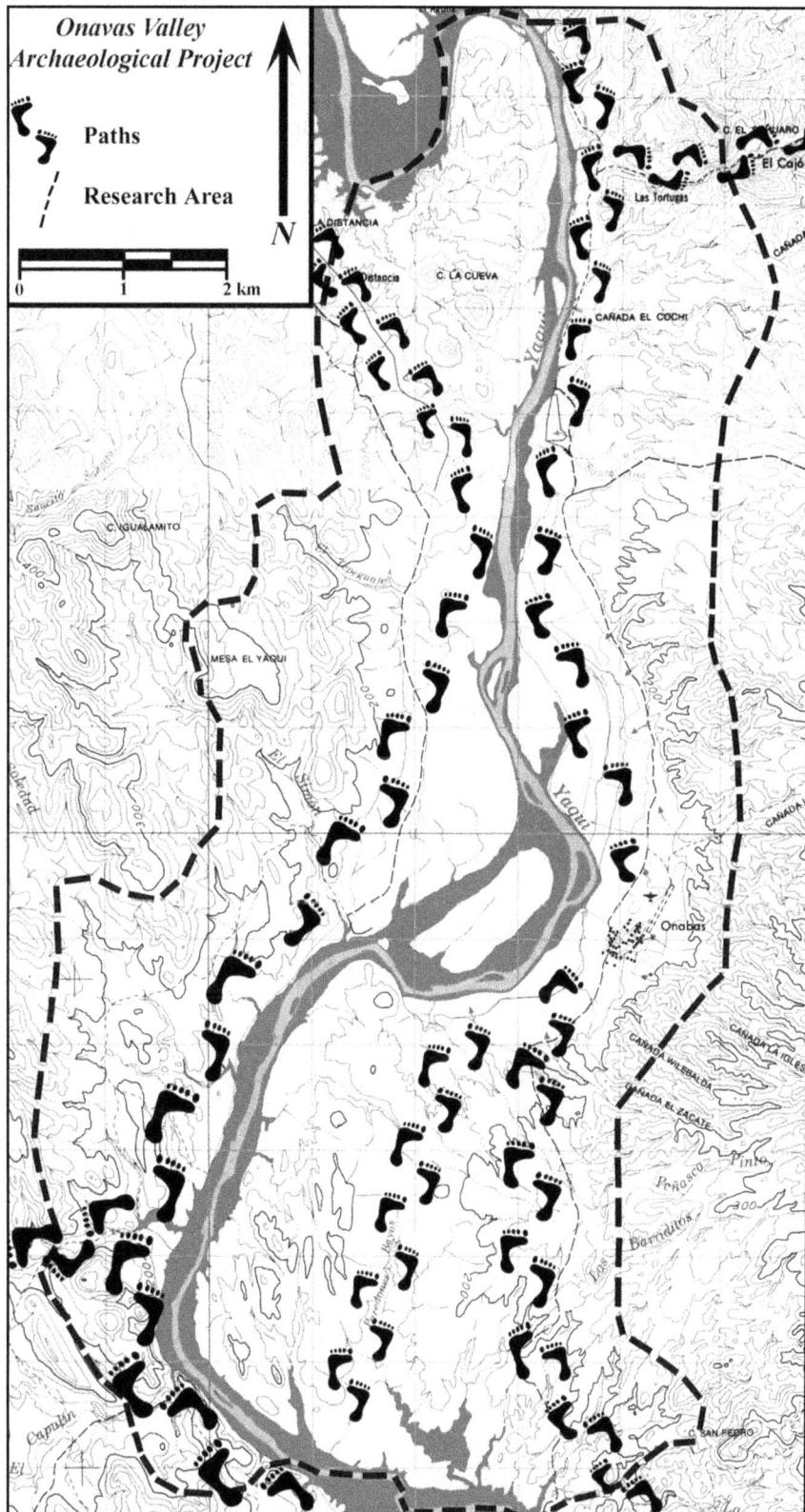

Figure 7.12. Identified trails at the Onavas Valley.

scape as the results of "stereotyped actions, including specific acts and sequences of acts, that represent the socially prescribed orders by which communities define, legitimize, and sustain their occupation of their traditional homelands." Even more so than in settlement ecology or settlement pattern, human agency and cultural knowledge are factors in the construction of ritual landscape, both of a material and imagined nature (Dobres and Robb 2000; Earle 1997; Feld and Basso 1996; Yoffee et al. 1999). The sequence of acts, such as ceremonies, rituals, or feasts, creates a social memory that enhances community affiliation and integration among members of a community and between different communities that may or may not have a political structure to bond them (Potter 2004; Rappaport 1979), such as the Yaqui communities (Radding 1997; Spicer 1983, 1992, 1994). Basso explains that traditional wisdom often is tied to places, inscribing the landscape with history, legend, knowledge, and power that help to structure activities and organize relationships (Basso 1996). In other words (Anschuetz et al. 2001:178):

> Ethnohistorically known groups have full ritual calendars and a rich cosmology that structure, organize, and inform on much of their landscape, which community members perceive and with which they interact.

The importance of these activities and continual increase in knowledge might easily lead to the construction of public architecture (constructed landscape). In some cases, the repetition and reuse of a specific area to perform such activities may result in significant or substantial archaeological remains to be associated to a particular ritual landscape (Anschuetz et al. 2001; Ashmore and Knapp 1999). Such material remains may take the form of "public buildings, monuments, squares or plazas, petro-

glyphs or pictographs, and various vernacular markers" (Anschuetz et al. 2001:178).

Natural or conceptual elements of the landscape may also serve as markers, even without the addition of any significant material culture; such elements may include rivers, mountains, caves, forests, water sources, or peaks (Ashmore and Knapp 1999; Feld and Basso 1996; see Figure 7.5). However, such markers are difficult to identify archaeologically as ritual spaces without the presence of ethnohistorical information. The natural markers identified by the OVAP were based mostly on ethnographic data from neighboring groups, and on how they interact with their landscape, as well as from ethnohistorical accounts from rituals.

The OVAP recorded material evidence for public and/or ceremonial architecture. To date, these features are the ones that shape our fragmentary understanding of the ritual landscape. A brief description of them follows.

Stone Altar

Two stone altars were recorded. One at SON P:10:70, identified as the southern village, This structure was identified as an altar on top of a small hill, and consists of two stone slab platforms. The lower one measures 8 x 6 m in area by 0.50 m high and the second upper one measures 3 x 3 m in area by 0.50 m high, using the slope of the hill as a base (Figure 7.13). No archaeological artifacts were found on or near this feature. The altar was made of local stone from the surrounding hills and dry laid as no remains of any type of mortar was encountered. Its orientation appears relevant because of its alignment with the higher peak of the Sierra on the east side of the valley. Although the OVAP was not able to confirm this, the Sierra Madre Occidental peaks may have been used as astronomical markers. From the location of this feature, the entire site and the central valley

Figure 7.13. El Altar, SON P:10:70 (Photograph by Emiliano Gallaga).

can be observed.

The second altar was found at SON P:6:10, identified as a ranchería. This is smaller than the first and is located on the southwest portion of the site above the river. This feature was made of two layers of river cobbles, the first 3 x 1.50 m in area by 0.25 m high and the second of 1 x 1 m in area by 0.25 m high. Several plain wares sherds were associated with this feature. Considering the difference in size and manufacture, this feature may have served as a family or household altar as opposed to a public altar, like the one described for SON P:10:70 site.

Although Colonial documents frequently mention sorcery, idolatry, ceremony and rituals among the Indians in this region, they provide very little description of the rituals or details about them. Regardless, Catholic priests mention the used of stone idols and altars at the hills near by the communities. On this subject Pérez de Ribas (1999: 189, 246, 236, 494, 495) mentions the use of stone altars and stone idols among the Indian communities on the Sierra Madre Occidental, and in particular, that "some of these idols they erect in the form of altars or shrines that consist of piled-up stones and dirt" (1999:495).

Plaza

A possible open plaza was identified on the northside of SON P:10:70. The distribution of the surface material and the location of the domestic and public/ceremonial structures around a flat open area to the north of the site suggest that the area could have been used as an open plaza. Notably, a good view of the altar exists from this location. Colonial documents mention the use of plazas and the performance or speeches of chiefs or caciques from house roofs to Indians congregated in open places (Pérez de Ribas 1999:276). Similar performances could have take place at these architectural features.

Earth Mound

A small earthen mound was recorded at SON P:10:12. This site was identified as the northern village. The mound is the first recorded in this area (see Figure 7.14). The feature measured 16 x 7 m in area by 2.5 m high, and consists of packed earth. It was likely covered by large river cobbles, as some still covered the ground surface on the west side.

Unfortunately, disturbance by human and animal activities have succeeded in systematically destroying the site and only a fraction of the cobbles appear to remain in situ. Some sherds and flake materials were found in association with the mound, but the absence of a clear pattern prohibits the determination of a particular use or activity. However, apart from all the evidence to support a Prehispanic origin or manufacture, it is possible that this earth mound forms part of the activities associated with the construction of a small modern irrigation canal. In 1999, ranchers poured a small cement irrigation ditch. Regrettably, nobody from the locality could confirm or deny the mound's possible modern construction or pro-

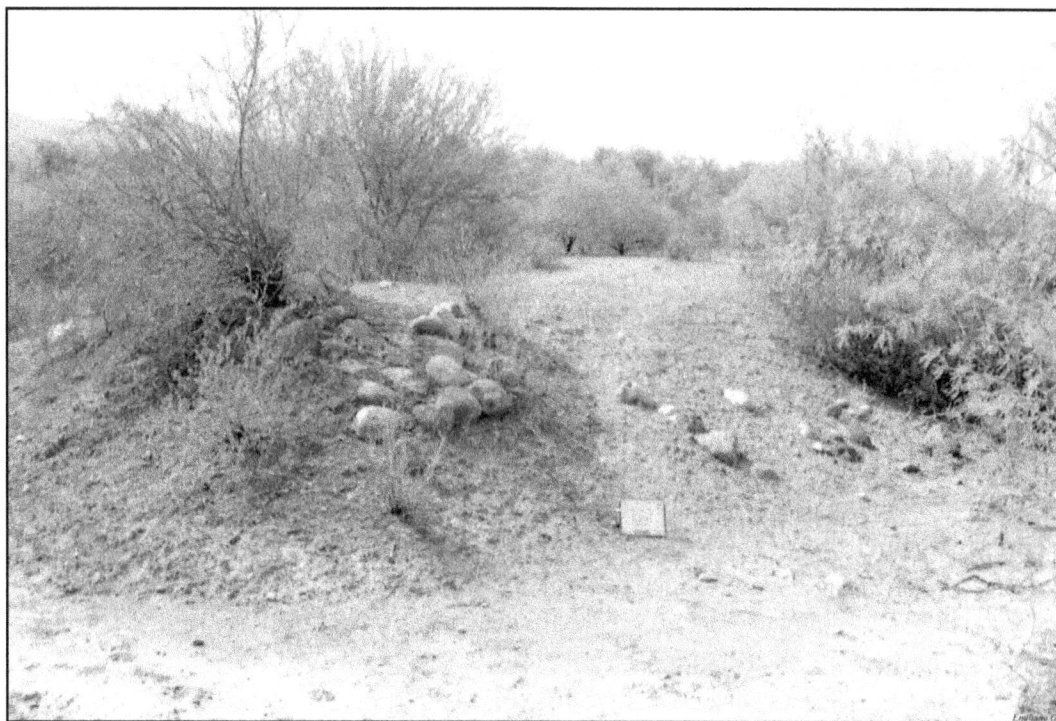

Figure 7.14. Possible Platform mound, SON P:10:12 (Photograph by Emiliano Gallaga).

vide any other relevant information regarding its origins. I should note, however, that the concrete canal ends about 50 m south of the mound. In addition to this earthen mound, the remains of an agriculture terrace more than 100 m long was found on the alluvial plain, just 50 to 60 m west of the earth mound. This terrace consists of a rock alignment. Unfortunately, mechanized agriculture activities have destroyed a substantial part of the feature. The terrace divides the floodplain into two areas, one higher than the other, and may have served to control the erosion and irrigation of the land. The location of this particular feature is relevant because it may indicate the use of irrigation systems in the area by Prehispanic communities, the distribution of different features in the landscape beside settlements, and the exploitation of the resources in the area by those communities. This feature may serve as evidence supporting Colonial accounts of use of irrigation techniques in the area by the Prehispanic communities.

The use of the mound is unknown, but it was probably built for the purpose of extending the elevated area to create additional surface, a platform for the possible construction of additional habitation structures, or as a public arena. Although the mound is not impressive in size, its construction may have required communal effort thus qualifying it as public architecture.

Funerary Mound

A funerary mound, SON P:10:8, was recorded and excavated near the community of Onavas. This mound is a large feature of 100 x 65 m in area by approximately 2 m high. Unfortunately, the site has been slowly destroyed over the years by several invasive and destructive activities, including pot hunting, farming, ranching, the construction of roads, and the placement of irrigation canals and, electric posts. At the time

of the OVAP excavations of this mound, less than a third of the site remained more or less intact. Considerable amounts of archaeological materials are scattered on the surface as a result of these destructive activities. As discussed earlier in the chapter on the excavation, local informants mentioned that when they built a concrete canal in the area in 1999, the canal cut the mound in half. At that time, several inhumations and cremations were observed and looted. In addition to the funerary evidence, a substantial amount of domestic material was found at the site, such as metate fragments, large amounts of ceramic and lithic materials, and small pieces of daub as well.

Preliminary results from the excavation unit, and new research data from a excavation project at the site, indicate that the cemetery ceased to function as such at the beginning of Onavas III phase, and is highly possible that was reused as a midden, explaining the high frequency of domestic material on top of it.

This is the first feature of its type recorded in the Sonoran archaeological record and the third for the Northwest Mexico region published to date. The first funerary mound recorded and excavated, with more than 166 burials, was at the site of Guasave, Sinaloa by Gordon Ekholm in 1942 in an area that is described as the northern limits of Mesoamerica (Carpenter 1996; Ekholm 1942; Gallaga 2004b). A second funerary mound was reported at the site of Mochicahui, Sinaloa, where a mound one meter high containing possibly more than 40 burials existed (Talavera 1995). In both cases, considerable domestic material was also recorded.

In the Prehispanic context, the identification of cemetery features implies that this society reached a level of social organization that favored the planned establishment and distinction of a resting area for the ancestors (Beck 1995; Gallaga 1999; Hodder 1980; Saxe 1970). Colonial documents mention some burial practices among the Nébomes, but they refrain to mention the use of cemeteries among them, but seem a common practice for the Huatabampo region. The finding of this a feature in the Onavas Valley is important as it suggests that this high level of political, social, and religious organization at the Prehispanic communities of the Onavas Valley was present.

Pictographs

SON P:10:5 was recorded by the PROCEDE and it is the only rock art identified in the Onavas Valley to date. This is a rock panel located on El Obispo drainage relatively high in the mountains, 4 km away on the west side of the Río Yaqui. The panel consists of 15 paintings of geometric designs (zigzag lines, circles, spirals, rhombs, and lines) made with red, blue, purple, and brown colors. No other features or archaeological material were recorded in association with the rock art (INAH 1998). The location and type of painting suggests that the site was related to the drainage and/or its water. As mentioned above, following the course of the drainage further into the mountains leads to several cliff dwelling sites. It may be possible that the paintings functioned in association with these sites as a marker of some sort, perhaps territorial or clan-based, if those sites are related and contemporaneous.

Geoglyph

One geoglyph in a shape of a star was recorded (SON P:10:20, see Figure 7.15). Located on the mesas near the floodplain along the Río Yaqui, the stone arrangement features a small triangular enclosure of less than 4 m². From each of the three corners a small river cobble stone alignment extends for 1 to 2 m. On the surface, little archaeological material (domestic and non-domestic) was discovered in relation to the curious alignment. No habitation sites

were recorded near this feature. The closest sites (SON P:10:19 and SON P:10:80) are about 250-300 m away.

Geoglyphs are common in the Sonoran Desert. Such features have been reported at La Playa site in the Trincheras region (Montane 1996:178), in the Pinacate area, and at Isla Tiburon (Bowen 1976a; Montane 1996:178). At least in two mores sites, the Río Boquillas, near La Playa site and in the Isla Tiburon (Figure 7.16), geoglyphs in the shape of a star had been reported (Montane 1996:178). The Onavas example thus appears not to be an isolated event in the Sonoran archaeological record. Their specific uses remain unknown, but they are typically associated with ritual and ceremonial activities. A similar interpretation is posited for this star-shaped feature in the Onavas Valley.

Other Features

Besides these possible examples of public/ceremonial and residential architecture, the OVAP recorded other features. At least seven medium size stone circles originally recorded as hearths in the field were encountered at different sites (SON P:6:8, SON P:10:26; SON P:10:56, SON P:10:83; SON P:10:86, SON P:10:98, and SON P:10:99) (See Appendix I and II).

The circles consistently measured 0.80 cm in diameter and lacked ash or charcoal in the interior, or fire-cracked-stone in or around the circles. It is possible that these features are the remains of the base for a storage container, such as those found in the cliff dwelling sites in the Sierra Madre Occidental of Chihuahua identified as *cuexcomates* (Di Peso et al. 1974; Guevara 1986). A cuexcomate is a storage container of a semi-spherical shape and a circular base common in Prehispanic communities.

Other reported features were concentrations of fire-cracked stone that were recorded as ovens. At least 25 of these features are identi-

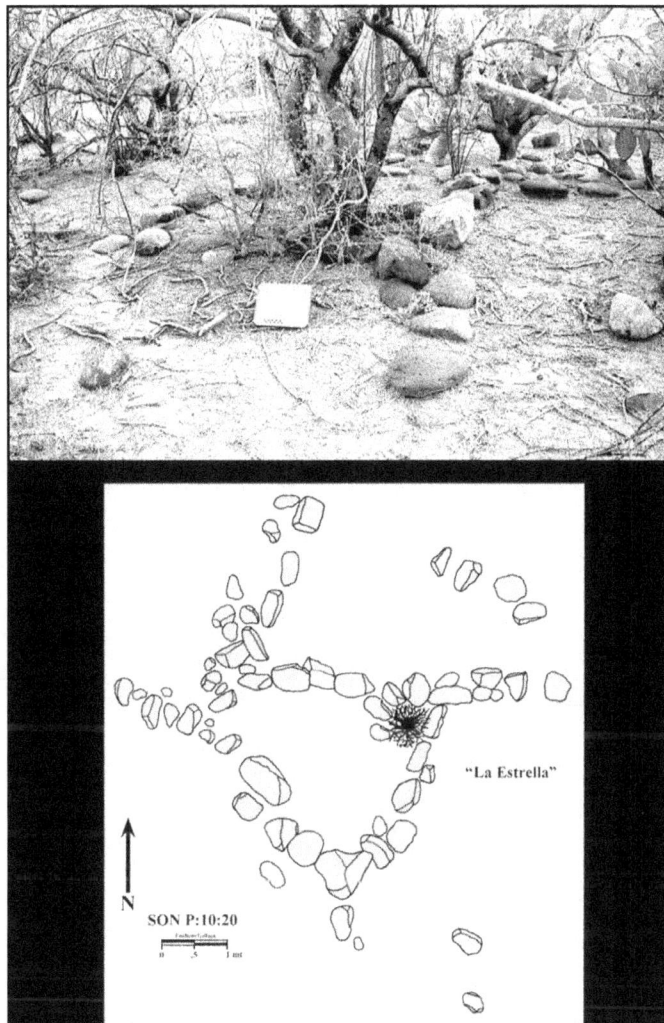

Figure 7.15. La Estrella, SON P:10:20 (Photograph by Emiliano Gallaga).

fied. Those are related to food preparation or agave processing areas.

Lastly, burials, most likely human were also recorded by the OVAP. Human and natural destruction and perturbation of sites inevitably exposed some burials, leaving bones and material visible on the surface. All the burials recorded were inhumations and around site compound, but it was not possible to identify the anatomical position of the interments or to identify burial pits for any of the burials, with the exception of the two inhumation found at

the SON P:10:08 excavation unit (see excavation unit description in Chapter 6). In total 19 burials were identified. Only one of them was found in direct association with a residential unit.

The descriptions and analyses of the habitation, public and ceremonial structures, and other elements show that the Onavas Valley exhibits a great diversity of features in spite of the constant destruction of the archaeological record. These features may indicated religious and ceremonial activities performed by the Pre-

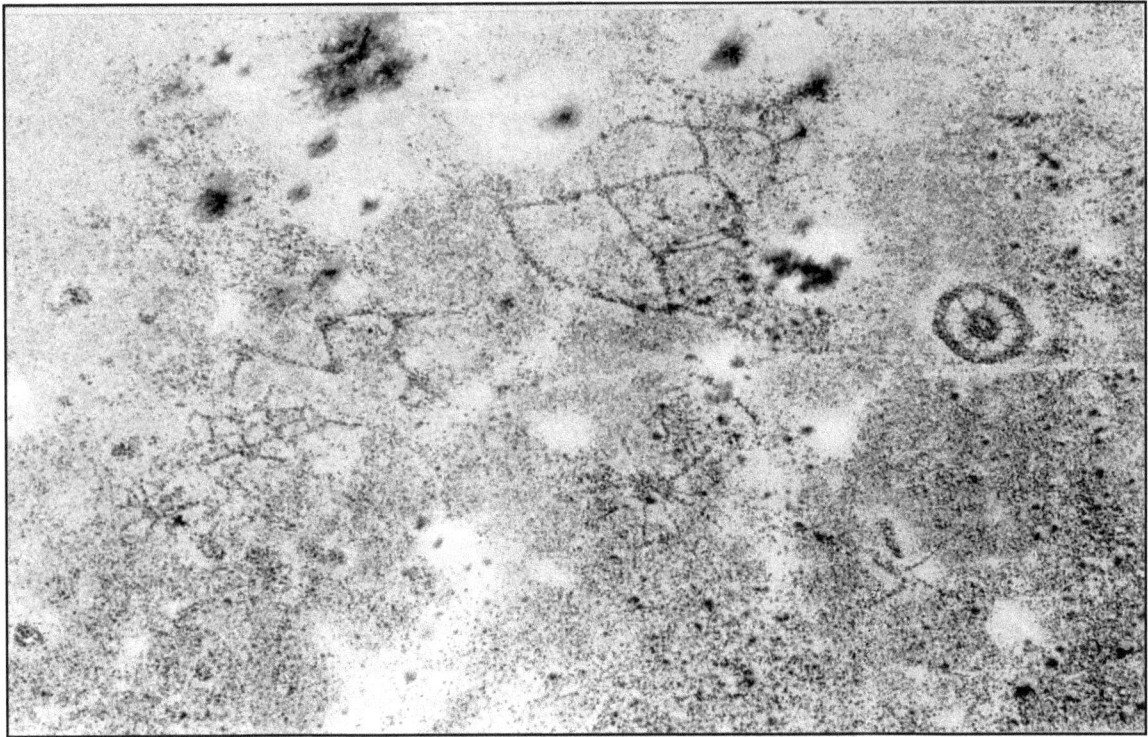

Figure 7.16. Star geoglyphs at Isla Tiburon (Bowen 1976a: Figure 21).

hispanic communities of the area in one hand, and the exploitation of resources and use of the landscape on the other. The spatial distribution analysis of those sites and features tell a great deal about how the Prehispanic communities might have envisioned their landscape.

In addition to the features described above and identified as part of the constructed ritual landscape of the Onavas Valley, natural or conceptual landscape markers must have existed in the socially constructed mythical and magical worlds of the Prehispanic Nébome communities. As Basso (1996:34) states:

> For Indian men and women, the past lies embedded in features of the earth—in canyons and lakes, mountains and arroyos, rocks and vacant fields—which together endow their lands with multiple forms of significance that reach into

their lives and shape the ways they think.

Many natural markers, such as rivers, mountains, caves, forests, water sources, or mountain peaks, can be inferred to have played such roles even if there is an absence of any associated material evidence (e.g. Brody 1988). Pérez de Ribas (1999:368) made a similar remark when an old Yaqui woman replied to him "Father, look across the river; do you see all those hills, mountains, peaks, and heights there? Well, we revered all of them and there we practiced and celebrated our superstitions." It is extremely difficult to identify such markers based on the presence of archaeological material alone (Anschuetz et al. 2001; Ashmore and Knapp 1999). Oral histories, legends, or myths recorded from local indigenous groups about the use or knowledge of such features can provide information that facilitates their identification in the archaeological record.

As mentioned earlier, three illustrative examples of these natural markers have been recorded ethnographically in neighboring regions. First, the Sierra del Bacatete among the Yaqui communities is recognized as a traditional marker of Yaqui territory (Hu Dehart 1995; Olavarria 1995; Spicer 1983, 1992, 1994). According to Yaqui history, their traditional Yaqui land was settled by the "prophets" who appeared before the elders and walked the region marking the limits of their territory. One of those natural markers was the Sierra del Bacatete (Spicer 1994). The second one is the Río Mayo that serves the Mayo community as a mythical entity for its role as a source of life in the valley, as well as a food and freshwater resources (Crumrine 1983; Crumrine and Crumrine 1967; Figure 7.17).

In a third instance, an oral history provided by the Yaqui informant Mariano Tapia, recorded and translated by Giddings in the early 1940s, exemplifies what may be suggested by such extrapolation. Tapia narrated the story of "Suawaka" (a Yaqui Indian hero) and describes that "[i]n earlier times, there used to be serpents with seven heads. These lived northeast of Guaymas near a hill that had two little points; it is called Takalaim…" (Giddings 1993:138). The hill described with two little points is now commonly referred to as the "tetas de cabra" hill (goat's tits). These hills, which are ethnographically identified as the location of seven-headed serpents, thus move beyond their apparent function as natural feature to marking mythical significance. Although the ethnographic record of the Nébome or Lower Pima appears to be thin in terms of oral his-

Figure 7.17. Mayo Indians at the Río Mayo celebrating San Juan day (Photograph courtesy of the University of Arizona, Arizona State Museum, Photographic Collections, Edward H. and Rosamond B. Spicer Collection, Album IX).

tory, legends, or myths detailing the Onavas Valley, examples like this must be considered and explored further to start identifying and understanding natural or conceptual landscape markers in the valley.

For the OVAP area, the Río Yaqui must have served as a similar conceptual marker. The importance of the river consisted not only of sustaining life in the valley and providing resources to the Nébome communities, but also of running its course as a cyclical natural force that gives and takes life. As such, the Río Yaqui undoubtedly served as a fundamental element in the mythical world of Prehispanic communities settled in the area. Similar to other river communities, the Nébomes most likely had rituals or ceremonies associated with the Río Yaqui, to its yearly floods, and to its resources. Pérez de Ribas (1999:291) recorded this type of activities in his Colonial writings as:

> …[he] brought back four kinds of sorcery that he used for various effects and events: one to prevent the fields from drying up, another to prevent the river from flooding, and others for similar frauds.

From this account, it appears likely that the local indigenous population had magical items and particular ceremonies/rituals to pray for water for agricultural purposes, albeit in moderation so as not to destroy the fields. In another account, the Jesuit Father mentions:

> When someone's wife, sons or close relatives died and the person was buried, the widower, widow, or the deceased's next of kin was taken to a river, and there facing west, he was submerged in the water three times (Pérez de Rivas 1999:179).

The account thus indicates that the river played an important role in the magical/spiritual world of the Prehispanic Indian communities. More

recently, Pennington (1980:149) recorded a fertility ceremony or rite called dutki'adat, dukitč (when the water comes), where the Río Yaqui is also used ritually:

> Several women participated…the chosen women went to the monte (ša'igam) from several days. During this time they saw no one but each other. They then returned to the village and danced for one or two days on a board placed over a large olla (haha) that was buried in the ground containing corn, squash, and bean seeds. When planted these seeds were certain to grow… at the dance ended a group of men formed a line extending from the dancing place to the Río Yaqui. The women then ran to the river, disrobing en route, and jumped into the water.

Here, albeit some hundred years later, the Río Yaqui played an important role in the closure of the ritual/ceremony. No archaeological material or sites were identified in direct association with such ritual activities for the river, in spite of these compelling ethnohistorical descriptions. A possibility exists that the SON P:10:20 site, La Estrella (the star), may be associated with the river.

Beside the Río Yaqui, the Nébomes must have valued other natural markers as well, in particular caves or mountain peaks, and probably included them in their mythical world, just as the old Yaqui Indian women told Father Pérez de Ribas (1999:368) in their account during the early seventeen century. Many Prehispanic communities worldwide exhibit a magical-ritual perception of mountains and caves. For example, Mesoamerican caves were often considered portals to the underworld serving as and reflecting metaphorical connections between the supernatural and mortal world, houses of gods, or places of origin (Broda 1991; López Austin 1973, 1995; Taube

2003).

Ethnographic research describes the presence of rock shelters among the Lower Pima further up in the Sierra, but not in the Onavas Valley (Dunnigan 1983). The OVAP survey did not include the mountainous area that is known to have archaeological sites, which provide information about the use of these areas by the Prehispanic communities. Furthermore, natural markers in the Onavas Valley were certainly present in Prehispanic times, but the inherent limitations of the material record in archaeology prohibited identification during the OVAP. More interdisciplinary research is necessary to collect the data necessary to interpret the presence of certain conceptual or natural markers in the Nébome ritual landscapes.

The OVAP recorded several examples of possible constructed landscape and pointed to possible natural or conceptual markers indicative of ritual landscapes in the Onavas Valley. One possible earthen mound, two likely stone altars, a geoglyph, rock art, a possible plaza, and a mortuary mound comprise the available evidence of such constructed markers and serve as the securely identified material representation of ritual landscape surrounding the Nébome communities.

ETHNIC LANDSCAPE

Ethnicity is a very dynamic, multi-sensual, and constantly changing cultural process (Barth 1998; Jenkins 1997). Nonetheless, this process uses and leaves material remains behind that can thus shed light on the humans who used, created, and discarded those items. The problem lies in the determination of to whom—individually or collectively—that material belongs, or to which sector—lower or upper class—of the community it belongs, and when and where it was acquired as raw material, manufactured, used, and finally discarded (Cameron 2005).

Archaeologists often lack the answers for all those questions. Without the actual living humans present, cultural materials must be used instead to archaeologically identify social and political interactions, migration, or cultural processes in general. Yet we must remind ourselves that although those diagnostic distributional maps depict strong geographical or temporal boundaries, they are merely a partial material representation of Prehispanic spatial interactions.

To complement the archaeological material record, landscape archaeology has developed to facilitate the consideration and inclusion of both ritual and ethnic landscapes into archaeological investigation. Anschuetz et al. (2001:179) describe ethnic landscapes as:

> ...spatial and temporal constructs defined by communities whose members create and manipulate material culture and symbols to signify ethnic or cultural boundaries based on customs and shared modes of thought and expressions that might have no other sanction than tradition.

Of course, ethnic landscapes are notoriously hard to identify archaeologically especially when no diagnostic material or material culture assemblage exists to point to or associate with a particular human group, such as the Nébomes in the Onavas Valley. But because the identification and analysis of ethnic landscapes are interrelated with ritual landscapes: thus, the recording of ritual and public markers helps decipher the ethnic landscape.

One must be careful not to fix such markers as limited or set boundaries to define an ethnic group's distribution or interactions. Ethnicity per se is not tied to physical spaces or may not manifest itself in explicit association with particular geographic markers (Barth

1998; Jenkins 1997). After all, ceremonies, rituals, or other such activity that identifies an ethnic group may be performed outside its original geographical location without signifying a loss in community affiliation. An example of this is the Yaqui community who has their traditional territory in southern Sonora where they maintain a set of cultural activities that identify them as Yaqui (Hu Dehart 1995; Olavarria 1995; Spicer 1992, 1993, 1994). Due to certain political events and their general socio-historical context, Yaqui communities are found today well-outside their traditional territory, in places such as Tucson and Phoenix in the United States, or Yucatan in southern Mexico, and Cuba (Spicer 1994; Padilla 1995). In those communities certain ceremonies and ritual activities that identify them as Yaquis are still performed, such as the Pascola (Figure 7.18). The endurance of the Yaqui community and ethnic group affiliation is based on the maintenance of the group language, memory of holy places and events, sacred laws, special songs, dances, and rituals, and the maintenance of communities or voluntary organizations (Hu Dehart 1995; Olavarria 1995; Spicer 1992, 1993, 1994). Clearly these activities can be performed without being confined to a particular geographical place such as the Yaqui Valley or the Bacatete mountains.

Although some ethnographic and ethnohistoric data exist for the study area, it is very limited and offers a rather general cultural pattern for the Nébome area as well as for neighboring regions. In addition, without archaeological research for comparison, it is still difficult to determine which cultural activities and material originated in Prehispanic times and which ones were introduced by the Spanish colonists.

The OVAP provides the first material assemblage for the Onavas Valley, and some artifact types have not been previously recorded in southern Sonora. These were: (1) the masonry stone slab structures and (2) the local decorated ceramic material name Onavas Purple-on-Red (see Figure 6.3). Until further research proves otherwise, these materials are identified as the best available material representation of the Prehispanic Nébome group.

The masonry stone slab structures could be a local expression or adaptation of a southern construction technique. As mentioned above, the closest similar masonry stone slab structures have been recorded are in the upper Río Fuerte region, at the Buyubampo site, in northern Sinaloa (John Carpenter personal communication 2005). On the other hand, Pérez de Ribas (1999: 289, 391) wrote that the Nébomes constructed houses with stone bases and structures made with sturdy earth walls.

Secondly, the Onavas Purple-on-Red is a local decorated ceramic type. This ceramic type may prove to be diagnostic for this particular area, pending further research on both on the ceramic technology (e.g., chemical analysis and/or petrography) and in the region in general. Onavas Purple-on-Red has not previously been recorded among the Sonora ceramic types or those from the northern Sinaloa. As mentioned in the ceramic analysis chapter, based on superficial analysis and on experimental archaeology in ceramic manufacture with local clays and local potters the manufacture of this ceramic type appears to be local. Petrographic analysis must be performed next on local clay sources and ceramic sherds to sustain this preliminary conclusion further.

Material associated with dress and ornamentation emerges as promising directions as the words of Pérez de Ribas describing local dress (Pérez de Ribas 1999:391-392) (see on page 139). The OVAP recovered a small metate with remains of red ochre during the survey. The Jesuit father also mentions the use of shell beads among the Nébome: "they would hang some type of votive or offering, such as the white beads made from little sea snails with

Figure 7.18. A Yaqui Indian dressed as a chapayeka *for Easter celebration at Hermosillo, Sonora, Mexico (Photograph by Emiliano Gallaga).*

which they adorn themselves" (1999:404). Such shell items, among others, were found by the OVAP (see Figure 6.9). Descriptions of nearby cultural groups, also offer possible indications of the use of certain materials as ethnic markers. However, numerous cultures in this region used ochre and shell adornments, but types and quantities of use and context change. Detailed analysis on species and manufacture techniques could start to distinguished cultural traditions. Pérez de Ribas emphasizes the use of cotton, turquoise, and the color blue as corporal decoration among the Yaqui:

> They adorned their ears by piercing the edge of the ear and hanging some little charms from ribbons of blue cotton thread. Even the men did this, in addition to hanging some small, valuable emerald-like stones [turquoise?] from the cartilage of their nose (Pérez de Rivas 1999:329).

Pérez de Ribas mentions that almost all the Indian nations from the region decorated themselves accordingly. Several turquoise pieces were recorded by the OVAP suggesting prolific use of this material in the area. Pérez de Ribas mentions the use of turquoise among the Yaquis may further point to extra-regional interactions and denotes that this precious material could be obtained via the Río Yaqui, passing though the Onavas Valley.

These are just some preliminary thoughts on how to start identify Nebome archaeological material culture and tie that to a human group that the historical documents call the Nebomes. As we mentioned before, the ethnic landscape is the most difficult and problematic to interpret, but not impossible.

LANDSCAPE DISCUSSION

This chapter summarizes and interprets the archaeological data gathered in the OVAP survey of the Onavas Valley. In conjunction with ethnohistoric and ethnographic data, the archaeological landscape of this valley was presented. The settlement ecology or settlement analysis indicates that the Prehispanic communities of the Onavas Valley followed a clustered settlement pattern with some formal and structured inter-site interactions. The regional center or the Prehispanic Onavas community and the well-placed villages may have influenced such interactions, possibly enhanced by ritual and public performances. As expected, sites are concentrated near water sources and arable lands. Only six sites were located near the hills, all camps. Much of this pattern appears to coincide with the geographical characteristics of the valley. The variety of material and site types reflect the diversity of natural resources that the Nébomes had at their disposal and a land use classification was provided as a result. Arable land, in particu-

lar, proved important to discuss and formed the basis upon which a population estimation analysis was made arriving at a reasonable figure of circa 3,000 Nébome Indians for the Prehispanic period. The presence of non-local material reveals that the valley was not isolated and probably played an active and significant role in the transmission of goods and ideas. The probable presence of paths would affirm that the valley enjoyed good communication, at least geographically speaking, with neighboring areas, especially with the coast. However, the analysis of archaeological materials indicated, that the valley appears to have been more related to the Huatabampo tradition than to the Río Sonora archaeological tradition.

In terms of ritual landscape, the archaeological material evidence, ethnohistorical and ethnographic data to provide some useful insights about possible ritual activities and contexts. Several constructed landscape features and possible natural or conceptual markers were described as part of ritual landscapes at the Onavas Valley. How were they used? What types of activities or rituals were performed there? These are some questions that emerge, but may never receive an answer. The presence of public architecture suggests that these Prehispanic communities achieved a social and political development that allowed and enabled the persuasion of community members to construct larger structures for the common good and not just residential structures for their immediate families. The distribution of the public architecture features in the valley reveals that most of the ceremonial and public architecture was located either at sites identified as villages, in the case of the earthen mound, the plaza, and the stone altar, or in complete isolation, such as the La Estrella geoglyph and the rock art. This difference might distinguish open and public performances from more secluded activities. An example of such use of spaces in rituals can be perceived in the description of the fertility ceremony or rite called *dutki'adat, dukitč* (when the water comes) as recorded by Pennington (1980:149). A selected group of people performed secluded activities outside the community away from the rest of the members before the ceremony became public, involving the rest of the community members, and ending in a communal bath in the Río Yaqui. Similar performances may have taken place at constructed and natural markers in Prehispanic times.

The presence of rock art and geoglyphs presents a familiar scenario in terms of common ritual and magical practices in the Sonoran archaeological record, but the identification of stone altars and a mortuary mound suggest a more sophisticated and complex religious and ritual structure for the valley than previously known (Pailes 1972, 1994a, 1994b). In the case of the cemetery mound feature, Alvarez (2003:9) mentions that for sites affiliated to the Huatabampo archaeological tradition, a mortuary pattern is discernable and consists of communal spaces, such as cemeteries, while other groups such as the Totorame region preferred inhumation under house floors. It is possible that the cemetery concept employed in the Onavas Valley originated in the Huatabampo area. Future research and excavation on the mortuary mound will uncover more information required to form a more precise understanding of the mortuary practices of the Nébomes, to expand our knowledge of the Nébome material record, and to start deciphering the ritual landscape of this group. Current exploration of the cemetery mound by archeologist Cristina Moreno, will provide more information about these topics.

In spite of its limitations, this landscape analysis has provided archaeological insight into a little known archaeological area previously assumed to be part of the Río Sonora archaeological tradition.

Having gone as far as is possible with survey data alone, I now turn outward to neighboring archaeological areas. I compare the results of the OVAP to the data gathered by three systematic survey projects conducted in Northwest Mexico and the U.S. Southwest so that we can better understand the lifeways and culture of past peoples in the study region.

Chapter 8
Cultural Landscapes in the Northwest Mexico/ U.S. Southwest

Requiring neither extended analysis nor rational justification, sense of place rests its case on the unexamined premise that being from somewhere is always preferable to being from nowhere. All of us, it asserts, are generally better off with a place to call our own. Places, it reminds us, are really very good (Basso 1996:87; *emphasis in original*).

The OVAP provided the opportunity to analyze a delimited geographical area archaeologically as a whole and to depict an initial understanding of life in the Prehispanic communities of that area. The cultural patterns defined archaeologically for the Onavas Valley reflect cultural decisions made by the Nébomes based upon the valley and their people cultural, economic, political, and natural characteristics. A remaining research goal of the OVAP is the comparison of those patterns found in the valley with other areas in the Northwest Mexico/U.S. Southwest.

The areas selected for this comparative analysis share similar geographical characteristics with the Onavas Valley, most notably arid conditions, desert vegetation, and a high dependability on seasonal waters. In addition to geographical conditions, the areas were chosen based on the completion of systematic archaeological surveys. Although systematic surveys are common in the Southwest U.S. archaeology today, they are not common in the Northwest of Mexico. The OVAP is one of a small number of systematic surveys conducted to date in the state of Sonora. Hopefully more of such surveys will follow in the near future.

Based on the geographical conditions and the completion of systematic surveys, three areas were used to draw comparisons with the Onavas Valley, one located in Arizona, one in Chihuahua, and one in Sonora. First, in Arizona, the Marana Community Survey Project (MCSP) provided enough data to understand how the Marana Hohokam community related to its surrounded area. This project thus serves to illustrate the effectiveness of the full-coverage survey as a research methodology in the Southwest U.S. (Doyel et al. 2000; Fish et al. 1990, 1992). Secondly, in Chihuahua, the Casas Grandes Regional Survey Project (CGRSP) established an accurate and comprehensive picture of the full range of influence of the site of Paquimé, Chihuahua (Minnis and Whalen 2004; Whalen and Minnis 1999, 2000, 2001, 2003). Finally, in Sonora, the Cerro de Trincheras Settlement and Land Use Survey Project (CTSS) delineated the area of settlement development of the Cerro de Trincheras site and determined that culture's land use through time (Fish and Fish 2004; McGuire and Villalpando 1993). Notably, the achievements of the Marana Community project—first begun in 1981—motivated the undertaking of such a project in the Cerro de Trincheras area in 1999.

Before providing a comparative discussion of the three survey projects in relation to the OVAP, I summarize the results of the three projects. For more detailed presentations of these projects, I refer the reader elsewhere (e.g., Doyel at al. 2000; Fish and Fish 2004; Fish et al. 1990, 1992; Fish and Fish 2004; McGuire and Villalpando 1993, 2011; Minnis and Whalen 2004; Whalen and Minnis 1999, 2000, 2001, 2003). Here, I focus on similarities and differences relevant to the OVAP results.

THE MARANA COMMUNITY SURVEY PROJECT

During the early 1980s, considerable knowledge already existed for the Phoenix Basin— the core of the Hohokam area—providing a general archaeological understanding of the Hohokam culture. The same did not hold true for neighboring areas, such as the Tucson Basin. The unevenness of research seriously limited the overall interpretation of the Hohokam tradition. To bolster the state of archaeological knowledge on the Hohokam people, several researchers decided to undertake a full-coverage survey in the Tucson Basin area.

Suzanne Fish, Paul Fish, and John Madsen (1992) coordinated a systematic foot survey in the northern portion of the Tucson Basin about 35 km north of Tucson. The following research goals guided this full-coverage survey:

> (1) "the recovery of spatial relationships among remains of all sizes, representing ephemeral activities as well as habitation; (2) the ability to evaluate settlement pattern against a full range of environmental variation; and (3) the ability to define territorial units of interrelated sites that included relatively low densities and dispersed distributions" (Fish et al. 1992:xi).

The research goals spoke directly to the need to increase our knowledge about the Hohokam settlement pattern and cultural development in the Tucson Basin (Doyel et al. 2000; Fish et

al. 1990, 1992). The aims of the project also entailed an evaluation of the full-coverage survey method for its ability to provide reliable data upon which to build a comprehensive understanding of the Marana Hohokam and the Hohokam in general.

Although full-coverage or systematic surveys are time and resource-consuming, the location and geographical conditions of the Marana area showed that a survey of that area was a worthwhile initiative (Fish et al. 1990). Free of major geographical obstacles, such as rivers, canyons, or rugged mountains, and still relatively undisturbed by urban development during the early 1980s, the Marana area provided favorable survey conditions. Located close to the city of Tucson, archaeologists further benefited from easy access to the research area. Furthermore, these archaeologists experienced a sense of urgency, rapid urban expansion of the city of Tucson and the Marana community threatened the area, as did the Central Arizona Aqueduct Project in later years.

The geographical and climatic conditions of the area also facilitated the systematic survey. Fish et al. (1990:192) summarize the conditions at Marana as follows:

> …annual rainfall is just under 300 mm. Mountains bounding the basin to the east rise to a height of approximately 9,000 ft. To the west, a lower chain typifies the topography of more recent volcanic activity. The seasonally flowing Santa Cruz River drains the basin and ultimately joins the Gila. Major and minor drainage cross the valley slopes or bajadas. Some carry runoff from orographic rainfall in the mountains, and some originated in storm-fed bajadas watersheds. The full range of environmental variation exists within an average horizontal distance of 15 mi

between mountains on the east and west. No internal barriers are present to inhibit travel, communication, and exchange.

Favorably, a lack of moisture translated into arid vegetation, enabling archaeologists to survey the area easily. More importantly, limited vegetation signified that remains likely survived relatively unaffected by plant growth. Frequently obfuscating the archaeological record, plant growthis a potentially destructive formation process (Schiffer 1987).

The Marana Project covered a total of 1800 km². To focus on the mound sites within that area, 470 km² was studied by full-coverage survey. The remaining area was surveyed with transects (Fish et al. 1992). In the full-coverage research area more than 700 sites were recorded and "thousands of scatters and isolated artifacts" (Fish et al. 1990:193) were found. Furthermore, the survey enabled the identification of key features and sites to excavate and analyze later—tasks that are still ongoing today (Fish et al. 2000).

The entire project and its subsequent analysis illustrated that the Prehispanic Hohokam community at Marana consisted of an area of 146 km². The community was composed of several hundred sites located on terraces of both major and tributary streams, at mountain front edges, and on alluvial fans that extended from the Santa Cruz River to the Tortolita Mountains. This location proved significant, as researchers until then had believed that Hohokam communities tended to settle along the river valleys and typically not in the foothills (Doyel et al. 2000; Haury 1976; Fish et al. 1990, 1992). In addition to this rather direct observation, the MCSP revealed many details about the Hohokam in the Tucson Basin that further adjusted the general archaeological interpretation of the Hohokam culture. Here, I summarize those relevant details for the OVAP beginning with the cultural development of the Marana community.

During the Pre-Classic Period (A.D. 600–1150), two discrete communities with ball courts were located on opposite sides of the river in the northern Tucson Basin and were surrounded by several sites that comprised the Marana community. Over time, these two conglomerations gave shape to the Classic Marana community (A.D. 1150–1300) that consisted of one principal mound site measuring about 1.5 km in length and 0.5 km in width. The location of the mound site replacing the earlier Pre-Classic ball court sites was at the center of the Marana community (Doyel et al. 2000; Fish and Fish 2000; Fish et al. 1990, 1992).

Although the Marana Mound Site (AZ AA:12:251 [ASM])—referring to the Marana community during the Hohokam Classic period—lies centrally in the basin, its location affords no availability of optimal farming land nor direct access to water. To address both of these fundamental needs, a 10 km long canal was constructed from the Santa Cruz River to the fields of the Marana Mound Site. The canal supplied water to the Marana community and to the surrounding farming lands. In addition to farming activities specialized agricultural production, such as agave cultivation, took place in nearby areas. Pondering the question why the Marana Mound was located in this location, Fish and Fish explain that the "construction of the Marana platform mound in a geographically central position with few other advantages suggests communal concern with a symbol to integrate the expanded Classic Period community" (2000:247). Fish and Fish also expound that the terms 'tribe' or 'chiefdom' fail to accurately represent the Marana community, which is a middle-range society. Rather than postulating that kin-based systems underlie Hohokam centralized organization, they argue that architectural symbols of integration reflect a Hohokam ideology and territorial affiliation (Fish et al. 2000; Whitecotton 1977). From this perspective, they interpret that the central position of the site places its members in a privileged position for exchange and control over the Tucson Basin. Controlling the production and/or trade of exotic and/or prestige items both for internal and external distribution, and through the ceremonial role of the platform mound, the community exerted its power through material and ideological means.

The settlement pattern analysis of Marana's pre-Classic and Classic sites reveals additional cultural trends of interest in the Hohokam habitation of the Tucson Basin. During the Pre-Classic period a settlement pattern emerged that remains consistent throughout the Hohokam period: a primary village, distinguished by the presence of non-habitation structures, with surrounding smaller villages and hamlets. Pre-Classic settlements are, moreover, composed of agglomerations of houses facing each other thus shaping open courtyards, and ball courts—a non-habitation structure. This pattern changes during the Classic Period. Settlements are then comprised of adobe residential compounds that consist of a range of one to several houses and platform mounds. During this process, a remarkable increase in population occurred. During the Classic Period, the area the Hohokam inhabited increased almost threefold from that occupied during the Pre-Classic. From approximately 2,000,000 m² the residential area expanded to 6,000,000 m². To explain this increase, Marana researchers argue that the local population experienced an influx of immigrants at the peak of Hohokam habitation of the Tucson Basin (Fish and Fish 2000; Fish et al. 1990, 1992).

In terms of population numbers, the Marana Mound site alone is estimated to have housed between 400 to 800 members (Fish and Fish 2000:252). Three to five times that number could have lived in the larger area of the Marana community. Considering the entire estimated residential area amounting to 6,145,000 m² (Fish and Fish 2004:59), an estimated population of more than 6,000 people could have inhabited the Marana community area (Craig 2000:159).

The full-coverage survey also allowed the researchers to evaluate the full range of environmental diversity of the basin. They defined six land use zones for productive activities based on environment, site types, and material evidence. Zone 1 consisted of alluvial fan residence and floodwater agriculture. A runoff agave cultivation area formed zone 2. Zone 3 corresponded to the intense exploitation of upper bajada plant resources. Mountain pediment residential areas, floodwater and runoff cultivation, and upper bajada and riparian resources comprised zone 4. Zone 5 served for riverine residential areas, irrigation and floodwater agriculture, and riparian resources. Lastly, zone 6 corresponded to a terraced hillside residential areas and agriculture, upper bajada resources, and lithic quarries (Fish et al. 1992:31). A concentrated number of rock pile features recorded in zone 2 received special attention and were identified as an indication of specialized production activities meant to increase food supplies in a particularly marginal agricultural area.

The archaeological record indicates that Marana community members appeared to have pursued subsistence activities in one or more of the identified land use zones. As Fish and Fish explain, the "irrigation networks, series of adjacent floodwater fields, and the large rock pile complexes all involved common interest and efforts for subsets of community members" (Fish and Fish 1992:102). Honing in on the social component of such subsistence strategies, associated social interactions between different sites in the basin are interpreted as mechanisms to enhance community coherence and to cement social and economic interrelationships.

Moving into the project's theoretical

implications, the MCSP provided new data to look into questions of complexity, inequality, and hierarchy related to Hohokam society and relevant for archaeology at large. The Hohokam communities differ in important ways from the Mississippian Prehispanic tradition that has provided, at least in the United States, much of the data upon which the theory of chiefdoms is based (Neitzel 1999; Pauketat 1994, 1997, 2000). However, material evidence illustrates that the Hohokam society developed beyond egalitarian decision-base structures, identifying the Hohokam as a middle-range society (Doyel et al. 2000; Fish and Fish 1992, 2000; Gumerman 1991; Mills 2000). Unfortunately, leaders and elites prove difficult to identify and/or recognize in the material record in most of Northwest Mexico and Southwest U.S., the principal obstacle to postulate or confirm such agent-based approaches as chiefdom societies. Nonetheless, the presence of monumental architecture or non-residential structures suggests some form of leadership or social organization capable of mounting a group effort for their construction (Harry and Bayman 2000; Fish and Fish 2000a, 2000b).

The neo-evolutionary models used to identify and characterize the social, political, and economical organization of Prehispanic societies in the Northwest Mexico and Southwest U.S. have proved inadequate or problematic. In response to this problem, in the 1990s archaeologists formulated new models (Mills 2000), such as the dual-processual model proposed by Blanton et al. (1996). Briefly, this model posits two types of leadership strategies: a network-based strategy, where a leader's prestige derives from linkages with individuals from other communities, and a corporate-based strategy, where a leader's position depends mainly on support from kinship-based groups inside the community. The dual-processual model proved useful for examining the Hohokam archaeological remains important

for interpreting the Hohokam socio-political scenario.

Without leaders and/or elite sectors evident through the archaeological record, and if ball court structures can be considered indicative of an inclusionary system, the archaeological data on the pre-Classic Period Hohokam communities at Marana appear to reveal a corporate leadership mode. By the Classic Period, however, the presence of platform mounds may be taken to indicate a shift to a network oriented strategy (Abbot et al 2007; Harry and Bayman 2000; Fish and Fish 2000a, 2000b). Analysis of the Marana Platform Mound Site material confirmed a "lack of economic differentiation between the residents of the platform mound site and shared access to exchange networks between the residents of the Marana Mound compound and... [neighboring] sites" (Harry and Bayman 2000:150)—evidence suggesting a corporate strategy. The architectural characteristics of the platform mound, such as limited access and encircling compound walls, however, point to an exclusionary socio-political system emerging within the Marana community. Externally, then, the Marana Mound community appeared to be engaged in a corporate strategy based on a shared exchange network between sites. Simultaneously and internally, the community adopted a network strategy based on an exclusionary system. I should note, however, that the latter appears not through limited access of goods but through the architecture of the platform mound itself (Harry and Bayman 2000; Fish and Fish 2000a). As Fish and Fish (2000a:167) conclude:

Although both increasingly centralized and exclusionary tendencies appear over the course of the Classic period, the context of power and privilege remained primarily corporate and embodied in the institutions of civic-territorial organizations.

In addition to the dual-processual model, Fish and Fish interpret the socio-political structure of Marana as a community. The civic-territorial organization mentioned by Fish and Fish is embodied in the concept of the community as an important characteristic. Generally, the community concept has been defined as a "set of interrelated sites within a bounded community territory...such a community contains a center with public architecture of a kind and/or magnitude that is not duplicated in other community sites" (Fish and Fish 2000a:160). Membership in a particular community appears to regulate and control access to the region's natural resources. The size and limits of a community are marked by the limits of another cluster of settlements with public architecture and by the "demands and constrains of subsistence, communication, and integration" (Fish and Fish 2000a:161). Systematic or full-coverage surveys provide the necessary settlement pattern data to identify the characteristic community elements, such as a center with public architecture and the limits of the community.

The principal contribution of the Marana Community Survey Project was to have provided data and insight into the development over time of a complete settlement pattern of a Hohokam community outside the Hohokam core area. Settlement pattern analysis revealed patterns in addition to farming that indicated a community response to the geographical conditions of the area. The discovery of diverse production patterns resulted in the understanding that a diversification of sites or settlements occurred as well as the expansion of traditional settlement areas, such as river beds, into less favorable areas. The excavation of selected features and sites, previously identified through survey, provided additional information that documented a complex society beyond the egalitarian-decision structure. Although the material assemblage differed little from that of the Hohokam communities in the Phoenix Basin, the assemblage illustrated how the Marana Hohokam exploited their surrounding environment. Moreover, the assemblage indicated likely extra-regional interactions through which they obtained exotic materials, such as marine shell. Lastly, Fish and Fish documented the economic and nutritional value of the agave cultivation in Prehispanic times and its likely importance for the Marana Hohokam.

THE CASAS GRANDES REGIONAL SURVEY PROJECT

In the history of Northern Mexico and Southwest U.S. archaeology, the state of Chihuahua has occupied an important place. The northern area of Chihuahua functioned as a key player in the Prehispanic cultural development of the region. Furthermore, the archaeological site of Casas Grandes, also known as Paquimé, has captured the imaginations of many visitors. As early as the first Spanish conquistadors in the early seventeenth century to the twenty-first century archaeologist, travelers and professionals have indicated their interest in the site. This large, 70 ha, adobe pueblo site, of which only 30 ha has been explored to date (Cano 2001:82), has been recognized as the largest settlement in the region as well as a primary regional center that maintained interactions with neighboring communities located in the modern international four corners (Di Peso et al. 1974; Gamboa 2001; Minnis and Whalen 2004; Whalen and Minnis 2001).

A major research question explored at Paquimé is the degree and intensity of the local, regional, and extra-regional interactions. In the early 1960s, Charles R. Di Peso from the Amerind Foundation of the United States and Eduardo Contreras from INAH, Mexico, directed a colossal archeological research project, the Joint Casas Grandes Project (JCGP).

Through the JCGP, they undertook the task of exploring the role of Paquimé in the Prehispanic traditions of the international four corners (Di Peso et al. 1974). After three years of excavation and ten additional years of analysis, the JCGP published eight comprehensive volumes of data and research results. Di Peso et al. (1974) reached the conclusion that the Paquimé was formed through the influence of Mesoamerican pochtecas, or traders, around the Late Prehispanic Period and that as a prime regional center Paquimé directly influenced the surrounding area of almost 88,000 km² (Di Peso et al. 1974:2:667). In spite of an impressive accumulation of data, analysis, and research undertaken at the site, Paquimé was interpreted against a vacuum of archaeological research. The lack of even minimal excavation in any of the immediately neighboring communities or any systematic surveys meant that no one could deny or affirm on the basis of archaeological evidence the conclusions reached by the JCGP (Minnis and Whalen 2004; Whalen and Minnis 1999, 2000, 2001). In the last decades this situation has fortunately changed. Nonetheless, although considerable archaeological research and re-analysis of Di Peso's results in Chihuahua has been undertaken, archaeologists will agree that what we know or think we know of Paquimé today is still largely based on the results of the JCGP.

To fill the gaps in our knowledge, two American archaeologists, Paul Minnis and Michael Whalen, began the Casas Grandes Regional Survey Project (CGRSP). With this project, they hoped to "remedy this situation and to turn these data to consideration of the origin, extent, and nature of the system of regional interaction that focused on Paquimé" (Whalen and Minnis 1999:55). In their aim to broaden and elaborate the understanding of Paquimé and its sphere of influence, these researchers designed their archaeological exploration guided by the opinion that an understanding of regional systems can be achieved "only through careful study of all of their components, not simply those at the top" (Whalen and Minnis 1999:54). The initial goal of the CGRSP was to fill the gap between the impressive data collected by Di Peso at Paquimé and the virtual absence of information from the surrounding area. The CGRSP principally aimed to gather data to determine the area's full regional settlement pattern and the local and regional interactions of Paquimé as a primary regional center with its surrounding areas based on data from the surveys. To meet these aims, Minnis and Whalen designed a regional survey consisting of four research areas or units: the Santa Maria unit to the south of Paquimé, the San Pedro unit to the north, the Carretas unit to the far north, and the Paquimé unit. The latter constitutes a survey of the area around the site of Paquimé, excluding the site itself.

The entire research area is located between two major geographical zones: the Chihuahuan Desert to the east with a basin-and-range topography and the Sierra Madre Occidental to the west with peaks ranging between 2400 m to 3000 m above the valley. The areas are characterized by a semiarid to arid climate, with an annual precipitation of 600 mm in the Sierra and 250 mm in the Chihuahuan Desert. The location of Paquimé in this valley is no coincidence. The Sierra's precipitation creates a fertile drainage where "major streams like the Ríos Santa María, Casas Grandes, and San Pedro offer a combination of water and arable land unmatched anywhere else in the region" (Whalen and Minnis 1999:55). The drainage areas formed an important pull factor and attracted most of the human inhabitants to this region. In addition, the region is characterized by a diversity of vegetation provided by the range of natural resources available in the Sierra on the one side and the Chihuahua Desert on the other. Different types of ecosystems offer a variety of resources, a diversity of game for hunting, and many fruits for harvesting (Minnis and Whalen 2004; Whalen and Minnis 1999, 2000, 2001).

Several field seasons between 1989 and 1995 resulted in the systemic survey of nearly 270 km² and the recording of a total of 291 sites. In addition, unsystematic exploration outside the intensive survey areas resulted in 90 additional sites, amounting to a total of 381 archaeological sites. Furthermore, nearly 500 isolated occurrences were recorded in the systematically and unsystemically surveyed areas (Whalen and Minnis 2001:93). I should point out that the 270 km² does not form a continuous area, but represents the total of the four distinct survey areas mentioned earlier. Minnis and Whalen decided to focus on important drainage areas that would provide better information and data about the Prehispanic development in areas they describe as the "most populous segment of the landscape in the late prehistoric times" (Whalen and Minnis 2001:93). Systematic surveys of those areas offered the optimum approach to discover and identify key sites for later excavation. Subsequent excavation thus provided stronger and more comprehensive data to confirm, reject, or modify the preliminary conclusions of the initial survey analysis (Whalen and Minnis 2001:174-175).

Although researchers caution that the survey project results are preliminary and still under study, some observations can be made about the project's achievements. First, the material data collected in the survey enabled the researchers to divide the area into two zones: the Inner zone and the Middle zone. The Inner zone comprises an area of 124 km² that extends from Paquimé to a distance of 30 km. A total of 171 sites were recorded in this Inner sphere. The Middle zone amounts to 145 km² and stretches from 30 km to 80 to 100 km from Paquimé. During the survey, 210 sites were recorded in this area. Although Whalen and Minnis refrain from mentioning it, referring to an Inner and a Middle zone suggests that an 'outer zone' exists. Ostensibly, the "outer zone" corresponds to the area where Paquimé's influence is minimal and against which the Inner and Middle zone are defined.

Secondly, based upon the analyzed ceramic assemblages and structural remains, sites were divided into settlements belonging to two time periods: the Viejo Period, A.D. 700-1200/1250, and the Medio Period, A.D. 1200/1250-1450. Upon completion of this analytical division, 15 sites corresponded to the Viejo Period, of which four belonged to the Inner zone and 11 to the Middle zone. A total of 309 sites pertain to the Medio Period with 141 located in the Inner Zone and 168 in the Middle Zone. A remaining 57 sites resisted such classification (26 for the Inner Zone and 31 for the Middle Zone) and were designated as unknown (Whalen and Minnis 2001).

Although only 20 percent of the sites dated to the Viejo Period, some patterns still emerge from those data. Ranging from 0.01 to 2.5 ha, most of the Viejo sites were small in size and a few were of middle size. Whalen and Minnis (2001:100) report a mean of 0.69 ha (s.d.: 0.62) and mention that some large sites were recorded as well. The Viejo sites consist mostly of pithouse structures and a few surface level structures. Researchers postulate that the low number of Viejo sites recorded might be because of the superposition of Medio Period sites rendering the Viejo sites invisible to archaeological survey (Stewart et al. 2005; Whalen and Minnis 2001, 2003). Further, most of the Viejo sites were settled along the well-watered valleys of major streams. Although data are still scarce, Whalen and Minnis noticed an increase in the size of Viejo communities at the end of the Viejo Period. Interpreted as an expansion of the Viejo population, this observation is taken as a probable beginning of what becomes the Medio Period (Minnis and Whalen

2004; Whalen and Minnis 2001, 2003).

The archaeological record for the Medio Period is rather different. Nearly 80 percent of the sites recorded during the CGRSP belong to this period. In general, the surveyors noted mounds of melted adobe known to contain pueblo adobe room blocks. The Medio Period sites were found to share a similar artifact assemblage with the same proportion of local and imported wares, and they had a comparable ceramic density. Site size analysis revealed no distinctions in artifact assemblage's sites between the two zones. When focusing on characteristic Paquimé features and facilities associated with the sites, however, such as ball courts, birdcages, extensive upland agricultural terrace systems, and large ovens, a sharp distinction appears. Sites with these distinctive features were encountered in the Inner zone, but were almost absent from the Middle zone. This discovery provided a suitable material indicator to measure the real extension of Paquimé's influence over the region (Whalen and Minnis 1999, 2001, 2003).

Besides those features and facilities associated with the site of Paquimé, another medium of influence or control in the region was the distribution of exotic material. In terms of trade items, Whalen and Minnis agree with Di Peso's conclusions that exotic items such as marine shell, copper items, and parrots are irrefutable evidence of extra-regional trade, but they disagree with the hypothesis that those exotic items are evidence of the stockpiling of goods for mercantile exchange (Whalen and Minnis 2001, 2003). Rather, they argue that exotic materials must be "seen as prestige goods that were procured, accumulated, and distributed by the elites of society as an important source of power and authority" (Whalen and Minnis 2001:206). They consider it more likely that such distribution occurred in exchange for labor or to gain community members, to augment their alliances with Paquimé

elites, and to support local kinship networks.

Similar to Fish and Fish's interpretation of the Marana community, Whalen and Minnis understand Paquimé not as a tribe nor as chiefdom, but as a midlevel or intermediate society. They envision Paquimé developing from an egalitarian socio-political structure in the Viejo Period to greater complexity in the Medio Period without the realization of any formal social stratification, bureaucratic administration, or strong decision-making hierarchies (Whalen and Minnis 2000:176). While it remains unclear how this qualitative change really happened, from the data documented by the CSRSP Whalen and Minnis postulate that competition between emergent sites and elites to gain supremacy of the region likely resulted in the rise of a primary center, such as Paquimé.

The CGRSP further made several interesting contributions in terms of population figures. According to an estimation of resource carrying capacity of the fertile floodplain valley of a 5-km radius around Paquimé, the site could support 3,300 people (Whalen and Minnis 2001:72). I would like to note that the site of Paquimé is excluded from this discussion and also from the following population estimate. Paquimé alone has been estimated to have had around 2,250-2,500 individuals (Gamboa 2001:50; Whalen et al. 2010:546).

Although the CGRSP does not provide an exact figure for the research area or for the separate zones, other data such as the number of room blocks and the total area of residential space facilitate the calculation of some contrasting rudimentary population figures. A total of 393 room blocks were recorded in the research area for the Medio Period covering an area of 412,933 m² (Whalen and Minnis 1999:57). As mentioned earlier, Craig (2000:159) calculates population figures in the Hohokam area on the basis of 10 people per residential hectare. Applying Craig's estimation to the CGRSP research area of total residential area of 412,933 m², or 41.3 ha, results in a population estimate of 413 people.

Yet, a different approach to the same data is possible and provides another population figure. Assuming for the sake of calculation that the number of rooms all correspond to contemporary habitations, multiplying the total number of rooms reported for the research area by 3 to 6 members per room provides an estimated figure of 1,179 and 2,558 inhabitants, not including those of the site of Paquimé. This estimate approximates the population estimate obtained first based upon the area's resource availability and would therefore seem to be the most accurate for the area around Paquimé.

In sum, the data collected by the CGRSP in the zones around Paquimé enabled several observations about the Casas Grandes tradition. First, the survey and subsequent analysis illustrated that the real direct influence of the primary center of Paquimé was no more than 10 percent of what Di Peso (1974:2:314-15) originally proposed. Whalen and Minnis indicate that the material evidence documented indicated that the Inner core with a 15 km radius appeared to be directly under the influence of the center. They also confirmed that settlements located between 15 and 30 km radius were closely tied to Paquimé but retained a certain degree of autonomy. Beyond the 30 km radius and into the closest drainage, Whalen and Minnis identified a Middle zone that functioned as the outermost limits of Paquimé political influence. The areas identified as the Middle Zone such as Santa María to the southwest, Carretas and Animas to the northwest, and the Sierra Madre to the West appeared to have existed outside the direct control of the primary center, but nonetheless shared certain cultural characteristics such as ball courts and ceramic assemblages. Finally, far away areas (nearly 100 km), such as Villa Ahumada to the east and Babícora to the south, appear to have had

minimal contact with the center and existed autonomously of Paquimé.

The CGRSP further confirmed that like these far away areas, neighboring regions that were removed from the influence of Paquimé existed, such as the Jornada Mogollon, the lower Río Grande, the Mimbres area, the northern Animas area, and southern Chihuahua (Kelley et al. 1999; Stewart et al. 2005; Whalen and Minnis 2001). In all those areas archaeological excavation has uncovered Paquimé ceramic types, but they only exist as a minimum component of a larger assemblage dominated by local wares. Such material evidence documents the importance of the primary center of Paquimé, but does not confirm direct influence over neighboring areas typical of a powerful regional center. Instead, the evidence suggests Paquimé functioned as a link, albeit an important one, in the Prehispanic trade network.

Finally, Whalen and Minnis estimate that Paquimé's influence in the region consisted of a limited interaction sphere approximately 70,000 to 100,000 km². While similar to the 88,000 km² proposed by Di Peso (1974:2:667), an important difference exists. The interaction sphere proposed by Whalen and Minnis implies "some sorts of social and economic relation among the area's populations" (Whalen and Minnis 2001:194), while the one Di Peso determined assumed a "single, uniformly high level of regional integration" (Whalen and Minnis 2001:195).

THE CERRO DE TRINCHERAS SETTLEMENT AND LAND USE SURVEY PROJECT

Geographically, the Trincheras tradition extends from the northernmost coast and coastal plain of the Gulf of California, along the Concepción, Magdalena, and Altar drainages to the Río San Miguel in the east, and to the north begins approximately at the international border extending to Desemboque in the south. The Trincheras Purple-on-red specular ceramic type, cerros de trincheras sites (hills with human-made terraces), and the Cerro de Trincheras site in northern Sonora characterize this tradition (McGuire and Villalpando 1993, 1995, 2011). Spanish colonists and early explorers first reported these sites, but archaeological investigation was not carried out until the past few decades (Gallaga and Newell 2004). The Cerro de Trincheras and La Playa, both in the Río Magdalena Valley, are the two major and most intensively studied sites of this tradition.

In the Río Magdalena Valley stands the Cerro de Trincheras, the largest cerro de trincheras site of this tradition. The site is an isolated volcanic hill rising 160 m above the valley and covering an area of 100 ha. The hill has more than 900 terraces, 300 stone circles, several square structures, and at least two ceremonial structures, La Cancha and El Caracol (Gallaga 1998; Martinez n.d., 2011; McGuire and Villalpando 2011). The Cerro de Trincheras community occupied the site from around A.D. 1300 to 1450, and it has been broadly estimated that almost 2,000 people lived at the site at some point (McGuire et al. 1999:136).

Early researchers were particularly drawn to this area to study the acquisition, exploitation, and exchange of marine shell. Prior to excavation, marine shell was believed to have been a major good traded by the Trincheras communities intra- and inter-regionally, especially with the Hohokam communities of southern central Arizona (Kelley and Villalpando 1996; McGuire and Villalpando 1993, 1995; Vargas 1999).

The excavation of the Cerro de Trincheras site provided a great deal of information and understanding about the site (Gallaga 1997; McGuire and Villalpando 1993, 1995, 2011; McGuire et al. 1999; O' Donovan 2002, Villa-

lpando and McGuire 2009), but little about the surrounding area. Remedying this situation a few years later, in 1999, Suzanne Fish and Paul Fish undertook a systematic survey focusing on the core of the Trincheras archaeological tradition in northern Sonora.

The Cerro de Trincheras Settlement and Land Use Survey Project (CTSS) forms a continuation of an ongoing research collaboration between Mexican and American archaeologists in Sonora and a further step in the knowledge of the cultural development of the Trincheras archaeological tradition in Sonora. The CTSS followed from previous archaeological research conducted in the area: the excavation of the Cerro de Trincheras Site, excavations at the La Playa site, and the Altar Valley Survey Project (McGuire and Villalpando 1993, 1995, 2011; McGuire et al. 1999; Sanchez et al. 1996). Good relationships with local officials and communities built by the researchers of previous projects facilitated the planning and realization of the CTSS (Fish 1999b:1). In addition, the destruction of nearby cerros de trincheras sites pressed the archaeologists to undertake this survey project.

In 1999, Suzanne Fish and Paul Fish designed and supervised a systematic survey project covering an area of 20 km² located nearby and around the Cerro de Trincheras site. Shortly after the project's start, the coverage area was increased to 75 km² to include some unexpected cerros de trincheras sites both inside and outside the full coverage survey area. These sites promised to add valuable data about the development of the Cerro de Trincheras as a primate center in the area and to provide insights on its territorial organization.

The CTSS strove to achieve two immediate research goals. Establishing the settlement pattern around the primary center of Cerro de Trincheras site formed the first to analyze the territorial organization and population dynamics at the center. Secondly, the systematic survey would yield enough data to estimate the agricultural potential of the area. This information would then contribute to an understanding of agricultural subsistence for the primary center of Cerro de Trincheras and the surrounding settlements in the basin over time (Fish 1999b:1).

The survey area lay in the Río Magdalena valley, in the basin-and-range topography province, and in the Sonoran desert environmental zone. A semiarid to arid climate with annual precipitation of 300 mm and summer temperatures above 100° F characterizes the region. The usual natural resources typical of Sonoran desert zones are found in this area, such as deer, javalina, and rabbits, as well as leguminous trees and columnar cacti. On the flood plain, vegetation consists of riparian plant communities such as ironwood and mesquite (Fish 1999; McGuire et al. 1999). Annual precipitation is insufficient to sustain agricultural activities alone. Prehispanic communities must have used irrigation to concentrate and/or channel water to agricultural fields from formerly perennial or seasonal flows (Fish 1999b; Fish and Fish 2004; McGuire et al. 1999).

After 12 weeks of fieldwork, 75 km² were systematically surveyed and more than 240 archaeological sites were recorded. Great diversity was found to characterize the sites, which ranged from pre-ceramic to pre-Revolution hacienda sites. Ceramic assemblages analyzed during previous archaeological research in the area—enabled the identification of the recorded sites (Gallaga 1997; McGuire and Villalpando 1993, 2011; McGuire et al. 1999; Fish and Fish 2004). Site distribution broke down as follows: one Paleoindian site, 47 Archaic sites, 89 Early Ceramic sites, 141 Late Ceramic sites, 18 Historic Papago sites, and 17 Historic European sites (Fish and Fish 2004:56). The study documented a long and permanent occupation in the Magdalena River Valley, extending from the Archaic to modern times. Although all the data gathered by the CTSS proved important, researchers focused on the ceramic period to understand the rise of the Cerro de Trincheras site as a primate center (Fish 1999b; Fish and Fish 2003, 2004).

The Cerro de Trincheras community occupied the site from around A.D. 1300-1450. Early Ceramic sites preceded that occupation, while Late Ceramic sites—the subsequent phase—were more or less contemporaneous. Early Ceramic sites were found throughout the survey area and likely relied on irrigation and floodwater farming. Survey also revealed that during the next phase, the Late Ceramic, sites increased in number as did the evidence of floodwater farming, particularly in the southern portion of the survey area around the Cerro de Trincheras site. The growth in site numbers for the Late Ceramic phase has been interpreted as a possible local and regional social aggregation or re-accommodation process. The Cerro de Trincheras site is thought to have been an important pull factor. Furthermore, archaeologists discovered the abandonment of larger Early Ceramic sites occurring prior to the Late Ceramic phase, social re-location may explain this finding (Fish 1999b; Fish and Fish 2003, 2004).

In terms of population estimates, McGuire et al. provide the only figures for the area when they mention that 2,000 people inhabited the Cerro de Trincheras (McGuire et al. 1999:136). Fish and Fish, however, provide data on the total site area for the Early and Late Ceramic phases thus enabling demographic calculations. The Early Ceramic phase sites amount to 2,249,700 m² (225 ha) and 3,954,300 m² (395.4 ha) correspond to the Late Ceramic phase (Fish and Fish 2004:59). Using Craig's (2000:159) estimation of 10 people per hectare and assuming that all sites were contemporaneous, 2,250 people inhabited the area during the Early Ceramic phase and 3,954 people during the Late Ceramic phase. From the former to the latter, population appears to have almost doubled in the valley and tripled when adding the 2,000 people estimated to have lived at the Cerro de Trincheras.

In a separate analysis, Fish and Fish postulate that the valley's Prehispanic potential farming area amounted to around 875 ha (Fish and Fish 2004:55). This area can hypothetically support around 2,034 and 5,087 (see Population Density in Chapter 7 for potential farming resources per family discussion). According to these estimates, the valley's potential farming capabilities could indeed sustain the population figures for both phases of occupation.

The CTSS resulted in a preliminary model explaining the social and cultural development of the Cerro de Trincheras in the area and possibly for the rest of the Trincheras tradition. Mapping the cerros de trincheras sites in the area—the primary research goal—allowed archaeologists to compare the sites complexity. Temporal identification of sites, based on the ceramic assemblage, revealed a likely scenario of social development. Cerros de Trincheras sites from the Early Ceramic phase lack the typical corral or rounded enclosure that researchers have associated with ritual/ceremonial activities at the summits of these sites. In the Late Ceramic phase, cerros de trincheras sites appeared more abundant, but dispersed. Located over a generally well-spaced distance from one another in the valley, this distribution might represent a mechanism for communal observances of special ceremonies/ritual. Moreover, most of the Late Ceramic sites had corral structures at the summit. This finding strengthens the interpretation of a regional institutionalization of specialized functions, which was probably coordinated by the Cerro de Trincheras site as a primate center in the area (Fish 1999b; Fish and Fish 2003, 2004; McGuire et al. 1999).

CTSS further provided data for an analysis of site size to better assess the roll of the Cerro de Trincheras in the area. That no contemporaneous Late Ceramic phase site recorded in the valley equals the Cerro de Trincheras site in size convinced the archaeologists of the "differential aggregation of area population at this preeminent site" (Fish 1999b:7). As a critical concluding thought, however, Fish and Fish explain that the survey did not cover enough area to be able to assess the occurrence of the abandonment of and movement from less desirable farming areas located away from the river and the Cerro de Trincheras to irrigable floodplains and lower basin alluvial fans located near the primary center. Fish and Fish suspect this change may have taken place simultaneously to the re-location of population in and around the Cerro de Trincheras that occurred during the Late Ceramic phase. The rise of the Cerro de Trincheras and the construction of its residential, public, and ceremonial structures appear to further reflect the hierarchy of the site and the socio-political importance of this center in the Río Magdalena basin. Based on CTSS and earlier excavations in the area (McGuire and Villalpando 1993; McGuire et al. 1999; Sanchez et al. 1996) Fish and Fish interpret the Cerro de Trincheras as a primate center housing a population that negotiated and coordinated the increasing social interactions of its surroundings (Fish and Fish 2004:63).

COMPARISON WITH THE OVAP

Comparisons with similar projects in neighboring areas may facilitate further insights into the Prehispanic context surveyed in the Onavas Valley. The survey projects described above—the MCSP, the CGRSP, and the CTSS—stand out as valuable comparative contexts.

Geographical Setting

Three of the four areas are located in Northwest

Mexico. Currently, Marana in the northen Tucson Basin is situated north of the international border in the U.S. Southwest. In Prehispanic times prior to the modern border, all research areas belonged to the same geographical region. In terms of environment, the four areas share similar desert environment conditions as the Sonoran Desert envelops the Marana, Trincheras, and Onavas areas while the Chihuahuan Desert surrounds Paquimé.

Topographic and morphological differences, however, distinguish the four areas. The Marana and Trincheras research areas are situated practically in open valleys in basin-and-range topography. The environmental zone of the Sierra Madre Occidental protrudes into the Onavas Valley and the Casas Grandes Valley. An open valley in the basin-and-range zone also characterizes the Casas Grandes research area, but the Sierra Madre Occidental topography cannot be ignored. The Onavas Valley, in contrast, constitutes a boxed, narrow river valley situated in the western portion of the Sierra Madre Occidental (Fish and Fish 2004; Fish et al. 1992; McGuire et al. 1999; Whalen and Minnis 2001). When considering the areas' topographic and environmental similarities and differences, the Onavas Valley emerges as being comparatively unique in nature due to its restricted topography. The Prehispanic settlement pattern of the valley reflects this characteristic.

Inhabitants of all four areas faced a hot desert climate and a scarcity of water. Permanent and even perennial rivers therefore formed important pull factors in the choice of which areas to settle. Logically, in the four areas settlements were erected near permanent and perennial rivers, such as the Santa Cruz River for Marana, the Río Magdalena for Trincheras, the Río Casas Grandes for Paquimé, and the Río Yaqui for Onavas. Of all these rivers, the Río Yaqui carries the most water and does so year-round, providing communities with fresh-water resources, such as fish, the entire year.

For all four traditions, the desert offered a variety of natural resources, such as cholla buds, prickly pear, sahuaro fruit, agave, and mesquite seeds. Marana, Casas Grandes, and especially Onavas inhabitants also benefited from access to high altitude forest and the natural resources that such an environment provides. Located further away from forested areas, Trincheras depended entirely on its desert surroundings. In terms of farming soil, the Casas Grandes and Onavas areas profited in Prehispanic times from the best arable land. Farming land in the Trincheras area, follow by the Marana area, required more soil preparation to raise crops successfully (Fish and Fish 2004; Fish et al. 1992; McGuire et al. 1999; Whalen and Minnis 2001).

Of course, cultural/adaptive responses are as much a reflection of the natural characteristics of the area as they adhere to social and political patterns. To assess these variables, the systematic surveys in the four areas proved worthwhile as a method. By providing comprehensive recording and analysis of the Prehispanic material records as well as the natural environments, the systematic surveys enabled archaeologists to interpret the full cultural landscape of their areas' Prehispanic inhabitants.

Settlement Density and Structure

An optimal comparison of settlement density and structure is possible between the four data sets because all four projects undertook systematic surveys that followed similar methodology. A preliminary comparison between these projects is made for the Late Prehispanic period (A.D. 1250/1250-1450/1500).

As Table 8.1 illustrates, the survey projects in the areas of Casas Grandes and Marana covered the most ground, followed by Trincheras and then Onavas. I should note

Table 8.1. Comparative statistics of the total site area for the OVAP, MCSP, CGRPS, and CTSS

Project	Survey area (km^2)	Total site area (km^2)	Site area per km²
Marana	146	6,145,000	42,100
Trincheras	75	3,954,300	52,700
Casas Grandes	270	412,933	1,530
Onavas	67	415,646	6,204

in respect to this observation that the Casas Grandes and Marana projects lasted several years, while the latter two consisted of a single field season. Table 8.1 also indicates a rather sharp difference in total site area, placing Marana and Trincheras in one side and Casas Grandes and Onavas in the other. It is possible, however, that the total site area for Marana and Trincheras constitutes of the whole site area, whereas Casas Grandes total site area includes solely adobe room block space not the entire site area (Whalen and Minnis 1999, 2001). For Onavas, the total site area represents the whole area reported, however most of the sites were destroyed by mechanized farming activities and only scattered surface material was visible and recorded. Table 8.1 indicates that the Marana and Trincheras total site area are 1:14.7 and 1:9.5, respectively, larger than the total site area of the Onavas Valley.

In terms of settlement area per km², again the total number of sites for Marana and Trincheras covered more surface area than did the Onavas sites with ratios of 1:6.3 and 1:8, respectively. The presence of more flat areas for site development at Marana and Trincheras and the absence or scarcity of flat areas in the Onavas Valley might very well explain these different ratios. Considering the geography of each area further, some degree of competition

for land between farming and habitation could also explain these ratios. Furthermore, cerros de trincheras sites are located on volcanic hills and cover a large amount of surface area that exceeds those of sites situated in flat areas. Comparatively, then, the Trincheras area may be effectively inflated to some degree.

Because the estimated settlement are for Casas Grandes data corresponds not to the entire site area, but only to room block area, the site area estimates in the Onavas Valley may be underestimated. In a narrow boxed valley, such as the Onavas Valley, habitation surface is likely to have overlapped with or stood in competition with farming land. It is conceivable then that the Marana and Trincheras site areas correspond more accurately to habitation site area, whereas in the Onavas Valley the amount of recorded site area may include farm land.

In addition, because of the area's geographical characteristics, the Onavas survey of 67 km² recorded smaller sites that were generally located in the valley, or more homogenously in similar topographic settings. Virtually no sites appeared nearby or in the hills and higher mountains. At Marana, Trincheras, and Casas Grandes, where survey covered larger surface areas, more sites were recorded. Situated in river valleys, hills, and mountains, those sites were further located in more heterogeneous topographic settings than those in the Onavas Valley.

Primary Site and Population Density

The four systematic surveys indicate that during the Late Prehispanic period in all four areas a primary site dominated or at least influenced its surrounding areas. Although the OVAP did not identify a prominent Prehispanic site through the archaeological survey, it has been argued in preceding chapters that a principal Nébome site stood in Prehispanic times at the location of the Onavas town. In spite of differences among the four areas, Marana, Trincheras, Casas Grandes, and Onavas all featured a site prominent in its respective regional setting. Of the four areas, the Marana Platform Mound site was the largest primary site, covering an area larger than 150 ha. The Cerro de Trincheras site forms the second largest with 100 ha followed by Paquimé with 80 ha and Onavas with approximately 10 to 15 ha.

In spite of this comparison in size, Paquimé emerges as the most complex and elaborate site, followed by the Marana Platform Mound, Cerro de Trincheras, and finally Onavas. At 80 ha, Paquimé consists of more than 1,780 adobe rooms distributed over several buildings of four to five stories high (Whalen and Minnis 2001:107). In addition, platform mounds, ball courts, and water systems render Paquimé the site with the most elaborate public and ceremonial architecture in the Casas Grandes Inner Zone and one of the most socially complex Prehispanic communities in the Northwest Mexico and the U.S. Southwest.

At 150 ha the Marana Platform Mound is larger than Paquimé and, "containing more than 25 compounds is the largest site in its 146 km² community and the only village site in which all residents lived in walled compounds" (Fish and Fish 2004:59). In addition, a 10 km-long canal illustrates the social and political power of the Marana Platform Mound site. The Cerro de Trincheras is the third largest site in the region at 100 ha. This primary site contains more than 900 stone terraces, 350 stone circles, and at least two distinctive public and ceremonial structures, La Cancha and El Caracol. It was also the largest site in its region with the greatest population density. Furthermore the Cerro de Trincheras located on the largest hill itself served as a public architectural statement.

The Onavas settlement clearly constitutes the smallest of the four with an area of approximately 10 to 15 ha. The site is likely to have included some kind of public or ceremonial structures. Considering that the two second largest sites in the valley (SON P:10:12 and SON P:10:70, See Appendix I and II) did have such structures, however, it is not inconceivable to reason that the region's primary site would have had such architecture as well. In addition, this site enjoys a central position in the valley.

From the above comparison of the areas' primary sites, the Onavas Valley's Prehispanic community emerges as the least elaborate and complex community of the four presented here. Placement of these primary sites in their respective regional context, especially considering settlement hierarchy and estimated population density, provides further insights.

In terms of settlement site hierarchy, Paquimé and Cerro de Trincheras were at least ten times larger than the next largest settlement site, in their respective archaeologically defined traditions. Beyond Paquimé, the CGRSP indicated that the second largest site reported covered an area between 10,000 and 15,000 m² of mound area (Whalen and Minnis 2001:138). For the Marana and Onavas communities, the distances between the prominent site and the second rank site(s) is less striking. Research indicates that the Marana community comprised at least 11 sites larger than 100,000 m², three of which amounted to more than 500,000 m². In the Onavas community, survey recorded 15 sites larger than 10,000 m², of which three measured greater than 20,000 m². The latter figure suggests that primary centers in general had higher population densities as a reflection of their socio-political status in their communities.

Population density estimates, particularly for the primary centers, provide additional contrasts of interest. Beginning with the primary sites, the maximum population number for the site of Paquimé has been estimated as more than 2,200 inhabitants. The estimate for the Marana Platform Mound site amounts approximately 900 members, while the Cerro de Trincheras is thought to have housed around 2,000 residents. In lieu of concrete and substantial archaeological evidence of the postulated primary site at Onavas, no estimation exists for the Prehispanic primary center of the Onavas Valley. Colonial reports written after the Jesuits had established a mission church at Onavas provide some vague indications, although they require a strong cautionary note as these accounts occurred at least 150 years after Europeans arrived to the New World. Father Cabero in 1662 and Father Zapata in 1678 provide census figures for the Onavas settlements that indicate that 400 to 800 inhabitants lived in the town of Onavas settlement alone (Pennington 1980:33; Zapata 1678:361-362). Were these numbers to be proven accurate, the Onavas primary site housed significantly fewer inhabitants than the primary sites of the other three archaeological traditions.

Estimations of population density reveal a similar picture as that described above on the basis of absolute population numbers. Along with the earlier site size discussion, population density was the highest in the architecturally compact Paquimé. The Cerro de Trincheras exceeds the Marana Platform Mound in terms of population density. Relying on a low suggested number of absolute populations, the Onavas settlement is likely to have had the lowest population density figure.

Total population estimations for the survey areas also offers interesting analytical insight. On the whole, such estimations resulted mostly from calculations of farming resource capacity and/or from accounts of residential area in the form of accumulated site area or room blocks in the case of Casas Grandes (Craig 2000, Fish and Fish 1994). Interestingly, as Table 8.2 illustrates, all four survey areas have similar population estimations: around 3,000 people. Population density, however, provides a highly divergent picture, depicting Trincheras area with the highest level, follow by Onavas, Marana, and lastly Casas Grandes. Of course, the material evidence in the four areas, as discussed earlier, points to density levels suggesting a nucleated population during Prehispanic times in these archaeologically defined regions. Having already established the presence of a population dense community then, a comparison between the areas of the estimations within their regional setting forms a necessary step to contextualize the Onavas Valley and its internal population density relationships.

As Table 8.2 summarizes, population densities of some of the four survey areas are relatively higher than those of other traditions. When contemplating the total Casas Grandes area the CGRSP yielded a low density. According to the MCSP the complete Marana community area presented a medium-high level of population density. On the other end of the spectrum, the survey projects in the Trincheras and Onavas areas recorded relatively high population densities for those regions. Because larger projects yielded considerably lower density levels than smaller survey projects, the size of the survey area clearly requires consideration as an important factor of bias. Nonethe-

Table 8.2. Total population estimations for the four projects			
Project	Survey area (km^2)	Total population	Persons per km²
Marana	146	3,000-4,000	20-27
Trincheras	75	4,000	52.6
Casas Grandes	270	3,300	12.2
Onavas	67	3,000	44.7

less, the results coincide with the observation that in open valleys, such as Marana, Casas Grandes, and even Trincheras, settlement was more dispersed resulting in lower population density levels. A boxed river valley area, such as the one encountered in the Onavas Valley, restricted and concentrated settlement, where a limited amount of land was available to meet residential requirements as well as farming needs.

Marine Shell Manufacture and Trade of Finished Goods

Another aspect that the four areas share is material evidence for intra- and inter-regionally interactions. The geographically strategic position of the Marana Platform Mound site seems to reflect the control of exotic goods distribution in the region. The Cerro de Trincheras seems to have functioned as an important manufacture center of marine shell goods, albeit mostly for local consumption. The Casas Grandes area has been recognized as a major consumer of exotic goods, especially marine shell. And last, the Onavas Valley seems to have had a participant role, as a consumer and manufacturer of marine shell goods, on a likely important trade route between the coast and the interior.

For all four areas, survey projects recorded and recovered non-local materials that archaeo-logical analysis identified as exotic or prestige goods. Examples are marine shell, copper, decorated ceramics, specific animal remains, turquoise, and/or obsidian. Of these items, marine shell is the most commonly shared item between the four areas. Its favorable preservation in the field, the ease of spotting shell on the surface, and its frequent presence meant that marine shell served as a productive primary exotic good to analyze and compare between regions.

Throughout the Prehispanic region of modern Northwest Mexico and the U.S. Southwest, we assume marine shell formed a coveted item (Braniff 1989; Nelson 1991). Appreciation of its natural beauty and guided by the cultural values ascribed to this material meant that marine shell as a raw material or as a finished good constituted an important trade item. Ethnographic and ethnohistoric research in Central Mexico illustrates the great importance some cultures (e.g., Mexica) attributed to marine shells as a symbol, a ceremonial/ritual item, even a representation of a god, or as a marker of social and political status (López Austin 1995). Of the values or cultural concepts potentially associated with shell, its association with water undoubtedly proved most significant in the Northwest Mexico and the U.S. Southwest. Shell goods are a coveted commodity in deser conditions. Marine shell is relatively easy to obtain along the coast, but not in the interior, and was likely transported either as a raw material, pre-forms, or as finished goods to non-coastal communities in exchange for their region's resources (Bradley 1993, 1999; Nelson 1991; Suárez 1974; Vargas 2004; Villalpando 1988, 2000a).

Table 8.3 provides statistics on the marine shell collected from the surface by the four projects under consideration. That shell appeared on the surface in all areas signifies extra-regional interaction, as none of the areas is situated near the coast.

At the Marana community, survey recovered only 51 items from the surface of 35 sites. None of this material was positively identified as workshop debris (Fish and Fish 2004:62). Although additional research and excavation of the area was later undertaken on documented shell manufacture inside the community (Bayman 1996), surface material indicates that this exotic material was not as common as other exotic items. It appears more likely that Marana inhabitants obtained such material from sporadic extra-regional trade. In addition, as only 5 percent of the sites inside the Marana community reported marine shell, the internal distribution of this exotic material seems to have been limited.

The survey project of the Trincheras area, in contrast, provides a rather different picture. Out of a total of 233 sites recorded, archaeologists recorded marine shell at the surface of 71 sites, amounting slightly more than 30 percent of the site sample. Material analysis of more than 700 shell items revealed that half of the shell assemblage consisted of workshop debris and finished goods constituted the other half of the assemblage. These results suggest that the production of marine shell goods took place at the Cerro de Trincheras community, perhaps much of it for local consumption (McGuire and Villalpando 2011; Vargas 2004:72). In addition, several stone items used for shell goods manufacture, such as reamers, were found at the Cerro de Trincheras site and at the survey area that supported the marine shell manufacturing industry (Vargas 2004). Shell distribution inside the Trincheras survey area indicates that both larger and smaller sites had access to this material. In the absence of research to the contrary, archaeologists have taken this to point to a lack of centralization over the circulation of this exotic material (Gallaga 2004a; Vargas 2004).

For the Casas Grandes area, researchers for the CSRSP survey mention that marine shell was "too rare to play any part in this analysis"

Table 8.3. Shell statistics for the four projects

Project	Number of sites	Sites with shell	Number of shell items
Marana	712	35	51
Trincheras	233	71	710
Paquimé	381	54*	93*
Onavas	122	51	1,191

* Personal communication Michael Whalen November 2005.

(Whalen and Minnis 2001:150). Whalen (personal communication 2005) states that only 93 pieces of shell were recorded from the surface of 54 sites. Of those, 61 pieces were identified as freshwater shell, leaving only 28 marine shell items (4 pieces were identified as indeterminate), which represent a very low number of shell artifacts. Regardless, in their discussion they summarize that "only 11.5 percent of Inner Zone room blocks had shell on the surface, while the comparable Middle Zone figure is 26.3 percent, or more than twice as large" (Whalen and Minnis 2001:117). Interestingly, the marine shell distribution in the smaller sites of the Middle Zone was higher than that in the small sites of the Inner Zone. This observation suggests an unequal distribution of this exotic material between the primary center of Paquimé and the Inner Zone sites and Paquimé and the Middle Zone sites. This further suggests the likelihood that the Middle Zone sites did not depend entirely on Paquimé to obtain this exotic material. It is noteworthy to mention that at the site of Paquimé more than 3.9 million pieces of shell were recovered from the late 1950s and 1960s excavations (Di Peso et al. 1974). That finding certainly appears to confirm that the Paquimé site played an important role on the distribution and control of this exotic material, at least in the Inner Zone (Whalen and Minnis 2001).

In comparison, the amount of the marine shell recovered from the surface of Prehispanic sites in the Onavas Valley exceeds those found in the three other areas by the following ratios: 1:23.3 times more than the MCSP, 1:1.7 for the CTSS, and 1:13 times more than the CSRSP. At Onavas, 51 sites yielded 1,191 pieces of collected shell that represents more than 41 pecent of the site recorded. The analysis of that material indicates that almost two-thirds of that total consisted of workshop debris while the remainder constituted to finished goods. Albeit small, 1 percent of the sample was identified as

raw material, providing additional support to the local manufacture hypothesis. The marine shell analysis thus depicts the communities of the Onavas Valley as both consumers and manufacturers of this exotic material. The high amount of debitage suggests that the Onavas communities manufactured goods not only to satisfy local consumption but also to trade with communities farther inland, possibly as far as the site of Paquimé. The latter highlights the likelihood of the Río Yaqui as one important trade route.

CHAPTER SUMMARY

The projects featured in this chapter indicate that in spite of the arid and desert-like conditions, societies characterized by complex forms of organization beyond egalitarian organization do arise and flourish. Each of the projects recorded that public and ceremonial structures were constructed, hence documenting a type of community social organization that was capable of undertaking activities beyond the basic family social structures. Furthermore, the identification of a pyramid-shaped settlement hierarchy, with a prominent site at the top and many small sites at the bottom, strengthens the possibility of a middle-range socio-political structure. Of the four areas, the primary center of Paquimé exerted the strongest, most measurable, and direct territorial influence over its surrounding area. The Marana Mound, the Cerro de Trincheras, and the Prehispanic center at Onavas appear to have had some influence over the surrounding communities of their respective valleys, but not as strong as Paquimé. Analysis of artifacts and features from surface and excavation, as conducted in some of the projects, illustrated that in light of alternative leadership models such as the dual-processual model (Blanton et al. 1996), a corporate leadership strategy applies for at least the Marana Platform Mound, Cerro de Trincheras, and Paquimé. The analyses of material type, distribution, and amount indicate that no single sector ran the socio-political structure of the site or/and controlled the distribution of goods. It seems likely then that several groups competed with each other to acquire power. Furthermore, in the absence of leaders identified or identifiable in the material record at those areas, a corporate model certainly seems more appropriate. The presence of apparently exclusive ceremonial structures reveals that some sort of elite or special social sector operated at those sites and may indicate that a network leadership strategy was in place, or emergent (Blanton et al. 1996). The presence of exotic material such as turquoise, non-local decorated ceramics, and marine shell, demonstrates that the three areas also participated in intra- and inter-regional interactions to obtain those exotic materials. Most likely such networks and exotic materials were used by the Prehispanic communities and social groups inside a community as one means to achieve or acquire local power.

In addition to the dual-processual model, Fish and Fish apply the concept of "community" to the Marana research area (Fish et al. 1992). This concept focuses on the spatial boundaries of a community and entails a notion of territorial affiliation tying the members of any particular community to the area inside the boundaries. The spatially bound territory corresponds not only to the settlement or residential areas, but to the affiliation of its residents and their rights to use the surrounding natural resources (Fish and Fish 2000:161). The spatial boundaries also build cultural/ritual landscapes to bind community members in the social realm and into the geographical space the community holds.

The Nébome communities at Onavas represent the least complex societies of the four areas under consideration. The lack of further excavation material and contexts make it difficult to achieve a deeper level of interpretation regarding the internal social complexity of Nébome[1] society. Nonetheless, the presence of public and ceremonial structures, on one hand, and the amount and types of exotic goods, such as marine shell on the other hand, suggests a middle-range level community. But at this point in the research, an argument can be made that the mortuary mound 'public structure' could be identified with an individual in a leadership position; that of a chief versus the middle-range level community structure. In addition, it can be argued that small public architecture in the absence of large public architectural endeavors requires a more organized community effort. The distribution of exotic goods suggests that they are more common at the larger sites rather than at the smaller ones. This suggests some measure of distributional control over these exotic goods. A clustered settlement pattern indicates that the Prehispanic sites in this valley could be part of a single territorial organization. In this regard, the term community may be applied to the Nébome settlements of the Onavas Valley. Future excavation of key features and sites will provide additional information to clarify this rudimentary picture. In order to provide a better picture of the cultural patterns discussed here research in adjacent valleys is needed.

Finally, the comparative analysis of archaeological projects undertaken in similar geographical environments with comparable methodologies has demonstrated its utility in several directions. In all four areas, systematic surveys provide initial insights into the area's distinct archaeological record and cultural tradition. A comparative examination of settlement patterns in the research areas revealed how the Prehispanic communities developed.

---

1   The analysis of the data from Cristina Garcia project's of SON P:10:8 El Cementerio is underway.

Data gathered by these projects allowed researchers to build cultural frameworks that can be further tested with the excavation of selected sites or features, identified previously by the survey project. In the end, those cultural frameworks become stronger because they incorporate a wealth of data gathered with broad (systematic survey) and specific (excavation) perspectives.

Chapter 9
Conclusions and Final Thoughts

…I am telling you, those are not house foundations!! I know what those look like and those are definitively not houses!!!... So tell me what are they? (Comment by an Onavas rancher 2004).

OVAP field investigations and analyses fulfilled several research objectives: a preliminary definition of the cultural landscape, a description of the material assemblage of the Nébomes, a definition of the local archaeological tradition, and a proposal for a local chronology for the Onavas Valley. Much was learned. Much more remains to be done to comprehend more fully the internal and external Prehispanic population, economic, and social dynamics of this region. The approach pursued by the OVAP, which included a combination of full-scale survey and settlement pattern analysis, as well as ethnohistorical and ethnographic analysis of landscape structure, illustrate the potential of this research strategy for understanding under-researched areas such as the Onavas Valley.

Previous archaeological surveys in similar river valley areas in Sonora, such as the Río Sonora and the Río Bavispe in northern Sonora or the Cuchujaqui drainage and the Río Mayo in southern portion of the state (Doolittle 1988; Douglas and Quijada 2004a, 2004b; Pailes 1972), show that Prehispanic sites in this type of environment and geographical setting are usually found near water sources and arable lands, and mostly on top of small mesas or elevated areas. The OVAP confirmed a similar pattern for the Onavas Valley. Landscape structure analysis supplemented artifact and settlement pattern analysis to illustrate the almost total concentration of residence and ancillary activities in areas with water availability for agriculture and land suitable for farming throughout the Prehispanic sequence.

A clustered settlement pattern indicated that the Prehispanic Onavas community was composed of a structured set of inter-site relationships, most likely with a socio-political structure beyond that of a tribal/egalitarian organization. Although chiefs or principales are mentioned in Colonial documents among the Nébomes, at this point in the field research it remains impossible to document their presence archaeologically. The community concept or model, as a socio-political and identity unit, offers a more advantageous fit than just a settlement pattern analysis to describe the archaeological remains recovered in the valley. But the community model by no means denies the possibility that the Prehispanic Onavas society had a certain degree of complexity that is reflected on the settlement pattern identified by the OVAP. The fact that these valleys, specifically the Nebomes/Opatas Valley, accepted the new social structure of the Spaniards, indicated that they were accustomed to a certain degree to socio-political complexity, and that social and political inequality existed already (Gallaga and Newell 2012).

Artifact analyses provided preliminary insights into the Nébome material culture, from which some cultural and economic patterns were inferred. The amount and diversity of material collected suggested the existence of well-established sedentary communities that engaged in several activities such as farming, gardening, craft manufacture, fishing and hunting. Those activities illustrated how well the Nébomes utilized the local resources that the valley had to offer. The identification of non-local decorated sherds, turquoise, obsidian, and large amounts of shell reveals that the Onavas Valley had wide ranging exchange relationships and contacts. It is premature, however, to suggest the degree and type(s) of extra-regional interactions in which the Prehispanic residents of the Onavas Valley communities might have been engaged. Two new ceramic types, the Onavas Plain and the Onavas Purple-on-Red, were identified, thus increasing the known variety of Sonoran ceramic types. Based mostly on local and non-local decorated ceramic and projectile point materials, a preliminary local chronology was defined that awaits further testing. The amount and types of marine shell goods recorded suggest that the valley's Prehispanic populations not only acquired this exotic material, but also dedicated considerable amounts of time to the manufacture of shell goods. Again, it is premature to determine whether this production was for local consumption, for trade with neighboring areas, or both. Also, it cannot yet be determined how the valley acquired this exotic material: directly from the coast, indirectly via traders, or both.

Overall, the material analysis indicates that the Prehispanic Onavas communities were engaged in multiple craft production industries, such as ceramics, shell goods, textiles, and lithic ornaments and tools. A great deal of that craft production was most likely for local consumption, but some may have been used for trade outside the local economic realm of the Onavas Valley. The large quantities and manufactured items suggest regional trade. Paquime is most likely to be one of them.

One of the most relevant research contributions that emerged from the integrated material, settlement pattern, landscape structure, and ethnohistorical analyses was to challenge the existing assumption that this portion of the Middle Río Yaqui belonged to the Río Sonora archaeological tradition. The data strongly suggest that the Onavas Valley shared more characteristics with the Huatab-

ampo archaeological tradition, probably with those communities identified by Pailes (1972) of the Cuchujaqui phase in the lower foothills in southern Sonora. The lack of incised and textured Río Sonora wares and the presence of more than one residential structure type, not only the few Río Sonora double stone foundation residential structures, directly contradicts the previously existing assertion that the Onavas area belonged to the Río Sonora archaeological tradition. The presence of red wares with similar interior shell scraping as those of Huatabampo sites, high density of marine shell, and a funerary mound (Alvarez 2003:9; Ekholm 1942:125; Pailes 1972:334) suggests an affiliation with the Huatabampo archaeological tradition instead. It is also possible to envision this area as a transition region between the Rio Sonora and the Huatabampo traditions that later might have evolved into the Nébome culture described by the Spaniards in the seventeenth century.

To this point, I will briefly mention the results of the marine shell analysis that emerged from the comparison of the four surveys in the Marana-Hohokam, Paquimé, Cerro de Trincheras, and Onavas areas. While the MCSP, CGRSP, and CTSS recorded 854 pieces of shell all together, the OVAP reported close to 1200 pieces. I should note that the presence of a large amount of shell on the surface of many Onavas sites is a direct result of recent mechanized farming activities and may reflect a possible source of bias. The large number of shell artifacts recovered indicates that the Onavas had a close relationship with the coast, either directly or indirectly, further increasing the likelihood that the Onavas area had more cultural ties with the Huatabampo tradition than with the Río Sonora tradition. Although a better temporal affiliation is needed for the shell and recognizing that some percentage of the total amount of finished shell goods may have been destined for local consumption, the archaeological record places the Río Yaqui as a viable general trade route between the coast and the interior. Finally, the comparative analysis between the OVAP and three archaeological survey projects, which were undertaken in the general region using a rather similar multidimensional analytical approach to the OVAP, illustrated that the Onavas Valley Prehispanic communities achieved a socio-political complexity albeit not as pronounced as that characterizing the three neighboring areas.

As part of this conclusion, a summary statement is in order for the two models used in this research: the Cultural Landscape Analysis and the Community Model. These models provided the preliminary interpretation of the archaeological record of the valley and suggest several points of departure for future research in the area.

THE CULTURAL LANDSCAPE ANALYSIS APPROACH

Developed in the last decade, landscape archaeology has been adopted as a practical methodological approach to interpret past cultural landscapes. Its rapid acceptance in the archaeological field can be verified through the increasing number of articles, books, and papers on the subject. Proceeding from the already well-established settlement pattern analysis, landscape archaeology incorporates additional aspects of the human condition that are less tangible in the material record, such as ritual and ethnic landscapes, thus enriching the archaeologist's interpretation of past cultures. In spite of the limitations inherent in relying on the material record to interpret how humans envisioned and lived their natural surroundings, cultural landscape analysis (CLA) has proven to be a strong but flexible methodological framework to discern the territorial distribution of human features across space and time. One important aspect of the CLA is its capacity to study a landscape on the regional level based on the analysis of natural elements that human populations may choose to use or to avoid, such as water sources, soils, forest resources, game, or plants. This characteristic meant that the CLA formed a reliable methodological framework to use in an area where little to no archaeological research had preceded. As has been discussed in this research, the CLA framework provides fuller interpretations with additional information obtained from other fields such as ethnohistory and ethnography. The implementation of a full-coverage systematic pedestrian survey ensured the acquisition of the maximum amount of available archaeological data from the field. This accommodated and facilitated the CLA yielding the optimum understanding of the region, its natural setting, and the distribution of natural resources that proved essential to comprehend the regional dynamics of this particular community.

As mentioned earlier, the CLA has been useful for examining ecological aspects of settlement patterns and for envisioning the landscape through the magical, ceremonial, and religious realms of the studied communities. A preliminary depiction of the ritual landscape for the Onavas Valley proved interesting. Although the results in this direction were not as comprehensive as I desired, they illustrated nonetheless a more accurate perspective of the landscape as it was likely encountered and imagined by the Nébome Indians. This preliminary interpretation of the Nébome ritual realm was possible through the interrelation of data sets obtained from archaeological, ethnohistorical, and ethnographic records. Thus, the application of an archaeological landscape analysis for the first time in Northwest Mexico proved to be a very useful methodological approach to start understanding the Prehispanic communities of this area. Of course, all analyses here presented, based mostly on the surface material context, offer provisional cultural patterns for the Onavas Valley that must be contrasted with further research and excavation of key features and sites.

THE COMMUNITY MODEL APPLICATION

Previous personal experiences from past projects had already indicated the difficulty in identifying the presence of leaders, big men, caciques, chiefs, or individuals who wielded notable socio-political power in the archaeological record of this large region. At best, the material context illustrates some general indications of some extent of material inequality, which are identified as corporate strategies (Blanton et al. 1996). Ethnohistorical records document Nébome chiefs at Onavas Valley communities in the seventeenth century, but finding material remains of such figures through surface survey is almost an impossible quest. Considering this situation, the OVAP incorporated the community model in its research design to provide a feasible explanatory framework for the archaeological data recorded. This model is presented as a feasible alternative to the chiefdom concept. The community model is explained as a socio-political and territorial unit configuration identified by a set of related settlements representing all its members and surrounding environmental resources. In addition, community membership corresponds to a self-identification as a social group and affiliation to a specific territory. However, the use of the community concept does not mean that the Prehispanic inhabitants of the Onavas Valley did not achieve sociopolitical complexity.

Similar to the CLA, the community model is flexible enough to be used in an area or region where archaeological knowledge is thin or non-existent and can be applied to the regional level analysis as well. Due to the fact that this model does not focus on the individual level (chiefs), but on the community as a whole, the model enabled a broader interpretation of the archaeological record and the surrounding landscape that has facilitated the identification

of key components for subsequent research in the area. Using the community model as a base framework of interpretation in several distinct areas will help us better understand the variability in community life that might have existed in the Prehispanic past. Furthermore, this model is designed to be interdisciplinary and accommodate complementary information or data from other fields, such as ethnohistory, ethnography, history, and geography. This particularity makes it especially useful in areas where archaeological research is in its early phase and must rely on all available sources of information. Due to these characteristics, the community model has risen in importance in the field of archaeology and is seen to apply in more and more areas, among them Northwest Mexico and the U.S. Southwest.

Questions remaining for future research in the Onavas area are: Whether the community valley organization identified at the Onavas Valley repeats itself in other portions of the Río Yaqui? If those communities are identified, do they share the same patterns as Onavas? Are non-residential structures present? What type of residential structures do they exhibit? Is the use of the landscape similar for all communities along the Río Yaqui?

WHERE DO WE GO FROM HERE?

The completion of the OVAP fieldwork and analyses form a valuable contribution to the knowledge of the Prehispanic development of the Northwest Mexico and the U.S. Southwest. The OVAP, as a systematic archaeological research project in the valley, has provided not only a much needed material record for the area, but also a settlement pattern, a landscape analyses, and a provisional chronology. It revealed a long human occupation of the valley (since the Paleoindian to date), a high Prehispanic population density, and a diverse and rich material record for the Nébome Indian group. In providing some rudimentary answers about the archaeology of the area, many more questions have emerged that can be answered with more research and excavation of sites at the Onavas Valley and in neighboring areas.

Now that the basic archaeological data set and regional level analysis have been obtained, what are the next steps to be taken in the Onavas Valley? Two research directions stand out: discern the internal organization of the Onavas communities; and identify the presence and nature of settlements in the nearby high mountains and their relationship with the valley communities.

First, the OVAP described several residential and non-residential Nébome structures for the first time, but does not go beyond this preliminary description. In spite of the physical destruction of most of the Prehispanic sites, mostly by mechanized farming activities, several sites remain fairly undisturbed and may provide significant information about the internal organization and distribution of activities of the Nébome communities. Of course, productive excavation requires that sites remained relatively undisturbed to answer specific research questions, such as refining ceramic seriation, establishing continuous occupation, identification of activity areas, specific natural resources consumption, and/or obtaining ^{14}C dates to test the preliminary chronology. Accordingly, three sites top the list: SON P:6:5, SON P:10:56, and SON P:10:08 (Appendix I and II). The first two, identified as "aldeas," evidenced at the surface at least 16 and 11 residential structures each, a low degree of perturbation, and some compound arrangement. The research and excavation of one of these sites is likely to uncover the internal organization of those communities, probably establishes how space was distributed and used, and eventually compares compound organization with other sites such as Marana or Paquimé. In addition, if possible, excavation of smaller but well-preserved sites such as

SON P:10:27, SON P:10:55, SON P:78, SON P:10:88, or SON P:10:102 (Appendix I and II), will provide a good comparison between smaller and bigger residential sites inside the Onavas community, and/or on a smaller scale such as personal or individual items analysis.

Further excavation of the SON P:10:8 site (See Appendix I and II), the funerary mound, is necessary to clarify the preliminary functions established from the limited excavation unit # 1 (funerary mound, midden, or both). Current research and analysis of mortuary remains show physical characteristics unknown to the region for the Nébomes group, such as cranial deformation and dental modification that tied them more to southern and archeological traditions than northern Sonora. ^{14}C samples will provide data to refine the local chronology, and the analysis of the material associated to the burials will offer data to establish a possible material hierarchy.

Secondly, local inhabitants living in and around the Onavas town commented on the existence of archaeological sites high up in the Sierra. The identification of such sites is important not only for its recording and preservation as archaeological sites, but also as one more element of the territorial distribution of human features in this regional landscape. Are the mountain sites related to the valley communities? If they are, what characterizes that relation? Are they culturally connected? Are they seasonal or permanent sites? Do they share the material assemblage identified at the Onavas Valley? What are their local and regional interactions? These are only some of the research questions that may be addressed. Furthermore, the mountain's remains are virtually unexplored archaeologically in southern Sonora, because the little research conducted in the region (southern Sonora), including the OVAP, has exclusively focused on the valleys. This type of research, however, poses new challenges, not only related to the lack of archaeological investigations, but also of a logistic nature due to the extreme geographical conditions.

Another promising topic for research in the area, concerns the analysis of trade and exchange items, and trade patterns and networks. Increasing archaeological research is expanding the material data sets in Northwest Mexico allowing for better analysis and comparisons between the materials. In particular, the marine shell that OVAP collected provides a well-documented and analyzed data set that can be contrasted with other areas in order to provide a preliminary analysis of consumption patterns, manufacture techniques, and socio-political uses of such materials. Relevant questions to answer are: Is marine shell as abundant in other sections of the Río Yaqui as in the Onavas Valley? What is the role of the Middle Río Yaqui communities in the trade routes between the coast and the interior? Who undertook the trade, a specialist, or was it a secondary activity? Marine shell appears to be coming to Onavas communities from the coast, but what materials go out in return? With Onavas communities trading shell farther inland, what was received in return? These are some interesting questions that still await answers in addition to many other and related questions to archaeological material, such as: What is the geographical distribution of Onavas Purple-on-Red? If the tracing of turquoise sources were possible, what would be learned?

In addition to these suggestions for future research supplied from an archaeological perspective, ethnographic research in the valley promises insights as well. Although current residents of the valley do not consider themselves Pimas, they still hold some of the keys to understanding how the landscape might have been exploited with traditional technologies. A "salvage" ethnography that focuses on the land tenure systems used before the damming of the Rio Yaqui would prove informative especially in regards to inundation farming and the management of its widely fluctuating cir-

cumstances. An ethnography on the techniques and strategies that the Onavas residents used for such farming might relate to the farming in Prehispanic times. Several Colonial documents mention the use of annual river fluctuations to irrigate and fertilize the farming soils of the floodplain of the Río Yaqui valley. They also narrate times when the river covered farming soils with sand. Inundation farming is not as reliable as irrigation farming stated by Suzanne Fish (personal communication 2006). Consequently, members of the Onavas community might have had to rely on alternative food sources, such as irrigation farming, orchards, hunting, and gathering. The upper El Novillo dam, constructed in 1963, today prevents the river's yearly inundations of the Onavas Valley. Elders in the community remember the life in the valley before the construction of the dam. Collection of this information and other topics are important in an effort to understand a farming system differing from irrigation, to discover alternative subsistence systems, and to arrive at a model to compare in similar geographical valleys.

DEPARTING THOUGHT: WHERE DID THEY GO FROM HERE?

Unfortunately, at the time the OVAP was conducted, no local indigenous people, or people that identify themselves as such, survived in the area (see Figure 9.1). Ethnographic data collected by Pennington (1980) at the end of the 1960s reveal that the Lower Pima once lived in the Onavas Valley. Ethnohistoric research and data from Colonial documents illustrate that the term *Lower Pima* or *Pima bajo* was used for the Indian population of the valley after the late seventeenth century. Before the late seventeenth century, these same people were called the Nébome (Dunnigan 1983; Pennington 1980; Pérez de Ribas 1999). The first record of the Nébomes in the Jesuit Colonial

Figure 9.1. Panoramic of the Onavas town after a walking day in the field (Photohraph by Emiliano Gallaga).

documents was made in 1591 when Jesuit missionaries visited a group of Nébomes from the community of Nuri that had left that town to settle in the Spanish community of Bamoa at the Sinaloa River (Dunnigan 1983; Spicer 1992; Pennington 1980; Pérez de Ribas 1999). The Nébome group who founded the town of Bamoa were part of the Indian committee that came with Alvar Nuñez Cabeza de Vaca in 1536 (1993, Covey 1998), but he failed to mention the name of that particular Indian group. Diego de Guzman provides the first account of the Nébomes ever in the Colonial documents, when his expedition reached Cumuripa in 1533, the lowermost Nébome village on the Río Yaqui (Carrera Stampa 1955:172; Sauer 1932:12). Before the OVAP, with the exception of the PROCEDE project, no archaeological research or data existed for this region and no attempts were made to interpret any archaeological material culture to link the historic Nébomes with their prehispanic counterparts. To be sure, much remains to be done in the Onavas valley to determine more fully who the Nébomes were and where they went.

References Cited

Abbot, David; Alexa Smith, and Emiliano Gallaga
    2007   Ballcourts and Ceramics: The Case for Hohokam Marketplaces in the Arizona Desert. *American Antiquity*, 72(3):461-484.

Abbot, Tucker.
    1996   *Seashells of North America. A Guide to Field Identification.* St. Martin's Press, New York.

Adams, Jenny L.
    1997   *Manual for a Technological Approach to Ground Stone Analysis.* Center for Desert Archaeology, Tucson.

Adams, R. McC.
    1981   *Heartland of Cities: Surveys of Ancient Settlement and Land Use on the Central Floodplain of the Euphrates.* University of Chicago Press, Chicago.

Adler, Michael A.
    1996   Settlement Pattern. In *Encyclopedia of Cultural Anthropology,* Vol. 4, edited by David Levinson and Melvin Ember, pp. 1154-1160, Henry Holt and Company, New York,

Almada, Francisco R.
    1990   *Diccionario de Historia, Geografía y Biografía Sonorenses*, # 21, Instituto Sonorense de Cultura. Sonora, Mexico.

Alvarez, Ana Maria
    1990   Huatabampo: consideraciones sobre una comunidad agrícola prehispánica en el sur de Sonora. *Noroeste de México* 9:9-93.

    1996   Sociedades agricolas. In *Historia general de Sonora*, vol. 1, pp. 197-232. Gobierno del Estado de Sonora, Hermosillo, Mexico.

    1999   Estructura territorial Cahita en el momento del contacto. El caso de las naciones Yaqui y Mayo. *Noroeste de México*, special edition, pp. 111-118.

    2003   *!Que tiempos aquellos, señor Don Simón! Balance y perspectivas del proyecto Huatabampo a muchos años de su realización.* Paper presented at the "30 Años del INAH en Sonora: Mesas de Análisis, Balance y Perspectivas en arqueología, historia y antropología," Hermosillo, Sonora.

Amsden, Monroe
    1928   Archaeological Reconnaissance in Sonora. *Southwest Museum Papers,* No. 1, Los Angeles.

Anell, Bengt
    1969   Running Down and Driving of Game in North America. *Studia Ethnographica Upsaliensia* No. 30, Lund, Sweden.

Anschuetz, Kurt F., Richard H. Wilshusen, and Cherie L. Scheick
    2001   An Archaeology of Landscapes: Perspectives and Directions. *Journal of Archaeological Research* 9(2):157-211.

Ansley, John
    1993   Points, Preforms, Fine Bifaces, and Drills. In *An Archaeological Survey of the Altar Valley, Sonora, Mexico,* edited by Randall McGuire and Elisa Villalpando, pp. 55-60. Anthropological Papers of the University of Arizona No 184. University of Arizona Press, Tucson.

Ashmore, Wendy, and A. Bernard Knapp (editors)
    1999   *Archaeologies of Landscape: Contemporary Perspectives.* Blackwell Publishers, Oxford.

Bandelier, Adolph
    1890-1892   *Final Report of Investigations Among the Indians of the Southwest United States...1880-1885.* Archaeological Institute of America Series, No. 3 and 4, Cambridge.

Banning, E. B.
    2000   *The Archaeologist's Laboratory: The Analysis of Archaeological Data.* Interdisciplinary Contributions to Archaeology. Kluwer Academic and Plenum Publishers.

Barnett, Frankling
    1991   *Dictionary of Prehistoric Indian Artifacts of the American Southwest.* Northland Publishing, Flagstaff.

Barth, Frederik (editor)
    1998   *Ethnic Groups and Boundaries: The Social Organization of Culture Difference.* Waveland Press, Inc., Illinois.

Basso, Keith H.
    1996   *Wisdom Sits in Places: Landscape and Language among the Western Apache.* University of New Mexico Press, Albuquerque.

Bayman, J. M.
    1996   Shell Ornament Consumption in a Classic Hohokam Platform Mound Community Center. *Journal of Field Archaeology* 23:403-418.

Beals, Ralph L.
    1943   *The Aboriginal Culture of the Cahita Indians.* Ibero-Americana, No. 19, University of California Press, Berkeley.

Beck, Lane A. (editor)
    1995   *Regional Approaches to Mortuary Analysis.* Plenum Press, New York.

Blanton Richard E., Gary M Feinman, Stephan A. Kowaleski, and Peter N. Peregrine
    1996   A Dual-Processual Theory for the Evolution of Mesoamerican Civilization. *Current Anthropology* 37:1-14.

Bowen, Thomas
    1976a *Seri Prehistory. The Archaeology of Central Coast of Sonora, Mexico.* Anthropological Papers of the Univeristy of Arizona No 27. University of Arizona Press, Tucson.

    1976b Esquema de la historia de la cultura Trincheras. In *Sonora: Antropología del Desierto.* Edited by Beatriz Braniff and Richard S. Felger, pp 347-363. Colección Cientifica 27, INAH, SEP, México.

    2000   *Unknown Island: Seri Indians, Europeans, and San Esteban Island in the Gulf of California.* University of New Mexico Press, Albuquerque.

2002   Not by Design: The Arizona State Museum's 1966-67 Survey of the Trincheras Culture. *Kiva* 68(1):5-22.

n.d.   *A Survey and Re-evaluation of the Trincheras Culture, Sonora, Mexico.* Ms. on file, Arizona State Museum, Tucson.

Bradley, Ronna J.
1993   Marine Shell Exchange in Northwest Mexico and the Southwest. In *The American Southwest and Mesoamerica: Systems of Prehistoric Exchange,* edited by Jonathon E. Ericson and Timothy G. Baugh, pp. 121-158. Plenum Press, New York and London.

1999   Shell Exchange within the Southwest: The Casas Grandes Interaction Sphere. In *The Casas Grandes World,* edited by Curtis F. Schaafsma and Caroll L. Riley, pp. 213-228. University of Utah Press, Salt Lake City.

Brand, Donald
1935   The Distribution of Pottery Types in Northwest Mexico. *American Anthropologist* 37:287-305.

Braniff, Beatriz
1989   *Arqueomoluscos de Sonora, Noroeste y Occidente de Mesoamérica.* Cuaderno de trabajo No. 9, INAH, Mexico City.

1992   *La Frontera protohistórica Pima-Opata en Sonora, México.* Colección Cientifica 240 (1-3). INAH, Mexico City.

Braniff, Beatriz (editor)
2001   *La Gran Chichimeca: El Lugar de las Rocas Secas.* Jaca Book and CONACULTA, Mexico City.

Broda, Johanna
1991   Cosmovisión y observación de la naturaleza: el ejemplo del culto de los cerros en Mesoamérica. In *Arqueoastronomía y etnoastronomía en mesoamérica,* edited by Johanna Broda, Stanislaw Iwaniszewski, and Lucrecia Maupomé, pp. 461-500. Universidad Nacional Autónoma de México, Mexico City.

Brody, Hugh
1988   *Maps and Dreams: Indians and the British Columbia Frontier.* Douglas & McIntyre, Vancouver and Toronto.

Brooks, Richard H., and Sheilagh T. Brooks
1985   Archaeological, Ethnological and Historical Implications of the Game "Cuatro" in Northwestern Mexico. In *The Archaeology of West and Northwest Mesoamerica,* edited by Michael S. Foster and Phil C. Weigand, pp. 365-380. Westview Press, Boulder.

Cameron, Catherine M.
2005   Exploring Archaeological Cultures in the Northern Southwest: What Were Chaco and Mesa Verde? *Kiva* 70(3):227-273.

Cano, Olga
2001   Paquimé y las Casa Acantilado, Chihuahua. *Arqueología Mexicana* 9 (51): 80-87.

Canuto, Marcello A., and Jasón Yaeger (editors)
2000   *The Archaeology of Communities: A New World Perspective.* Routledge. London and New York.

Carpenter, John
1996   *El Ombligo de la Labor: Differentiation, Interaction and Integration in Prehispanic Sinaloa, Mexico.* Unpublished Ph.D. dissertation, Department of Anthropology, University of Arizona, Tucson.

Carpenter, John, and Guadalupe Sánchez
2001   La Arqueología de los Grupos Yutoaztecas Tempranos. In *Avances y Balances de Lenguas Yutoaztecas,* edited by Jose Luis Moctezuma and Jane H. Hill, pp. 359-373. INAH, Mexico City.

Carrera Stampa, Manuel
1955   *Memoria de los servicios que había hecho Nuño de Guzmán, desde que fue nombrado Gobernador de Panuco en 1525.* Jose Porrúa e Hijos, Mexico City.

Chang, K. C.
1967   Major Aspects of the Interrelationships of Archaeology and Ethnology. *Current Anthropology* 8(3):227-243.

Covey, Cyclone (translator and editor)
1998   *Cabeza de Vaca's Adventures in the Unkown Interior of America.* University of New Mexico Press, Albuquerque.

Craig, Douglas B.
2000   The Demographic Implications of Architectural Change at the Grewe site. In *The Hohokam Village Revisited,* edited by David, E. Doyel, Suzanne K. Fish, and Paul R. Fish, pp.139-166. Southwestern and Rocky Mountain Division of the American Association for the Advancement of Science, Colorado State University Press. Boulder.

Crumrine, N. Ross
1983   Mayo. In *Southwest,* edited by Alfonso Ortiz, pp. 264-275. Handbook of North American Indians, volume 10, W. Sturtevant, general editor. Smithsonian Institution, Washington, D.C.

Crumrine, N. Ross, and Lynne S. Crumrine
1967   Ancient and Modern Mayo Fishing Practices. *Kiva* 33(1):25-33.

Dean, Jeffrey S. and John C. Ravesloot
1993   Chronology of Cultural Interaction in the Gran Chichimeca. In *Culture and Contact, Charles C. Di Peso's Gran Chichimeca,* edited by Anne I. Woosley and John C. Ravesloot, pp. 83-104. Amerind Foundation and University of New Mexico Press, Dragoon and Albuquerque.

Di Peso, Charles C.
1956   *The Upper Pima Indians of San Cayetano del Tumacacori.* The Amerind Foundation Series 7, Amerind Foundation, Dragoon, Arizona.

1974   *Casas Grandes, a Fallen Trade Center of The Gran Chichimeca 2: The Medio Period.* Amerind Foundation Series 9, Dragoon.

Di Peso, Charles C., John B. Rinaldo, and Gloria J. Fenner
1974   *Casas Grandes: A Fallen Trading Center of the Gran Chichimeca.* Amerind Foundation, Dragoon, Arizona.

Dirst, Victoria A.
1979   *A Prehistoric Frontier in Sonora.* Unpublished Ph. D. dissertation, Department of Anthropology, University of Arizona, Tucson.

Dobres, Marcia-Anne, and John Robb (editors)
  2000   *Agency in Archaeology.* Routledge, London.

Doolittle, William E.
  1988   *PrehispanicOccupance in the Valley of Sonora, Mexico: Archaeological Confirmation of Early Spanish Reports.* Anthropological Papers of the University of Arizona No 48. University of Arizona Press, Tucson.

Douglas, John E., and Cesar Quijada
  2004a Between the Casas Grandes and the Río Sonora Valleys: Chronology and Settlement in the Upper Bavispe Drainage. In *Surveying the Archaeology of Northwest Mexico,* edited by Gillian E. Newell and Emiliano Gallaga, pp. 93-112. University of Utah Press, Salt Lake City.

  2004b Not so Plain After All: First Millennium A.D. Textured Ceramics in Northeastern Sonora. *Kiva* 70(1):31-52.

  2005   Di Peso's Concept of the Northern Sierra: Evidence from the Upper Bavispe Valley, Sonora, Mexico. *Latin American Antiquity* 16(3):275-293.

Doyel, David E., Suzanne K. Fish, and Paul R. Fish (editors)
  2000   *The Hohokam Village Revisited.* Southwestern and Rocky Mountain Division of the American Association for the Advancement of Science, Colorado State University Press. Boulder.

Dunnigan, Timothy
  1983   Lower Pima. In *Southwest*, edited by Alfonso Ortiz, pp. 217-230. Handbook of North American Indians, volume 10, W. Sturtevant, general editor. Smithsonian Institution, Washington, D.C.

Earle, Timothy
  1997   *How Chiefs Come to Power: The Political Economy in Prehistory.* Stanford University Press, Stanford, California.

Ebert, James I.
  1992   *Distributional Archaeology.* University of New Mexico Press, Albuquerque.

Ekholm, Gordon
  1937-1940   Sonora-Sinaloa Archaeological Project. American Museum of Natural History Archives, New York.

  1939   Results of an Archaeological Survey of Sonora and Northern Sinaloa. *Revista mexicana de estudios antropológicos* 3:7-11.

  1942   *Excavations at Guasave Sinaloa, Mexico,* Anthropological Papers No. 38, American Museum of Natural History, New York.

Escársega E., Jesús A.
  1996   Geología de Sonora. In *Historia General de Sonora, tomo 1: periodo prehistórico y prehispánico,* pp. 25-96. Gobierno del Estado de Sonora, Hermosillo, Mexico.

Feinman, Gary, and Jill Neitzel
  1984   Too many Types: An Overview of Sedentary Prestate Societies in the Americas. In *Advances in Archaeological Method and Theory,* vol. 7, edited by Michael B. Schiffer, pp. 39-102. New York: Academic Press.

Feld, Steven, and Keith H. Basso (editors)
  1996   *Senses of Place.* School of American Research Press, Santa Fe, New Mexico.

Fenton, William N.
 1962 Ethnohistory and its Problems. *Ethnohistory* 9(1)1-21.

Fish, Paul R., and Thomas Gresham
 1990 Insight from Full-Coverage Survey in the Georgia Piedmont. In *The Archaeology of Regions: A Case for Full-Coverage Survey*, edited by Suzanne Fish and Stephen A. Kowalewski, pp. 147-172. Smithsonian Institution Press, Washington, D.C.

Fish, Paul R., and Suzanne K. Fish
 1994 Southwest and Northwest: Recent Research at the Juncture of the United States and Mexico. *Journal of Archaeological Research* 2:3-44.

Fish, Paul R., Suzanne K. Fish, George J. Gumerman, and J. Jefferson Reid.
 1994 Toward an Explanation for Southwestern "Abandonment". In *Themes in Southwest Prehistory*, edited by George J. Gumerman, pp. 135-163. School of American Research Press, Santa Fe.

Fish, Suzanne K.
 1999a How Complex Were the Southwestern Great Towns' Polities? In *Great Towns and Regional Polities:In The Prehistorical American Southwest and Southeast*, edited by Jille E. Neitzel, pp. 45-58. The Amerind Foundation New Word Studies Series No. 3. University of New Mexico Press, Albuquerque.

 1999b The Cerro de Trincheras Settlement and Land Use Survey. Preliminary Report submitted to the National Geographic Society, Grant #5856-97.

Fish, Suzanne K., and Paul R. Fish
 1992 The Marana Community in Comparative Context. In *The Marana Community in the Hohokam World*, edited by Fish, Suzanne K., Paul R. Fish, and John H. Madsen, pp. 97-106. Anthropological Papers of the University of Arizona No 56. University of Arizona Press, Tucson.

 1994 Multisite Communities as Measures of Hohokam Aggregation. In *The Ancient Southwestern Community: Models and Methods for the Study of Prehistoric Social Organization*, edited by W. H. Wills and Robert D. Leonard, pp. 119-129. University of New Mexico Press, Albuquerque.

 1996 Conceptos mesoamericanos, asimilacion Hohokam. *Noroeste de Mexico* 13:11-22.

 2000a The Institutional contexts of Hohokam Complexity and Inequality. In *Alternative Leadership Strategies in PrehispanicSouthwest*, edited by Barbara Mills, pp. 154-167. University of Arizona Press, Tucson.

 2000b Civic-Territorial Organization and the Roots of Hohokam Complexity. In *The Hohokam Village Revisited*, edited by David, E. Doyel, Suzanne K. Fish, and Paul R. Fish, pp. 373-390. Southwestern and Rocky Mountain Division of the American Association for the Advancement of Science, Colorado State University Press. Boulder.

 2003 Cerros de Trincheras secundarios en perspectiva regional. Paper presented at the "30 Aniversario, Centro INAH, Sonora, 2003" in Hermosillo, Sonora, Mexico.

 2004 In the Trincheras Heartland: Initial Insights from Full-Coverage Survey. In *Surveying the Archaeology of Northwest Mexico*, edited by Gillian E. Newell and Emiliano Gallaga, pp. 47-64. University of Utah Press, Salt Lake City.

Fish, Suzanne K., Paul R. Fish, and James M. Bayman
 2000 *Research Design. Power and Economy at the Marana Platform Mound Site: Structure of an Early Clas-*

sic Center near Tucson, Arizona. Ms. on file at the Borderland Studies, Arizona State Museum, University of Arizona, Tucson.

Fish, Suzanne K., Paul R. Fish, and John H. Madsen (editors)
   1992   *The Marana Community in the Hohokam World.* Anthropological Papers of University of Arizona No 56. University of Arizona Press, Tucson.

Fish, Suzanne K., Paul R. Fish, and John H. Madsen
   1990   Analyzing Regional Agriculture: A Hohokam Example. In *The Archaeology of Regions: A Case for Full-Coverage Survey,* edited by Fish, Suzanne K. and Stephen A. Kowalewski, pp. 189-218. Smithsonian Institution Press, Washington, D.C.

Fish, Suzanne K., and Stephen A. Kowalewski (editors)
   1990   *The Archaeology of Regions: A Case for Full-Coverage Survey.* Smithsonian Institution Press, Washington, D.C.

Gallaga, Emiliano
   1997   *Analisis de la ceramica policroma del sitio cerro de Trincheras, Sonora, México.* Unpublished licenciatura thesis, Escuela Nacional de Antropología e Historia, Mexico.

   1998   Informe de area A1: "La plaza de el caracol." Ms. on file, Cerro de Trincheras Excavation Project, Centro INAH Sonora, Hermosillo.

   1999   *An Evaluation of the Cemetery Concept at Snaketown: A Re-analysis of Old Data.* Unpublished Master thesis, Department of Anthropology of the University of Arizona, Tucson.

   2004a A Spatial Distribution Analysis of Shell and Polychrome Ceramics at the Cerro de Trincheras Site, Sonora, Mexico. In *Surveying the Archaeology of Northwest Mexico,* edited by Gillian E. Newell and Emiliano Gallaga, pp. 77-92. University of Utah Press, Salt Lake City.

   2004b Catalogue: archaeological material from the Gordon F. Ekholm (1937-40) archaeological project in Sonora, Mexico. Electronic publication at http://anthro.amnh.org/

   2004c Heaven and Hell: My Summer in Jail! *SMRC Revista,* 38(141):11-18.

Gallaga, Emiliano, and Gillian E. Newell
   2004   Introduction. In *Surveying the Archaeology of Northwest Mexico,* edited by Gillian E. Newell and Emiliano Gallaga, 1-26. University of Utah Press, Salt Lake City.

   2012   Comunidades de rango medio en el norte de México: el caso del Valle de Onavas, Sonora. In *El Poder Compartido. Ensayos sobre la arqueología de organizaciones políticas segmentarias y oligárquicas.* Edited by Dannels, Annick and Gerardo Gutierrez, CIESAS and El Colegio de Michoacan, A.C, Mexico.

Gamboa, Eduardo
   2001   Paquimé y el mundo de la cultura Casas Grandes. *Arqueología Mexicana* 9(51):46-54.

Gandara, Manuel
   1992   *La Arqueología Oficial Mexicana: Causas y Efectos.* Colección Divulgación. INAH, Mexico City.

Gasco, Janine, Greg C. Smith, and Patricia Fournier
   1997   *Approaches to the Historical Archaeology of Mexico, Central & South America.* Monograph 38, The Institute of Archaeology, University of California, Los Angeles.

Gentry, Howard S.
  1942 *Río Mayo Plants: A Study of the Flora and Vegetation of the Valley of the Río Mayo, Sonora.* Publication No. 527. Carnegie Institution of Washington.

Giddings, Ruth Warner
  1993 *Yaqui Myths and Legends.* University of Arizona Press, Tucson.

Gilpin, Dennis
  2003 Chaco-Era Site Clustering and the Concept of Communities. *Kiva* 69(2): 171-206.

Gladwin, Harold S., Emil W. Haury, E. B. Sayles, and N. Gladwin
  1938 *Excavation at Snaketown: Material Culture.* Medallion Papers 25, Gila Pueblo, Globe.

Gladwin, Winifred, and Harold S. Gladwin
  1929 *The Western Range of the Red-on-Buff Culture.* Medallion Papers No. 5, Gila Pueblo, Globe.

Goldstein, Paul S.
  2000 Communities without Borders: The Vertical Archipelago and Diaspora Communities in the Southern Andes. In *The Archaeology of Communities: A New World Perspective,* edited by Marcello A. Canuto and Jason Yaeger, pp. 182-209. Routledge, London.

Grove, David C., Kenneth G. Hirth, David E. Buge, and Ann M. Cyphers
  1976 Settlement and Cultural Development at Chalcatzingo. *Science* 192:1203-1210.

Guevara S., Arturo
  1986 *Arqueología del área de las Cuarenta Casas, Chihuahua.* INAH-SEP, Colección Científica No. 151. Mexico City.

Gumerman, George J. (editor)
  1991 *Exploring the Hohokam: Prehistoric Desert Peoples of the American Southwest.* Amerind Foundation New World Studies Series No. 1. Amerind Foundation Dragoon, Arizona and University of New Mexico Press, Albuquerque.

Guzmán, Diego
  1615 Carta del Padre Diego Guzmán al Padre Provincial de septiembre de mil seiscientos veinte y nueve. Historia 15. Memorias para la historia de la provincia de Sinaloa. Archivo General de la Nación, Mexico City.

Hallenbeck, Cleve
  1987 *The Journey of Fray Marcos de Niza.* Southern Methodist University Press.

Hammond, George
  1940 *Coronado's Seven Cities.* United States Coronado Exposition Commission, Albuquerque.

Hammond, George, and Agapito Rey (translators)
  1928 *Obregón's History of 16th Century Exploration in Western America.* Wetzel Publishing Company, Los Angeles.

  1940 *Narratives of the Coronado Expedition 1540-1542.* University of New Mexico Press, Albuquerque.

Harry, Karen, and James M. Bayman
  2000 Leadership Strategies among the Classic Period Hohokam: A Case Study. In *Alternative Leadership*

Strategies in the PrehispanicSouthwest, edited by Barbara Mills, pp. 136-153. University of Arizona Press, Tucson.

Haury, Emil W.
1950   *The Stratigraphy and Archaeology of Ventana Cave, Arizona.* University of Arizona Press, Tucson and University of New Mexico, Albuquerque.

1976   *The Hohokam, Desert Farmers and Craftsmen: Excavations at Snaketown, 1964-1965.* University of Arizona Press, Tucson.

Heckman, Robert A.
2000   The Trincheras Tradition. In *Prehistoric Painted Pottery of Southeastern Arizona,* edited by Robert A. Heckman, Barbara K. Montgomery, and Stephanie M. Whittlesey, pp. 75-82. Technical Series 77. Statistical Research, Tucson, Arizona.

Hedrick, Basil C., and Carroll L. Riley (translators)
1976   *Documents Ancillary to the Vaca Journey.* In Research Records of the University Museum and Art Galleries University Museum Studies, Southern Illinois University, # 5.

Heredia, José
1969   Relación del Capitán Diego de Guzmán. In *Memorias y Revista del Congreso Mexicano de Historia* I:123-143.

Hinton, Thomas B.
1955   A Survey of Archaeological Sites in the Altar Valley, Sonora. *Kiva* 21(3-4):1-12.

Hirsch, E.
1994   Landscape: Between Place and Space. In *The Archaeology of Landscape: Perspectives on Place and Space,* edited by Hirsch E. and O'Hanlon, M., pp. 1-30. Clarendon Press, Oxford.

Hodder, Ian.
1980   Social Structure and Cemeteries: A Critical Appraisal. *Anglo-Saxon Cemeteries, 1979,* edited by Philip Rahtz, Tania Dickinson, and Lorna Watts, pp. 161-169. BAR British Series No. 82.

Hopkins, Armando
1988   *Imágenes prehispánicas de Sonora: La expedición de Don Francisco de Ibarra a Sonora en 1565, Según el Relato de Don Baltasar de Obregón.* Hermosillo, Sonora, Mexico.

Hu-Dehart, Evelyn
1995   *Adaptación y resistencia en el Yaquimi: Los Yaquis durante la colonia.* Colección Historia de los Pueblos Indígenas de México, CIESAS, INI, Mexico.

Huntington, Ellsworth
1912   The Fluctuating Climate of North America—The Ruins of the Hohokam. *Annual Report of the Board of Regents of the Smithsonian Institution,* pp. 383-387. Smithsonian Institution Press, Washington, D.C.

Hurdaide, Diego Martinez de
1610-1617   *Informes desde Culiacán y Sinaloa.* Ms. on file, Special Collection, University of Arizona, Tucson.

Instituto Nacional de Antropología e Historia, Sonora, Archives
1998   PROCEDE field notes and report. Archaeology Department Archives, Hermosillo Sonora, Mexico.

Instituto Nacional de Estadistica, Geografica e Informatica

1993   *Espaciomapa, Yecora, Hoja* H12-12.

1994   *Fotoarea.* 01/04/1994, Zona H12-12, linea 70 and 71.

Jacome, Felipe Carlos

1936   *The Nogales Wash Site.* Pimeria Alta Historical Society, Nogales.

Jenkins, Richard

1997   *Rethinking Ethnicity: Arguments and Explorations.* SAGE Publications, London.

Jernigan, Wesley E.

1978   *Jewelry of the Prehistoric Southwest.* School of American Research and University of New Mexico Press, Albuquerque.

Johnson, Alfred E.

1960   *The Place of Trincheras Culture of Northern Sonora in Southwestern Archaeology.* Unpublished MA thesis, University of Arizona, Tucson.

1966   Archaeology of Sonora, Mexico. In *Handbook of Middle American Indians,* edited by Gordon F. Ekholm and Gordon R. Willey, pp. 26-37. Handbook of Middle American Indians, Vol. 4, R. Wauchope general editor, University of Texas Press, Austin.

Johnson, Gregory A.

1972   A Test of the Utility of Central Place Theory in Archaeology. In *Man, Settlement and Urbanism,* edited by Peter J. Ucko, Ruth Tringham, and G. W. Dimbleday, pp. 769-785. Hertfordshire: Duckworth.

Justice, Noel D.

2002   *Stone Age Spear and Arrow Points of the Southwestern United States.* Indiana University Press, Bloomington and Indianapolis.

Keen, Myra

1971   *Sea Shells of Ttropical West America.* Stanford University Press, Stanford.

Kelley, J. Charles

2000   Aztatlán Mercantile System: Mobile Traders and the Northwestward Expansion of Mesoamerican Civilization. In *Greater Mesoamerica: The Archaeology of West and Northwest Mexico,* edited by Michael S. Foster and Shirley Gorenstein, pp. 137-154. University of Utah Press, Salt Lake City.

Kelley, Jane H., Joe D. Stewart, Art C. MacWilliams, and Loy C. Neff

1999   A West Central Chihuahuan Perspective on Chihuahuan Culture. In *The Casas Grandes World,* edited by Curtis F. Schaafsma and Carroll L. Riley, pp. 63-77. University of Utah Press, Salt Lake City.

Kelley, Jane H., and Elisa Villalpando

1996   An Overview of the Mexican Northwest. In *Interpreting Southwestern Diversity: Underlying Principles and Overarching Patterns.* Edited by Paul R. Fish and Jefferson Reid. Arizona State University Anthropological Research Papers 48:69-77, University of Arizona Press, Tucson.

Kintigh, Keith W.

1990a   Protohistoric Transitions in the Western Pueblo Area. In *Perspectives on Southwestern Prehistory,* edited by Paul Minnis and C. L. Redman, pp. 258-275. Westview Press, Boulder.

2003   Coming to Terms with the Chaco World. *Kiva* 69(2): 93-116.

Kowalewski, Stephen A
1996   Clout, Corn, Copper, Core Periphery, Culture Area. In *Pre-Columbian World Systems,* edited by Peter N. Peregrine and Gary M. Feinman, pp. 51-64. Prehistory Press, Madison.

Krech III, Shepard.
1991   The State of Ethnohistory. *Annual Review of Anthropology* 20:345-75.

Lazalde, Jesus F.
1992   *Puntas de Proyectil: Catalogo. Museo Regional UJED.* Impresiones Graficas, Durango, Mexico.

Lekson, Stephen H.
1991   Settlement Pattern and the Chaco Region. In *Chaco and Hohokam: Prehistoric Regional Systems in the American Southwest,* edited by Patricia L. Crown and W. James Judge, pp. 31-55. School of American Research Press, Santa Fe.

1999   Great Towns in the Southwest. In *Great Towns and Regional Polities: In the Prehistorical American Southwest and Southeast,* edited by Jille E. Neitzel, pp. 3-22. Amerind Foundation New Word Studies Series No 3. University of New Mexico Press, Albuquerque.

Lightfoot, Kent G.
1995   Culture Contact Studies: Redefining the Relationship between Prehistoric and Historical Archaeology. *American Antiquity* 60(2):199-217.

Lister, Robert H.
1958   *Archaeological Excavation in the Northern Sierra Madre Occidental, Chihuahua and Sonora, Mexico.* Series in Anthropology No. 7, University of Colorado Studies, Boulder.

Little, Barbara
2002   *Public Benefits of Archaeology.* University of Florida Press, Gainesville.

López Austin, Alfredo
1973   *Hombre-dios: religión y política en el mundo Náhuatl.* Universidad Nacional Autónoma de México, Mexico.

1995   La religión, la magia y la cosmovisión. In *Historia Antigua de México: VIII: el horizonte posclásico y algunos aspectos intelectuales de las culturas mesoamericanas.* Edited by Linda Manzanilla and Leonardo López, pp.419-458. INAH, UNAM, Porrua editores, Mexico City.

López Austin, Alfredo, and Leonardo López Luján
2001   *El Pasado indígena.* Fondo de Cultura Económica and Colegio de México, México

Lumholtz, Carl
1912   *New Trails in Mexico.* Charles Scribner's Sons, New York.

MacMahon, James A.
1985   *Deserts.* The Audubon Society Nature Guides, New York.

Magaña, Maricruz
2004   *Informe final del análisis realizado a los materiales de concha del Proyecto Arqueológico Valle de*

Onavas, Sonora. Unpublished report. Onavas Valley Archaeological Project, Sonora, Mexico.

Majewski, Teresita, and James E. Ayres
  1997   Toward an Archaeology of Colonialism in the Greater Southwest. *Revista de Arqueología Americana* 12:55-86.

Marcus, Joyce
  2000   Toward an Archaeology of Communities. In *The Archaeology of Communities: A New World Perspective,* edited by Marcello A. Canuto and Jason Yaeger, pp. 231-242. Routledge, London.

Marshall, John and Todd W. Bostwick
  2003   Projectile Points from Brown's Ranch Rock Shelter. In *Archaeological Testing of AZ U:1:25 (ASM), The Brown's Ranch Rock Shelter Site, in Northern Scottsdale, Maricopa County, Arizona,* edited by Thomas E. Wright, pp. 103-132. The Arizona Archaeologist No. 33. Arizona Archaeological Society, Phoenix.

Martinez, Jupiter
  n.d.   Informe Area B5. Ms. on file, Cerro de Trincheras Excavation Project, Centro INAH Sonora, Hermosillo.

  2011   Área B5, La Cancha. In *Excavations at Cerro de Trincheras, Sonora, México,* edited by Randall H. McGuire and Elisa Villalpando, pp. 579-596. Anthropological Papers of the University of Arizona No 204. University of Arizona, Tucson.

McGee, William J.
  1895   The Beginning of Agriculture. *American Anthropologist* 8:350-375.

  1896   Expedition to the Papagueria and Seriland. *American Anthropologist* 9:93-98.

  1898   The Seri Indians. *Seventeenth Annual Report of the Bureau of American Ethnology.* Smithsonian Institution, Washington, D.C.

  2000   *Trails to Tiburon: The 1894 and 1895 Field Diaries of W. J. McGee.* Transcribed by Hazel McFeely Fontana. University of Arizona Press, Tucson.

McGuire, Randall H.
  1997   Crossing the Border. In *Prehistory of the Bortherlands: Recent Research in the Archaeology of Northern Mexico and the Southern Southwest,* edited by John Carpenter and Guadalupe Sanchez, pp. 130-137. Arizona State Museum Archaeological Series #186, University of Arizona Press,Tucson.

McGuire, Randall H., Charles Adams, Ben A. Nelson, and Katherine Spielman
  1994   Drawing the Southwest to Scale: Perspectives on Macroregional Relations. *Themes in Southwest Prehistory,* edited by George J. Gumerman, pp. 239-266. School of American Research Press, Santa Fe, New Mexico.

McGuire, Randall H., and Elisa Villalpando (editors)
  1989   Prehistory and the Making of History in Sonora. In *Columbian Consequences,* edited by D. H. Thomas, pp.213-228. Smithsonian Institution Press, Washington, D.C.

  1993   *An Archaeological Survey of the Altar Valley, Sonora, Mexico.* Anthropological Papers of the University No 184. University of Arizona Press, Tucson.

  1995   Excavacíon arqueológica de Cerro de Trincheras: informe preliminar de la temporada de campo 1995. Informe al Consejo de Arqueología del INAH, Mexico City.

2011   Excavations at Cerro de Trincheras, Sonora, México (2 volumes). Anthropological Papers of the University of Arizona No 204. University of Arizona, Tucson.

McGuire, Randall H., Elisa Villalpando, Victoria Vargas, and Emiliano Gallaga
    1999   Cerro de Trincheras and the Casas Grandes World. In *The Casas Grandes World,* edited by Curtis F. Schaafsma and Caroll L. Riley, pp. 134-148. University of Utah Press, Salt Lake City.

Mills, Barbara (editor)
    2000   *Alternative Leadership Strategies in the Prehispanic Southwest.* University of Arizona Press, Tucson.

Miller, Wick R.
    1983   Uto-Aztecan Languages. In *Southwest,* edited by Alfonso Ortiz, pp. 113-124. Handbook of North American Indians, volume 10, W. Sturtevant, general editor. Smithsonian Institution, Washington, D.C.

Minnis, Paul E., and Charles L. Redman (editors)
    1990   *Perspectives on Southwestern Prehistory.* Westview Press, Boulder.

Minnis, Paul E., and Michael E. Whalen
    2004   Chihuahuan Archaeology: An Introductory History. In S*urveying the Archaeology of Northwest Mexico,* edited by Gillian E. Newell and Emiliano Gallaga, pp. 113-126. University of Utah Press, Salt Lake City.

Moctezuma, José Luis
    1991   Las lenguas indigenas del noroeste de méxico: pasado y presente. In *El Noroeste de México: sus culturas etnicas,* edited by Donaciano Gutierrez and Josefina Gutierrez, pp. 125-136. Museo Nacional de Antropología, INAH, Mexico City.

Montane, Julio Cesar
    1993   *Atlas de Sonora.* Gobierno del Estado de Sonora, Hermosillo, México.

    1996   Desde los orígenes hasta 3000 años antes del presente. In *Historia general de sonora, tomo 1: periodo prehistórico y prehispánico,* pp. 151-195. Gobierno del Estado de Sonora, Hermosillo.

Nabhan, Gary Paul
    2004   *Gathering the Desert.* University of Arizona Press, Tucson.

Nakayama, Antonio
    1974   *Relación de Antonio Ruiz: La Conquista en el Noroeste.* Colección Científica # 18, INAH, México.

Neitzel, Jill E. (editor)
    1999   *Great Towns and Regional Polities in the Prehistoric American Southwest and Southeast.* Amerind Foundation, New World Studies Series No. 3, Amerind Foundation, Dragoon, and The University of New Mexico Press, Albuquerque.

Nelson, Margaret C.
    1996   Chipped Stone Analysis: Food Selection and Hunting Behavior. In *Short-term Sedentism in the America Southwest. The Mimbres Valley Salado,* edited by Ben A. Nelson and Steven A. LeBlanc, pp. 141-176. Maxwell Museum of Anthropology and University of New Mexico Press, Albuquerque.

Nelson, Richard S.
    1991   *Hohokam Marine Shell Exchange and Artifacts.* Anthropological Papers of the University of Arizona No 179. University of Arizona Press, Tucson.

Nentuig, Juan
    1977   *El rudo ensayo: descripción geografica, natural y curiosa de la provincia de Sonora, 1764.* Colección Cientifica No. 58, Etnología, INAH, Mexico City.

Newell, Gillian, and Emiliano Gallaga (editors)
    2004   *Surveying the Archaeology of Northwest Mexico.* University of Utah Press, Salt Lake City.

Núñez Cabeza de Vaca, Alvar
    1993   *Naufragios y Comentarios.* Colección Austral, No. 304, Mexico.

O'Donovan, Maria
    2002   *New Perspectives on Site Funtions and Scale of Cerro de Trincheras, Sonora, Mexico: the 1991 Surface Survey.* Anthropological Papers of the University of Arizona No 195. University of Arizona, Tucson.

Olavarria, Maria Eugenia
    1995   Los Yaquis. *Etnografía Contemporánea de los Pueblos Indigenas de México: Región Noroeste,* pp. 529-574. INI, Mexico City.

Olsen, Stanley J.
    1968   *Fish, Amphibian and Reptile Remains from Archaeological Sites, Part 1: Southeastern and Southwestern United States.* Papers of the Peabody Museum of Archaeology and Ethnology, Vol. 56, no.2, Harvard University.

Ortega N, Sergio
    1996   El sistema de misiónes Jesuitas: 1591-1699. In *Historia general de Sonora, tomo ii: de la conquista al estado libre y soberano de Sonora,* pp. 37-78. Gobierno del Estado de Sonora, Hermosillo.

Padilla, Raquel
    1995   *Yucatán, Fin del Sueño Yaqui: El Tráfico de los Yaquis y el otro Triunvirato.* Gobierno del Estado de Sonora, Secretaria de Educación y Cultura y el Instituto Sonorense de Cultura. Hermosillo, Sonora, Mexico.

Pacheco, Angelica
    2003   *Desarrollo tecnológico y aprovechamiento de materias primas en el Noroeste de México: La industria de lítica lasqueada en la región de Bavispe, Sonora.* Unpublished Licenciatura tesis, Escuela Nacional de Antropología e Historia, Mexico.

Pailes, Richard A.
    1972   *An Archaeological Reconnaissance of Southern Sonora and Reconsideration of the Río Sonora Culture.* Unpublished Ph. D. dissertation, Department of Anthropology, Southern Illinois University, Carbondale.

    1980   The Upper Río Sonora Valley in Prehispanic Trade. In *New Frontiers in the Archaeology and Ethnohistory of the Greater Southwest,* edited by C. L. Riley and B. C. Hedrick, pp.20-39. Transactions of the Illinois State Academy of Science, vol. 72, no. 4, Springfield.

    1984   Agricultural Development and Trade in the Río Sonora. In *Prehistoric Agricultural Strategies in the Southwest,* edited by Susanne K. Fish and Paul R. Fish, pp. 309-326. Anthropological Research Papers no.33. Arizona State University, Tempe.

    1993   Recientes investigaciones arqueológicas en el sur de Sonora. In *Noroeste de Mexico* 12:81-88, INAH-Sonora, Hermosillo.

    1994a Recientes investigaciones arqueológicas en el sur de *Sonora.* In *Sonora: antropología del desierto,*

Noroeste de México no. 12, edited by Beatriz Braniff and Richard S. Felger, pp. 80-88. INAH, Sonora, Mexico.

1994b Relaciones Culturales Prehistoricas en el Noroeste de Sonora. In *Sonora: antropología del desierto., Noroeste de México no. 12,* edited by Beatriz Braniff and Richard S. Felger, pp. 117-122. INAH, Sonora, Mexico.

Parsons, Jeffrey R.
   1990   Critical Reflections on a Decade of Full-Coverage Regional Survey in the Valley of Mexico. In *The Archaeology of Regions: A Case for Full-Coverage Survey,* edited by Suzanne Fish and Stephen A. Kowalewski, pp. 7-32. Smithsonian Institution Press, Washington, D.C.

Pauketat, Timothy R.
   1994   *The Ascent of Chiefs: Cahokia and Mississippian Politics in Native North America.* University of Alabama Press, Tuscaloosa and London.

   1997   Specialization, Political Symbols, and the Crafty Elite of Cahokia. *Southeastern Archaeology* 16: 1-15.

   2000   The Tragedy of the Commoners. In *Agency in Archaeology,* edited by Marcia-Anne Dobres and John Robb, pp. 113-130. Routledge, London and New York.ç

Pennington, Cambell W.
   1969   *The Tepehuan of Chihuahua: Their Material Cultura.* University of Utah Press, Salt Lake City.

   1980   *The Pima Bajo of Central Sonora, Mexico,* vol. 1. University of Utah Press, Salt Lake City.

   1982   La cultura de los Eudeve del Noroeste de México. *Noroeste de México* 6: 9-35.

Peregrine, Peter N.
   1992   *Mississippian Evolution: A World Systems Perspective.* Monographs in World Archaeology No. 9. Prehistory Press, Madison.

Pérez Bedolla, Raúl G.
   1996   Geografía de Sonora. In *Historia general de sonora, tomo 1: periodo prehistórico y prehispánico,* pp. 97-150. Gobierno del Estado de Sonora, Hermosillo.

Pérez de Ribas, Andres
   1999   *History of the Triumphs of Our Holy Faith amongst the Most Barbarous and Fierce Peoples of the New World,* translated by Daniel T. Reff, Maureen Ahern, and Richard K. Danford. University of Arizona Press, Tucson.

Pfefferkorn, Ignaz
   1989   *Sonora: A Description of the Province,* translated by Theodore E. Treutlein. Southwest Center Series. University of Arizona Press, Tucson.

Pogue, J. E.
   1912   The Aboriginal Use of Turquoise in North America. *American Anthropologist* 14(3):437-466.

Pollard, Helen P.
   1997   Recent Research in West Mexican Archaeology. *Journal of Archeological Research* 5(4): 345-384.

Potter, James M.
    2004   The Creation of Person, The Creation of Place: Hunting Landscape in the American Southwest. *American Antiquity* 69(2):322-338.

Radding, Cynthia
    1997   *Wandering Peoples: Colonialism, Ethnic Spaces, and Ecological Frontiers in Northwestern Mexico, 1700-1850.* Duke University Press, Durham and London.

Rapoport, Amos
    1982   *The Meaning of the Built Environment.* University of Arizona Press, Tucson.

Rappaport, Roy A.
    1979   *Ecology, Meaning, and Religion.* North Atlantic Books, Richmond, California.

Ravesloot, J. C., J. S. Dean, and M. S. Foster.
    1995   A Re-Analysis of the Casas Grandes Tree-Ring Dates: A Preliminary Discussion. In *Arqueología del norte y del occidente de México: Homenaje al Doctor J. Charles Kelley,* edited by B. Dahlgren and M. D. Soto, pp. 325-332. UNAM, Mexico City.

Rea, Amadeo M.
    1998   *Folk Mammalogy of the Northern Pimans.* University of Arizona Press, Tucson.

Reff, Daniel T.
    1991   *Disease, Depopulation, and Culture Change in Northwestern New Spain,* 1518-1764. University of Utah Press, Salt Lake City.

Rice, Glen E.
    1985   *Studies in the Hohokam and Salado of the Tonto Basin.* OCRM Report No. 63. Office of Cultural Resource Management, Arizona State University, Tempe.

Rice, Glen E., and John C. Ravesloot
    2001   *Who Used the Areas Between Villages? The Role of Camps, Activity Areas and Fields in the Study of Prehistoric Landscapes.* P-MIP Technical Report N0. 2002-09. Department of the Interior United States Bureau of Reclamation Arizona Projects Office, Phoenix, Arizona.

Rice, Glen E., and Charles L. Redman
    2000   Compounds, Villages, and Mounds: The Salado Alternative. In *The Hohokam Village Revisited,* edited by David, E. Doyel, Suzanne K. Fish, and Paul R. Fish, pp.317-340. Southwestern and Rocky Mountain Division of the American Association for the Advancement of Science, Colorado State University.

Rice, Prudence M.
    1987   *Pottery Analysis: A Sourcebook.* University of Chicago Press, Chicago.

Riley, Carroll
    1987   *The Frontier People.* University of New Mexico Press, Albuquerque.

    1990   A View from the Protohistoric. In *Perspectives on Southwestern Prehistory,* edited by Paul Minnis and Charles L. Redman, pp. 228-239. Westview Press, Boulder.

    1999   Sonoran Statelets and Casas Grandes. In *The Casas Grandes World,* edited by C. F. Schaafsma and C. L. Riley, pp. 193-205. University of Utah Press, Salt Lake City.

    2005   *Becoming Aztlan: Mesoamerican Influence in the Greater Southwest,* AD 1200-1500. The University of Utah Press, Salt Lake City.

Roberts, Brian K.
1996   *Landscapes of Settlement: Prehistory of the Landscape.* Routledge, London and New York.

Rossignol, Jacqueline, and LuAnn Wandsnider (editors)
1992   *Space, Time, and Archaeological Landscapes.* Plenum Press, New York and London.

Sánchez, G., John. P. Carpenter, and E. Villalpando
1996   Proyecto La Playa: Five Thousand Years of Occupation in the Boquillas Valley, Sonora, Mexico. Paper presented at the 61st Meeting of the Society for American Archaeology, New Orleans.

Sanoja, Mario, and Iraida Varjas
1994   La creacion de los primeros centros de poder. In *Historia antigua de Mexico, vol :1 El Mexico antiguo, sus areas culturales, los origenes y el horizonte Preclasico,* edited by Linda Manzanilla and Leonardo Lopez, pp. 247-278. Porrua, INAH, UNAM, Mexico City.

Sauer, Carl O.
1925   The Morphology of Landscape. *University of California Publications in Geography* 2:19-53.

1932   *The Road to Cibola.* Ibero-Americana No. 3. University of California Press, Berkeley.

1934   *The Distribution of Aboriginal Tribes and Languages in Northwestern Mexico.* University of California Press, Berkeley, California.

Sauer, Carl and Donald Brand
1931   Prehistoric Settlements of Sonora with Special Reference to Cerros de Trincheras. *University of California Publication in Geography* 5(3):67-148.

Saxe, A. A.
1970   *Social Dimensions of Mortuary Practices.* Unpublished Ph. D, Dissertation, Department of Anthropology, University of Michigan, Ann Arbor.

Schiffer, Michael B.
1987   *Formation Processes of the Archaeological Record.* University of Utah Press, Salt Lake City.

Schuyler, Robert L.
1988   Archaeological Remains, Documents, and Anthropology: A Call for a New Culture History. *Historical Archaeology* 22:36-42.

Segesser, Philipp
1945   The Relation of Phillip Segesser: The Pimas and Other Indians. *Mid-America: An Historical Review* 27(3): 139-187.

Sheridan, Thomas
1988   How to Tell the Story of a "People Without History:" Narrative versus Ethnohistorical Approaches to the Study of the Yaqui Indians Through Time. *Journal of the Southwest* 30(2):168-189.

1999   *Empire of Sand: The Seri Indians and the Struggle for Spanish Sonora,* 1645-1803. University of Arizona Press, Tucson.

Slaughter, Mark C.
1993   Production and use of Flaked Stone Artifacts from los Hornos. In *In the Shadow of South Mountain:*

The Pre-Classic Hohokam of La Ciudad de los Hornos, 1991-1992 Excavation, vol. 1, edited by Mark L. Chenault, Richard V. N. Ahlstrum, and Thomas Motsinger, pp. 285-315. Archaeological Report No 93-30. SWCA, Tucson.

Slaughter, Mark C., L. Fratt, K. Anderson, and R. V. N. Ahlstrom
    1992   *Making and Using Stone Artifacts: A Context for Evaluating Lithic Sites in Arizona.* Arizona Historical Preservation Plan, Arizona State Parks. Environment Consultants, Tucson.

Sliva, Jane
    1997   *Introduction to the Study and Analysis of Flaked Stone Artifacts and Lithic Technology.* Center for Desert Archaeology, Tucson.

Smith, Carol A.
    1976   *Regional Analysis.* Academic Press, New York.

Snead, James E.
    2004   Ancestral Pueblo Settlement Dynamics: Landscape, Scale, and Context in the Burnt Corn Community. *Kiva* 69(3):242-270.

Spence, Michael W., Phil C. Weigand, and Dolores Soto de Arechavaleta.
    1993   El intercambio de obsidiana en el Occidente de México. In *Evolución de una civilización pre-hispanica,* edited by Phil C. Weigand, pp. 203-210. El Colegio de Michoacán, Morelia, Mexico.

Spencer, Ch. S., and E. M. Redmond.
    1997   *Archaeology of the Cañada de Cuicatlan, Oaxaca.* Anthropological paper of the American Museum of Natural History No. 80, New York.

Spicer, Edward
    1983   Yaqui. In *Southwest,* edited by Alfonso Ortiz, pp. 250-263. Handbook of North American Indians, volume 10, W. Sturtevant, general editor. Smithsonian Institution, Washington, D.C.

    1992   *Cycles of Conquest: The Impact of Spain, Mexico, and the United States on the Indians of the Southwest,* 1533-1960. University of Arizona Press, Tucson.

    1993   Yaquis. In *Southwest,* edited by Alfonso Ortiz, pp. 250-263. Handbook of North American Indians, volume 10, W. Sturtevant, general editor. Smithsonian Institution, Washington, D.C.

    1994   *Yaquis: historia de una cultura.* Instituto de Investigaciones Históricas, Serie Historiadores y Cronistas de Indias No. 9. UNAM, Mexico City.

Spores, R.
    1980   New World Ethnohistory and Archaeology, 1970-1980. *Annual Review of Anthropology* 9:575-603.

Stewart, Joe D., Jane H. Kelley, A. C. MacWilliams, and Paula J. Reimer
    2005   The Viejo Period of Chihuahua Culture in Northwestern Mexico. *Latin American Antiquity* 16(2): 169-192.

Suárez, Lourdes.
    1974   *Técnicas prehispánicas en los objetos de concha.* Colección científica No.14. INAH, Mexico City.

    2002   *Tipología de los objetos prehispánicos de concha.* Editorial Miguel Ángel Porrúa, 2da edición, CON-ACULTA-INAH, Mexico City.

Talavera González, Jorge Arturo
  1995   *Mochicahui, Sinaloa: un asentamiento prehispánico en la frontera septentríonal de Mesoamerica (un estudio arqueológico).* Unpublished licenciatura thesis, Escuela Nacional de Antropología e Historia, Mexico.

Taube, Karl
  2003   Ancient and Contemporary Maya Conceptions about Forest and Fields. In *The Lowlands Maya Area: Three Millennia at the Human-Wildland Interface,* edited by Arturo Gómez-Pompa, Michael F. Allen, Scott L. Fedick, and Juan J. Jiménez-Osornio, pp. 461-492. Food Products Press, New York.

Tolstoy, Paul
  1971   Utilitarian Artifact in Central Mexico. In *Archaeology of Northern Mesoamerica (part one),* edited by Gordon F. Ekholm and Gordon R. Willey, pp. 270-296. Handbook of Middle American, Vol. 10, R. Wauchope general editor, University of Texas Press, Austin.

Trigger, Bruce
  1983   American Archaeology as Native History: A Review Essay. *William and Mary Quarterly* 40(3):413-452.

  1985   *Natives and Newcomers: Canada's "Heroic Age" Reconsidered.* McGill-Queen's University Press, Kingston.

Upham, Steadman
  1986   Imperialist, Isolationist, World Systems and Political Realities. In *Ripples in the Chichimec Sea,* edited by Francis J. Mathien and Randall H. McGuire, pp. 205-219. Southern Illinois University, Carbondale and Edwardsville.

Varela, Juan
  1626   *Anua de 1626 en las misiones de San Ignació.* Ms. on file, Special Collection, University of Arizona Press, Tucson.

Vargas, Victoria
  1998   *Shell Trade within Northwestern Mexico: Cerro de Trincheras and Casas Grandes.* Paper presented at the 64th Annual Meeting of the Society for American Archaeology, Seattle.

  1999   *The Shell Artifact Assemblage from the Cerro de Trincheras Survey Project.* Ms. on file, Arizona State Museum, University of Arizona Press, Tucson.

  2004   Shell Ornaments, Power, and the Rise of the Cerro de Trincheras: Patterns through Time at Trincheras Sites in the Magdalena River Valley, Sonora. In *Surveying the Archaeology of Northwest Mexico,* edited by Gillian E. Newell and Emiliano Gallaga, pp. 65-76. University of Utah Press, Salt Lake City.

Varien, Mark D.
  1999   *Sedentism and Mobility in a Social Landscape: Mesa Verde and Beyond.* University of Arizona Press, Tucson.

Velázquez, Castro Adrián.
  1999   *Tipología de los objetos de concha del Templo Mayor de Tenochtitlan.* Colección científica No.392. INAH, Mexico City.

Villalpando, Elisa
  1988   Rutas de intercambio y objetos de concha en el noroeste de México. *Cuicuilco* 21:77-81.

1989   Los que viven en las montañas: correlación arqueológica-etnográfica en isla San Esteban, Sonora, México. *Noroeste de México* No. 8, Centro Regional Sonora, INAH.

1997   La tradición Trincheras y los grupos costeros del desierto Sonorense. In *Prehistory of the Borderlands: Recent Research in the Archaeology of the Northern Mexico and the Southern Southwest,* edited by John Carpenter and Guadalupe Sanchez, pp. 95-112. Anthropological Papers of the University of Arizona No 186. University of Arizona Press, Tucson.

2000a   Conchas y caracoles. Relaciones entre nómadas y sedentarios en el Noroeste de México. In *Nómadas y sedentarios en el Noroeste de México: homenaje a Beatriz Braniff,* edited by Marie-Areti Hers, Jose Luis Mirafuentes, Maria Dolores Soto, and Miguel Vallebueno, pp. 525-546. UNAM, Mexico City.

2000b   The Archaeological Traditions of Sonora. In *Greater Mesoamerica: The Archaeology of West and Northwest Mexico,* edited by Michael S. Foster and Shirley Gorenstein, pp. 241-254. University of Utah Press, Salt Lake City.

2001a   Los pobladores en Sonora. In *La gran Chichimeca: El lugar de las rocas secas,* edited by Beatriz Braniff, pp. 211-236. Jaca Book and CONACULTA, Mexico City.

Villalpando, Elisa, and Paul R. Fish
1997   Prefacio. In *Prehistory of the Borderlands: Recent Research in the Archaeology of the Northern Mexico and the Southern Southwest,* edited by John Carpenter and Guadalupe Sanchez, pp. ix-xi. Anthropological Papers of the University of Arizona No 186. University of Arizona Press, Tucson.

Villalpando, Elisa, and Randall McGuire
2009   *Entre Muros de Piedra: La Arqueología del Cerro de Trincheras.* Instituto Sonorense de Cultura-INAH, México.

Wasley, William W.
1966-1967   *Arizona State Museum Sonora-Sinaloa Project.* Arizona State Museum Archives, Tucson.

Webster, G. S.
1996   Social Archaeology and the Irrational. *Current Anthropology* 37(4):609-627.

Weigand, Phil C., and Garman Harbottle
1993   The Role of Turquoise in the Ancient Mesoamerican Trade Structure. In *The American Southwest and Mesoamerica: Systems of Prehistoric Exchange,* edited by Jonathon E. Ericson and Timothy G. Baugh, pp. 159-178. Plenum Press, New York and London.

1995   Minería pre-hispanica en las regiones noroccidentales de Mesoamérica, con énfasis en la turquesa. In *Arqueología del Occidente y Norte de México,* edited by Eduardo Williams, and Phil C. Weigand, pp. 115-138. El Colegio de Michoacán, Morelia, Michoacan.

Wells, E. Christian, Glen E. Rice, and John C. Ravesloot
2004   Peopling Landscape between Villages in the Middle Gila River Valley of Central Arizona. *American Antiquity* 69 (4):627-652.

West, Robert C.
1993   *Sonora: Its Geographical Personality.* University of Texas Press, Austin.

Whalen, Michael E., and Paul Minnis
1999   Investigating the Paquimé Regional System. In *The Casas Grandes World,* edited by Curtis F. Schaafsma and Carroll L. Riley, pp. 54-62. University of Utah Press, Salt Lake City.

2000   Leadership at Casas Grandes, Chihuahua, Mexico. In *Alternative Leadership Strategies in the Prehispanic Southwest,* edited by Barbara J. Mills, pp.168-179. University of Arizona Press, Tucson.

2001   *Casas Grandes and its Hinterland: Prehistoric Regional Organization in Northwest Mexico.* University of Arizona Press, Tucson.

2003   The Local and the Distance in the Origin of Casas Grandes, Chihuahua, Mexico. *American Antiquity* 68 (2):314-332.

Whalen, Michael E., A. C. MacWilliams, Todd Pitezel
2010   Reconsidering the Size and Structure of Casas Grandes, Chihuahua, Mexico. *American Antiquity* 75 (3):527-550.

Whitecotton, Joseph W.
1977   *The Zapotec: Princes, Priests, and Peasants.* Norman, University of Oklahoma Press.

Wilcox, David
1986a The Tepiman Connection: A Model of Mesoamerican-Southwestern Interaction. In *Ripples in the Chichimec Sea: New Considerations of the Southwestern-Mesoamerican Interactions,* edited by Frances J. Mathien and Randall H. McGuire, pp. 135-154. Southern Illinois University Press, Carbondale.

1986b A Historical Analysis of the Problem of Southwestern-Mesoamerican Connections. *In Ripples in the Chichimec Sea: New Considerations of the Southwestern-Mesoamerican Interactions,* edited by Frances J. Mathien and Randall H. McGuire, pp. 9-44. Southern Illinois University Press, Carbondale.

1999   A Peregrine View of Macroregional Systems in the North American Southwest, A. D. 750-1250. In *Great Towns and Regional Polities: In the Prehistorical American Southwest and Southeast,* edited by Jill E. Neitzel, pp. 115-143. Amerind Foundation New Word Studies Series No 3, University of New Mexico Press, Albuquerque.

Willey, Gordon R.
1953   *Prehistoric Settlement in the Virú Valley, Peru.* Bulletin No. 155, Bureau of American Ethnology, Washington, D.C.

William, Eduardo (editor)
1994   *Contribuciones a la arqueología y etnohistoria del Occidente de México.* El Colegio de Michoacán.

Wilson, Samuel M.
1993   Structure and History: Combining Archaeology and Ethnohistory in the Contact Period Caribbean. In *Ethnohistory and Archaeology: Approaches to Postcontact Change in the Americas,* edited by Daniel J. Rogers and Samuel M. Wilson, pp. 19-30. Plenum Press, New York.

Woodbury, Richard
1954   *Prehistoric Stone Implements of Northeastern Arizona.* Papers of the Peabody Museum of American Archaeology and Ethnology No. 34. Harvard University, Cambridge.

Yetman, David
1996   *Sonora: An Intimate Geography.* University of Arizona Southwest Center, Tucson, and University of New Mexico Press, Albuquerque.

Yoffee, Norman
2005   *Myths of the Archaic State: Evolution of the Earliest Cities, States, and Civilizations.* Cambridge University Press, Cambridge.

Yoffee, Norman; Suzanne Fish, and George R. Milner.
   1999   Communities, Ritualities, Chiefdoms: Social Evolution in the American Southwest and Southeast. In
          Great Towns and Regional Polities: In The Prehistorical American Southwest and Southeast, edited by Jill
          E. Neitzel, pp. 261-272. Amerind Foundation New Word Studies Series No 3. University of New Mexico
          Press, Albuquerque.

Zapata Ortiz, Juan
   1678   *Relación de las Misiones que la Compania tiene en el Reyno y Provincias de Nueva Vizcaya en la Nueva
          España.* Ms. on file, Special Collection, University of Arizona, Tucson.

Appendix I

Summary of Material Data for All Sites

Site	Size (m^2)	Site type*	Habitation structures	Public Architecture	Burials	Water System	Hearth	Storage Area	Shell	Shell Reamers	Onavas Lisa	Red Wares	Onavas P/R	Non-local Wares	Points	Stone Tools	Obsidian	Turquoise
Son P:6:3	100	I	1								11	1						
Son P:6:4	20,300	II	4		4				80		243	7	7			4	1	1
Son P:6:5	17,600	II	17		1				23		329		13		5	2	7	
Son P:6:6	900	C-2										X**				X		
Son P:6:7	104	C-2									17	7						
Son P:6:8	13,000	I	1					1	8		109	2			3	4	6	
Son P:6:9	225	C-1					1				47							
Son P:6:10	10,200	I		1			2+				98				8		1	
Son P:6:11	400	C-2									37	1			1			
Son P:6:12	400	C-2									28							
Son P:6:13	100	C-4														1		
Son P:6:14	225	C-4									16							
Son P:6:15	600	C-2									65	6						
Son P:6:16	5,500	I	1						6		76	1						
Son P:6:17	100	C-2									27	1						
Son P:6:18	900	I	1								93							
Son P:6:19	600	C-2/I	1						1		17						1	
Son P:10:02	875	I	3				1+				X					X		
Son P:10:03	10,000	II	1						9		122				1	1		
Son P:10:04	10,000	I					1+		X		X			X		X		
Son P:10:05	10	C-5																
Son P:10:06	8,400	I							X		92		5			3		
Son P:10:07	7,200	I	1						X		X	X				X		
Son P:10:08	5,000	C-5			1	1+			442	7	2648	9	223	15	9	18	47	3
Son P:10:09	7,200	I									X	X				X		
Son P:10:10	736	C-2									X	X						
Son P:10:11	100	C-2									X	X						
Son P:10:12	15,000	III			1		1		59		50	7	2			3		
Son P:10:13	2,520	C-2									46				2		3	
Son P:10:14	9,600	I	1		2				15		98	6	2		4			
Son P:10:15	900	C-2									49	1						
Son P:10:16	3,600	I					2		14		93	5			2	4	5	
Son P:10:17	7,600	I	1						8		167				1	1	1	
Son P:10:18	3,600	I							5		129	6	2			1		
Son P:10:19	1,200	C-2							8		39					1		
Son P:10:20	120	C-5		1							1							
Son P:10:21	100	C																
Son P:10:22	500	C																
Son P:10:23	3,000	C-1			1		4		X		X	X			X	X	X	
Son P:10:24	4,000	C-1							X		X					X	X	
Son P:10:25	40	C-1														X		
Son P:10:26	27,500	I					7	1	2		112	3		1	12	1	1	
Son P:10:27	15,600	I	2					1	28		336	2	1			1	2	1
Son P:10:28	6,000	I							4	1	123	2	6			5	1	
Son P:10:29	1,350	C-2							2	2	121	1	11			2		
Son P:10:30	1,200	C-2									72	1	5			1		
Son P:10:31	520	C-2							1		102		2					
Son P:10:32	1,050	C-2					1				116	X				1		
Son P:10:33	200	I				1												

Site	Size (m²)	Site type	Habitation structures	Public Architecture	Burials	Water System	Hearth	Storage Area	Shell	Shell Reamers	Onavas Lisa	Red Wares	Onavas P/R	Non-local Wares	Points	Stone Tools	Obsidian	Turquoise
Son P:10:34	400	C-2									20	1	1					
Son P:10:35	100	C-2									37							
Son P:10:36	400	C-2						2			46	5						
Son P:10:37	144	C-2									25	1						
Son P:10:38	100	C-2									16	2						
Son P:10:39	100	C-3									40							
Son P:10:40	3,600	I	2						1		174		1			3	2	
Son P:10:41	5,400	I			1				8		221		7			3		1
Son P:10:42	100	C-2									27					1		
Son P:10:43	100	C-2									7	1						
Son P:10:44	1,500	I							3	1	137		15			1		
Son P:10:45	100	C-2									18	2				1		
Son P:10:46	100	C-2									12							
Son P:10:47	2,000	C-2									41					1		
Son P:10:48	225	C-2									25	1						
Son P:10:49	225	C-2									31	1						
Son P:10:50	25	C-1														1		
Son P:10:51	100	C-2							3		14							
Son P:10:52	3,000	C-1					1+				106					2		
Son P:10:53	225	C-1									45					1		
Son P:10:54	225	C-2									22					1		
Son P:10:55	8,000	I	3						6		119		1			3	1	
Son P:10:56	18,900	II	10		1	1+		1	11		414		1	2		2	1	
Son P:10:57	144	C-2									15							
Son P:10:58	144	C-2									14					1		
Son P:10:59	1,200	C-2									67	2		1				
Son P:10:60	2,000	C-2									74							
Son P:10:61	25	C-4									5							
Son P:10:62	64	C-4									52							
Son P:10:63	1,200	C-2									39	2	1					
Son P:10:64	4,000	I						4			105	5						
Son P:10:65	3,000	C-2						20			73	2	1				3	
Son P:10:66	100	C-3									45							
Son P:10:67	400	C-2									59		2					
Son P:10:68	2,000	C-2									74							
Son P:10:69	1,125	C-2									53	5						
Son P:10:70	16,800	III	3	2	1				66		162	1	10		2	5	6	
Son P:10:71	64	C-4									7							
Son P:10:72	25	C-2									8							
Son P:10:73	2,800	I	6								43							
Son P:10:74	144	C-1									30							
Son P:10:75	100	C-1									69					1		
Son P:10:76	25	C-2									48							
Son P:10:77	25	C-4									16							
Son P:10:78	2,000	I	5						1		18					1		
Son P:10:79	4	C-3																
Son P:10:80	4,800	I	1				1		2		28	1						
Son P:10:81	9	C-4									61							
Son P:10:82	4	P																

Site	Size (m²)	Site type	Habitation structures	Public Architecture	Burials	Water System	Hearth	Storage Area	Shell	Shell Reamers	Onavas Lisa	Red Wares	Onavas P/R	Non-local Wares	Points	Stone Tools	Obsidian	Turquoise
Son P:10:83	400	I	1					1			123	4						
Son P:10:84	2,000	C-2							3		68				1			
Son P:10:85	2,400	I									103					1	3	
Son P:10:86	11,700	I						1	1		157	1			2	2	2	
Son P:10:87	3,600	I							2		40				1			
Son P:10:88	2,800	I	3			1					22							
Son P:10:89	25	C-2										52						
Son P:10:90	4,500	I	1						5		68		1			1		
Son P:10:91	6,550	I			1		3?		17		107	1			2	4		1
Son P:10:92	625	C-2									22					1		
Son P:10:93	4,400	I	2						2		67	4				2		
Son P:10:94	2,100	C-2									28					1	1	
Son P:10:95	25	C-2									16							
Son P:10:96	800	C-2							3		34	1			1		5	
Son P:10:97	400	C-2									66		1				2	
Son P:10:98	9,600	I	2		4			1	250		213		34		4	9	32	5
Son P:10:99	400	C-2					1				35				2		1	
Son P:10:100	225	C-1									14							
Son P:10:101	20,000	I	6		1				12		80		1		17	3	14	1
Son P:10:102	6,600	I	3						22		87	2			3	2	5	
Son P:10:103	5,000	C-2							9		17	6			4	1	14	
Son P:10:104	900	C-2							2		12				6	1	8	
Son P:10:105	100?	C-2							2		16						3	
Son P:10:106	900	C-2									15					1		
Son P:10:107	3,200	C-2							1		56					1	1	
Son P:10:108	2,400	C-2							1		53					1		
Son P:10:109	100	C-4									4	3						
Son P:10:110	10,800	I							19		91		2					
Total	415,696		83	6	18	4	25	7	1193	11	10,105	175	328	17	99	110	179	13

Notes:

*Site type:
I: Household/Rancheria
II: Hamlets/Big Rancheria
III: Central Site/Villages
IV: Regional Center

C-1: Food Gathering
C-2: Agricultural Field
C-3: Material Source Recollection Area
C-4: Hunting Area, Trails, and Pot Burst
C-5: Shrines/Altars2

**Blocks marked with an "X" are sites that were recorded in 2004 and where specific material was observed at the surface but that were not collected and not included in the material analysis.

Appendix II

Summary of Time Period Data for All Sites

Site	Size (m²)	Site type*	Quaternary	Paleoindian-Archaic	Late Archaic-Early Agricult	Early Ceramic	Onavas Period	Onavas I	Onavas II	Onavas III	Onavas IV	Habitation structures	Public Architecture	Burials	Water System	Hearth	Storage Area	Shell	Shell Reamers	Onavas Lisa	Red Wares	Onavas P/R	Non-local Wares	Points	Stone Tools	Obsidian	Turquoise
Son P:6:3	100	I					x	x				1								11	1						
Son P:6:4	20,300	II					x	x	x			4	4					80		243	7	7			4	1	1
Son P:6:5	17,600	II		x	x		x	x	x			17	1					23		329		13	5		2	7	
Son P:6:6	900	C-2																			X**				X		
Son P:6:7	104	C-2					x	x												17	7						
Son P:6:8	13,000	I			x		x	x		x		1					1	8		109	2			3	4	6	
Son P:6:9	225	C-1					x									1				47							
Son P:6:10	10,200	I			x		x			x			1			2+				98				8		1	
Son P:6:11	400	C-2			x		x	x	x											37	1			1			
Son P:6:12	400	C-2					x													28							
Son P:6:13	100	C-4	x																						1		
Son P:6:14	225	C-4					x													16							
Son P:6:15	600	C-2					x	x												65	6						
Son P:6:16	5,500	C-3					x	x				1						6		76	1						
Son P:6:17	100	C-4					x	x												27	1						
Son P:6:18	900	C-5					x					1								93							
Son P:6:19	600	C-6					x					1						1		17						1	
Son P:10:02	875	C-7					x					3				1+				X					X		
Son P:10:03	10,000	C-8	x				x	x				1						9		122				1	1		
Son P:10:04	10,000	C-9					x									1+		X		X			X		X		
Son P:10:05	10	C-10																									
Son P:10:06	8,400	C-11					x	x										X		92		5			3		
Son P:10:07	7,200	C-12					x					1						X		X	X				X		
Son P:10:08	5,000	C-13					x	x	x	x	x	1	1+					442	7	2648	9	223	15	9	18	47	3
Son P:10:09	7,200	C-14					x													X	X				X		
Son P:10:10	736	C-15					x													X	X						
Son P:10:11	100	C-16					x													X	X						
Son P:10:12	15,000	C-17					x	x	x			1		1				59		50	7	2			3		
Son P:10:13	2,520	C-18	x				x													46				2		3	
Son P:10:14	9,600	C-19					x	x	x			1		2				15		98	6	2		4			
Son P:10:15	900	C-20					x	x												49	1						
Son P:10:16	3,600	C-21			x		x	x									2	14		93	5			2	4	5	
Son P:10:17	7,600	C-22			x		x					1						8		167				1	1	1	
Son P:10:18	3,600	C-23					x	x	x									5		129	6	2			1		
Son P:10:19	1,200	C-24					x	x										8		39					1		
Son P:10:20	120	C-25					x								1					1							
Son P:10:21	100	C-26																									
Son P:10:22	500	C-27																									
Son P:10:23	3,000	C-28					x							1		4		X		X	X			X	X	X	
Son P:10:24	4,000	C-29					x											X		X					X	X	
Son P:10:25	40	C-30	x																						X		
Son P:10:26	27,500	C-31			x		x	x								7	1	2		112	3		1	12	1	1	
Son P:10:27	15,600	C-32					x	x	x			2				1		28		336	2	1			1	2	1
Son P:10:28	6,000	C-33					x	x	x									4	1	123	2	6			5	1	
Son P:10:29	1,350	C-34					x	x	x									2	2	121	1	11			2		
Son P:10:30	1,200	C-35					x	x	x											72	1	5			1		
Son P:10:31	520	C-36					x	x	x									1		102		2			1		
Son P:10:32	1,050	C-37					x	x								1				116	X				1		
Son P:10:33	200	C-38												1													
Son P:10:34	400	C-39					x	x	x											20	1	1					
Son P:10:35	100	C-40					x													37							
Son P:10:36	400	C-41					x	x										2		46	5						
Son P:10:37	144	C-42					x	x												25	1						
Son P:10:38	100	C-43					x	x												16	2						
Son P:10:39	100	C-44					x													40							
Son P:10:40	3,600	C-45					x	x	x			2						1		174		1			3	2	

Site	Size (m²)	Site type	Quaternary	Paleoindian-Archaic	Late Archaic-Early Agricult.	Early Ceramic	Onavas Period	Onavas I	Onavas II	Onavas III	Onavas IV	Habitation structures	Public Architecture	Burials	Water System	Hearth	Storage Area	Shell	Shell Reamers	Onavas Lisa	Red Wares	Onavas P/R	Non-local Wares	Points	Stone Tools	Obsidian	Turquoise
Son P:10:41	5,400	I					x	x	x					1				8		221		7			3		1
Son P:10:42	100	C-2					x													27					1		
Son P:10:43	100	C-2					x	x												7	1						
Son P:10:44	1,500	I					x	x	x									3	1	137		15			1		
Son P:10:45	100	C-2					x	x												18	2				1		
Son P:10:46	100	C-2					x	x												12							
Son P:10:47	2,000	C-2					x													41					1		
Son P:10:48	225	C-2					x	x												25	1						
Son P:10:49	225	C-2					x	x												31	1						
Son P:10:50	25	C-1				x																			1		
Son P:10:51	100	C-2					x											3		14							
Son P:10:52	3,000	C-1					x	x								1+			106					2		
Son P:10:53	225	C-1					x												45					1		
Son P:10:54	225	C-2					x												22					1		
Son P:10:55	8,000	I					x	x				3						6		119	1				3	1	
Son P:10:56	18,900	II			x		x	x				10			1	1+	1	11		414	1		2		2	1	
Son P:10:57	144	C-2					x	x												15							
Son P:10:58	144	C-2					x													14					1		
Son P:10:59	1,200	C-2					x	x		x										67	2		1				
Son P:10:60	2,000	C-2					x													74							
Son P:10:61	25	C-4					x													5							
Son P:10:62	64	C-4					x													52							
Son P:10:63	1,200	C-2					x	x	x											39	2	1					
Son P:10:64	4,000	I					x	x										4		105	5						
Son P:10:65	3,000	C-2					x	x	x									20		73	2	1				3	
Son P:10:66	100	C-3					x													45							
Son P:10:67	400	C-2					x		x											59		2					
Son P:10:68	2,000	C-2					x													74							
Son P:10:69	1,125	C-2					x	x												53	5						
Son P:10:70	16,800	III			x		x	x	x			3	2	1				66		162	1	10	2	5	6		
Son P:10:71	64	C-4					x													7							
Son P:10:72	25	C-2					x													8							
Son P:10:73	2,800	I					x					6								43							
Son P:10:74	144	C-1					x													30							
Son P:10:75	100	C-1					x													69					1		
Son P:10:76	25	C-2					x													48							
Son P:10:77	25	C-4					x													16							
Son P:10:78	2,000	I					x					5						1		18					1		
Son P:10:79	4	C-3				x																					
Son P:10:80	4,800	I					x	x				1				1		2		28	1						
Son P:10:81	9	C-4					x													61							
Son P:10:82	4	P	x																								
Son P:10:83	400	I					x	x				1					1		123	4							
Son P:10:84	2,000	C-2			x		x										3		68					1		
Son P:10:85	2,400	I					x												103					1	3	
Son P:10:86	11,700	I		x	x		x	x									1	1		157	1			2	2	2	
Son P:10:87	3,600	I			x		x	x									2		40					1		
Son P:10:88	2,800	I					x					3	1						22							
Son P:10:89	25	C-2							x												52						
Son P:10:90	4,500	I					x	x	x			1					5		68	1				1		
Son P:10:91	6,550	I					x	x							1	3?	17		107	1			2	4		1
Son P:10:92	625	C-2					x													22					1		
Son P:10:93	4,400	I					x	x				2					2		67	4				2		
Son P:10:94	2,100	C-2					x												28				1	1		
Son P:10:95	25	C-2					x													16							
Son P:10:96	800	C-2			x		x	x									3		34	1				1	5	
Son P:10:97	400	C-2					x		x											66		1				2	
Son P:10:98	9,600	I			x		x	x	x			2		4			1	250		213	34			4	9	32	5
Son P:10:99	400	C-2			x		x										1		35					2	1	
Son P:10:100	225	C-1					x													14							

Site	Size (m²)	Site type	Quaternary	Paleoindian-Archaic	Late Archaic-Early Agricult.	Early Ceramic	Onavas Period	Onavas I	Onavas II	Onavas III	Onavas IV	Habitation structures	Public Architecture	Burials	Water System	Hearth	Storage Area	Shell	Shell Reamers	Onavas Lisa	Red Wares	Onavas P/R	Non-local Wares	Points	Stone Tools	Obsidian	Turquoise
Son P:10:101	20,000	I	x	x			x	x	x			6		1				12		80		1		17	3	14	1
Son P:10:102	6,600	I			x		x	x				3						22		87	2			3	2	5	
Son P:10:103	5,000	C-2					x	x			x							9		17	6			4	1	14	
Son P:10:104	900	C-2			x		x											2		12				6	1	8	
Son P:10:105	100?	C-2					x											2		16						3	
Son P:10:106	900	C-2					x													15				1			
Son P:10:107	3,200	C-2					x	x										1		56						1	1
Son P:10:108	2,400	C-2			x		x	x										1		53				1			
Son P:10:109	100	C-4					x	x												4	3						
Son P:10:110	10,800	I					x	x	x									19		91		2					
Total	415,696											83	6	18	4	25	7	1193	11	10,105	175	328	17	99	110	179	13

Notes:

*Site type:

I: Household/Rancheria

II: Hamlets/Big Rancheria

III: Central Site/Villages

IV: Regional Center

C-1: Food Gathering

C-2: Agricultural Field

C-3: Material Source Recollection Area

C-4: Hunting Area, Trails, and Pot Burst

C-5: Shrines/Altars2

**Blocks marked with an "X" are sites that were recorded in 2004 and where specific material was observed at the surface but that were not collected and not included in the material analysis.